A SHORT HISTORY OF ENGLISH

BY THE SAME AUTHOR

STUDIES IN ENGLISH RHYMES FROM SURREY TO POPE. A Chapter in the History of English. 5s. net.

THE HISTORICAL STUDY OF THE MOTHER TONGUE. An Introduction to Philological Method. 9s. net.

THE GROWTH OF ENGLISH. An Elementary Account of the Present Form of our Language and its Development. 5s. net.

THE TEACHING OF READING IN TRAINING COLLEGES. 3s. net.

THE PLACE OF THE MOTHER TONGUE IN NATIONAL EDUCATION. 1s. net.

A SHORT HISTORY
OF ENGLISH

WITH A BIBLIOGRAPHY OF RECENT BOOKS
ON THE SUBJECT, AND LISTS OF
TEXTS AND EDITIONS

By HENRY CECIL WYLD

AUTHOR OF 'THE HISTORICAL STUDY OF THE MOTHER TONGUE'
'A HISTORY OF MODERN COLLOQUIAL ENGLISH'
'STUDIES IN ENGLISH RHYMES FROM
SURREY TO POPE', ETC., ETC., ETC.

THIRD EDITION
REVISED AND ENLARGED

NEW YORK
E. P. DUTTON AND COMPANY INC.

FIRST EDITION	.	.	.	.	Oct. 1914
SECOND EDITION	.	.	.	.	Feb. 1921
Reprinted	.	.	.	.	Apr. 1923
Reprinted	.	.	.	.	Oct. 1924
Reprinted	.	.	.	.	Dec. 1925
THIRD EDITION, *revised and enlarged*	.				Mar. 1927
Reprinted	.	.	.	.	Nov. 1929

Printed in Great Britain

PREFACE TO THE REVISED EDITION

IT is now thirteen years since the first edition of this book appeared, and the revision of it, first contemplated six or seven years ago, has been delayed by the urgency of other work. It is a satisfaction to me to feel that whatever the drawbacks of procrastination, which in this case has entailed repeated re-printing of the book in almost its original form, this new edition has gained considerably by the delay. I refer in particular to the completion of two considerable pieces of investigation with which I have been associated, carried out by former pupils—that on the *West Midland Dialects of Middle English*, by Dr. Mary Serjeantson of Lady Margaret Hall, and that on the *History of the Early London Dialect* (including that of the adjacent areas) by Miss B. Mackenzie, B.Litt., of Somerville College. A brief abstract of the former has appeared during the present year (1927) in the *Review of English Studies*, while the latter is being prepared for publication and will, I hope, appear shortly. Both of these monographs are attempts to answer questions which confronted myself and my pupils in the course of our work on the innumerable problems of M.E. Grammar. Although I have, as I believe, always specifically acknowledged the help derived from the work of others in the course of the present book, I wish to record here how much I owe to both the afore-mentioned ladies, in respect of minute details and more general pieces of information drawn from their copious stores of material, and for the many references to texts and monographs with which they have supplied me. Miss Mackenzie's work on the London dialect carries the conclusions obtained by Heuser in his *Alt-London* several stages farther, and the general result, which I have attempted to summarize in the proper place below, is I believe to clear up much that was formerly obscure.

I only wish that minute surveys on the same scale as these two on West-Midland and on the London-Middlesex area were available for the other great dialect areas of Middle English.

Quite apart from the debt already acknowledged, I owe special thanks to Miss Serjeantson for generous practical help of many kinds in the work of revision. Not only has she copied out many paragraphs from my handwriting, at the best a tedious task, and one trying to the eyesight, including the new list of M.E. texts, arranged with some minuteness according to their assumed district or county—all of this so far as the West and Central Midland areas are concerned being based on her own investigations—but she has also rendered me invaluable assistance in determining the re-arrangement and re-numbering of paragraphs, and in indicating precisely what was to be cut out from the old, and where the new matter was to be fitted in. Any one who has undertaken to revise, and partly to re-write, a book of this kind knows how troublesome this work is. The re-statement of the genealogical grouping of the M.E. dialects which appears in the present volume was greatly facilitated by the admirable maps showing dialect boundaries, and comparative tables of dialect forms, with which Miss Serjeantson supplied me. Last but not least, Miss Serjeantson has read all the proofs and suggested many corrections and improvements.

In conclusion let me express the hope that this book may at least serve the purpose of provoking further investigation in the many fields of inquiry here touched on, but too often, alas, left unharvested.

HENRY CECIL WYLD.

MERTON COLLEGE, OXFORD,
July, 1927.

PS.—The greater part of this book was already in proof when I received Professor Zachrisson's new book, *English Pronunciation at Shakespeare's Time, As Taught by William Bullokar.* It will take some time to estimate the full bearing of this most important work, which presents fresh matter in the nature of 'occasional spellings', and a new critical examination of the statements of the early Ortho-epists, together with some weighty palaeographical evidence. While Professor Zachrisson agrees in the main with the views expressed in

Chap. vii of the present volume, he differs from some of them in detail, and from others in principle. I think it probable that, as a result of his new investigations, we shall have cause to modify some of the opinions which have prevailed hitherto concerning the pronunciation of the age of Shakespeare. In the present volume I have, unfortunately, only been able to make a few changes in deference to some of the new facts brought to light by Professor Zachrisson.

H. C. W., *September*, 1927.

CONTENTS

BIBLIOGRAPHY

I

A. Historical Grammars and Histories of the English Language.

Bradley, H. The Making of English. London, 1904.

Emerson, O. The History of the English Language. London, 1894.

Jespersen, O. Growth and Structure of the English Language.

Kaluza, M. Historische Grammatik der englischen Sprache. I. (Introd., Phonetics, Phonology, and Accidence of O.E.), 1900. II. (Phonol. and Accidence of M.E. and Mod. Engl.), 1901.

Kluge, E. Geschichte der englischen Sprache. Strassburg, 1899 (in Paul's Grundr.², pp. 926, &c. Also published separately).

Lindelöf, U. Grundzüge der Geschichte der englischen Sprache. Teubner, 1912.

Luick, K. Historische Grammatik der englischen Sprache. (Leipzig, 1913-21; to p. 548. Contains valuable bibliographical information relating to texts and monographs.)

Morris, R. Historical Outlines of English Accidence (Revised Kellner and Bradley), 1897.

Sweet, H. A New English Grammar, Logical and Historical. Part I. (Introd., Phonol., and Accidence.) Oxford, 1892. Part II. (Syntax.) 1899.
History of English Sounds. Oxford, 1888.

Wyld, H. C. The Historical Study of the Mother Tongue. An Introduction to Philological Method. John Murray, 1906, &c.

Works dealing chiefly with Development of Vocabulary.

Greenough, J. B., and **Kittredge, G. L.** Words and their Ways in English Speech. London, Macmillan, 1902.

Skeat, W. W. Principles of English Etymology. Oxford. 2 Vols.

Pearsall Smith, L. The English Language. Williams & Norgate.
To this category also belong the works of Bradley and Jespersen cited above.

The New English Dictionary. Ed. Sir J. Murray, Henry Bradley, William Craigie, and C. T. Onions. Oxford.

B

B. The Old English Period.

(For List of O.E. Texts and Editions see Chapter V on O.E. Sounds.)

I. DICTIONARIES AND GLOSSARIES.

(See also under IV below.)

Bosworth-Toller. An Anglo-Saxon Dictionary. Oxford, 1882-98. Supplement, 1908.

Napier, A. S. Old English Glosses. Oxford, 1900.

Sweet, H. A Student's Dictionary of Anglo-Saxon. Oxford, 1897.

II. GRAMMARS.

Bülbring, K. Altenglisches Elementarbuch. I. (Lautlehre.) Heidelberg, 1902.

Dieter, F. Altenglisch. In Dieter's Laut- und Formenlehre d. altgerm. Dialekte: Lautlehre, Pt. I, Chaps. 4 and 10; Formenlehre, Pt. II, Chaps. 16 and 22. Leipzig, 1898-1900.

Sievers, E. Angelsächsische Grammatik. (3rd Edition.) Halle, 1898.

Sweet, H. Grammatical Introduction to Anglo-Saxon Reader. Oxford. (Though merely a sketch, this is an original and reliable work.)

Wardale, E. E. An Old English Grammar. Methuen, 1922

Wright, J. and E. M. An Old English Grammar. Oxford, 1908.

III. GRAMMARS AND MONOGRAPHS OF THE VARIOUS O.E. DIALECTS.

1. *West Saxon.*

EARLY W.S.

Cosijn, P. J. Altwestsächsische Grammatik. 's Graven Haag, 1888. (Deals with the language of Alfred's Cura Pastoralis and of the Parker Chron.)

LATE W.S.

Brüll, H. Die altenglische Latein-Grammatik des Ælfric. Berlin, 1904.

Dunkhase, H. Die Sprache der Wulfstanschen Homilien. Jena, 1906.

Fischer, F. The Stressed Vowels of Ælfric's Homilies. (Publ. of Mod. Lang. Assoc. of America, Vol. I.) Baltimore, 1889.

Schüller, O. Lautlehre von Ælfric's 'Lives of Saints'. 1908.

Trilsbach, G. Die Lautlehre der spätwestsächsischen Evangelien. Bonn, 1905.

Wilkes, J. Lautlehre zu Ælfric's Heptateuch und Buch Hiob. Bonner Beitr. xxi. Bonn, 1905.

2. *Saxon 'Patois'.*

Boll, P. Die Spr. d. altenglischen Glossen in MS. Harley 3376. Bonn 1904.

Hardy, A. K. Die Sprache der Blickling-Homilien. Leipzig, 1899.

3. Kentish.

Williams, Irene. Grammatical Investigation of the Old Kentish Glosses. (M.S. Vespas. D. VI.) Bonner Beitr. xix. Bonn, 1906.

Wolf, R. Untersuchung der Laute in den kentischen Urkunden. Heidelberg, 1893.

4. Mercian.

Brown, E. M. Sprache der Rushworth Glossen (Rushw.[1]). 1891-2, Göttingen.

Chadwick, H. M. Studies in Old English. (Deals with the old Glossaries.) Cambridge, 1899.

Dieter, F. Über Sprache und Mundart d. ältesten englischen Denkmäler. Göttingen, 1885.

Zeuner, R. Die Sprache d. kentischen Psalters. (Vespas. A. I.) Halle, 1881. (Now recognized as Mercian, long known as the 'so-called Kentish Ps.' !)

5. Northumbrian.

Carpenter, H. C. A. Die Deklination in der nordhumbrischen Evangelienübersetzung d. Lindisfarner Hs. Bonn, 1910.

Füchsel, H. Die Spr. d. nordhumbrischen Interlinearversion z. Johannes-Evangelium. (Lindisfarne.) Anglia, xxiv.

Kellum, M. D. Language of the Nthmbr. Gloss to St. Luke. Yale Studies, 1906.

Kolbe, Th. Die Konjugation der Lindisfarner Evangelien. Bonn, 1912.

Lea, E. M. The Language of the Northumb. Gloss to the Gospel of St. Mark. (Lindisfarne MS.) Anglia, xvi.

Lindelöf, U. (1) Die Spr. d. Rituals von Durham. Helsingfors, 1890. (2) Die südnordhumbrische Mundart. (Spr. d. Glosse Rushw.[2]) Bonn, 1901.

Müller, R. Über die Namen des nordhumbrischen Liber Vitae.

Stolz, W. Der Vokalismus . . . d. Lindisfarn. Evangelien. Bonn, 1908.

Williams, O. T. The Dialect of the Text of the Northumbr. Genealogies. M. L. R., iv. 1908-9.

6. Poetical Texts.

Thomas, P. G. Dialect in Beowulf. Mod. Lang. Review I. 1905-6.

Weightman, Jane. The Language and Dialect of the later O.E. Poetry. University Press, Liverpool, 1907. (See references in this work.)

IV. GLOSSARIES OF INDIVIDUAL TEXTS.

WEST SAXON.

Harris, M. A. Glossary of the West Saxon Gospels. Boston, 1899.

MERC.

Grimm, C. Glossar z. Vesp. Psalter und Hymnen. Heidelberg, 1906.

Thomas, P. G., and H. C. Wyld. A Glossary of the Mercian Hymns in Vespas. A. I. Otia Merseiana IV. Liverpool, 1904.

NORTHUMBR.

Lindelöf, U. (1) Wörterbuch zur Interlinearglosse d. Rituale Eccl. Dunelm. (Durham Ritual.) Bonn, 1901.
(2) Glossar z. altnorthumbr. Glosse Rushw.[2] Helsingfors, 1897.

Cook, A. S. A Glossary of the Old Northumbrian (Lindisfarne) Gospels. 1894.

SAXON 'PATOIS'.

Förster, Max. Lexikalisches z. Vercelli-Codex CXVII. (in Festgruss an Morsbach, pp. 148, &c.). Halle, 1913.

Morris, R. Glossary to Blickling Homilies, in Edition of these (Pt. III), E.E.T.S., 1880.

POETICAL.

Simons, R. Cynewulfs Wortschatz. Bonner Beitr. z. Anglistik, iii. Bonn, 1899.

GENERAL.

Very important are **A. S. Napier's** Contributions to O.E. Lexicography. (Trans. Phil. Soc. 1906, pp. 265–351.)
A laborious discussion of the distinctive Vocabulary of Dialects is found in **R. Jordan's** Eigentümlichkeit des anglischen Wortschatzes. Heidelberg, 1906 (Anglistische Forschungen, 17).

V. FOREIGN LOAN-WORDS IN O.E.

MacGillivray, H. S. The Influence of Christianity on the Vocabulary of O.E. Pt. I. Halle, 1902.

Pogatscher, A. Zur Lautlehre der griechischen, lateinischen, und romanischen Lehnwörter im Altenglischen. Strassburg, 1888 (Q. und F. 64).

VI. O.E. WRITING AND RUNES.

Keller, W. Angelsächsische Palaeographie (II Parts). Part II has facsimiles and transcriptions. 1906 (Palaestra XLIII. 1 and 2).

Viëtor, W. Die nordhumbrischen Runensteine. Marburg, 1905.

C. Middle English Period.

(See also under London Dialect.)

(*For List of M.E. Texts and Editions, see Chap. VI on M.E. Sounds.*)

I. DICTIONARIES.

(a)

Mayhew, A. L., and **Skeat, W. W.** A Concise M.E. Dictionary. Oxford, 1888.

Stratmann, F. H., ed. **H. Bradley.** A Middle English Dictionary. Oxford, 1891.

(Most English Editions of M.E. Texts, in E.E.T.S., and those published by Clarendon Press, are furnished with fairly exhaustive Glossaries.)

(b)

Dictionaries and Glossaries compiled during L.M.E. Period.

Catholicon Anglicum. An Eng.-Lat. Wordbook, dated 1483 (Yorks.). Ed. S. J. H. Herrtage. Camden Soc., 1882.

Vocabularies and Nominales (eleventh, thirteenth, fifteenth centuries) in Anglo-Saxon and Old English Vocabularies. Thomas Wright, re-edited by R. P. Wülcker. London, Trübner, 1884. 2 Vols.

Promptorium Parvulorum. The First Eng.-Lat. Dictionary, 1440 (Norfolk). Ed. A. L. Mayhew. E.E.T.S., Oxford, 1908.

II. GENERAL M.E. GRAMMAR.

Ekwall, E. Ortsnamenforschung ein Hilfsmittel f. d. engl. sprgesch. Studium. Germ.-Rom. Monatschrift, v, p. 592.

Morsbach, L. Mittelenglische Grammatik. Halle, 1896. (First Pt. only, pp. viii + 192. Deals with Sources ; Grouping and Characteristics of chief M.E. Dialect Types ; Quantity, and Qualitative treatment of O.E. short vowels and part of O.E. *ā*.)

Jordan, R. (1) Die mittelenglischen Mundarten. Germ.-Rom. Monatschrift, ii, pp. 125–34.

    (2) Handbuch d. mittelengl. Grammatik, Th. I. Lautlehre. Heidelberg, 1925.

Wright, J. and **E. M.** An Elementary M.E. Gr. Oxford, 1925.

Wyld, H. C. (1) S.E. and S.E. Midland Dialects in Middle English. Essays and Studies, by Members of Engl. Assoc. vi, 1921, pp. 112–45.

    (2) (With the assistance of **M. S. Serjeantson**.) Place-Names and English Linguistic Studies (Ch. VII of Introduction to the Survey of English Pl. Ns. Pt. I. 1924).

III. INVESTIGATIONS OF SPECIAL TEXTS AND DIALECTS.

(Useful bibliographical information in **J. M. Booker's** Dates, Dialects, and Sources, twelfth, thirteenth, and fourteenth century Monuments and MSS. Heidelberg, Winter, 1912 ; and Forschungsberichte: Englische Sprachkunde, **J. Hoops**, Stuttgart-Gotha, 1923.)

(a) *Kentish.*

Danker, O. Laut- und Flexionslehre der mittelkentischen Denkmäler (Diss.). Strassburg, 1879.

Dölle, R. Graphische und lautliche Untersuchung von . . . Ayenbite of Inwyt. Bonn, 1912.

Heuser, W. Zum kentischen Dialekt im Mittelenglischen. Anglia, xvii, pp. 73–90.

Jensen, H. Die Verbalflexion in Ayenbite (Diss.). Kiel, 1908.

Konrath, M. Zur Laut- und Flexionslehre d. Mittelkentischen. Archiv, 88 and 89.

Morris, R. Introduction to Edition of Ayenbite. E.E.T.S., 1886. (Study of Kentish in general and of Ayenbite in particular.)

Philippsen, H. Deklination in den Vices und Virtues. Erlangen, 1911.

Wallenberg, J. K. The Vocabulary of Ayenbite of Inwyt. Upsala, 1923.

Weightman, Jane. Vowel Levelling in Early Kentish ; and the use of the symbol *ʒ*. E.S., Vol. 35, 1905.

(b) *South-West.*

Breier, W. Eule und Nachtigall. Halle, 1910.

Heuser, W. Zur Sprache d. Legenden St. Editha und St. Etheldreda. 1887.

Lucht, P. Lautlehre d. älteren Laʒamonhandschrift. Palaestra, 49, 1905.

Mohr, F. Sprachliche Untersuchungen z. den Legenden aus Gloucestershire. 1888.

Napier, A. S. Introduction to Holy Rood Tree. E.E.T.S., 1894.

Ostermann, H. Lautlehre d. germ. Wortschatzes d. Ancren Riwle. Bonner Beitr. 19. i. 1905.

Pabst, F. Die Sprache d. mittelenglischen Reimchronik d. Robert v. Gloucester. Berlin, 1889; also Anglia, 13. 202, 245.

Pfeffer, R. Die Sprache d. Polychronicons John Trevisas (Diss. Bonn). Düren, 1912.

Wyld, H. C. The Surrey Dialect of the 13th Century, English Studies (Holland), Apr. 1921.

(c) *East Midland.*

Boerner, O. (1) Die Sprache Robert Mannyngs of Brunne. Halle, 1904.

(2) Reimuntersuchung über die Qualität der betonten langen *e*-Vokale bei Robert of Brunne, in Festgruss für Morsbach, pp. 298–351. Halle, 1913.

Hallbeck, E. S. Language of the M.E. Bestiary. Christianstad, 1905.

Lambertz, P. Die Sprache d. Ormulum. Marburg, 1904.

Meyer, H. Zur Sprache d. jüngeren Teile d. Chronik von Peterborough. 1889.

Morris, R. Introduction to his Edition of Genesis and Exodus. E.E.T.S. Revised, 1873.

Schultz, E. Die Sprache d. English Guilds aus d. Jahre 1389. Hildesheim, 1891.

Serjeantson, M. S. The Dialect of the Earliest Complete Engl. Prose Psalter, English Studies (Amsterdam), Vol. VI, pp. 177–99, Dec. 1924.

Wyld, H. C. (See article in Essays and Studies cit. under M.E. Period II, above.)

(d) *West Midland.*

Hirst, T. O. Phonology of the London MS. of the Earliest Complete English Prose Psalter. Bonn, 1907.

Hulbert, J. R. The West Midland of the Romances. Mod. Philology, xix, pp. 1-16, 1921.

Menner, R. J. 'Sir Gawain and the Green Knight' and the W.Midl. P.L.M.A. xxxvii, pp. 503-26, 1922.

Morris, R. Preface to his Ed. of Early English Alliterative Poems. E.E.T.S. (2nd Ed. Revised), 1869.

Mühe, Th. Über den Text MS. Cotton Titus D. XVIII. der Ancren Riwle. 1901.

Rasmussen, J. K. Die Sprache John Audelay's. (Laut- und Flexionslehre.) Bonn, 1914.

Schlütter, A. Über die Spr. und Metrik der Lieder d. MS. Harleian 2253. Archiv, 71, pp. 153, &c., and 357, &c. (These are the lyrics contained in Boeddeker's Altenglische Dichtungen.)

Schüddekopf, A. Sprache und Dialekt d. me. Gedichtes Will. of Palerne. Erlangen, 1886.

Serjeantson, M. S. The Dialects of the West Midlands in Middle English, Rev. Engl. Studies, Vol. III, Nos. 9, 10, 11, 1927.

Stodte, H. Spr. und Heimat der Katherine-Gruppe (Diss.). Göttingen, 1896.

Williams, Irene. The Cleopatra MS. of Ancren Riwle. Anglia, 28, p. 300, &c.

(e) *Northern.*

Baumann, I. Die Spr. d. Urkunden aus Yorkshire. Anglist. Forsch. 11, 1902.

Heuser, W. Die ältesten Denkmäler und die Dialekte d. Nordenglischen. Anglia, 31. 276, &c.

Morris, R. Introduction to Prick of Conscience. E.E.T.S.

Perrin, L. P. Thomas von Castleford's Chronik. 1890.

Ullmann, J. Studien z. R. Rolle von Hampole. Engl. Studien, 7. 415

Vikar, A. Contributions to the History of the Durham Dialects Malmö, 1922.

Wetzlar, A. Die Sprache . . . d. nordenglischen Homiliensammlung 1907.

(f) *Scotch.*

Curtis, F. J. The Middle Scotch Romance of Clariodus. Anglia, 17, pp. 1-68; 125-60.

Murray, J. A. H. The Dialect of the Southern Counties of Scotland Trans. Phil. Soc., 1873. (Deals with the early language as well as with Mod. Dialect.)

Ostermann, L. Untersuchungen z. Ratis Raving. Bonner Beitr. 12, pp. 41, &c. 1902.

Smith, Gregory. Introduction to Specimens of Middle Scots. Blackwood, 1902.

(g) *Irish English.*

Heuser, W. Introduction to Die Kildare-Gedichte. (Fourteenth-century poems written in Ireland.) Bonner Beitr. Bonn, 1904.

IV. DETAILED MONOGRAPHS, ETC., ON SPECIAL PROBLEMS
OF MIDDLE ENGLISH.

Björkman, E. Orms Doppelkonsonanten, Anglia, xxxvii, pp. 350-81, and 494-6, 1913-14.

Brandl, A. Z. Geographie d. altengl. Dialekte. Berlin, 1915.

Bryan, W. F. The Midland Present Plural Indicative Ending in -*e(n)*. Mod. Philol., xxiii, Jan. 1921.

Bülbring, K. D. (1) Geschichte d. Ablauts der st. Zeitwörter innerhalb d. Südenglischen. Q. und F. 63. Strassburg, 1889.
(2) Über die Erhaltung d. ae. kurzen und langen *æ*-Lautes im Mittelenglischen. Bonner Beitr. z. Anglistik, 15, pp. 101, &c. Bonn, 1904.
(3) Die Schreibung *eo* im Ormulum. Bonner Beitr. 17, pp. 51, &c. Bonn, 1905.

Cornelius, H. Altenglische Diphthongierung durch Palatale im Mittelenglischen. Studien z. engl. Phil. 30. Halle, 1907.

Eilers, F. Dehnung vor dehnenden Consonanten. Stud. z. engl. Phil. 26. Halle, 1907.

Ekwall, E. (1) Ortsnamenforschung ein Hilfsmittel für das engl. Sprachgeschichte-Studium. (Deals with OE. *ā* and *ȳ* in Lancs. in M.E.) Germ.-Rom. Monatschrift, v, Nov. 1913, pp. 592-608.
(2) Contributions to the Hist. of O.E. Dialects. Lund, 1917.

Flasdieck, H. M. Ein südost me. Lautwandel, Eng. Stud. LVIII. 1-23.

Funke, O. Zur Wortgeschichte d. französ. Elemente im Englischen, Englische Studien, LV. 192.

Hackmann, G. Kürzung langer Tonvokale in einsilbigen Wörtern im Mittel- und Neuengiischen. Stud. z. engl. Phil. 10. Halle, 1908.

Haussen, H. Die Geschichte der starken Zeitwörter im Nordenglischen (Diss.). Kiel, 1906.

Hemken. Das Aussterben alter Substantiva im Verlaufe d. engl. Sprachgeschichte. Kiel, 1906.

Heuser, W. Festländische Einflüsse im Mittelenglischen. Bonner Beitr. 12. Bonn, 1902.

Horn, W. Beiträge z. Geschichte d. engl. Gutturallaute. Berlin, 1901.

Knopff, P. Darstellung d. Ablautverhältnisse in der schottischen Schriftspr. (Diss.). Bern, 1904.

Luick, K. (*Lengthening of ĭ and ŭ in open Syllables.*)
(1) Untersuchungen z. engl. Lautgeschichte, 1896, pp. 229, &c.
(2) Studien z. engl. Lautgeschichte. 1903.
(*Shortening of long vowels in words of three Syllables*, &c.)
(3) Quantitätsveränderungen im Laufe d. englisch. Sprachentwicklung. (Beitr. z. engl. Gr. III.) Anglia, xx, pp. 335, &c. 1898.
(4) Der Ursprung d. neuenglischen *ai-au*-Diphthonge. E. St. 27, pp. 89-100. 1900.

Mackenzie, B. A. A Special Dialectal Development of OE. *ēa* in M.E. E. Studien, Bd. 61, 1927.

Mařik, Josef. *W*-Schwund im Mittel- und Frühneuenglischen. Vienna and Leipzig, 1910.

Mettig. Die französischen Elemente im Alt- und Mittelenglischen (800–1258). E. Studien, 41, pp. 177, &c.

Oberdörffer. Aussterben altengl. Adjectiva und ihr Ersatz im Verlaufe der englischen Sprachgesch. (Kiel. Diss.). 1908.

Offe. Aussterben alter Verba und ihr Ersatz, &c. (Kiel. Diss.). 1908.

Serjeantson, M. S. (1) Distribution of Dialect Characters in M.E. English Studies (Amsterdam), 1922.

(2) The Development of O.E. *ēag, ēah,* in M.E. Journ. of Engl. and Germanic Phil., Vol. XXVI, 1927.

Teichert, F. Über das Aussterben alter Wörter im Verlaufe d. engl. Sprachgesch. (Kiel. Diss.). Erlangen, 1912.

Wackerzapp, A. Geschichte d. Ablaute d. starken Zeitwörter innerhalb d. Nordenglischen (Diss.). Münster, 1890.

Weick, Fr. Das Aussterben d. Präfixes *ge-* im Englischen. Darmstadt, 1911.

Wyld, H. C. (1) Contributions to the Hist. of the Guttural Sounds in Engl. Trans. Phil. Soc., 1899–1900.

(2) History of Initial ʒ- in Middle and Modern Engl. Dialects. Otia Merseiana, II, 1901.

(3) Treatment of O.E. *y̆* in the Dialects of the Midl. and S.E. Counties in M.E. E. St. 47, pp. 1–58. 1913. (Deals with Pl. Ns. of 27 Counties, and with West Midl. Texts.)

(4) O.E. *y̆* in the Dialects of the South and S.W. Counties in M.E. E. St. 47, pp. 146–66. 1914. (Deals with Pl. Ns. of 9 Sthn. Counties.)

Zachrisson, R. E. (1) Contribution to the Study of Anglo-Norman Influence on English Place Names. Lund, 1909.

(2) Two instances of Fr. Influence on Engl. Pl. Ns. Utg. af Nyfilologiska Sällskapet i Stockholm. Upsala, 1914.

D. The London Dialect and Rise of the Literary Language.

Brugger. Zur lautlichen Entwickelung d. englischen Schriftsprache im Anfang d. 16. Jahrh. Anglia, xv, pp. 261–344.

Dibelius, W. John Capgrave und die englische Schriftsprache. Anglia, vols. xxiii and xxiv. (A minute investigation of fifteenth-century English.)

Dölle, E. Zur Sprache Londons vor Chaucer. Halle, 1913.

Delcourt, Joseph. Essai sur la langue de Sir Thomas More d'après ses œuvres anglaises. Paris, Didier, 1914.

Flasdieck, H. M. Forschungen z. Frühzeit d. neuengl. Schriftspr. (Pts. I and II.) Halle, 1922.

Frieshammer, J. Die sprachliche Form der Chaucerschen Prosa. Halle, 1910.

Fuhr, K. Lautuntersuchungen zu Stephen Hawes Pastime of Pleasure. Marburg, 1891.

Heuser, W. Alt-London, mit besond. Berücksichtigung d. Dialekts. Osnabrück, 1914.

Hitchcock, E. V. Pecock's Language, in *Introduction* to the Folewer to the Donet, pp. xxiv–lxxi. E.E.T.S., 1924.

Hoelper, E. Die englische Schriftsprache in Tottel's Miscellany. Strassburg, 1894.

Hoffmann, A. Laut- und Formenlehre in Reginald Pecock's Repressor (Diss.). Greifswald, 1900.

Lekebusch, J. Die Londoner Urkundensprache von 1430–1500. Halle, 1906.

Mackenzie, B. A. Contributions to the History of the Early London Dialect. 1927.

Morsbach, L. Über den Ursprung der neuenglischen Schriftsprache. Heilbronn, 1888.

Neumann, G. Die Orthographie der Paston Letters von 1422–1461. Studien z. engl. Philologie, vii. Marburg, 1904.

Reaney, P. H. (1) On certain Phonological features of the dialect of London in the twelfth century, E. Stud., Bd. 59, pp. 321–345. 1925.
(2) The dialect of London in the thirteenth century. E. Stud., Bd. 61, pp. 9–23. 1926.

Römstedt, H. Die englische Schriftsprache bei Caxton. Göttingen, 1891.

Rudolf, E. Die englische Orthographie von Caxton bis Shakespeare (Diss.). Marburg, 1904.

Swearingen, G. F. Die englische Schriftsprache bei Coverdale (Berlin. Diss.). Weimar, 1904.

Schmidt, F. Studies in the Language of Pecock (Diss.). Upsala, 1900.

Süssbier, K. Die Sprache der Cely-Papers (Berlin. Diss.). 1905.

ten Brink, B. Chaucers Sprache und Verskunst. (2nd Ed., F. Kluge.) Leipzig, 1899.

Wild, F. Sprache d. wichtigeren Chaucer-Hss., Wiener Beiträge, 44. Leipzig, 1915.

Wille, J. Die Orthographie in Roger Ascham's Toxophilus und Scholemaster (Diss.). Marburg, 1889.

E. English of the Modern Period.

(See also under LONDON DIALECT, &c.)

I. SPECIAL MONOGRAPHS AND ARTICLES.

Diehl, L. Englische Schreibung und Aussprache im Zeitalter Shakespeares (Diss.). Giessen, 1906, and Anglia, xxix.

Ellis, A. J. Early English Pronunciation. Pts. I–IV.

Holmqvist, E. On the history of the Engl. present inflections, particularly *-th* and *-s*. Heidelberg, 1922.

Horn, W. (1) Historische neuenglische Grammatik. (Pt. I, Lautlehre.) Strassburg, 1908.

(2) Untersuchungen zur neuenglischen Lautgeschichte. Strassburg, 1905 (Q. und F. 98).

Jespersen, O. (1) John Hart's Pronunciation of English (1569 and 1570). Heidelberg, 1907.

(2) A Modern English Grammar on Historical Principles. Pt. I, Phonology. Heidelberg, 1909; II, Syntax, 1914.

Kihlbom, Asta. Contribution to the Study of Fifteenth Century English. Uppsala, 1926.

Luick, K. (1) Untersuchungen zur englischen Lautgeschichte. Strassburg, 1896.

(2) Studien zur englischen Lautgeschichte. Vienna and Leipzig, 1903.

(3) Beiträge zur englischen Grammatik :—Anglia, xiv, 1892, pp. 268–302 ; xvi, 1894, pp. 451–511 ; xx (1898), pp. 335–62 ; xxx (1907), pp. 1–55.

Müller, E. Englische Lautlehre nach James Elphinston (1765, 1787, 1796). Heidelberg, 1914.

Price, H. T. History of Ablaut in the Strong Verbs from Caxton to the end of the Elizabethan Period. Bonn, 1910.

Spira, T. Die englische Lautentwickelung nach französischen Grammatiker-Zeugnissen. Giessen, 1908.

Viëtor, W. (1) Shakespeare's Pronunciation. I. Phonology and Rhyme Index, 1906 ; II. Shakespeare Reader, 1907. Marburg.

(2) Die Aussprache d. Englischen nach den deutsch-englischen Grammatiken vor 1740. Marburg, 1886.

Wyld, H. C. (1) Class Dialect and Standard English, in A Miscellany presented to John Macdonald Mackay, pp. 283–91. University Press, Liverpool, 1914.

(2) Spoken English of Early Eighteenth Century. Mod. Lang. Teaching, June and July, 1915.

(3) A History of Modern Colloquial English. Fisher Unwin, 1920, 3rd impression, 1925.

(4) Studies in English Rhymes from Surrey to Pope. Murray, 1923.

Zachrisson, R. E. (1) Pronunciation of English Vowels, 1400–1700. Göteborg, 1913.

(2) Shakespeares Uttal (Studier i modern Språkvetenskap). Utg. af Nyfilologiska Sällskapet i Stockholm, v. 2. Upsala, 1914.

(3) The English Pronunciation at Shakespeare's Time, as taught by William Bullokar. Upsala, 1927.

(See also the introductions to reprints of the early Grammarians.)

II. DICTIONARIES AND GLOSSARIES.

Onions, C. T. A Shakespeare Glossary. Oxford, 1911.

Skeat, W. W. A Glossary of Tudor and Stuart Words. Edited, with Additions, by A. L. Mayhew. Oxford, 1914.

II

SELECTED LIST OF WORKS ON ENGLISH PRONUNCIATION

Of sixteenth- and seventeenth-century books, this list includes only those of which reprints exist. Many of the following have been published in a series entitled *Neudrucke frühneuenglischer Grammatiken*, under the general editorship of Rudolf Brotanek, by Niemeyer, Halle. Those published in this series have an asterisk in front of the author's name.

1530. **Palsgrave, J.** Lesclarcissement de la langue françoise. (Reprinted F. Genin, Paris, 1852.)

1532. **Du Wes, G.** An Introductorie. (Reprinted in Genin's Ed. of Palsgrave.)

1547. **Salesbury, W.** Account of English Pronunciation. (See Ellis's E. E. Pronunciation, 768–87).

1567. **Salesbury, W.** Account of Welsh Pronunciation. (Ellis's E. E. P. 743–68.)

1568. ***Smith, Sir Thomas.** De Recta et Emendata Linguae Anglicae Scriptione Dialogus. Ed. Deibel, Halle, 1913.

1580. ***Bellot, J.** Le Maistre d'Escole Anglois. Ed. Theo. Spira, Halle, 1912. (See also Zachrisson, English Pronunciation, 1400–1700, pp. 9–16.)

1580. **Bullokar, W.** Booke at large for the amendment of Orthographie for English Speech. Ed. M. Plessow, in Fabeldichtung in England. Palaestra, 52, pp. 237, &c. Berlin, 1906.

1621. **Gill, A.** Logonomia Anglica. Ed. J. Jiriczek, Q. und F. 90, 1903.

1622 and 1633. ***Mason, George.** Grammaire Angloise. Ed. Brotanek, 1905.

1634. ***Butler, Charles.** English Grammar. Ed. A. Eichler, 1910.

1640. ***Daines, Simon.** Orthoepia Anglicana. Ed. Rössler and Brotanek, 1908.

1685. ***Cooper, C.** Grammatica Linguae Anglicanae. Ed. J. D. Jones, 1912.

1701. ***Jones, John.** Practical Phonography. Ed. E. Ekwall, 1907.

1725. **Lediard.** Grammatica Anglicana Critica. (Full account in Ellis, pp. 1040, &c.)

1753. **Bertram, Carl.** The Royal English-Danish Grammar. Copenhagen, 1753.

1801. **Walker, John.** Rhetorical Grammar. (2nd Ed.)

1809. **Bachelor, T.** Orthoepical Analysis of the Engl. Language.

III

SHORT LIST OF WORKS FROM FIFTEENTH CENTURY TO EARLY EIGHTEENTH, CHIEFLY OF A COLLOQUIAL CHARACTER

To illustrate the familiar Style of this period and the Spellings which throw light on Pronunciation.

1424–1506. **The Paston Letters.** Ed. Gairdner.

1447–50. **Shillingford, John** (Mayor of Exeter). Letters and Papers of. Ed. Moore. Camden Soc., 1871.

1449. **Pecok, Bp. Reginald.** The Repressor, 2 vols. Ed. Babington. Rolls Ser., 1860; The Donet, E.E.T.S. 1921; The Folewer to the Donet, E.E.T.S. 1924, Ed. E. V. Hitchcock.

1467 (before). **Gregory, William** (Ld. Mayor of London). Chronicle, in Collections of a Citizen of London. Ed. Gairdner. Camden Soc., 1876.

1473–88. **Cely Papers.** Ed. Maldon. Camden Soc., 1900.

1482. **Monk of Evesham.** Revelation of. Arber's Reprints.

c. 1500. **Hymn to the Virgin** (English in Welsh spelling). MS. Brit. Mus. Addit. 14866. Ed. Idris Bell. Anglia, 36, p. 116, &c. 1912.

1501. **Reception of Catherine of Aragon.** In Letters and Papers. Vol. I. Ed. Gairdner. Rolls Ser.

1545. **Ascham, Roger.** Toxophilus. Arber's Reprints.

1549. **Latimer, Bp.** Seven Sermons preached before Edw. VI. Arber's Reprints.

1550–3. **Machyn, Henry.** Diary of. Camden Soc. Nichols, 1848.

1573–80. **Harvey, Gabriel.** Letter Book. Ed. C. J. L. Scott. Camden Soc., 1884.

1575. **Laneham, Robert.** Letter from, in Captain Cox his Ballads and Books. Ed. Furnivall. Ballad Soc., 1871.

1582–1602. **Queen Elizabeth's Letters to James VI.** Camden Soc., 1849.

1593. **Queen Elizabeth's Englishings.** (Transl. of Boethius, &c.) Ed. Pemberton. E.E.T.S., 1899.

1580–1661. **Alleyne Papers.** Ed. Payne Collier. Shakespeare Soc., 1843.

1593–1626. **Alleyne, Edward.** Memoirs of. Ed. Payne Collier. Shakespeare Soc., 1843.

1625–43. **Letters of Lady Brilliana Harley.** Camden Soc., 1853.

1634–75. **Correspondence of Dr. Basire.** Ed. W. N. Darnell. 1831.

1639–96. **Memoirs of the Verney Family.** Ed. Lady Verney. 4 vols. 1894.

1705–39. **The Wentworth Papers.** Ed. J. J. Cartwright. 1883.

CHAPTER I

INTRODUCTORY. SCOPE OF THE INQUIRY
GENERAL CONSIDERATIONS

§ 1. THE earliest documentary knowledge of English which we possess consists in a few rather scrappy Charters of the last years of the seventh century and the first few years of the eighth. These Charters are in Latin, but contain English Place and Personal names. (See Sweet's *O.E.T.*, pp. 426, etc., chs. i, ii, iv, and v.)

From the end of the seventh century, then, we can trace the development of English, in various forms or dialects, by means of documents which become increasingly numerous as years go on.

§ 2. During the 1200 odd years over which our knowledge of English extends, changes of very considerable extent have taken place.

To begin with, the spelling of the words is very different in different ages, so much so, that at first sight it is hardly possible to recognize the identity of the present-day forms with those of their ancestors in bygone ages. We attribute these changes in the spelling, on the whole, to an attempt, more or less successful, to adapt this to the changing pronunciation of the different periods.

Again, we find that the vocabulary changes. While many words remain and retain their old meaning, others, which in one age were in common use, disappear altogether, or they alter their meaning; new words come into use and take the place of those which have dropped out of use. We observe that this process of loss and gain and of change of meaning is for ever going on in the English vocabulary.

Nor do grammatical forms or inflexions enjoy immunity from change. Many are lost altogether and their places taken by others which had originally a different function and now have extra work thrown upon them. Other inflexions are simply lost without anything being put in their place, and without any loss in intelligibility or definiteness of expression. But the ravages made in the inflexional system of English often involve a new form of sentence, a new construction, a new Syntax.

§ 3. All these changes—in Pronunciation, in Vocabulary, in Accidence and Syntax—would have to be considered and described in a complete account. The description of these phenomena constitutes the *History of English*.

But the changes referred to do not take place all over the country precisely at the same time, nor in the same way. From the beginning of its career in these islands, English was not a uniform language, but existed in several different forms, or *Dialects*. As time went on this diversity increased, so that in the thirteenth and fourteenth centuries the speech of no two counties was exactly alike, and more or less different forms of English were spoken in different parts of the same county. Some of these differences find utterance in the written language.

§ 4. A complete history of English would take into account all the facts in the development of every form of English from the earliest period till the present day.

It is obvious that such a multitude of facts could not be compressed into the compass of one small volume, but would fill a respectable library of large books.

§ 5. Fortunately, at the present time, the great majority of the English Dialects are of very little importance as representatives of English speech, and for our present purpose we can afford to let them go, except in so far as they throw light upon the growth of those forms of our language which are the main objects of our solicitude, namely, the language of Literature and Received Standard Spoken English.

We shall have a good deal to say later concerning both Literary and Standard Spoken English. It is enough here to say that they are very closely related ; that the origin of both is the same; that the starting-point was in the language of London as spoken by the Court and the upper ranks of Society and in the transaction of official business from the fifteenth century. The problem of the history of this form of English is made complex and difficult by two important facts. First, the dialect of London was, from the geographical position of the city, a border dialect, subject to various dialectal influences from the surrounding areas—from Middlesex itself, where a variety of Saxon was spoken, from Hertfordshire on the North, from Bucks. to the West, and especially from Essex to the East, whence S.E. Midland influence gradually penetrated to the capital. This regional dialect of London, which partook of the characters of several dialect types, when it attained to the position of a common standard, developed a particular variety which became a Class dialect. Secondly, this *Received Standard* English, having become the language of the upper classes, was subject to the influence of fashion, and from the later fifteenth century onwards exhibits an ebb and flow in the type of speech, in the pronunciation, and in grammatical forms, in conformity with what is current at different times among those classes or groups of speakers who are recognized as models of 'correctness' in speech and manners, if not always perhaps in every other respect. The early history of Standard English is that of a *Regional* dialect, modified by surrounding types of regional speech ; the later history of Received Standard, and of the leading form used in literature, is mainly that of a *Class* dialect, modified by other Class dialects, rather than by Regional speech.

To understand the rise of Literary and Standard Spoken English, therefore, it is necessary to know something at least of the early dialects of the S. and S.E. Midlands, many of whose features are common to that dialect which has become the language of Literature and of polite society. We have also to take into account the influence of fashion in causing a shifting of standards of correctness.

We may, therefore, to some extent, though not wholly, narrow down our inquiry to the problem of the origin and development of that form of English which is now spoken by educated and well-bred people, and, what is to all intents and purposes the same thing, of that form which is the vehicle of literature, and which for the last four or five centuries has also been that used in the composition of private or public documents, no matter what the native form of speech of the writers might be.

§ 6. [1] After the end of the fourteenth century, the other dialects, excepting always those of Lowland Scotch, gradually cease to be the vehicle of literary expression, and are no longer of importance to us as independent forms of English. We cannot afford, however, to let them altogether out of our sight, because the dialectal composition of the Standard Language varies slightly ; it adopts or discards this or that element or feature from time to time for reasons, no doubt mainly social, which we cannot determine with exactitude.

---

[1] This depended, however, largely upon the education of the writer. Thus the Life of S. Editha (Wilts., circa 1420) is written in a very rustic form of English, while the Letters of John Shillingford, a native of Devonshire and Mayor of Exeter, about thirty years later, betray but few typically Southern deviations from London English. (See these Letters, Ed. Moore, Camden Soc., 1871.)

§ 7. In this book, therefore, the developments of the Modern provincial English dialects are not considered unless they can throw light on the history of Standard English.

And while we concentrate mainly upon the history of the dominant form of English, and limit our efforts to an attempt to describe the growth of this, we must further, within this field, make a careful choice of material.

While we are bound to take cognizance of many particular and general facts of development in the dialects of Old and Middle English, we must of necessity leave unchronicled many details which are of great interest and importance for the special student of these early periods. We cannot attempt a complete account of Old or Middle English, but must confine ourselves, in the main, to such facts as are of significance for our chief theme, the origin and subsequent development of the dominant dialect which emerges towards the end of the M.E. period.

§ 8. We have already enumerated the various aspects of English which have to be considered in a complete treatment —its sounds, its vocabulary, its inflexions, and its syntax. Of these, it is perhaps most important to give as clear an account as possible of the development of the sounds and inflexions. The reason of this is, first, that pronunciation and accidence are the most characteristic features of a dialect, and, secondly, that the history of sounds is especially capable of treatment in terms of general laws or tendencies of change.

A couple of examples will serve to make clear the importance of the history of pronunciation in determining the dialectal character. In Standard English we use the form *fire* [faiə]. This is from a M.E. *fīr* and an O.E. *fȳr*. The modern form can only be of either Northern or N. East Midland origin. It can only be derived from the M.E. *fīr*. But other types of this word existed in M.E.—*fuir* [fȳr], the type in use in the West and Central Midlands and in the South and S. West, and *fēr*, the Kentish and South-eastern type. Had these types survived into Mod. Engl., the former would have become **fure* and the latter **fere* [fiə]. Again, take the word *knell*. This goes back to M.E. *knellen* and to O.E. *cnellan*. The type shown in these three forms is S. Eastern or Kentish. The West and Central Midland and Southern type was in O.E. *cnyllan*, M.E. *knullen*, which would develop in Mod. Engl. into **knull*. The corresponding N. East Midland type would result in a Modern **knill*, M.E. *knillen*. These two illustrations are enough to show the importance of pronunciation as a characteristic feature of dialect. Furthermore, the principles, of which these two words are isolated examples, can be formulated in terms of regular laws, which apply to all words containing the same original sounds. The history of sound changes within the various dialects of O. and M.E., therefore, and the development of the sounds through the Modern period, is bound to form an important section in a book dealing with the history of the English Language.

§ 9. The history of English Accidence is partly the history of the treatment of sounds in unstressed syllables, partly also the history of the substitution of one form for another through the influence of the principle known as *Analogy* (see § 70 below).

§ 10. The changes in English Syntax are due partly to the loss of inflexional syllables and the subsequent recasting of the sentence, partly to the influence of Latin and French sentence structure and idiom.

§ 11. Lastly, there is the question of Vocabulary. This is a side of the history of English which requires very judicious handling. Although, for reasons explained in the Preface, this aspect of the history of English is not dealt with here, a few words may be said upon it. It cannot be supposed that in a small book a detailed account of the introduction, origin, and development of meaning of every individual word should be attempted. This would involve, not a statement of general principles, but a series of isolated and disconnected articles. Such work is the business of the lexicographer pure and simple.

It seems better to avoid all treatment of individual words as such in a history of a language, and in tracing in outline the history of the vocabulary to subordinate everything, as far as possible, to principles, citing words merely as illustrations of these.

Thus it would be quite out of place to give lists of words borrowed from Malay, Chinese, Hungarian, Polish, etc., with any attempt at completeness, because it is far more important to understand how words get from one language into another, and what happens to them, as regards their form, when they do get there, than to have a mechanical knowledge that a particular word was borrowed from some language of which we are entirely ignorant. Any one who knows, say, Greek or Chinese, will have no difficulty in distinguishing the words in English which have been adopted from those languages.

Again, it would be improper to take a few hundred native words, haphazard, and describe with minuteness the changes in meaning, perhaps very considerable, which they have undergone, unless the principles of change in meaning, so far as these can be brought under a generalized statement, are first explained, and the particular words cited merely to illustrate the principle.

The same view applies to the method of dealing with loan-words in a short history of a language. It is important and necessary to state what are the principal languages which have contributed to the English vocabulary, how and when the speakers of these languages came in contact with the English, what classes of words we acquired from the various sources, and the history of the external form of the words when once they had become part and parcel of English speech. Armed with these general points, each of which should have been sufficiently illustrated by specific examples, the student will be in a position to discover for himself the sources of many of the principal foreign loan-words, and if he is in doubt, as indeed any one may be, on such a point, there are the Etymological Dictionaries to settle the point for him.

§ 12. It cannot be too strongly emphasized that the study of the history of English in such a book as this, or in a hundred others, many of which may be larger and better, is a barren and lifeless pursuit if divorced from the study of the language itself as it exists in the actual documents of the different periods. If we would feel and realize the drama of linguistic evolution, we must penetrate by patient study into the spirit and life of the language at each period—a long and slow process—and then, when we can ' look before and after ', we shall gradually gain a sense of growth and development. No statistical and descriptive account can give this vital knowledge, no amount of laws, and tables, and paradigms. All that the best history of English ever written can do for the student is to act as a guide to the path which he must tread anew for himself.

There is a real danger at the present time for the student of English in the very multiplicity which exists of grammars, histories of the language, monographs on minute points of phonology and syntax, and 'aids to study' of all kinds, a danger that the weary pilgrim will never reach his goal—namely, a first-hand knowledge of the language itself as it exists in the literature. It is to be feared that the formidable and ever-increasing array of books and articles *about* English make it, in some ways, more and more difficult to get to the reality. The only means of salvation lies in a constant reference, on the one hand, to the actual texts, and, on the other, to the living spoken English of to-day, in which the great impulses of change are ever at work, and where we can observe history being made under our very eyes.

For we must never forget that while, from the nature of the case, the past history of a language must necessarily be traced by means of written records, these are to be regarded as affording us merely an indication of what was actually taking place in the spoken language itself. Change in language implies a change in the mental and physical habits of the living human beings who speak the language. The drama of linguistic history is enacted, not in manuscripts nor inscriptions, but in the mouths and minds of men.

CHAPTER II

POSITION OF ENGLISH AMONG LANGUAGES. DIALECTAL AND CHRONOLOGICAL DIVISIONS

§ 13. ENGLISH was introduced into these islands in the fifth century by Germanic tribes who came, in the first instance, under colour of helping Vortigern, the British king, against the Picts. But soon, seeing the 'nothingness of the Britons, and the excellence of the land', the Jutes, who were the first comers, sent for their kinsmen, who, coming in large numbers, murdered and pillaged their way to the possession of the best part of the country, causing the Britons to flee before them 'like fire' into the mountains of the west.

In about a century, the various tribes had settled down, and the thoroughness of their grip on the country may be gauged from the purely English character of most names of places in the South and Midlands, except of course those on the borders of Wales and in Cornwall.

The principal tribes were the Jutes, the Angles, and Saxons, who came respectively from Jutland, Schleswig, and Holstein.

The Jutes settled Kent, perhaps part of Surrey, part of Hampshire, and the Isle of Wight. The various tribes of Saxons took possession of the rest of the South and West, between the Thames and the Humber. The Angles settled in the North and Midlands.

§ 14. But if the Germanic invaders of Britain were in many respects savages, they were also noble savages, and in their character lay the seeds of much that was worthy and admirable.

In the oldest fragments of heathen poetry, side by side with the fierceness and cruelty which we expect, there are also displayed the excellent qualities of high courage, loyalty to a leader or a cause, a tenderness and a love of nature which spring from what ten Brink calls the 'pious soul of English heathendom'. The pirate who in the fifth century put forth 'through the mists of ocean' to seek his fortune in an unknown land, and to face, undaunted, risks and dangers, first among the stormy waves, and then amid strange peoples, far from 'his home where he was reared', may have been bloodthirsty and unscrupulous, but he was certainly neither ignoble in spirit nor contemptible as a man. His descendants, turned farmers, country gentlemen, devotees of the chase, peaceful rulers in their district, protectors of their households, faithful servants of their chief or king, had time and opportunity to cultivate the gentler virtues. But their swords, meanwhile, were not allowed to rust ; there was plenty of fighting during the first few centuries of the English settlement. The introduction of Christianity, while it gave a sanction to the innate qualities of altruism, faithfulness unto death, and deep-rooted tenderness which reside in the Germanic peoples, did not destroy, but merely disciplined, and gave a nobler and better controlled direction to the sterner elements in the national character. In Beowulf, the ideal king and warrior of Germanic heathen chivalry, we find essentially the same character and virtues as in Alfred, the Christian monarch and soldier, than whom no nobler figure is to be found in the annals of any nation.

§ 15. Throughout Old English history and literature there appears the expression of a national character, in which what are often regarded as chiefly heathen elements are inextricably blended with the gentler and sweeter qualities that find their natural incentive in Christianity. Thus it is a very superficial criticism which would divide our old poetry into the National (meaning thereby purely heathen) and the Christian, for there is no fundamental difference of spirit between them—both are equally 'national'. Different aspects of the national genius are indeed emphasized in the poetry of heathen and Christian periods, but all the elements and spirit of each are found in both ; there is no sudden break, no new departure. As we turn over the pages of the History of the Church in England, we are struck with something like amazement that such an engaging personality as that of St. Bede, with his serene and lofty outlook upon the world, his tenderness and pathos, his sound historical method, his captivating gift of narrative, his profound piety, could emerge from a people separated by but three generations from heathenism, and by less than three centuries from the ruthless followers of Hengest. From these rude ancestors were to spring, in the course of a few centuries, a long and splendid line of kings, rulers, warriors, and legislators ; of poets, mystics, and scholars ; of bishops, saints, and martyrs, whom no Englishman of to-day can look back upon without a glow of pride at the thought that he belongs to the same race.

§ 16. The Dialects of Old English.

The language of the Germanic invaders, which in the earliest times can have been but slightly differentiated, had become split up, in the age of the earliest documents, into four still very similar, but nevertheless quite definitely marked dialects. We distinguish the Saxon dialects, the Kentish dialect (that of the Jutes), and the Anglian dialects. Anglian is divided into Northumbrian, the speech of the Angles North of the Humber, and Mercian, that of the Angles of the Midlands. Mercian and Northumbrian, while having several features in common which distinguish them from the Saxon and Kentish dialects, are also characterized severally by distinctive marks. Thus while we can often speak of a characteristic simply as Anglian, we have also to observe carefully the points in which Mercian and Northumbrian differ. We unfortunately know nothing of the early form of the East Anglian dialect.

Of the Saxon dialects, the most important by far is that of Wessex, which we refer to as West Saxon. This form of English is much more fully represented in literature than any other of the early dialects. In fact West Saxon was the nearest approach to a standard literary dialect which existed in Old English. Its prestige gave it currency beyond the bounds of a single province. This is the dialect which is studied first by students of the old language, and indeed there is little to read, and nothing worthy the name of *literature*, in prose, in any other form of Old English, except some interesting homilies in a dialect which it is now the fashion to refer to as a Saxon Patois. Kentish, Mercian, and Northumbrian are mainly known to us in Charters, Glossaries, in Glosses, or in paraphrases of the Gospels and the Psalms.

A very curious and interesting form of Old English is the Saxon Patois of the Blickling Homilies, and of what are known as the Harleian Glosses, which will be referred to more particularly later on. The view now held is that these are indeed in a Saxon dialect, which has many features in common with the West Saxon literary language of Alfred and Ælfric, while it also shows well-marked deviations that rather resemble Mercian in some respects. It is believed that this dialect developed within the Saxon area, and that it is not due to actual contamination from without. Unfortunately we do not know precisely in what part of the Saxon area this *Patois* was spoken.

§ 17. The Name of the People and their Language.

The country as a whole is called by our ancestors *Englalond*, 'land of the Angles'; the people, unless some specific tribe is designated, are called *Angel cynn*, 'Angle kin', and the language is known as *Englisc*. Bede uses the expression *Angli sive Saxones*, implying that both terms mean the same thing, but he generally calls the people *Angli*, and their language *Sermo Anglicus*, as a generic term, even when referring to the language of the Jutes.

The great and good Alfred, King of the West Saxons, the founder of West Saxon prose, calls his own language *Englisc*, and Ethelbert of Kent, the first English Christian King, applies the word *Angli* to himself and his people. Much later, the Abbot Ælfric, who wrote pure West Saxon, speaks of turning his Homilies *of Ledenum ğereorde to Englisċre sprǣċe*, 'from the Latin language into English speech'. *Lingua Saxonica*, *Saxonice* are but rarely used, unless in specific reference to the Saxon dialects. The expression *Anglo-Saxon* seems to have been coined in the eighteenth century, and is now less and less used among scholars. It is better to follow ancient precedent in this matter, and to call the language of the oldest periods *Old English*. We speak of this or that dialect of Old English, and also of Old Kentish, Old Mercian, etc.

§ 18. Relation of the O.E. Dialects to other Languages.

Old English belongs to the West Germanic branch of Germanic speech. Parent, or Primitive Germanic, was divided into three great branches: North Germanic, represented by the Scandinavian languages; East Germanic, represented chiefly by Gothic; and West Germanic. The principal divisions of the latter are Old Saxon, Old Frisian, Old English, and the Old High German dialects. Of these, Old Saxon and Old Frisian are most nearly related to English, the latter indeed having so many characteristics in common with O.E. that many scholars are inclined to assume an original unity which they call Anglo-Frisian, and suppose to have differentiated subsequently into Old English on one hand, and Old Frisian on the other. This assumption, however, is open to many criticisms into which we need not now enter.

The Old High German dialects underwent in the sixth century certain considerable changes in the original conso-nantal sounds, changes which we now find reflected in Modern German. On the other hand, Old High German adheres far more closely to the ancestral system of vowel sounds than any other West Germanic dialect, and also retains the original inflexions with remarkable fidelity.

By the help of Old Saxon and Old High German, both of which are in many respects nearer to the primitive West Germanic type than O.E., at the time of the oldest documents, we are able to form a very fair idea of a form of O.E. earlier than any which we find recorded, and also to reconstruct West Germanic itself. If we find a feature preserved only in O.H.G. among W. Gmc. dialects, but occurring also in Gothic, and perhaps in Nth. Gmc. as well, we are pretty safe in assuming that it was not only a West Germanic feature, but had survived from Primitive Gmc. itself. Such a feature is, for example, the survival of the old diphthong *ai* in O.H.G. (written *ai, ei*) as in *stein* 'stone', which in Goth. is *stains*, and in old Norse *steinn*. We have no doubt that this was a West Gmc. sound, though O.E., O.Sax., and O.Fris., have all lost it.

§ 19. The Chronological Divisions of English.

If we bear in mind that language changes gradually, and that it is perpetually changing, it will be evident that it is impossible to define with precision the exact date at which a language passes out of one stage and enters upon a new era of its existence. The process is a continuous one, and one period passes by insensible gradations into another. At any given moment there exist side by side with young speakers, whose language represents the 'latest thing' in speech development, an old generation who still represent an order of things which has passed away except in the speech of themselves and their exact contemporaries, and also an intermediate generation whose speech shows some characteristics both of the new and the old.

It is nevertheless the case, that round about a particular period of time, we can observe certain tendencies arising, and gaining ground as time goes on. We are thus able to mark off the course of any language whose records cover a considerable extent of time into more or less rough chronological divisions, each of which has definite features which distinguish it from what is before and after.

From this point of view, and for the sake of convenience, we make the following more or less rough and approximate chronological divisions of English:

Old English
- Earliest O.E. End of seventh century.
- Early O.E. Eighth and ninth centuries.
- Late O.E. From beginning of tenth century to about 1050.

Early Transition English.   From 1050–1150.

Middle English {
Early M.E.   1150–1250.
Central M.E.   1250–1370.
Late M.E..   1370–1400.
}

Modern English {
Early Modern.   1400–1500.
Seventeenth century.
Eighteenth century.
Present day.   From 1800.
}

Such divisions as these are necessarily arbitrary, and will largely depend upon what features are selected as distinguishing tests.   Some will prefer to consider the Modern period as beginning about 1450, and will apply the form Early Modern to English as it existed between this date and the middle of the following century.

CHAPTER III

THE SOUNDS OF SPEECH

§ 20. IT is not proposed to give here an elaborate treatise on Phonetics, but as Sounds are the realities of Speech, and as much confusion of thought often prevails concerning the nature and mode of formation of these, it seems desirable to include a few remarks concerning them.

In the first place it is important to use a clear terminology, and to use it consistently. A good phonetic terminology is one which expresses briefly, and unambiguously, the facts of utterance.

As experience has convinced the present writer that Sweet's method of classifying and describing sounds is the most exact and adequate, it will be employed throughout this chapter, and generally in this book.

NOTE. Symbols placed in brackets, as [þ], are phonetic symbols, which will be used in this work when necessary.

§ 21. Voice and Breath.

A very important organ of speech is the Glottis, which contains two membranes capable of vibration, and known as the vocal chords. When the vocal chords are drawn across the Glottis, so as to close it, the air when driven from the lungs passes in a series of puffs through the chords, and makes them vibrate. This vibration causes a buzzing sound which is known as *Voice*. Sounds which are accompanied by this vibration are known as Voiced Sounds. If, on the other hand, the vocal chords are not drawn tight, but lie folded back against the walls of the Glottis, the air passes through the throat without any hindrance, there is no vibration of the chords, no Voice. Sounds produced under these conditions, and without any vibration of the Chords, are called Voiceless, Un-voiced, or *Breath* sounds.

Examples of Voiced Sounds are the consonants *z* as in *buzz*, *v* as in *vice*, and the *th* [ð] in *this*. Vowels, as their name implies, are usually voiced in nearly all languages.

Examples of Voiceless, or Breath Sounds, are *s* in *sit*, *f* in *fat*, and the *th* [þ] in *think*.

§ 22. **Consonants and Vowels.**

The fundamental difference between Consonants and Vowels depends upon the degree of opening of the *Mouth Passage.*

Thus in a Consonant the mouth passage is either *completely stopped* for a moment, as in [p, t, k], or sufficiently closed or narrowed to produce a perceptible friction, as in [f], *sh* [ʃ] in *ship*, or *th* [þ] in *thin*.

In forming vowel sounds, on the other hand, the passage is never narrow enough to cause friction when the air-stream passes through. This can be realized at once if we compare the consonant [v] with the first vowel in *father* [ā].

Consonants formed by a momentary closing or *stopping* of the air-passage, as in [p, t, k], are called **Stops,** or **Stop-consonants;** those formed by merely narrowing the passage and causing friction [f, þ, ʃ] are called **Open Consonants,** or by some writers **Continuants.**

§ 23. **Classification of Consonants.**

There are three points to be observed in describing a Consonant sound : **Where is it made? How is it made? Is it voiced or not?**

§ 24. **The question 'Where?'**

Consonantal articulation, that is, the production either of Stops or Open Consonants, may take place in the Throat or in the Mouth Passage. Throat open consonants occur in Arabic, and a Throat Stop (Glottal Stop) occurs in Danish, and, in a milder form, in German, and in several forms of Scots, but as a rule the consonants of the European languages are formed in the mouth. This being so, it is better to discard altogether the misleading term *Guttural* in dealing with the sounds of English and other European languages.

The majority of the Consonants formed in the mouth are made by different parts of the tongue ; some are made by the lips, and some by the combined activities of tongue and lips. In addition to these organs, the soft palate or Velum and the Uvula also function, the former functioning together with the tongue in forming back consonants: stops, open, nasals, etc., the latter vibrating against the tongue in the back trills.

§ 25. **Consonants made with the Tongue.**

It is possible to form consonants with every part of the upper surface of the Tongue, along its whole length from the Root to the Point or Tip. It is important to map out roughly the chief characteristic areas of the tongue, since each of these forms a typical kind of consonant sound. Starting at the *Back* and working forward, we have the following areas: *Back*; *Front* (or Middle of the tongue); *Blade* (the area just behind the *Point*); the *Point* itself.

As a rule, a consonant is formed between the tongue and that part of the roof of the mouth immediately above the tongue area which is being used.

§ 26. Back Consonants.

Typical sounds of this class are [k, g], *back voiceless*, and *back voiced stops* respectively. This is the class often unfortunately called *Gutturals*, a misleading and meaningless term in this connexion, because they are not formed in the *Throat* at all, but between the *Back of the tongue* and the *Soft Palate*.

Note that *Back Consonants* may be made with the *Root* (Root Cons.); by the part just in front of the Root (Full Back); or slightly further forward (Back Advanced). The Back area is, however, perfectly definite in extent, and if we try to form [k] or [g] first with the Root, and then further and further forward, we shall find there is a limit which we cannot pass without the resulting sound ceasing to be a typical *Back* [k] or [g] stop, and becoming something quite different. The *Full Back* stop is heard in the English *cart*, *cup*; the *Back Advanced* in *keep*, *kit*. The reason for this difference will be apparent later, when we deal with the articulation of vowel sounds.

§ 27. Front Consonants.

This class of sounds, made with the *Middle* or *Front* of the tongue, is exceedingly important in the History of English, and unfortunately its character is often misunderstood. Much of the confusion of mind which prevails concerning *Front* consonants arises from the misleading and vague term *Palatal* which is often applied to them. The word ought to be banished from the vocabulary of scientific students of language because it has no meaning. If *Palatal* means ' formed with the roof of the mouth ', then it may be said that all consonants made by the tongue are formed between this and some part of the roof of the mouth; if it be argued that the term refers only to the *Hard Palate*, then the reply is that in that case it would apply also to a totally different class, the *Blade* consonants. The important thing is to know *what part of the tongue* is being used in forming a given consonant. We therefore shall do well to get rid for ever of this unmeaning term.

We have only one *Front Consonant* in Modern English, namely the *Front Open Voiced* which we write *y*, as in *you*, *yacht.* The symbol generally used for this is [j]. In German not only this sound exists, as in *jung*, *Jahr*, but also the voiceless form of it, as in *ich* [ij̊]. The student should make a point of realizing, by practice, when he is using the *Front* area of the tongue, and should then proceed to form a Stop Consonant, both Breath and Voiced, with the same part of the tongue. The *Front Stops* undoubtedly existed for a time in Old English. The effect on the ear of a voiceless front stop is that of a peculiar kind of [t]; that of the voiced front stop, of a peculiar kind of [d]. For this reason we denote these sounds by the symbols [t̑] and [d̑] respectively.

It should be noted that when we pronounce a *Front Consonant*, the tongue is drawn up so that the *Middle* is brought into play, and the *Point* is curled round and down, so that it lies in the cavity below and behind the lower front teeth. If the Point is in any other position than this we may be sure that we are not pronouncing a *Front Consonant* at all. Unless the theory and practice of this class of sounds be well understood, a great deal that is written about ' Palatalization ' is entirely devoid of meaning. Students must take the trouble to learn this, to most Englishmen and Germans, entirely new class of Stops. *Front Stops* occur in Russ. дядя [d̑ád̑a] and in Swedish *kenna* [t̑énna] ; *Front Divided* in Italian *voglio* [vɔ˘lo] ; *Front Nasal* in French *montagne* [mɔ̃tan̑], Ital. *vergogna* [vɛrgɔ́n̑a].

§ 28. Blade Consonants.

To this class belong [s] and [z]. These are really the only members of the group which concern us much, though in Modern English it is probable that some speakers use *Blade Stops* instead of the ordinary *Point Stops*, especially before [ʃ, ž] in the combinations [tʃ] and [dž] in *hitch, bridge* respectively.

§ 29. Blade Point Consonants.

The typical *Blade Point* Consonants are *sh* [ʃ], as in *ship, schön, cher,* and the initial consonant in French *jamais* [ž], the final in *rouge*, the medial consonant in *pleasure* [plɛžə]. While we have both the Voiced and Voiceless *Blade Point Open* consonants in English and French, in German only the voiceless [ʃ] exists, [ž] being often very difficult for German speakers to acquire.

In articulating this class of sounds, the *Blade* is raised, the tongue is slightly retracted, and the *Point* is turned upwards and backwards. The air-stream has to pass over both *Blade* and *Point*.

§ 30. Point Consonants.

These are often loosely called 'Dentals', a term which is not applicable to English [d] and [t], in which the Point does not touch the teeth, but forms a stop against the upper gums or *Alveolars* just behind the teeth. Thus the English *Point Consonants* [t] and [d] may be called *Point Alveolars* if it is desired to be very exact. As a matter of fact, the difference between point-teeth [t] and point-alveolar [t] is hardly perceptible to the ear. In German and French [t] and [d] are genuine *Point-Teeth* consonants, or '*Dentals*'.

§ 31. Point-Teeth Consonants.

The only *Point Consonants* which are articulated against the upper teeth in English are the *Point-Teeth Open* consonants, [ð] as in *this*, and [þ] as in *think*. The difficulty which foreigners sometimes find in pronouncing these sounds is largely imaginary. The way to obtain them is to pronounce the P.-T. Stops, and then relax the pressure against the teeth, so that the air-stream can pass through with the characteristic hiss or buzz of this class of sounds. In English, some speakers form [þ, ð] merely by putting the point of the tongue lightly *against* the upper teeth, other speakers allow the point to protrude slightly between the upper and lower teeth.

§ 32. Lip Consonants.

These are made by the activity of both lips. The Stops [b] and [p] are typical examples of this class, and need no comment.

§ 33. Lip-Teeth Consonants.

These are made by bringing the lower lip against the upper teeth, and allowing the air-stream to pass between the narrow passage thus formed. The Open consonants of this group, [f] and [v], exist in most European languages.

§ 34. Lip-Back Consonants.

The *Lip-Back Open* are the sounds which concern us. These are the English [w], and [w̥] or Voiceless [w] written *wh*, as in *which*. These sounds are made by bringing the lips fairly close together, so that a slight consonantal friction is caused when the air-stream passes, and at the same time

raising the *Back* of the tongue. English [w] is a very important sound, not merely because of its occurrence in Modern
English, but because it is one of the oldest sounds in the
language. It has remained unchanged, apparently, not merely
since the West Germanic and Primitive Germanic periods, but
even from the Primitive Aryan mother-tongue.

Voiceless [w], or [w̥] occurs invariably in those words which
are written with initial *wh* (except *who, whole,* and one or two
more), in the pronunciation of Scotch and Irish speakers.
Many English people, even in the South, now use this sound,
but it is certainly not natural in English speech from the
Midlands downwards, and has been introduced comparatively
recently—within the last thirty and forty years—apparently
through Scotch and Irish influence, backed up by the spelling.
Many excellent speakers of Standard English never use the
sound at all.

§ 35. Lip-Front Consonants.

These are formed, as regards their consonantal element,
entirely with the lips, but with the activity of the latter is
combined the raising of the *Front* of the tongue. The *Voiced
Lip-Front Open* [β] occurs in French *huit* [βit], etc., and the
voiceless [ɸ] in the same language, when *ui* is written, after
a voiceless consonant, especially an Open voiceless, as in
fuite [fɸit].

§ 36. The Question 'How?' Consonants are formed.

Besides knowing the area in the mouth at which consonants
are formed, it is necessary to know also *how* the active part
is being used.

We distinguish five *modes* of forming consonantal sounds:
Stops, and *Open Consonants*—already described, *Divided*
articulation, *Nasalization,* and *Trilling*.

Some areas of the tongue, e. g. the *Back* and the *Point,* can
be used in all these ways.

NOTE. A trill is made either *with* the point of the tongue, or *against*
the back of the tongue, *with* the uvula.

§ 37. Divided Consonants.

These are what are popularly called 'l'-sounds. They are
made by forming a complete contact between some part of
the tongue and the corresponding area of the palate or the
teeth, while at the same time the edges or sides of the tongue
are allowed to sink slightly, so that the air-stream can pass
on either side of the point of contact. Thus the English and

German [l] sounds are made with the *Point* of the tongue. There is a complete stoppage at one place, but on either side of this there is an opening through which the air-stream passes. Thus the *Divided Consonants* have something in common both with *Stops* and *Open Consonants*, since there is complete contact at one point, but also there is an open passage so that the sound can be prolonged. The same mode is practicable with the back of the tongue. The *Back Divided* [ɫ] is heard in Russian, e. g. in былъ. In English, [l] is unvoiced after a voiceless consonant, as in *fling*, where [l] begins unvoiced, and is then voiced. In French *souffle* [sūfl̥] the [l] is unvoiced altogether.

§ 38. Nasal Consonants.

Nasalization is produced by opening the passage which leads from the throat to the *Nose,* so that the air-stream passes through the latter.

Any consonant may be nasalized, that is, the nose passage may be open, no matter what activities are going on in the mouth passage. At the same time, in most civilized European languages, the nasalization of consonants is confined to stops. The chief characteristic nasals are [n] *Point-nasal*; [ŋ] *Back-nasal,* as in *sing* [siŋ]; *Lip-nasal* [m], *limb* [lim]. We might say with perfect accuracy that [n] was a nasalized [d]; [ŋ] a nasalized [g]; and [m] a nasalized [b]. The student may practise passing from [g] to [ŋ], [d] to [n], etc., by the simple process of opening the nose passage, without releasing the stop.

In some languages, voiceless nasals occur, but they are not very common. Thus in French *rhumatisme* is often pronounced [rømatism̥] but also [rømatizm(ə)].

§ 39. Trills.

These sounds are popularly known as the 'r'-sounds. The two chief, if not the only *Trills,* are the *Point-Trill* [r], and the *Back-Trill* [я]. The former, which is heard among Scotch speakers, and probably occurred in Old and Middle English generally, is made by the rapid vibration of the *Point* of the tongue just behind the upper teeth. The latter, often heard in French, is produced by retracting the tongue, raising the Back of this organ, and allowing the *Uvula* to vibrate upon the raised surface.

Modern English [r] is not really a *Trill* at all, but merely a very weak *Point Open* consonant. The *r*-sounds, both in French and English, are unvoiced after voiceless consonants.

§ 40. The meaning of the third point to be considered in describing consonants, whether they are voiced or not, has already been explained (§ 21).

§ 41. If we combine the three points just discussed, we get the following table of consonant sounds:

	Back.		Front.		Blade.		Blade-point.		Point.		Lip.		Lip-teeth.		Lip-back.		Lip-front.	
	B.	V.	B.	V.	B.	V.	B.	V.	B.	V.	B.	V.	B.	V.	B.	V.	B.	V.
Open	χ	ʒ	i̥	j	s	z	ʃ	ž	þ	ð	p̥	ƀ	f	v	w̥	w	φ	β
Stop	k	g	ťt	d					t	d	p	b						
Divided	ł̥	ł	·ł̥	·ł					l̥	l								
Nasal	ŋ̥	ŋ	n̥	ṅ					n̥	n	m̥	m						
Trill	я̥	я							r̥	r								

NOTE. The Blade and Blade-point stops, Divideds, and Nasals are omitted from this Table because they occur as a rule only in combination with [ʃ, ž, s, z]. Some speakers no doubt tend to assimilate [t] to [ʃ] in [tʃ], but it is unnecessary for our present purposes to distinguish these sounds by special symbols.

§ 42. General Remarks upon the Consonants.

In order to realize the precise nature of each consonant, and the organic relation of one group to another, as well as of the individual sounds in each group, it is desirable to practise various exercises.

The student should practise in the first place the art of *Voicing* and *Unvoicing*, that is of alternately closing and opening the vocal chords without altering the position of the organs of the mouth.

The Open Consonants, Divided, and Nasals are the best for this purpose, as they can be prolonged: [s—z, þ—ð, ʃ—ž, j—j] etc. Another exercise is nasalizing and de-nasalizing. °Thus the process of opening and closing the nose passage should be practised by passing from [g] to [ŋ] and vice versa, and the same exercise should be tried with [b—m, d—n].

It is well to practise the consonants in organically related groups; all the *point*, all the *back*, all the *front* consonants in order. While it is highly desirable to learn to isolate sounds, and to pronounce consonants by themselves, it is useful also to add the vowel [ā] in pronouncing a consonant, thus—[ðā dā, nā, lā, rā], and so on with the consonants of each group.

It is particularly instructive to pass from Stop to Open, from Open to Stop of each group, gradually opening the Stop until the Open is fully formed. Besides practising the sounds in this vertical order, it is also an excellent thing to start with a *back* consonant, and shift the place of articulation gradually forward, until the *point* of the tongue is reached: [gā, 'gā, ɖā, dā] and so on. Practise this also with the *Open, Divided, Nasal,* and *Trill,* both *Voiced* and *un-Voiced.*

These exercises are all of them important for the student of the history of a language, because they illustrate the various possible changes in articulation which occur from time to time during the life of a language. A thorough mastery of these processes makes the history of a language more of a reality, and enables the student to get away from graphic formulae. Thus in stating Verner's Law [see Note 2 following § 352] it is essential to think in terms of sounds rather than of symbols, and to be able to say that under such and such conditions the Germanic *Voiceless Open Consonants,* derived from the corresponding Aryan or Indo-Germanic *Voiceless Stops,* were voiced, rather than to think of the process in terms of a graphic formula and to say that *p, t, k* which had become *f, þ, χ,* later, under the conditions stated by Verner, became *ƀ, ð, ǥ.*

§ 43. The Classification of Vowel Sounds.

There are four points which must be considered in describing and classifying a *Vowel Sound*: the *Height of the Tongue*; the *Part of the Tongue used*; the *Condition of the Tongue*; the *Participation or non-Participation of the Lips.*

§ 44. The Height of the Tongue.

The Tongue can be raised or lowered in the mouth, and these movements correspond to the movements of the lower jaw. We distinguish three degrees of *Height*: *High, Mid,* and *Low.* In the *High* position the tongue is usually raised as high as is consistent with the absence of friction. Thus in [i] as in *beat, viel, si,* the tongue is practically as high as is possible without passing into a consonantal sound. If the tongue be raised but very little from the position which it occupies in [i] it soon ceases to be a vowel, and becomes [j]. The *Mid* position is that which the tongue occupies when it is in the middle of the mouth. The *Low* position involves a still greater lowering of the tongue and sinking of the lower jaw, so that the mouth is, comparatively speaking, fairly wide open. The three degrees of height are illustrated in the

three English words [bɪt, bɛt, bæt] which in the Standard
pronunciation are *High*, *Mid*, and *Low*, respectively. It is
important to learn to realize the upward and downward
movements of the tongue, and the student may learn a great
deal at the beginning by merely deliberately moving the
tongue up and down silently and without attempting to utter
any particular sound.

§ 45. The Part of the Tongue Used.

The tongue may be drawn back in the mouth, so that the
back part comes into play; it may be advanced, so that
the *front* comes into play; or it may lie practically *flat* in the
mouth, so that its whole upper surface is used.

Vowels made with the *Back* of the tongue are called *back
vowels*; those made with the *Front* are *front vowels*; those
with the whole surface are known as *flat vowels*.

NOTE. Sweet, whose classification is here used, describes the last
class as *Mixed Vowels*. The term *Flat* is used in this book, as less
likely to lead to confusion, and as being more descriptive of the facts.

Examples of *back vowels* are [ā] as in *father*, *Bahn*, etc.;
[ɔ] as in English *saw*.

Front vowels are heard in the English words *bet*, *bat*,
French *si*, *dé*, and in German *Vieh*, *lehnen*, etc.

Flat vowels do not occur in French, but a typical English
sound occurring in *heard*, *worm*, *curl* [hād, wām, kāl] belongs
to this group, as does the common unstressed vowel [ə], as in
butter [batə], *Wordsworth* [wādzwəþ]. A *flat vowel* is also
heard in German in the unstressed syllables of *Vater*,
Knabe, etc.

NOTE. In *back* vowels the tongue *slopes* down from *back* to *front*; in
front vowels, from *front* to *back*. These two classes are sometimes called
sloped vowels. In the *flat* vowels there is no *slope*, hence the name.

§ 46. The Condition of the Tongue.

The condition referred to is the muscular condition, which
may be one of *Tenseness*, in which the tongue is braced and
hard, or, on the other hand, one of *Slackness*, in which the
tongue is relatively soft and slack. Vowels uttered with the
tongue *tense* have a clearer, shriller sound, and a higher pitch,
than those uttered with the tongue *slack*. We call the former
tense vowels, the latter, *slack* vowels.

NOTE. Sweet uses the term *Narrow* for *tense* vowels, and *Wide* for
slack. *Tense* and *Slack* are used here, after the example of many

phoneticians, as being more definitely descriptive of the facts, and less likely to give rise to misapprehensions.

The essential and characteristic difference between *tense* and *slack* vowels may be heard by contrasting the *mid-front-tense* [e], as in French *dé*, or German *Weh*, with the *mid-front-slack* vowel [ɛ], as in English *head, pen,* or German *fett, hell,* etc.   The student should also attempt to distinguish between the different muscular sensations felt in pronouncing alternately [e] and [ɛ].

§ 47.   It is rather important to warn students against confusing *Tenseness* with *Height,* as is done by the ambiguous terminology too frequently used.   Thus when a writer talks of an '*Open Vowel*' and a '*Close Vowel*', it is never quite clear what he means.   For some writers call [ɛ] '*open e*' (German 'offenes *e*'), as distinct from [e] which they call '*close e*'.   Here the real distinction is *purely one of Tenseness,* and not of *Height* at all.   But the same writers also refer to [ɔ], as in English *saw,* as '*open o*', as distinct from [o] in French *beau* or German *Lohn.*   Here the distinction *is* definitely one of *Height*; [o] being *mid-back-tense,* and [ɔ] *low-back-tense.*

There is no necessary connexion between *Height* and *Tenseness.*   There are two distinct series of vowels, one made with a tense tongue, the other with a slack, but differing in no other particular.   Thus, if we take the *Front* vowels, we can pronounce *High, Mid,* and *Low Tense,* and also vowels in the same three positions *Slack.*   It is a mistake to suppose, as some writers appear to suggest, that in passing from the *High Tense* to the *Low Tense* it is necessary to pass through several *slack* stages.   If, for instance, the tongue be slightly lowered from the *High Tense,* we do *not* get a *Slack* vowel, but merely a lowered *Tense* vowel, unless, of course, the tongue be deliberately slackened, which is not at all necessary. A *mid-tense* vowel is not *higher* than a *mid-slack* in the sense that the whole tongue is raised.   It is true, however, that when the tongue is made taut, the upper surface, or part of it, stands up rather more than when the tongue is slack and soft. In the same way we can raise our arm to a certain position, and while neither raising it nor lowering it, we can either make the muscles stand out in lumps or allow them to lie soft and unstrained.   But unless we deliberately choose to do so, we do not raise the arm when we stiffen the muscles.

All this, like any other fact in phonetics, the student must bring to the test of his own experience.

§ 48. **The Activity of the Lips.**

In pronouncing a vowel sound the lips may either be passive, or, in some cases, drawn right back from the teeth (spreading), or they may be slightly protruded, so that they take part in the articulation, and modify the sound uttered. Vowels in whose formation the lips take part are called *Rounded* vowels; those in whose formation the lips take no part are called *Unrounded*. In describing a vowel of the latter sort, the term *Unrounded* need not be used, as it is assumed that if no mention is made of *Rounding* this is absent. Examples of *Rounded* vowels are: [y] as in French *but* [byt], which is *high-front-tense-round*; [ø] as in German *schön—mid-front-tense-round*; [u] as in English *boot* [būt]—*high-back-tense-round*; [o] as in German *Bohne* [bōnë] or French *beau* [bo]—*mid-back-tense-round*, and so on.

It should be realized that as the movements of the lips are quite independent of those of the tongue, *Rounding* may be combined with any *Position*, or *Height*, or *Condition* of the tongue.

The student should therefore practise combining *Rounding* with every possible tongue position, and also, starting with familiar *Round* vowels, he should learn to unround these, without altering the tongue position.

§ 49. **Degrees of Rounding : Different Kinds of Rounding.**

Some vowels have more *Rounding* than others. Normally, this depends upon the *Height* of the tongue ; the higher the tongue, the greater the degree of *Rounding*. Some languages have abnormally *rounded* vowels, that is, vowels with greater or less rounding than normally belongs to that degree of *height* with which they are uttered. Vowels which have more than normal *rounding* are known as *over-rounded*, those which have less, as *under-rounded*. *Over-rounding* occurs in the German *ü* in *Bühne*, where a *mid-front-tense* has the degree of *rounding* which belongs to a *high* vowel, so that the *ü* here is really [ø] with increased *rounding*. Again, the Swedish *god* 'good' is a *mid-back-tense* with *over-rounding*.

The effect upon the ear of an *over-rounded* vowel is that of the next higher round vowel, so that the vowel in *Bühne* suggests [ȳ] and that in Sw. *god* [ū].

In *Back-round vowels* the shape of the lip-opening is roughly ○ , in *Front-round vowels*, roughly 0.

§ 50.　Table of Vowel Sounds.

Unrounded Vowels.

	Front.		Back.		Flat.	
	Tense.	Slack.	Tense.	Slack.	Tense.	Slack.
High	ſ i *he, Sie*	ſ i *Fisch*	]	]	ʇ ï Russ. сыръ	ʇ ĭ bit (Engl.)
Mid	ſ e *dé, sehr*	ſ ɛ *bell,* Germ. Bett	] a b*u*t (Engl.)	] a *father Mann*	ʇ ë *gute*	ʇ ə *father*
Low	ſ	ſ æ *hat* (Engl.)	]	] âpre	ʇ ʌ b*i*rd	ʇ

Rounded Vowels.

	Front.		Back.		Flat.	
	Tense.	Slack.	Tense.	Slack.	Tense.	Slack.
High	f y *lune*	f t*y*ttö (Finn.)	ʇ u w*ho,* sh*oo*t; r*u*h	ʇ u p*u*t, K*u*ss	f ü Swed. *fru*	f
Mid	f ø *le,* G*oe*the	f	] o b*eau*	ʇ o Germ. Gott	ʇ	ʇ b*o*nne
Low	f	ſ ö *beurre,* Götter	ʇ ɔ h*a*ll	ʇ ɔ h*o*t (Engl.)	ɪ	ɪ

§ 51.　Pitch of Vowels.

Every vowel sound has an inherent musical *pitch*, or note, which depends upon the shape of the mouth passage, the condition of the tongue, and the position of the lips. This inherent pitch is drowned in ordinary speech by the powerful vibration of the vocal chords, and is best heard by *Whispering* the vowel.

By *Whisper* phoneticians mean a definite contraction of the Glottis, which causes a slight friction of the air-stream against the walls of this organ.

The factors which determine pitch have been briefly mentioned, but it may make it clearer if it be said that *front* vowels are *higher* in pitch than *back* vowels; *high* are vowels higher in pitch than *mid, mid* higher in pitch than *low*; *tense* vowels have a higher pitch than *slack*; *unrounded* vowels are higher than *rounded* vowels.

§ 52. Quantity or Vowel Length.

The length or duration of a vowel sound is relative to other vowels in the language. In English our so-called short vowels are often of considerable length, as long as, or even longer, than what are considered long in other languages.

Although there is no necessary connexion between *Length* and *Tenseness*, many languages tend to make most of their *long* vowels *tense* and their *short* ones *slack*. In English and German *long* [i] and [u] are always *tense*, the same sounds when *short* always *slack*. This same is not true of French, however, where [i] and [u] are always *tense*, and generally short, except before *r*.

§ 53. Nasal Vowels.

All vowel sounds may be pronounced with the nose passage open, and vowels so uttered are called *nasal* or *nasalized* vowels. Such vowels, though frequent in French and in Polish, are unknown in Standard English and in German. They certainly existed, however, in prehistoric O.E., as well as in West Germanic and Primitive Germanic. We express them by placing [~] over the ordinary vowel symbol, thus [bɔ̃] = French *bon*.

§ 54. Intermediate Degrees of Height.

Although we only distinguish three characteristic degrees of *Height*, intermediate degrees occur in many languages and dialects. Thus in many forms of Provincial English a pure *mid-front-slack* is unknown, the sound being replaced by a *mid* vowel so much lowered in the direction of the *low-front* [æ] that to unaccustomed ears it is barely distinguishable from that sound. In Modern Dutch the *high-front-slack* seems to be lowered to the *mid-front*, while in words where this must once have existed the sound is lowered to the *low-front*. Thus *pit* 'lamp-wick' sounds like [pet], and *veldt* like [vælt].

In Danish [e] is raised almost to [i]. These facts are instructive in tracing the history of pronunciation in a language. For instance, when we find that in English an earlier [hēd] 'heed' has become [hīd], there can be little doubt that we have here the result of a process of gradual raising, and that at one time our ancestors must have pronounced a raised form of [e], not yet [i] but gradually tending towards it.

§ 55. Diphthongs.

A *diphthong* is a combination of two distinct vowel sounds, one of which only is *stressed* or accentuated. Only the stressed element in a true diphthong is syllabic, the other element being too much lacking in sonority, compared with the strong element, to function as a separate syllable.

§ 56. The Syllable.

The simplest account of what constitutes a syllable is to say that anything which maintains a unity of utterance produces the impression of a single syllable ; anything which tends to break up or destroy that unity produces the impression of more than one syllable.

The syllable is the unit of utterance, and may consist of a single vowel [a, ā] ; of a single consonant [l, v, b, p], etc. ; of a vowel + consonant [at, al] ; of two vowels dominated by one stress [ái, iá], etc. ; of a group of consonants uttered with a single impulse of stress [pst].

The factors which break up the unity of an utterance are differences of Stress and differences of Sonority.

§ 57. Stress.

If [ā] be uttered with gradually diminishing Stress or Loudness, the sense of unity remains, and the same is true of a long vowel uttered with equal loudness throughout its whole duration.

If, on the other hand, a long vowel be uttered with strong or loud beginning, then sudden diminution of stress, then sudden increase, and again a diminution, the result is not one long, but a series of short syllables [á a á a á a]. This series would consist of six syllables, three strong and three weak.

§ 58. Sonority.

Such combinations as [al, ad, aþ, ai] consist of a sonorous element followed by one less sonorous. The reduction in sonority is gradual, and does not break the sense of unity. On the other hand, if the sonority be reduced and then increased again, the effect is at once that of two syllables. Thus [ala, aþa, aia] cannot be other than two syllables. Here the sonority is reduced by [l, þ, i] respectively. [a] being a vowel is more sonorous than [l, þ] ; much more so than the latter, which is not only a consonant, but voiceless. [a] is more sonorous than [i] because, although the latter is a vowel, it is a high-vowel, and therefore has a narrower air-passage than the former, which is a mid-vowel.

Sonority then may be reduced in various ways: (1) by a pause, as in [a]/[a]; (2) by a Stop placed between vowels, which interrupts the sound altogether for a moment, if voiceless, and almost so, if voiced—[aba, apa]; (3) by an open consonant, which requires a narrower air-passage, and is therefore less sonorous than the highest vowel uttered with equal force [afa, apa, asa, aza], etc.; (4) by a less sonorous (higher) vowel, between two more sonorous (lower) vowels [aua, aia].

In combinations such as [æpl] we have the requisite conditions for the existence of two syllables—Sonorous sound + complete momentary cessation of sound in [p], followed by great increase of sonority in [l]. The last sound here becomes syllabic by contrast with the un-sonorous [p]. In [plɛit] there is only one syllable, because there is a gradual increase of sonority from the beginning of the word until the first element of the diphthong, and then a gradual reduction. [l] here is not syllabic because its sonority is drowned by the greater sonority of the vowel which follows.

§ 59. Limits of the Syllable.

The question, at what point one syllable ends and the next begins, is largely one of the incidence of fresh stress or impulse of breath.

The point of lowest stress constitutes the close of the syllable, and the next begins at the moment at which the new impulse is given. In *anigh* [ə/nai], the nasal consonant begins with the breath impulse, and it therefore belongs to the second syllable. In *an eye*, in careful speech [ən ai] the reduction goes on until the end of [n], and the new impulse begins with [ai]; in this case, therefore, [n] belongs to the first syllable.

In rapid, unstudied speech, the syllable-division in *an eye* tends to be precisely the same as in *anigh*, namely [ə/nai].

CHAPTER IV

GENERAL PRINCIPLES OF THE HISTORY OF LANGUAGE

§ 60. IT has already been pointed out, in the Introductory Chapter, that the drama of the development of Language takes place, so to speak, upon the lips and in the minds of living human beings, and not in books or written documents. In other words, language changes by being spoken.

We are therefore concerned to understand, so far as may be, how the activities of the speakers are related to the changes which these make in their language.

We must consider that if a nation gradually alters its language it is the individual speakers who are each and all responsible for what is happening. What is true of the individuals will be true also for the community as a whole, for this consists of a number of individuals.

§ 61. We can, then, begin by considering the behaviour of the individual as a speaker, that is, as a channel and transmitter of language. Why should he change his speech? Having learnt to speak, as his fathers have taught him, why should he not preserve his language unaltered and hand it on in his turn, unaltered, to the younger generations?

§ 62. The answer to this may be briefly summarized by saying that language is the expression of the thoughts and emotions of the human mind, by means of sounds, produced by certain movements of human bodily organs—the organs of speech.

This being so, there is a prima facie probability that language will not remain unchanged as it passes from generation to generation, for it is clear that the thoughts and feelings of humanity, even of such a portion of it as we call a single race, tribe, nation, are not at all times the same, but are capable of enrichment, expansion, and modification in a hundred ways, with the advance of civilization or the fortunes of its history. More than this, what can be more subject to alteration than the way in which a series of bodily movements are performed by human beings? If we remember that a slight change in the way of moving the organs of speech may cause a very considerable alteration in the sound which results, it does not surprise us that pronunciation should change.

§ 63. Now the individual, having acquired the sounds of his mother tongue, having, that is to say, mastered the various series of movements of the vocal organs necessary to the production of the different sounds, does not carry out these movements always in precisely the same way. He varies slightly, sometimes in one direction, sometimes in another. According to his personal habits he will tend to vary more commonly in one particular way, and thus he forms a new habit. From this new habit of using his organs of speech, the individual necessarily produces a slightly different sound from that with which he started. It must be noted that both the new way of using the speech organs, and the sound which results from this, deviate so slightly from the old that the speaker is quite unaware of the fact that anything is being changed. If he were by chance to diverge to an appreciable and recognizable extent from the pictures of sound and movement which exist in his mind he would at once feel that he had made a 'slip of the tongue', for his muscular sensations and his ear would tell him that he was 'wrong', and he would 'correct' himself. Thus no new habit could be started by a sudden, considerable, and appreciable divergence from the sound at which the speaker is unconsciously aiming. New departures in pronunciation, therefore, are necessarily unconscious, and *sound change is gradual*.

The tendency to variation is continuous, so that when the individual has formed a new habit he does not stick to it, but proceeds to diverge again from this fresh starting-point.

§ 64. But what is true of a single speaker is true also of all his companion speakers, of all the members of the community. They all tend to change their pronunciation, and they agree, on the whole, in the particular direction in which their tendency runs. This agreement in the direction of change is brought about by social intercourse, whereby speakers tend to assimilate their speech to that of the other persons among whom they live and with whom they consort most frequently and intimately. The closer the bond of union between the members of a group of speakers, the more closely the speech of all will agree. But no two individuals, however much they may resemble each other, are precisely alike in all respects. It is therefore inconceivable that all the members of a large community should agree exactly in their tendencies. We have to distinguish (*a*) tendencies which are shared by the whole community, and (*b*) tendencies which are not common to the whole but belong only to a comparatively few individuals. The groups of tendencies which come under (*b*) are got rid of and eliminated by the wear and tear of social intercourse, while the groups (*a*) pervade the whole community and become the universal tendency of the community. Thus it is possible to state as a general principle, that at a given time, in a particular community, a given sound will tend to be pronounced in the same way, and also, what is pretty much the same thing, will tend to change in the same direction. This remains true of all the words in which the sound occurs *under the same conditions.*

§ 65. The last expression needs some explanation. We distinguish two kinds of sound change, *Isolative* and *Combinative*. By Isolative sound change is meant change which occurs in a sound without any influence being exerted upon it by other sounds in the word or sentence. By Combinative sound change is meant a change in pronunciation brought about by the influence of other sounds in the same word or sentence. Thus the change of Primitive O.E. *ǣ* to *ē* in the Anglian and Kentish Dialects is an Isolative change. Whenever this sound *ǣ* occurs it is raised to *ē* : *wǣron* becomes *wēron*, *rǣd* becomes *rēd*, *scǣp* becomes *scēp*, and so on. On the other hand, the change of original *c* [k] to *ċ* [t] in O.E. is purely a Combinative change, since it only occurs before Primitive O.E. front vowels, or, when final, *after* front vowels : *ċēas* ' chose ', earlier **kæus* ; *ċin* ' chin ', earlier **kin* ; *ċetel* 'kettle', earlier **kætil* ; and so on.

Thus we must qualify the statement that the same sound always changes in the same way, by the addition of the words —*under the same conditions.* It sometimes happens that it takes a long time to discover the precise conditions which determine a sound change. Thus it took forty years after Grimm had formulated his Law of the changes of Indo-Germanic *p, t, k* in Germanic, before the conditions were discovered which determined the changes, apparently exceptional, of these sounds which appeared in certain words. Then, in 1877, Verner was able to supplement the original statement by supplying the conditions under which, instead of appearing in the Germanic Languages as the corresponding *Voiceless Open* consonants, the above sounds were voiced. This time it turned out that the ' exceptional ' voicing which had puzzled Grimm, his contemporaries, and immediate successors, was due to the place of the Accent. (See § 346.)

We proceed, then, with our investigations into the history of a language on the assumption of the principle that *Sound Laws admit of no exceptions*, subject to the limitations of time, dialect, and phonetic conditions just referred to.

If apparent exceptions appear, they may be capable of explanation : (*a*) by the discovery of the *Combinative Factors* at work ; (*b*) by the 'exceptional' form being borrowed from another dialect where the sound changes followed different lines ; (*c*) by the principle of *Analogy*, which will be discussed later on.

66. The Rise of Dialects.

We have so far considered sound change only as occurring regularly and uniformly throughout a single speech community. Outside the narrow limits of our community the same original sound may be treated in very different ways. This brings us to the question of the rise of Dialects, or varieties of speech, from what was once a uniform, homogeneous language.

The very conception of a Family of Languages, with a common ancestor, from which all the related languages have sprung, implies this *Differentiation of Dialect*, as we call it.

The existence of differences in speech, whether in modern England or ancient Germany, means that we have not a single community but many, not one Dialect but many.

§ 67. If we define *Speech Community* as a group of human beings between whom social intercourse is so intimate that their speech is practically homogeneous, then whenever we find appreciable speech differences we must assume as many communities, and it will follow that there will be as many Dialects as communities. Thus, any factors that split up one community into two or more are also factors of differentiation of dialect. The main factors which divide one group of human beings from another are : (1) *Geographical and Physical*—seas, rivers, mountain ranges, distance, any features of the country which actually separate communities by interposing barriers between them ; (2) *Occupational*—differences of employment, which lead, in modern society, to distinctions of *Class*; (3) *Political*, or divisions which depend not on physical boundaries but on arbitrary lines of demarcation, drawn for purposes of government—e. g. county, or even parish boundaries, or frontiers between countries.

The ideal condition of a community with a ring-fence round it, shutting it off from all other communities and their influence, is only realizable in districts remote from large centres of population, and where high mountains, deep valleys, broad rivers, moors, or deserts form natural means of isolation. Similarly, a community in the ideal sense, one in which there are no factors that divide the people up into more or less distinct groups, so that every individual has free and frequent social intercourse with every other, is hardly a conceivable phenomenon except under the most primitive conditions and when the population is small.

§ 68. What result does the division of one community into several exert upon the language? Why should it give rise to dialectal variety? Because when one part of a community is isolated from the rest, the balance of tendencies and of checks is altered. Individual tendencies, which under the old conditions were shared only by a small minority and therefore eliminated, exist in a different proportion under the new conditions, and survive unchecked by social intercourse as it now exists. In a word, different tendencies to variation flourish in the various parts of what was originally a single, undivided community. The result is that the speech changes in different directions, and on different lines, in each of the newly formed communities. Such is the beginning of Dialectal divergence, which if it continues for a long period of time produces differences of the kind and extent that we can witness in comparing the various Germanic languages with each other, and further, the far greater distinctions that are seen in comparing Germanic speech with Italic, or Celtic, and so on.

§ 69. The difference between a Dialect and a Language is one of degree and not of kind. If one form of speech is a mere variant of another, and shows but a slight divergence from it, one which only affects certain features, and these, perhaps, to a comparatively slight extent, so that the speakers of the two varieties are mutually intelligible, we should apply to such differences the term Dialect. When, however, the differences become so considerable, after a long independent development, that one set of speakers must acquire deliberately the mode of speech of the other before communication between them is possible, then we should say that here we have two separate languages. But even this terminology is rather popular than scientific, and philologists often employ the word *Dialect* where in popular phraseology *Language* would be used.

§ 70. Analogy.

By the side of sound change the other great factor in the development of language is *Analogy*. This principle has long been recognized among students of language, but a distinction was formerly made by Grammarians between 'true' and 'false' Analogy. The former was supposed to be a legitimate and natural process, the latter a corrupt and erroneous one. This distinction can no longer be maintained, and whatever the results may be, whether conservative and in accordance with past habits in the language, or whether, on the other hand, they lead to new departures, and, historically speaking, 'incorrect' forms, the process of Analogy is now recognized as being a perfectly natural one, of the same essential nature in all cases, and one which at every period of every language is necessarily in operation.

Briefly, analogy is the process whereby, in the first instance, words are associated in the mind in groups, whether it be according to *meaning, grammatical function, resemblance of sound*, to a combination of two of these, or even of all three. When once words have become associated together in the mind there is a tendency to connect them still more intimately and treat them as far as possible in the same way.

It is by virtue of the process of Analogy that we are able to conjugate the verbs, decline the nouns, form adverbs from adjectives, and so on, in any language which we know. As a rule, especially if the language be our native tongue, we arrive at the same results as the majority of speakers of our age and class. This means that, on the whole, our association-groups are the same as theirs. Thus we associate the Pl. of *cat* with thousands of other Pls. and unhesitatingly form [kæts] from the Sing. [kæt]; we do not find any difficulty in forming the adverb *cunningly*, etc., from *cunning*, etc., even if it should happen that we do not remember to have heard the particular adverb before. We have plenty of analogous forms to serve as a pattern. Similarly, we should not hesitate to form the Pret. *jeered* [džiəd] from the Vb. *jeer*, on the analogy of *cleared*, etc. All these happen to be in accordance with the habits of Standard English at the present time, and therefore the results are what the older school would call 'true' Analogy. But supposing that on the Analogy of *to clear*, *to fear*, *to jeer*, we formed the Pret. of *to hear* '*heared*' [hiəd]. This would be a perfectly natural process, and, indeed, identical with that whereby in the other cases we had arrived at 'correct' results, but the form in this case would not be in

E

accordance with the habits of educated speech. It so happens that in Standard English *hear*, as regards its Pret., is an isolated word which has to be learnt specially. If we have never noticed the form [hād] and do not know it, we cannot invent it; the ordinary Analogies do not work here. The old school would call this 'false' Analogy. It is as if in German, on the Analogy of *tragen*, Pret. *trug* [trūχ], we made a Pret. *sug* [sūχ] for *sagen*. As a matter of fact, the Pret. *frug* instead of *fragte* from *fragen* is often used, and it is clearly due to 'false' Analogy. It would be perfectly natural to use *sug* if we use *frug*, especially as *sagen* and *fragen* are associated in meaning as well as by sound. That this kind of thing continually happens in the history of a language, no one who has studied the subject doubts, and such 'false' Analogies constantly become the received and 'correct' forms.

This simply means that from age to age the association-groups of a community change their content. As it is, we find at the present day different association-groups among persons of different education and social class. This is well illustrated if we compare the standard language with the various popular dialects.

It often happens that in the declension of a noun, or the conjugation of a verbal tense, two quite distinct types or forms of the base or root arise, and that in the course of time the difference between the two forms becomes extreme, so that it is difficult to associate them together as merely Sing. and Pl. of the same noun or whatever it may be. Thus the O.E. Sing. type of *dæġ* 'day' in M.E. is *dei*, or *dai*, whereas the Pl., which in O.E. is *dagas, daga, dagum*, becomes in M.E. *dāwes*, etc. In Present-day English this difference would result in Sing. [deí], Pl. [dɔ̄z]. As a matter of fact, already in M.E. one or other type is usually eliminated in such a case as this, and the dialect settles down either upon the *day*-type, or the *daw*-type, and uses this for both numbers. No doubt, had there been a fair number of common words, sufficient to form an association-group of *-ei* or *-ai* as a Sing. form, and *-aw* as a Pl. form, the distinction might have been preserved longer, but as it is there was nothing to support a vowel change of this nature, combined with the addition of the Pl. suffix, so the Pl. type of the root disappeared. Those words which we call mutation-plurals—*teeth, geese, men*, etc., had in O.E. the mutated vowel in the Dat. Sing. as well as in the Nom. and Acc. Pl., whereas the un-mutated vowel occurred also in the Gen. and Dat. Pl. What happened was that in those few words which preserved mutation, the whole

Sing. was formed on the type of the Nom. and Acc. Sing. without mutation, and the whole Pl. on the type of the Nom. and Acc. Pl. with mutation. The case-sense, as we may call it, did not survive long in M.E. and, apart from the Possessive or Gen. case, a word was felt merely to be in the Nom. or case of the Subject, or else in the Acc. or case of the Object— the Dat. case relation being no longer felt.

Enough has been said to enable the student to understand what is meant by Analogy, and to guard him against surprise when he finds the far-reaching effects of the process in making new departures from the historically 'correct' usage.

§ 71. Foreign Contact.

When two communities, speaking different languages, or even different forms or dialects of the same language, come into close social contact, it generally happens that the speech of each is influenced by the other.

If the members of the two communities become so intimately intermingled that they intermarry, and gradually fuse into a single community, there is generally a period of bilingualism, during which all members of the community speak both tongues.

Then one or other of the two languages gradually ceases to be spoken and the other survives as the sole language.

Such conditions as these inevitably result in modification of the pronunciation of one or both languages, and in mutual exchanges in vocabulary. This actual physical contact between two groups of speakers brings about what we call *Direct* influence of one language upon the other.

The result of this intimate association upon pronunciation is that one language is spoken with a 'foreign accent', so that many or all the characteristic sounds of a language are given up in favour of those in the other which most closely resemble them. In many districts of Wales, where English has been spoken for generations alongside of Welsh, the English pronunciation is as foreign as that of a German or a Frenchman, and although there is extraordinary fluency and volubility, and even considerable 'correctness' in Grammar and Syntax, the sentence stress, the intonation, and all the sounds are purely Welsh and un-English.

Some such fate as this probably overtook Norman French as spoken in this country, some time before it died out.

The effect of bilingualism upon vocabulary is that speakers to whom two languages are equally familiar frequently introduce words from one language into their discourse when they are speaking the other.

The first words thus introduced will naturally be such as denote objects or ideas which are new to the people into whose language they are introduced, for which therefore there are no corresponding terms. But the process is soon extended to words for which native terms do exist. Thus the familiar words *skin, sky, they, their* were introduced from Scandinavian into English, as it might be said, without any adequate reason. Again, if the two languages thus brought into contact are closely related to start with, many words, though differing slightly in form in each tongue, are perfectly intelligible to all, in either form. This was the case for Old English and Old Norse, and there is no doubt that English speakers often used the English and Norse forms indiscriminately. This fact probably accounts for our present forms *give* and *get*, to mention no more, which certainly cannot be derived from the original pure English forms.

When at last one language dies out, and the other becomes the only form of speech, the survivor will have acquired, in the way just described, a more or less considerable number of *loan-words* from the language which has perished, and many of these will remain as permanent elements, used, sometimes instead of native words which they have ousted, sometimes by the side of these, to express an identical object or idea, or with a slight differentiation of meaning.

Words borrowed in this direct way usually have the nearest approximate pronunciation to the original which the borrowers can manage. The subsequent history of the pronunciation of these words is identical with that which the sounds which they contain undergo in native words in the language into which they have passed.

§ 72. The chief foreign linguistic influences which have been exerted *directly* upon English are those of the language of the Scandinavian invaders and settlers of England, and of Norman French. We must, however, include the early Latin loan-words acquired in Britain from Celtic speakers of Latin, and a great deal of the Latin which came in through the influence of the early Church, for many Latin terms used in connexion with religion, and learnt directly from public services, became familiar household words.

§ 73. By *Indirect* influence, we mean that exerted through literature. Words from ancient and modern languages are acquired by English writers from the authors they study, and are introduced by them into their own writings. Many of these remain purely literary words, or never gain currency at all ; others pass from literature into everyday speech. Modern scientific conceptions, new substances, and processes the result of scientific investigation, are commonly designated by Greek terms, often taken straight out of the dictionary.

The distinction between *popular* and *learned* words is an important one, though not always easy to draw. The character of a word from this point of view depends not upon its origin, but its usage. *Phonograph* is made up of two Greek words, and is therefore of learned origin, but with the spread of the machine among the people, the name has passed into popular usage. On the other hand, such words as *eftsoons, welkin, whilom,* and many more of the same kind, are pure English in origin, yet are in no sense *popular,* but rather, so far as they can be said to exist at all, at the present day, belong exclusively to learned, or literary language.

§ 74. We must not omit to mention the influence of one dialect, or variety, of the same language upon another. This has been of great importance in the history of English. The existence of various dialectal elements in Standard English has been determined by political, economic, and social causes. These may take the shape of spreading a particular sound change far beyond its original regional limits, or they may produce the wholesale importation of a particular dialectal type of certain words into a *Regional* or *Class Dialect* to which this was formerly quite alien.

The most typical features of dialect, it should be remembered, are pronunciation and grammatical forms. It is a far more difficult thing to localize vocabulary, and track it down to its original source. Most Standard English speakers use a certain number of ' Dialect' words, sometimes deliberately, knowing them to be such, sometimes without realizing the fact. This is particularly the case with terms relating to agriculture and sport. No Standard English speaker, except as a joke, would say, ' *us kep on tellin' he not to hurt un* ' [as kɛp ɔn tɛlin ī nɔt tu ʌ˞t ən], or talk about [rain, baɪl, baʃ, ūk, kʊm, ī] for [rein, bɔil, buʃ, hʊk, kam, hī] *rain, boil, bush, hook, come, he.* On the other hand, any one who turns over the pages of a Dialect Dictionary cannot fail to come across dozens of words with which he has been familiar all his life. This means, either that the reader is a ' Dialect speaker' without knowing it, or that the dictionary-maker has been unable to distinguish between ' Dialect' and Standard English.

CHAPTER V

HISTORY OF ENGLISH SOUNDS

I. THE OLD ENGLISH PERIOD

§ 75. Sources of our Knowledge of O.E.

FROM the point of view of the student of English Literature or Culture, everything which survives in the documents of the O.E. period is of more or less interest. In particular, the more imaginative poetical literature would claim our attention from these points of view; the philosophical and religious treatises which exist in the form of Homilies; the Laws, and the books on Medicine and on the use of herbs, and charms,—all have their claims on our consideration for various reasons. Again, the Lexicographer, and the student of O.E. as a mode of expression, would cast their net as widely as possible, and, to them, the precise dialect in which the literature was written would not be of prime concern.

In the present instance, however, our aim is to get a clear idea of the phonological peculiarities of each of the O.E. dialects, and for this purpose we must base our investigation upon those texts whose place or area of origin is pretty definitely known. Our list of sources, then, is a comparatively narrow one, and we are guided in our selection of the texts, not by their literary merits, but simply by their fitness to illustrate, in a reliable manner, particular dialects at a particular time. Apart from the texts mentioned below as definitely belonging to other dialects, most of the important O.E. documents which survive are written in a form in which the W.S. elements greatly predominate, but they often show a mixture of dialectal elements from other sources. This, as in the case of the poetry, is generally the result of the texts having been done into W. Saxon from another dialect, in which process some of the original features have been allowed to remain unaltered. Poetical texts not infrequently bear traces of having passed through several dialects, all of which have left their mark, as in Beowulf, in the form we possess.

Pure examples of the various dialectal types are found in the following works:

§ 76.　　　　**A. Northumbrian.**

1. Earliest Texts.

Fragments (poetical) in Sweet's Oldest English Texts
(O.E.T.), pp. 149, etc.　circa 737.
Liber Vitæ (Personal Names), O.E.T., pp. 153, etc.

Northern Area.

Genealogies. O.E.T., p. 167, etc.
Place and Personal Names in Moore MS. of Bede's
Eccl. Hist., O.E.T., p. 131, etc.　circa 737.
Ruthwell Cross Inscription, O.E.T., pp. 125, 126.
[There are no ninth-century Northumbrian Texts.]

2. Late Texts.

Northern Area.

Durham Ritual: Surtees Soc., vol. iv, 1849 (collated by
Skeat, Trans. Phil. Soc., 1879).
Durham Book, also called *Lindisfarne Gospels.* Ed.
Skeat, Gospels in Anglo-Saxon, 1871–1887.

Southern Area.

Interlinear version of the *Gospels of SS. Mark, Luke,
John,* in Rushworth MS., known as *Rushworth*[2]. Ed.
Skeat in Gospels cited above.

§ 77.　　　　**B. Mercian.**

1. Earliest Texts.

Epinal Glossary (circa 700) ⎫ Both in O.E.T., pp. 36–107.
Corpus Glossary (circa 750) ⎭
Eighth-Century Charters [in Latin; containing O.E.
words and names], O.E.T., pp. 429, etc.

2. Ninth-Century Texts.

Vespasian Psalter and Hymns, O.E.T., pp. 183, etc.

3. Late Texts.

Interlinear Gloss to St. Matthew (Rushworth[1], second
half of tenth century), Skeat's Gospels in Anglo-
Saxon.
Royal Glosses (fr. MS. Royal 2 A. 20). Ed. Zupitza,
in Zeitschr. f. d. A., Bd. xxxiii, pp. 47, etc.　circa 1000.

§ 78.   **C. West Saxon.**

Earliest Texts.

Charters: 1. (692 or 693); 2. (693–731); 3. (778).
O.E.T., pp. 426–427.

Ninth-Century Texts.

Works of King Alfred: { *Cura Pastoralis*, Sweet, E.E.T.S., 1871.
Orosius, Sweet, E.E.T.S., 1880.
Anglo-Saxon Chronicle: Parker MS. to 891, Plummer, Oxford. 2 vols. 1892–1900.

Late Texts.

Ælfric's Grammar and Glossary (circa 1000). Ed. Zupitza, 1880.
Ælfric's Homilies. Editions by Thorpe, and Skeat.
West Saxon Gospels (in C.C.C.C. MS.). Ed. Skeat, Gospels in Anglo-Saxon.

D. Saxon Patois.

Late O.E.

Blickling Homilies (dated 979). Ed. Morris, E.E.T.S., 1880.
Harleian Gloss (MS. Harl. 3376), printed in Wright-Wülker's Glossaries, vol. i. 192, etc.

§ 79.   **E. Kentish Texts.**

Earliest Texts.

Charters (seventh and eighth centuries), O.E.T., pp. 427, etc.

Ninth Century.

Charters, in O.E.T., pp. 441, etc.; three of these also in Sweet's *A.-S. Reader*, pp. 189, etc.
Bede Glosses (MS. Cotton C. II, circa 900), O.E.T., pp. 179, etc.

Late Texts.

Kentish Glosses, Zupitza, in Zeitschr. f. d. A., xxi, pp. 1, etc., and xxii, pp. 223, etc.; also in Wright-Wülker's *Vocabularies*, 55, etc.
Kentish Hymn, in Kluge's *Ags. Lesebuch*, and Sweet's *A.-S. Reader.*
Kentish Psalm (Ps. l), in Kluge's *Lesebuch.*

§ 80. Mode of Writing Old English.

The English, like all the Germanic tribes of Germany and Scandinavia, used at a very early period certain angular letters, which they graved upon horn, stone, wood, or metal. These letters, known as *Runes*, were chiefly used in charms, and inscriptions commemorating the dead or the illustrious upon monuments. Some of these inscriptions still exist in England and upon the Continent, but they are, for the most part, of no very great antiquity, not older indeed than the earliest manuscripts.

The ordinary mode of writing, which the English acquired after embracing Christianity, was a form of the Latin alphabet, which had come through an Irish source. Modern Irish is still written and printed in characters which closely resemble those of the O.E. MSS.

In writing and printing O.E. at the present day we use the ordinary alphabet; except that we borrow the signs *æ, þ,* and *ð*. The first had the value of the *low-front-slack* vowel, which we also denote in this way in phonetic transcription; the two others appear to have been used indifferently for the *point-teeth-open*, whether *Voiced*, or *Unvoiced*. Some editors also print ƿ for *w*, and ᵹ or ȝ for *g*, but this habit is very largely discarded now. ƿ and þ were taken over from the Runic alphabet.

NOTE. The names and forms of the various O.E. Runes are recorded in the *Runic Poem*, the text of which is given in *Bibl. d. ags. Poesie* (vol. containing Beowulf, etc.), 1883, p. 331, the text also by Bodkine, with a French translation, *La Chanson des Runes*, Havre, 1879. B. does not give the runes themselves. A table of all the known Germanic Runes, and an account of these, is given by Sievers in the section Schriftkunde in Paul's *Grundriss*. See also Bibliography above, B. vi.

§ 81. Pronunciation of O.E.

So far as we can discover, the following were the O.E. sounds:

SIMPLE VOWELS.

	Un-Rounded.		Rounded.	
	Front.	Back.	Front.	Back.
High	i, ī		H. y, ȳ	u, ū
Mid	e, ē	a, ā	M. œ, œ̄	o, ō
Low	æ, ǣ		L.	

§ 82.   DIPHTHONGS.

eo, ēo	ea, ēa	ie, īe
io, īo		

The diphthongs were pronounced pretty much as written ;
it should be noted, however, that whereas in *ĕo, ĭo*, the first
element was probably *tense*, and definitely *mid*, and *high*
respectively, in *ĕa* the first element was probably *slack*, and
low. *ĭe* occurs only in W. Saxon, and at an early period was
apparently levelled under *ĭ* in pronunciation, in part of the
Saxon area. Elsewhere, in Late W.S. *ĭe* was monophthongized
and rounded to [ў̆].

There were, in O.E., probably, both varieties of diphthongs
—*falling*, and *rising* diphthongs, e. g. *eo, eó*, etc.

In the latter, the first element was, originally, merely a glide-
sound. This class of diphthongs is of later development than
the other diphthongs which were developed in O.E. itself.

§ 83.   Examples of the occurrence of O.E. Vowels.

O.E. Symbol.	Analysis of Sound.	O.E. Words.
a	mid-back, as in Germ. *Mann.*	*assa* 'ass', *dagas* 'days', *faran* 'to go'.
ā	mid-back long, as in Germ. *Wahn.*	*hām* 'home', *stān* 'stone', *hlāf* 'loaf'.
e	mid-front, as in Fr. *été.*	*beran* 'to bear', *(ġe)seten* 'set' (p.p.), *helan* 'hide'.
e	mid-front, as in Engl. *hen.*	*menn* 'men', *seċġan* 'to say', *sendan* 'send'.
ē	mid-front long, as Germ. *lehnen.*	*fēdan* 'to feed', *gēs* 'geese', *mētan* 'to meet', *hēr* 'here', *wē* 'we'.
i	high-front, as in Germ. *Biss.*	*sittan* 'to sit', *sċip* 'ship'.
ī	ibid. long, as in Germ. *Biene.*	*sīþ* 'journey, time', *wrītan* 'to write'.
æ	low-front, as in Engl. *hat*, etc.	*sæd* 'sated, weary', *cræft* 'skill, trade'.
ǣ	ibid. long.	*sǣd* 'seed', *grǣdig* 'greedy'.
o	mid-back round, as in Germ. *Stock.*	*hopu* 'hope', *horn* 'horn', *brocen* 'broken'.
ō	mid-back-tense-round, as in Germ. *Hohn.*	*bōt* 'help, remedy', *bōc* 'book, charter', *blōd* 'blood'.
u	high-back-round, as in Engl. *put.*	*sunu* 'son', *full* 'full'.
ū	high-back-tense-round, Germ. *Stube.*	*hūs* 'house', *rūn* 'whisper, mystery'.
y	high-front-round, Germ. *küssen.*	*cynn* 'race', *byċġan* 'to buy', *wyrm* 'worm'.
ȳ	ibid. long, French *pure.*	*fȳlan* 'defile', *brȳd* 'bride', *hȳþ* 'landing-place, harbour' (*hithe*).

§ 84. Diphthongs.

O.E. Symbol.	O.E. Words.
ea	*ċeaf* 'chaff', *hleahtor* 'laughter'.
ēa	*ċēas* 'chose', *rēad* 'red', *lēas* 'false'.
eo	*eorþe* 'earth', *heofon* 'heaven', *feohtan* 'to fight'.
ēo	*ċēosan* 'to choose', *hlēoþor* 'sound, melody'.
ie	*hierde* 'shepherd', *Sċieppend* 'Creator'.
īe	*hīeran* 'to hear', *ċīesþ* 'he chooses'.

§ 85. The O.E. Consonants.

	Back.		Front.		Blade.		Blde.-Pnt.		Point.		Lip.	
	V.	B.	V.	B.	V.	B.	V.	B.	V.	B.	V.	B.
Open	g	h	ġ	ħ	s	s		sċ	ð, þ	ð, þ	ꝧ	
Stop	g	c	ċġ	ċ					d	t	b	p
Nasal	ng								n	hn	m	
Divided									l	hl		
Trill									r	hr		

	Lip-Back.		Lip-Teeth.	
	V.	B.	V.	B.
Open.	w	hw	f	f

NOTE. The symbols used in this table are not 'phonetic symbols' in the strict sense, but are those usually employed in writing and printing O.E. As they are fairly consistently employed to express the same sounds, they are, in a sense, 'phonetic'. The exceptions will be discussed directly.

§ 86.   The chief inconsistencies in the use of O.E. graphic symbols are found in that of *g* and *c*. The former is used to express both a *Front* and a *Back Open* consonant, and, probably by the tenth century, also a *Back Stop*. The combination *ċġ* nearly always expresses a *Front Stop*. *g* and *ċġ* nearly always express *Voiced* sounds.

g, no matter what its origin, when it occurs *initially*, in a word or syllable, before front vowels was the symbol of a *front-open-voiced* consonant [j]—*ġēar, ġiefan, heriġes*, etc. In grammatical works it is usually printed *ġ*, to distinguish it from the *back* consonant. Initially, before back vowels, and medially, in the same circumstances, it was in the earliest O.E., unquestionably, a *back-open-voiced* consonant (ʒ).

In this position, however, it probably became the present *stop* sound during the O.E. period, though it is impossible to say precisely when. Most authorities agree that, at any rate by the year 1000, *gōd* ' good ', *gān* ' to go ', etc., were pronounced with a *back stop*. In the middle of words, between original back vowels, the sound certainly remained an *open consonant* during the whole O.E. period. Thus *ăgan* ' own ', *folgian* (from **fulgōjan*) ' follow ', *sagu* ' saw, saying ', etc., must always be pronounced with a *back-open-voiced* consonant. Any other pronunciation is ridiculous in the light of the subsequent history of the sound in words. A *back-stop-voiced* was very rare, and was probably a late development, medially, in O.E., as it certainly was initially. The medial consonant in *frocga* ' frog ' is probably an example of this sound.

§ 87. There is the same ambiguity in the use of the symbol *c* in O.E. It expresses, always indeed, a *voiceless stop* sound, but sometimes a *back*, and sometimes a *front voiceless stop*. Before original *back* vowels *c* stands for [k], as in *cot* ' dwelling ', *catt* ' cat ', *cōl* ' cool ', etc. In the later MSS. *k* is sometimes written for this sound, but it is never consistently used, and *c* is by far the more usual symbol.

Before original O.E. front vowels, *c*, written *ċ* and *č* in grammatical works, is to be pronounced as a *front stop*—*ċiele* ' chill ', *ċīld* ' child ', *ċeaf* ' chaff '. The same rule applies when *c* occurs medially before -*i*—*rīċe* ' kingdom ', from **rīki*. Finally, after *front* vowels *c* was also a *front* consonant—*līċ* ' form, body ', *þæċ* ' roof '. The reason for the fronted *ċ* in *sēċan*, *þenċan* will appear in the discussion of the principal O.E. sound changes (§ 104).

O.E. *sċ* was probably [st], that is, *s* followed by a voiceless front stop. It may have become [ʃ] before the end of the O.E. period.

§ 88. *s* and *f* were pronounced as voiceless consonants [s, f] when final : *wæs* ' was ', *æs* ' food, meat ', *hlāf* ' loaf ', etc. ; initially, in the W. Saxon dialect, they were apparently voiced before vowels, as in Somersetshire and the South-West dialects at the present day (*s* was perhaps voiced initially in Kentish also) : *singan* ' sing ', *fæt* ' vessel, vat ', etc. ; medially, between vowels they were always voiced : *lufu* ' love ', *rīsan* ' rise ', etc., except when *s* was doubled as in *cyssan* ' kiss ', etc.

§ 89. *b* was originally a pure *lip-open-voiced* consonant [ƀ]. In early MSS. it is often written instead of the later *f*, between vowels—*hebuc* later *hafoc*, *heafoc* ' hawk '. Initially, it was probably pronounced as a *stop* in the historical period. The *lip-stop-voice* does not occur medially in O.E. except when doubled—*hebban* 'lift up', etc. [For the origin of this doubling cf. § 93.]

§ 90. *h*, originally a *back-open-voiceless* consonant [χ], was fronted later before and after front vowels, *ġesiht* 'sight', etc. Initially before vowels *h* was apparently a mere aspirate as at the present day, in the historical period. Medially, and finally before and after *back* vowels, *h* retained the pronunciation [χ].

§ 91. The combinations, *hl, hn, hr, hw*, should probably be pronounced with voiceless *l, n, r*, and *w* respectively : *hleahtor* 'laughter'; *hnǣgan* 'neigh'; *hring* 'ring'; *hwæt* 'what', etc.

§ 92. *ð* and *þ* are used for the *point-teeth-open*, both *voice* and *breath*, indiscriminately. Initially and finally the sound was probably voiceless everywhere at first ; medially between vowels *þ* and *ð* were voiced, and should be so pronounced.

§ 93. Doubled consonants should be pronounced long, with a fresh impulse in the middle of the sound. The chief sources of double consonants in O.E. are : (*a*) lengthening before -*j*-, e. g. *sittan*, earlier **sittjan*, from **setjan*; *sibb* 'relationship' from **sibjō* ; *reċċan* from **rakjan* 'narrate', etc., etc. After a long vowel or a diphthong the double consonant is simplified, e. g. *tǣċan* 'teach' from **tākjan*, W. Gmc. **taikjan*, earlier **taikkjan*. (*b*) The combination -*ln*- becomes -*ll*- in Gmc., e. g. Idg. **plno-*, Gmc. *full-*, O.E. *full* ; O.E. *wulle* 'wool', earlier **wulnā* ; cp. Lat. *lāna* from **wlana*.

NOTE. As we always mark the vowel quantities, and indicate whether *c* and *g* are fronted or not, the spelling of O.E. as it occurs in books for students is practically a phonetic transcription, apart from the slight inconsistencies just noted. It is not usually necessary to mark the fronted form of *h*, *h* = [j].

§ 94. **Accentuation or Stress.**

In O.E. as in other Germanic languages, the principal stress fell on the first, or 'root'-syllable of the word—*gōda* 'good', *heofon* 'heaven', *ternende* 'running'.

Prefixes, such as *bi-, on-, ġe-*, are always unstressed.

§ 95. **Plan of Treatment.**

It may make the following account of the history of the O.E. vowels clearer, if we give at once some hint of the plan and arrangement of the subject which is here attempted.

It may be well to point out that in tracing the development of the W. Gmc. vowels in O.E. we are dealing with changes which for the most part took place in this country, and therefore, although many of them occurred in the period before written documents, they are, in fact, a part of the 'History of English'. Some knowledge of the origin of the O.E. sounds is necessary to the proper understanding of their subsequent development. The subject is divided as follows:

(1) We first give an account of the principal sound changes, both *Isolative* and *Combinative*, which affected *all* the O.E. dialects.

(2) We then pass to changes which are specifically W. Saxon to the exclusion of other dialects.

(3) Peculiarities common to all dialects except W. Saxon.

(4) Features shared by the Anglian Dialects, but not by W. Saxon or Kentish.

(5) Features peculiar (*a*) to Mercian, (*b*) to Northumbrian.

(6) Kentish characteristics.

(7) Summary of points of agreement and disagreement between the various dialects.

§ 96. The O.E. Vowel Sounds compared with those of West Germanic.

By comparing the forms of words in the other W. Gmc. languages and in Gothic, we arrive at a view as to the original nature of Primitive O.E. sounds. The sounds, especially the vowels of the earliest historical period, are then seen to have undergone very considerable changes, both *Isolative* and *Combinative* (§ 65).

§ 97. Isolative Vowel Changes. Changes common to all Dialects of O.E.

(1) W. Gmc. *a* becomes O.E. *æ*: *dæġ* 'day', O.H.G. *tag*; *fæder* 'father', O.H.G. *fatar*, O.Sax. *fadar*; *wæġn* 'wagon', O.H.G. *wagan*.

NOTE 1. For subsequent treatment of *æ̆* in Kt. and Mercian see §§ 129, 137. In W.S. *æ* is written throughout the O.E. period, but the fact that the symbol *æ* is used very frequently in Ælfric to express the *ĕ*-sound rather points to the raising of *æ̆* to *ĕ* in L.W.S.

NOTE 2. For retention of W.Gmc. *a* in O.E. before a back vowel in following syllable, see § 107, Note.

(2) W. Gmc. *ā* becomes O.E. *ǣ*: *slǣpan* 'sleep', O. Sax. *slāpan*, O.H.G. *slāfan*.

(3) W. Gmc. *au* becomes in O.E. **æu, *æo, *æa, ēa*: *ēage* 'eye', O.H.G. *ouga*, Goth. *augō*; *ēare* 'ear', Goth. *ausō*.

NOTE. This *ēa* was monophthongized to *ǣ* in late O.E. Cp. for instance the occasional spellings: *dǣð* 'death', *ġelǣfa* 'faith', *ǣdiga* 'blessed', for *dēad, ġelēafa, ēadiġ.*

(4) W. Gmc. *ai* becomes O.E. *ā*: *hāl* 'whole' (adj.), Goth. *haīls*, O.H.G. *heil*; *āþ* 'oath', Goth. *aiþs*, O.H.G. *eid.*

(5) W. Gmc. *eu* becomes O.E. *ēo*: *þēod* 'nation, people', Goth. *þiuda*, O.Sax. *thioda.*

Combinative Vowel Changes common to all O.E. Dialects.

§ 98. (1) W. Gmc. *ã* becomes O.E. *ō*. The nasalized *ã* of Gmc. and W. Gmc. undergoes first a process of rounding—to *õ*, and then a lengthened vowel is substituted for the short, nasalized vowel: *brōhte* 'brought' from **braɲχta, *brãχta, *brõχta*; *fōn* 'take, seize' from **faɲχan, *fãχan, *fõhan*, etc.

§ 99. (2) (*a*) W. Gmc. *ã*, which as stated in § 97 is fronted to *ǣ* in Pr. O.E. by an isolative change, does not undergo this fronting if followed by *n* or *m*, but is rounded, and appears in the earliest historical period as *ō*:—*mōna* 'moon' from W. Gmc. **mānan-*, cp. O.H.G. *māno*, Goth. *mēna*; *nōmon* Pret. Pl. of *niman* 'to take' from **nāmum*, cp. O.H.G. *nāmum*, Goth. *nēmum*, etc. (*b*) W. Gmc. *ã* before *w*, or *g*, followed by a back vowel, remains in O.E.:—*sāwon, lāgon*, W. Gmc.**sāwum, *lãᵹum.*

§ 100. (3) **Pr. O.E. *ã* becomes *ō*.**

W. Gmc. *an-* (or *am-*), when it stood before the voiceless open consonants, *s, f, þ*, appears in the oldest English simply as *ō*. The *n* first nasalized *a* to *ã*, then this was rounded to *õ*, and as in the preceding case, nasalization was replaced by length, giving *ō*: O.E. *gōs* 'goose' from **gõs* from **gãs* from **gans*, cp. Germ. and Dutch *gans*; O.E. *tōþ* 'tooth' from original **tanþ*, cp. O.H.G. *zand*, O.Sax. *tand*; O.E. *sōfte* 'soft', O.H.G. *samfto.*

NOTE. This process, as regards the rounding, and substitution of length for nasalization, is identical with the preceding (§ 98 (1)), only whereas the nasal was lost before [χ] already in Pr. Gmc., and is thus absent in all Gmc. tongues, the loss of the consonant *n, m* before *s, f, þ* is an O.E. process. It is impossible to say at what period the various languages lost the nasalization of *ã.*

It will be seen later that *n* was always lost in O.E. before *s, f, þ*, just as it is lost in Gmc. before χ. The other vowels are merely lengthened after losing their nasalization, but undergo no qualitative change comparable to that from *ã-* to *õ, ō* (§ 113).

§ 101. (4) Original **an** becomes **on**.

W. Gmc. *a* before nasal consonants which remain in O.E. is generally rounded to *o* in the period of Alfred : *lond, hond, monn* instead of earlier *land, hand, mann*. In later O.E. *land, hand*, etc., again predominate. In no period are either the *an* or *on* forms used with perfect consistency in any of the texts.

§ 102. (5) **Fracture of Vowels before certain consonant combinations.**

Fracture is the term applied to the diphthongization of front vowels before *rr*, and *r* + another consonant ; *ll*, or *l* + another consonant ; *h*, *hh*, or *h* + another consonant. Examples : **Fracture of e :** O.E. *steorra*, O.H.G. *sterro* ; *eorþe* ʻearthʼ, O.H.G. *erda* ; *seolh* ʻsealʼ, O.H.G. *selah* > *selh ; *feoh* ʻmoney, propertyʼ, O.Sax. *fehu* ; *feohtan* ʻto fightʼ, O.H.G. *fehtan*. **Fracture of æ :** *earm* ʻpoorʼ, O.H.G. *arm* ; *eall* ʻallʼ, O.H.G. *all* ; *eald* ʻoldʼ, O.H.G. *alt* ; *eahta* ʻeightʼ, O. Sax. O.H.G. *ahto*. **Fracture of Pr. O.E.** ǣ : *nēah* from *nǣh, Goth. *nēƕ*.

NOTE 1. It is pretty certain that already in the late O.E. period, *ea* was monophthongized to æ and perhaps also raised to [ɛ]. Cp. § 97 Note, 120 Note. Such spellings as *swælt* for *swealt*, *swærtum* for *sweartum*, *andwærdum* for *andweardum*, *mærcode* for *mearcode*, all in Ælfric, taken in connexion with the M.E. development, seem to establish the monophthong in these cases.

NOTE 2. The process of ʻ*Fracture*ʼ consists in the development of a glide sound between the front vowel and the following *h*, *ll*, *rr*, *l*, *r*, or *h* + consonant. The cause of the development of this glide, which was originally of the nature of [w] or [u], lies in the nature of the following consonant. *h* was a back open consonant, a sound which easily tends to be lip-modified. *l* when doubled, or followed by another consonant, must have been pronounced with the fore part of the tongue hollowed. This gives a dull, ʻgutturalʼ effect to the sound, as is heard in many English and Scotch dialects at the present day. *r* when doubled, or followed by another consonant, was probably ʻinvertedʼ, i.e. uttered with the point of the tongue turned upwards and backwards, without trilling. This sound is now pronounced in many Southern English dialects. Each of these articulations involves a considerable glide, after a front vowel. A very similar effect to *Fracture* is heard in such Cockney pronunciations as [paiu(l)], etc., for *pale*. Note that *e* undergoes no Fracture before the *l*-combinations, except *lh, lc*. The Fracture of *i* is indistinguishable from that of *e*, except in Northumbrian (§ 132).

§ 103. **Mutation or ʻUmlautʼ.**

There are two kinds of *Mutation* in O.E.: one, A. which affects *back* vowels, is caused by a following *i* or *j* and results in fronting of the vowel; the other, B. which affects *front* vowels, is caused chiefly by *u*, or *o*, in some dialects also by *a*. The result of the latter process is to develop a vowel glide [*u*], which combines with the preceding front vowel to produce a diphthong. The former process is known as *i*- or *j*-mutation, the latter as *u*-mutation, or *o/a*-mutation, according to the vowel which causes it.

i-mutation is by far the more universal of these two processes in O.E.; it affects all dialects, and is less liable than *u*-mutation to be upset by Analogy. *u*-mutation, or its result, on the other hand, is distributed, in different dialects, in varying degrees of frequency. W. Saxon, apart from certain conditions (see § 110), tends to eliminate the diphthongized forms due to *u*-mutation, in favour of those with simple vowels, which may occur in certain cases of nouns, or persons of verbs. Since *i*- or *j*-mutation is a *fronting* process, and *u*, *o/a*-mutation one which depends largely on the development of a *back* element after front vowels, we may call the former *Front-Mutation*, and the latter *Back-Mutation*.

§ 104. **A. (6) i- or j-Mutation in O.E.**

The law may be simply stated as follows : all original back vowels when followed in the next syllable of a word by *-i-* or *-j-*, are *fronted*, to the corresponding front vowels. Further O.E. *æ*, derived by isolative change from earlier *a* (§ 97 (1)) under the same conditions, is raised from a low, to the mid vowel *e*. The process of *i*-, *j*-mutation was fully completed before the period of the earliest O.E. documents, that is, before the end of the seventh century. It may therefore have begun a century earlier. It certainly was carried out in England, because it affects loan-words which the English only learnt after their invasion of these islands.

The process of fronting the vowel was due to the front-modification of the intervening consonant by the following *-i-* or *-j-*. This front-modified sound then influenced, and fronted the preceding vowel. When the consonant was back, *c*, or *g*, it became a pure front *ċ*, *ġ*, or, if *g* was followed by *j*, *ċġ*; thus **lægiþ* becomes in the first instance **lǽġiþ* 'lays'; **sōkja* 'I seek' becomes **sōċi*; **bruggjō* 'bridge' becomes **bruċġ*, the phonetic values being [j, ẗ, d].

§ 105. *i*- or *j*-mutation of *ō*. Primitive O.E. *ō*, no matter what its origin, becomes first [ø], written *oe*, which in all dialects except W. Sax. survives nearly to the end of the O.E. period. In W.S. *oe* (*mid-front-round*) is unrounded to *ē* before the period of King Alfred, in whose works there are however some slight traces of the spelling *oe* :
bēċ Dat. Sing. and Nom. and Acc. Pl. of *bōc* 'book', from **bōki-* ; *sēċan* 'to seek', O. Sax. *sōkian*, Goth. *sōkjan* ; cp. O.E.

Pret. *sōhte* from *sōk-da; *fēdan* 'to feed' from *fōd-jan. cp.
O.E. *fōda* 'food'; *cwēn* 'queen', Pr. O.E. *cwōni, W. Gmc.
*kwāni, Gmc. *kwǣni (cp. § 99).

§ 106.   Pr. O.E. *ā* (earlier *ai*) becomes *ǣ*:—*dǣlan* from
*dāljan 'divide', cp. O.E. un-mutated *dāl* 'portion', O.H.G.
teil, Goth. *dails*. O.E. *dǣl* 'part' = *dāli also exists, and is
commoner than *dāl*. *tǣċan* 'teach' from *tākjan, cp. Pret.
tāhte.
lǣstan 'follow, carry out' from *lāstjan, cp. O.H.G. *leistan*,
O. Sax. *lēstian*, Goth. *laistjan*. O.E. has also the un-mutated
noun *lāst* 'track', etc.

§ 107.   *i-, j-*Mutation of O.E. *a* and *æ*: Pr. O.E. *a* becomes
æ: *hæbban* 'have' from *haƀƀjan; *slægen* 'slain' from *slagin.

NOTE. W. Gmc. *a* normally becomes *æ* by an Isolative change in
O.E. (§ 97 (1)), and on the Mutation of this see § 107 below; but *a*
remains, or is restored, if a back vowel follows, hence *dagas* N. and A. Pl.
of *dæġ*, *slagen*, one form of P.P. of *slēan* fr. *slagan. It happens sometimes, though comparatively rarely, that an O.E. *a* which had originally
a back vowel after it, is preserved as such till after the isolative tendency
which changed Pr. *a* to *æ* has passed away. If syllables containing such
a sounds receive a suffix with *i* or *j* later on, but before the period of
i- or *-j-*Mutation, the *a* undergoes fronting to *æ*. This is the case with
the forms *hæbban*, *slægen*, above.

Pr. O.E. *æ* becomes *e* by *i-* or *j-*mutation: *settan* 'to place',
from *sættjan, cp. Goth. *satjan*; *mete* 'food', from *mæti, cp.
Goth. *mat-s*, O.H.G. *maz*, O. Sax. *meti* (with mutation); *here*
'army' from **hæri-*, O.H.G. *hari*, Goth. *harjis*; *slegen*, P. P. of
slēan, from *slægin.

§ 108.   Pr. O.E. *ū* becomes *ȳ*: *mȳs* Pl. of *mūs* 'mouse',
from *mūsi; *brȳd* 'bride', Goth. *brūþ-s*, stem **brūþi-*; *cȳþan*
'make known', Goth. *kunþjan*, Pr. O.E. *kūþjan.

§ 109.   Pr. O.E. *ŭ* becomes *ў̆*: *fyllan* 'to fill' fr. *fulljan,
cp. O.E. *full*, Goth. and O.H.G. *fulljan*; *pytt* 'pit, hole',
O.H.G. *pfuzzi*, Early W. Gmc. loan-word from Latin *puteus*,
W. Gmc. form *puttja, Pr. O.E. *putti.

NOTE. An original Gmc. *ŭ* became *o* in W. Gmc. if *ō*, *a*, or *ā* followed
in the next syllable, but remained when followed by *-i-* or *-j-*. There are
many 'roots' which occur both with *ō* or *a* suffixes, and also with suffixes
containing *-i-* or *-j-*. In the former case we get *o* in the 'root' in O.E.,
in the latter *ŭ*. This *u*, later on, when the *i-*mutation period arrived,
became *ў̆*. Thus—*gold* 'gold' from **gulđa-*, but *gylden* 'golden' from
**gulđin-*; *god* 'god' from **guđa-*, but *gyden* 'goddess' from **guđin-*;
fox from *fuhsa, but *fyxen* 'vixen' from **fuhsin-*. In these and similar
cases, *y* is therefore the mutation of *ŭ* and not of *ŏ*.

Normally, ŏ cannot occur before -*i*- or -*j*-, (*a*) because ŏ in native words is not an original sound, but was developed in W. Gmc. out of *ŭ*, under the conditions just mentioned, and (*b*) because in those early loan-words where it occurred, it became *u* before -*i*- or -*j*-.

Thus if the sequence ŏ with -*i*- or -*j*- in the next syllable passed into W. Gmc. from Latin, as it sometimes did, *o* normally became *u*, and this naturally was mutated to *ў* later on, e. g. Latin *monēta* became *monīt-, whence *munit, whence O.E. *mynet* 'coin'.

Therefore *ĕ* as the mutation of ŏ is very rare, and when it is found, needs special explanation. For instance, *oxa* 'ox' has a Pl. *œxen, exen* by the side of commoner *oxan*. Original *uhsa- normally becomes *oxa* in O.E. If a form like *uhsin- existed it would naturally become *yxen, so that *exen* can only be explained by assuming that just before the period of mutation, but after the period at which ŏ followed by -*i*- became *ŭ*, a new formation *ŏhsin- was made, on the analogy of *ohsa; this new form *ohsin- then became *œxen, exen* in the mutation period. A similar explanation must be sought for *ele* 'oil' from Latin *oleum*, W. Gmc. *olja, *ulja, and for the Dat. Sing. *dehter* of *dohter* 'daughter'.

NOTE. In *þenċan, sendan, blendan, ende*, etc., the *e* probably does not represent the mutation of Pr. O.E. *o* from *a* before a nasal (§ 101)— *þankjan<*þoŋkjan, *ondi, etc., but earlier *þænċan, ænde*, etc., with raising of *æ* to *e* before *n* and cons. In some dialects -*æn*- must have remained into L. O.E. See § 161 (2).

For the effects of *i*-mutation on the Pr. O.E. Diphthongs, see §§ 116, 117, 118, 119, 124, 132, 139, which deal with the peculiar special developments of the various dialects.

§ 110. B. (7) Back-, or u-Mutation.

All the O.E. dialects are to some extent subject to this change, which consists in diphthonging *i*, *e*, and in Mercian *æ*, when *u*, or *o* (from earlier -*an*) followed in the next syllable, e. g. *hebun becomes *heofon*. The process is excellently described by Bülbring (*Elementarbuch*, § 229). What happened was that the *u* first 'lip-modified' the preceding consonant, which in its turn produced a lip- or rounded glide between itself and the preceding front vowel: *witum became *wit^w*um* and then *wi^w*t*^w*um*, whence *wiutum*, and later *wiotum*, later still *weotum*. (NOTE. *w* written after the symbol for a vowel or consonant sound implies that this was accompanied by a certain amount of rounding, or lip-modification.)

In W. Saxon this mutation takes place only (*a*) when the word begins with *w*, or any consonant followed by *w, sw*, etc., in which case it occurs no matter what consonant intervenes between the *i* or *e* and the following *u*; or, (*b*) when the intervening consonant is *l, r*, or a lip consonant—*p, m, f*. In words in which the *u* only occurs in certain cases—N. and Acc. Pl. Neuter, or Dat. Pl., Standard W. Saxon tends to give up the diphthongization, even in these cases, on the analogy of the undiphthongized forms of the other cases; thus *sċipu* (N. and Acc. Pl.) and *sċipum* (Dat. Pl.) 'ships', instead of *sċiopu* (*sċeopu*), etc., on the pattern of Sing. *sċip*, etc. The result is that this mutation is a far less prominent feature in W.S. than in any of the other dialects where no such tendency exists.

The *iu* and *eu* of this origin become *io* and *eo*, and in West Saxon are both levelled under *eo* as a rule.

æ never undergoes the process in pure W.S., except in the word *ealu* 'ale', which is the Common O.E. form (from **aluþ-*); never in Northumbrian, and only sporadically in a few forms, in one or two early Kentish charters, where it is probably due to Mercian influence. In Mercian the *u*-mutation of *æ* (*a*) to *ea* is a typical feature of the dialect (§ 138).

Examples in W. Saxon:—*cweocu* fr. *cwiocu*, earlier *cwiucu* from *cwicu* 'living'; *eofor* 'wild boar' from **efur*; *heorot* 'hart', from **herut*, cp. O.H.G. *hiruz*; *seolfor* 'silver', earlier **siluƀr*; *sweostor* 'sister', cp. O.H.G. *swester*.

NOTE. The combination *wiu* becomes *wu*, the *w* being lost after a consonant before *u*, so that we get *c(w)ucu*; *wudu* from *widu<wiudu*, *wuton<*wiutum*, etc., in all dialects except Kentish (§ 143). The type *cwic-*, on the analogy of *cwice*, occurs also in the form *cwicu*. This type not being diphthongized, does not change further, so that we find *cwicu*, *cucu*, and by a further cross analogy, also *cuce*, etc., at one and the same time.

§ III.   (8) 'Palatal Mutation'.

This term was suggested by Bülbring to denote primarily the loss in Anglian of the second element of the diphthong *ea* (which thus appears merely as *e*) before the consonant-groups *ht, hs, hþ*, when followed by a front vowel, or when final. Cf. § 90.

A very similar, though later process, affects also *eo, io*, in W. Sax., where we find *cniht* or *cnie·ht* 'boy', 'servant', instead of the normal, *cneoht* (as we might expect) from **cneht* with Fracture (§ 102). Here *eo* is fronted, and the first element raised to *i*. This only happens when the -*ht* is final, as in Nom.-Acc. Sing., or when a front vowel follows, as in Gen. and Dat. Sing. *cni(e)htes, cni(e)hte*; in the Pl. where back vowels occur in the suffixes, *eo* remains—*cneohtas, cneohta, cneohtum*; *Pihtisc* ' Pictish' but *Peohtas* ' Picts'.

NOTE. This is an important difference for the subsequent development of the language, since Mod. Engl. *knight* can only be derived from the O.E. *cniht* type, and not from *cneoht*-.

§ 112. (9) Loss of h between vowels and contraction of vowel groups.

Early in the historical period *h* disappears between vowels; thus **fōha* 'seize' becomes **fōa*, **sleaha* 'I strike' becomes **sleaa*, **feohes* (Gen. Sing. of *feoh*) 'property' becomes **feoes*, etc. These combinations of vowels are simplified by the loss of the unstressed vowel, but the remaining vowel or diphthong is lengthened, if short, thus : **fōa* becomes *fō*; **sleaa* becomes *slēa*; **feoes* becomes *feōs*, etc.; **pīhan* ' thrive' becomes **pīohan*, whence **pioan, pīon*.

Vowel Lengthening in O.E.
§ 113. (a) Lengthening replaces Nasalization.

We have seen (§ 100) that when the combinations *an-*, *am-* stand before *s*, *f*, or *þ*, the nasal consonant is lost, having previously nasalized the *a*, which is then rounded, and subsequently lengthened in compensation for the later loss of nasalization. Precisely the same nasalization, loss of nasal consonant, and gradual replacing of the vowel nasalization by vowel length, takes place when *i* or *u* stand before *n*, or *m*, followed by a voiceless open consonant. Nasalized *ĩ* and *ũ* before *h*, inherited from Germanic (cp. *ã*, §§ 98 and 100, Note), are lengthened in the same way. Examples: *sīþ* 'time, journey', fr. **sĩþ* fr. **sinþ*, Goth. *sinþs*; *gesīþ* 'companion', O.H.G. *gisindi*; *fīf*, fr. **fĩmf*, cp. Goth. *fimf*, O.H.G. *fimf*, O. Sax. *fīf*; *ūs* 'us', O.H.G. *uns*; *cūþe* 'could', cp. Goth. *kunþa*.

Examples of *ĩh, ũh* : O.E. *þēon* 'thrive', fr. **þiᵧχan—*þiχan*, Pr. O.E. *pīhan, pīohan*, etc. (§ 112); O.E. *þūhte* 'seemed', fr. **þuᵧχta—*þūχta*, Pret. of *þyncan*, fr. **þuᵧk-jan*.

§ 114. (b) Short vowels were lengthened before the combinations *nd*, *mb*, (*ng* ?), *ld*, *rd* : *findan, lāmb, sīngan* (?), *cīld, wōrd*, all of which had, originally, short vowels. The lengthening which took place, probably, early in the ninth century is of importance for the later history of the language, for Mod. [faind, tʃaild, koum], etc., can only be explained by assuming that the O.E. forms had long vowels. On the numerous cases such as *end, friend, wind*, where the Mod.

forms presuppose short forms, at any rate in M.E., see § 175 (7), below.

Sound Changes which occur only in West Saxon.

§ 115. (1) Diphthonging after initial Front Consonants.

After the *Front Consonants* *ċ*, *ġ* (whether earlier *g*, or *j*) and the combination *sċ* the Pr. O.E. vowels *æ*, *ǣ*, *e* are diphthongized, in the earliest period, to *ea*, *ēa*, *ie* respectively.

(a) After *ċ*: W. Saxon *ċeaster* 'city', etc. non-W. Sax. *ċæster*; *ċeaf* 'chaff', non-W.S. *ċæf*; *ċēace* from **ċǣce*, cp. Dutch *kaak*. There are no examples of *ċe-*.

(b) After *ġ* (=*g*): *ġeat* 'gate', non-W.S. *ġæt*; *ġeaf*, non-W.S. *ġæf*; *ġēafon* 'gave', Pret. Pl., Pr. O.E. *ġǣfon*; *ġielp* 'boast', cp. O.H.G. *gelf*, non-W.S. *ġelp*; *forġieldan* 'to pay for', non-W.S. *-ġeldan*: *ġ* = *j*—*ġēar* 'year', O.H.G. *jār*, Pr. O.E. *ġǣr*.

(c) After *sċ*: *sċeal* 'shall', earlier *sċæl*, Goth. *skal*; *sċēap* 'sheep', earlier *sċǣp*, cp. O.H.G. *scāf*; *sċieran* 'cut', cp. O.H.G. *sceran*.

NOTE 1.   In Late W.S. *ĕa* is frequently monophthongized to *ĕ* after front cons., so that we get *ċef*, *ġef*, *ġēr*, *sċēp*, etc. This does not take place before a following back vowel, so *ġeara*, *ġearum*, etc., remain.

NOTE 2.   The W.S. form *ċeaster* shows that the processes of fronting *c* before front vowels, and the subsequent diphthongization of this vowel after a front cons., were still in operation, if they did not actually begin after the English came to Britain, since *ċeaster* is a Latin loan-word first acquired from Latin-speaking people in this country.

NOTE 3.   The above process of diphthongization is later than that caused by Fracture, as may be seen from O.E. *ċeorl* 'churl' from earlier *ċerl*. The *eo*, which occurs in all the dialects, is the result of Fracture. Had **ċerl* remained unaltered until the period of diphthongization after front cons. this must have become **ċierl* in W.S.

§ 116. (2) i-, j-Mutation of the Pr. O.E. Diphthongs ēa, īo.

In W.S. alone, of all the O.E. dialects, *ēa* and *īo* when followed by *-i-* or *-j-*, are mutated to *īe*: (a) I. of *ēa* from **au**: *hīeran* 'hear', from **hēarjan*, cp. Goth. *hausjan*; *ġelīefan* 'to believe', cp. O.E. *ġelēafa* 'faith', Goth. *galaubjan*; *īeðe* adv. 'easily', from **ēaði*, cp. O.E. adj. *ēaðe* 'easy'; II. of **ēa** from **ǣ** (**W.Gmc. ā**) after front consonant:—*ċīese* 'cheese' from **ċēasi*, from **ċǣsi*, W. Gmc. **kāsjō*.

NOTE.   The W.S. form *ċīese* shows that *i*-mutation was a later process than that of diphthonging after front cons. (§ 115). Had the former process taken place earlier than the latter, Pr. O.E. **ċǣsi* would have remained unchanged by it, since *ǣ* suffers no *i*-mutation. *ċǣsi* then would have become **ċēasi* in W.S. The short diphthong *ie* in *ċietel*, etc., below (§ 117) tells the same story.

(*b*) Mutation of *īo* :—*cīesþ* 'chooses' 3rd Sing. Pres. of *cēosan*, from *cīosiþ*; *flīes* 'fleece' from **flīusi*; *ġetrīewe* 'faithful', cp. O. Sax. *gitriuwi*.

§ 117.   (3) ·i·Mutation of the Short Diphthongs.

The short diphthongs, *ĕa*, *ĭo*, no matter what their origin, become *ĭe* in W. Sax. through the influence of a following *-i-* or *-j-*.

(*a*) **Mutation of ĕa :** I. of ĕa, the result of Fracture (§ 102): *iermþu* 'poverty, wretchedness', from **earmiþu*, earlier **ærmiþu*, cp. O.H.G. *armida*; *fiellan* 'cause to fall, cast down', from **fealljan*, cp. *feallan* 'to fall'; *nieht* 'night', from **neahti*, earlier **næhti*, cp. Goth. *nahts*, stem **nahti-*; II. of ea from æ after front consonants (§ 115): *ćietel* 'kettle', from **ćeatil*, earlier **ćætil*, cp. Goth. *katils*; *ćiele* 'cold, chill', from **ćeali*, from **ćæli*, cp. O.E. *ćeal-d* 'cold'; *ġiest* 'stranger', from **ġeasti*, earlier *ġæsti*, cp. Goth. *gasts*, stem *gasti-*; *sćieppan* 'create', from **sćeappjan*, cp. Goth. *skapjan*; *sćiell* 'shell', from **sćeallj-*.

§ 118. (*b*) **Mutation of ĭo (iu), the result of Fracture :** *wierþ* 'becomes', from **wiorþiþ*, *wiurþiþ*, 3rd Sing. Pres. of *weorþan*; *hierde* 'shepherd', from **hiurdi*, **hiordi*, earlier **hirdi*, O.H.G. *hirti*; *ġesiehþ* 'sight', from -**siohiþu* from -**sihiþō*.

§ 119.   Later Treatment of W.S. īe.

Already in Alfred's time, *i* is often written for *ĭe*, no matter what the origin of this : *niht, cniht, sillan* (earlier *siellan*, from *sellan*), etc., and *ie* for original *i*, thus *wietan*, etc., for *witan*. This points to the conclusion that, at any rate in part of the W. Sax. area, *i* and *ie* had both been levelled under the one sound *i*. On the other hand, after and before *r*, *i* often appears as *y*, so that for instance *ryht* 'right' from *riht* > *rieht* > *reoht* is the regular Early W. Sax. form of this word.

In other parts of the W. Sax. area, on the other hand, *ĭe* is not levelled under *ĭ* but kept distinct, until in Late W.S. it is rounded to *ȳ*, which does not happen to original *i*. Thus in those Late W.S. texts which we possess, *ȳ* is the typical spelling, on the whole, for the earlier *ĭe* in all words of the classes illustrated in § 117. 3, above. Furthermore as in M.E. the [*ȳ*] sounds are still preserved in the words, in the Saxon area, we must assume that the change of *ĭe* to *ȳ* was typical of this area generally, although Alfred's forms do not in all cases appear to be consistent with this assumption. In Alfred's dialect, apparently, there was a tendency, already noted, of levelling *ĭe* under *ĭ*, which was not characteristic of the whole Saxon speech area.

NOTE.   *ĭe* and *īe* are typical E. W.S. sounds, and occur in no other dialect.   Further, that *ȳ* representing earlier *īe*, or anything else than the *i*-Mutation of *ŭ*, occurs in W.S. alone.

§ 120.   Pr. O.E. æ in W.Sax.

With regard to this sound, it is perhaps desirable to record the negative fact that it undergoes no alteration in the Saxon area, during the whole O.E. period, and indeed remains as a characteristic of Southern English (with the exclusion of Kentish) in the M.E. period (§ 162).   The other dialects have raised this *æ* (in *dǣd* 'deed', *sǣton*, pret. pl. of *sittan*, etc.) to *ē* before the period of the earliest documents.   This non-W. Sax. *ē* was tense, cp. § 123.

NOTE.   It is probable, however, that while the sound remained slack, it was raised to the mid [ẹ̄] in Late W. Sax.   Ælfric very often writes æ for original *ě*, *dǣriað* 'injures', *hǣfe* 'weight', *Sǣrgius* for *Sergius*, etc.   He even writes æ for *ē* occasionally, *gerǣfa*, *gecwǣmde*, and I have noted *gefretwodon* for *gefrǣtwodon*.

§ 121.   Late West Saxon Treatment of weo-.

It is typical of L. W.S. that the combination *weo-*, whether the diphthong be the result of *Fracture*, or *u-Mutation*, becomes *wu-* : *wurþan* fr. *weorþan*, *swurd* fr. *sweord*, *swustor*, fr. *sweostor*, *c(w)ucu* fr. *cweocu*.   A few cases of *wo-* occur in Alfred.

§ 122.   Unrounding of O.E. ȳ (i-Mutation of ŭ) in Late W.S.

In some L. W.S. texts, a tendency to unround O.E. *ȳ* to *ĭ* before front consonants and *n* is observable.   This is found more particularly in Ælfric's Grammar and in the Old Testament, though in the latter the *i*-forms are not quite universal.   The unrounded forms are less numerous in the W.S. Gospels, and still less so in Wulfstan's Homilies.   The Patois texts, Blickling Homilies, and Harleian Gloss generally preserve the rounded vowel before front consonants.   The words *cyning*, *cynn*, and *dryhten* appear fairly consistently, however, as *cinn*, *cining*, *drihten*.

It is clear that the unrounding tendency did not obtain over the whole W.S. area in the Late O.E. period, and this is confirmed by the M.E. forms.   In this period, *brugge*, *rugge*, etc., often appear in Sthn. texts, but the *i*-forms seem to be universal in *drihten*, *king*, *cyng*, etc.

NOTE.   *u* in M.E. *brugge*, etc., is a Norm.-Fr. symbol for the [y] sound (§§ 153, 158 (*c*), below).

Points in which all the non-W.Sax. dialects agree.

§ 123. (1) Raising of Pr. O.E. ǣ to ē.

As just noted in § 120, Northumbrian, Mercian, and Kentish all raise *ǣ* to *ē*. Thus all have *sēton*, W.Sax. *sǣton* 'they sat'; *rēd* 'council', W.S. *rǣd*; *scēp*, *mēd*, *strēt*, etc., *gēr* from *gǣr*, W.S. *gēar* (§ 115 (b)); *dēd* 'deed', W.S. *dǣd*; *grēdig* 'greedy', W.S. *grǣdig*, etc., etc. This change can be traced in Kentish at the end of the seventh century.

§ 124. (2) i-, j-Mutation of Pr. O.E. ēa.

Here again, all dialects except W.S. have *ē*: *hēran* 'hear', W.S. *hīeran*; *gelēfan* 'believe', W.S. *gelīefan*; *tēman* 'to teem, to bring forth', W.S. *tīeman*, from **tēamjan*, cp. O.E. *tēam* 'progeny'.

NOTE. The process whereby we have *ē* in non-W.S. instead of a diphthong is not clear. Was there a stage *ie* as in W.S., which was subsequently monophthongized? Or is it possible that the original diphthong when followed by -*i*- or -*j*- was monophthongized before the period of Mutation?

§ 125. (3) Frequency of Back-Mutation of e and i. (See § 110 above.)

All the non-W.S. dialects show a tendency to diphthongize *i* and *e* when followed by a back vowel, especially *u*, to an extent which is unknown in the literary dialect of Wessex. The results of the process are most fully developed in Kentish (see § 141), but the Anglian dialects also have them with great frequency, limited indeed only by smoothing (§ 127), which eliminates the second element of the diphthong. The non-W.S. dialects, unlike W.S., do not get rid of the diphthongized forms of words in favour of those without mutation, which may occur in particular cases of nouns, or parts of verbs. On the contrary, they tend rather to generalize the diphthongized forms as much as possible.

W.S. eliminates such a form as *geofu* 'gift', which is perfectly normal, in favour of *giefu* formed on the analogy of *giefe*, whereas Kentish tends to have the diphthongized forms everywhere: e. g. *begeotan, seondan, siondan* 'are', *agiaban* 'to give', *weada* 'woods', *sioððan* 'after', *siolf* (analogy of Dat. Pl. *seolfum*, etc.) 'self', etc., etc. All these are from Kentish Charters in the first half of the ninth century.

The so-called Saxon Patois of the Blickling Homilies also has the diphthongized forms to a far greater extent than the Court dialect of Alfred.

THE ANGLIAN DIALECTS.

Features common to both Northumbrian and Mercian.

§ 126. (1) **Absence of Fracture of æ, which appears as ă before ll and l + consonant; before -*ld* this is lengthened to ā.**

Anglian *all*, W.S. *eall*; *calf*, W.S. *ćealf*; *wall* 'wall', W.S. *weall*; *căld* 'cold', W.S. *ćeald*; *hāldan* 'hold', W.S. *healdan*; *bāld* 'bold', W.S. *beald*; *āld*, W.S. *eald* 'old', etc.

[Fracture of æ before the *r*-combinations is not found so consistently in Anglian as in W.S. Before *h*, etc., Fracture takes place originally, but the diphthong is simplified again (see § 127 below).
The *i-*, *j*-mutation of *a* before *ll* or *l* + cons. in Anglian is æ—*fællan*, W.S. *fiellan* (§ 117). Nthmb. *wærma* 'to warm' is probably to be regarded as = *warmjan*, with mutation of *a* to æ.]

§ 127. (2) Smoothing.

This is the name given by Sweet to the monophthongization of all diphthongs, both long and short, which took place in Primitive Anglian before *back* and *front* consonants. *ĕŭ, ĭŭ* become *ĕ, ĭ*; instead of *ĕā*, before back and front consonants, we get first *ǣ* and later *ē*. O.E. *ēā* was developed out of earlier *au* (§ 97 (3)) through the stages *æu, æo, æa*, and the short *ea* had a similar development. These diphthongs appear to have been overtaken by the Smoothing process while they were at the *æo* stage. The *ǣ* which results from the smoothing of the long diphthong is still found as a rule in eighth-century texts, but is later raised to *ē*. Thus the earliest (Moore) MS. of Bede has *lǣch*, whereas the later MSS. have *lēch* in the same passage; the Epinal Glossary has forms like *laec* 'vegetable', W.S. *lēāc*; *aec* 'also', W.S. *ēāc*; *herebāēcon* 'military standard', W.S. *bēācen*, while the ninth-century Leiden Riddle has *hēh*- 'high', W.S. *hēāh*; *suæðēh* 'however', W.S. *-ðēāh*. In the late Mercian Psalter and Hymns, *ē* is the commoner spelling—*hēh*, *ġeēcnað* 'increases', *bilēc* 'locked', W.S. *belēāc*, etc. The Lindisfarne Gospels have *hēh*, *bēcon*, *ēcan*, *ēc*, etc., but the more archaic spelling *ǣc* for the last word is far commoner.

The short *æ*, smoothing from *ĕā*, is usually not raised to *e*, cp. *dægas*, Pl. fr. *deagas* by back-mutation from *dægas* (§ 110), in the Mercian Hymns, and *middilsæxum* in an eighth-century Merc. Charter. Pr. O.E. *ǣ* remains in Nthumb. but becomes *e* in Merc.; cp. § 137 below.

§ 128.   (3) **Retention of ōē.**

The *i*-mutation of *ō*, originally *ōē* in all dialects (§ 105, above), remains in the spelling, and probably in the pronunciation, of the Anglian dialects throughout the O.E. period—*bōēċ*, W.S. *bēċ* 'books', *sōēċan*, W.S. *sēċan* 'to seek'.
(On *oe* in Kentish see § 144.)

Features which distinguish Northumbrian from Mercian.

§ 129.   (1) **Retention of Pr. O.E. ǣ** as in W.S. (§ 97 above), whereas the Mercian dialect of Vespas. Ps. agrees with Kentish in raising this to *e* (§ 137 below).

§ 130.   (2) **Traces of late Diphthonging after front con-sonants.** This is unknown in Mercian and Kentish, but characteristic of W.S., where, however, it is a primitive process. The Northumbrian process has been discussed with some minuteness by Bülbring, *Anglia*, Beibl. ix, and *Elementarbuch*, §§ 154, 155, 294–6, 302.

In Rushw.[2] *sċeal* 'shall', as in W.S., is found, and *sċīp* 'sheep' which according to Bülbring, § 154, is from **sċīep* with diphthongization of the Angl. *sċēp*, Pr. O.E. *sċǣp*.

NOTE.   This is surely later than the W.S. process, since it is later than the Angl. raising of *ǣ* to *ē*, though doubtless, as Bülbring says, much earlier than the Nthmb. diphthonging of *back* vowels after *sċ*.

The clearest cases of the diphthonging of back vowels in (Nthn.) Nthmb. are found after *sċ*, and must be very late, indicating a rising diphthong, i. e. one stressed on second element, if we take them seriously as diphthongal forms—*sċeān* 'shone', earlier *sċān*, pret. sing. of *sċīnan*, *sċeacca* 'to shake', *sċeōh* 'shoe', etc. The *e* in all these forms may be merely a graphic device to indicate that *sċ* is front.

§ 131.   (3) **Absence of back-Mutation of æ** (found in Mercian, § 138).

§ 132.   (4) **Distinction preserved between ēo and īo.**

In W. Sax. the old diphthong *īo* (Pr. O.E. *iu*) which only arose in W. Gmc. when *-i-* or *-j-* followed, became *īe* in the Mutation period unless there was a change of suffix (§ 118). In Anglian, no alteration was effected in the sound by the following *-i-* and the diphthong is preserved as *īo* in O. Nthmb. and remains distinct from *ēo* from Pr. *eu*, whereas in Mercian *īo* is levelled under *ēo* : Nthmb. *ðīostro* 'darkness', W.S. *ðīestru*, O. Sax. *thiustri* ; *gestrīona* 'gain, beget children', W.S. *gestrīenan*.

The same distinction is preserved in Nthmb. between the short diphthongs *ĭŏ*, *ĕŏ*: *wiurþit* in Bede's Death Song, W.S. *wierþ* from **wiurþiþ* from **wirþiþ* by Fracture; *hiorde* 'shepherd', W.S. *hierde*; *iorre* 'angry', W.S. *ierre*; *ġiornede* 'desired', W.S. *ġiernde*. (On the W.S. *ĭe*, later *ў̆*, in these forms, see §§ 118, 119, above.)

§ 133. (5) **Influence of initial w upon following vowels.**

The following changes are characteristic of late Nthmb.:

(*a*) *weo-* (Fracture) becomes *wo-*: *worða* 'become' from earlier *weorðan*, *worpa* 'throw' from *weorpan*, *sword* 'sword' from *sweord*.

(*b*) In Nthn. Nthmb. *weo-*, the result of *o-* or *u-*Mutation, also becomes *wo-*: *woruld* from *weoruld* from *weruld* 'world', *wosa* 'to be' from *weosan* from *wesan*. [According to Bülbring, § 267, in Sthn. Nthmb. *wosa* is the only form with *o* from *eo* as a result of *o-*Mutation; otherwise *weo-* remains—*weoruld*, etc.] This change is quite unknown in Mercian and Kentish. In late W.S. a somewhat similar change, that of *weo-* to *wu-*, occurs (§ 121).

(2) Initial *we-* becomes *wæ-* through rounding of the vowel: *wæġ* 'way' from *weġ*, *cwæða* 'speak' from *cweðan* (but *cweoðan* becomes *cwoða* (cp. (*b*) above), *wæs* 'be' Imperat. from *wes*. [Not quite unknown in Mercian, where such forms as *cwoeðaþ*, *woestenne* 'solitudine', occur sporadically.]

(*d*) In Late Nthn. Nthmb. *wē-* (Anglian form of Pr. O.E. *wǣ-*) becomes *wæ-*: *wǣpen* 'weapon', W.S. *wǣpen*, *wǣġ* 'wave', W.S. *wǣġ*.

[This change is unknown in Mercian.]

§ 134. (6) In **Southern Northumbrian**, W. Gmc. *au* (W. Sax. *ēa*) appears generally as *ēo*, being apparently arrested at the *ǣo* stage: *dēoþ* 'death', W.S. *dēaþ*; *dēof* 'deaf', W.S. *dēaf*; *hēofud*, W.S. *hēafod*; *ēore* 'ear', W.S. *ēare*, etc. Nthn. Nthmb. more commonly writes *ēa*, as in all other dialects.

§ 135. (7) **Northern Nthmb.** writes *ea* more frequently for Fracture of *e* before *rr* and *r* + consonant than *eo*: *hearte* 'heart', W.S. *heorte*; *earðu* 'earth'. In the Sthn. Nthmb. texts *eo* is more frequent.

[Mercian also shows some traces of *ea*, but *eo* is general.]

§ **136.** (8) **Southern Nthmb.** of the later period, on the other hand, generally writes *eo* instead of *ea* for the Fracture of *ǽ*: *eorm* 'arm', *hweorf* 'turned, wandered', W.S. *hwearf*.

[In Mercian, as in Kentish, *eo* sometimes occurs for *ea*, but rarely.]

Characteristic Mercian Features.

§ **137.** (1) **Raising of ǽ to ĕ.**

In distinction to Northumbrian and W.S., which retain *ǽ* throughout the O.E. period, but in agreement with Kentish, in part of the Mercian area this vowel is raised to *e* by an isolative change. This is most consistently shown in the ninth-century Vespasian Psalter and Hymns, and in the later Glosses in MS. Royal. The Mercian Matthew (Rushworth[1]), however, writes *æ* far more commonly. Examples (from Vesp. Ps. and Hymns) are: *hwet* 'what?', *deġes* (Gen. Sing. of *deġ* 'day'), *deġum* (Dat. Pl. on analogy of Sing.), *efter* 'after', *weter* 'water', *wes* 'was'.

The forms *dægas*, *dæga*, *cwæcung* in Vesp. Hymns are examples of Anglian smoothing from **deaga*, etc. See § 138 below.

§ **138.** (2) **Back-Mutation of Pr. O.E. æ.**

ġedeafenað 'befits', *iċ fearu* 'I go', *feadur* 'father' (Gen. Sing.), *ġehleadaþ* 'they load', *steaðelas* 'foundations'.

This mutation took place, in the dialect of the Vesp. Ps., also when *g* or *c* was the intervening consonant, but such forms as **deagas*, **cweacung* 'shaking' were smoothed to *dægas*, etc. This smoothing of *ea* is the chief source of *ǽ* in this text.

§ **139.** (3) **Levelling of ĭū, later ĭō, under ēŏ.**

Vesp. Ps. has *weotaþ* (Imperat. Pl.) 'know ye' from *wiutaþ*, *cweoþaþ* 'they speak', *cleopiu* 'I call' from **clipō ju*, whence **cliupō ju*, *ċēōseþ* 'chooses' from **cĭōsiþ*.

The same levelling occurs in the case of *ĭo* the result of Fracture of *ĭ*: *eorsian* 'become angry', *eorre* 'angry', *heorde*, W.S. *hierde* 'shepherd'.

NOTE. Such forms as *wreocende*, *spreocende* in Vesp. (Back-mutation of *e*), where we should expect Smoothing, must be due to the analogy of other verbs in the same class, where the diphthong normally remained unsmoothed, e. g. *beoran* 'bear', etc. *Steŏgun* 'climbed', from *stigun* (Pret. Pl.), may be explained on the analogy of *wreŏtun* 'they wrote'; but see also § 141 below.

Typical South-East Midl., S. Eastern, and Kentish Features.

§ 140.　(1) ǣ, the i-Mutation of Pr. O.E. ā raised to ē.

Most of the O.E. dialects preserve this ǣ unaltered during the whole O.E. period. Already in the Kentish Charters of the ninth century, we get forms such as *clēnra, ēniġ, mēst, ġemēnum* (Dat. Pl.) 'common', cp. Goth. *gamaini-*, and in the Surrey Charter of 871–89 *ġedēle*, W.S. *ġedǣlan* 'divide', Goth. *gadailjan* ; *lēsten* 'perform', Goth. *galaistjan* ; *hwēte-*, W.S. *hwǣte-* 'wheat', from **hwaiti-*, Pr. O.E. **hwāti*. A Suffolk Ch. of 991 has *dēle* ; another of 1038 has *ġelēsta, hlēfdiġen*. This change can be shown to be distinctly later than the raising of Pr. O.E. ǣ (§ 123 above) to ē which is common to all non-W.S. dialects. The later Kentish Psalm and Hymn write *æ* for both sounds, but owing to the early disappearance of the sounds (ǣ) in Kentish, the symbols *æ* and *e* are used indifferently for the mid-front sound. That *æ* is indeed used for a mid-front vowel is shown by the spelling *hǣr* for *hēr* 'here' in a Kt. Ch. of 831. In this word no one supposes that any old dialect ever had other than a mid-front vowel. The same confusion is shown in the spelling *swæstar* for *swestor* 'sister', where the short mid-front is certain.

[On preservation of this ē in M.E. see § 162 below.]

§ 141.　(2) **Typical Kentish Back-Mutation.**

We may consider such forms as *reogolweard* 'guardian of a (religious) rule', and *forespreoca* 'advocate', *breogo* 'prince', as typically Kentish, since W.S. does not admit of this mutation before a back consonant (cp. § 110) and, although it no doubt occurred under these conditions in early Anglian, it would be reduced by smoothing in the Anglian dialects (§ 127 above). Kentish influence may partly explain the forms in Vesp. Ps. discussed in § 139, note, above.

§ 142.　(3) **O.E. ȳ̆ (i-Mutation of ŭ), unrounded, and lowered to ē.**

In the Late Kentish Psalm, we find *sennum* 'sins' (Dat. Pl.), W.S. *synnum* ; *gelta* 'guilt', W.S. *gylt* ; *grammheġdiġ* 'cruel', W.S. *-hyġdiġ*; *snetera* 'wise', W.S. *snyter*, etc. In Early Kentish such spellings do not occur in *stressed* syllables, though the proper name *Hereġēþ*, W.S. *ġȳþ* is found, but the change, even in stressed syllables, is assured for the early period by the spelling *yfter* 'after' in a Ch. of 831, to represent Kt. *efter*, W.S. *æfter*. This spelling would be impossible unless Kt. scribes had already pronounced O.E. *y* as *e* in words where they still adhered to the traditional spelling (*y*). If they pronounced *e* whenever they saw or wrote *y*, of course *y* might come to be regarded as a symbol for the *e*-sound. The late O.E. Suffolk Ch. of 991 (Sweet's *Second A. S. Reader*, pp. 209–13), has several *e*-forms :—*breče* ' use ', *pette* ' pit ', *ğefelste* ' help ', etc.

ě, for original *ȳ*, continues to be one of the chief marks of Kentish dialect, or Kentish influence during the M.E. period (§ 158 (*b*)), and we have in Standard English to-day, words like *knell*, O.E. *cnyllan*, outside the Kentish dialect, which we know must be of S.E. Midl. or S.E. origin (§ 253, note 3, below).

NOTE. This feature extends in M.E. beyond the old Kentish area, and is found, in varying degrees of frequency, in S. Lincs., Northants, Essex, Suffolk, and Sussex. In the last quarter of the fourteenth century it is found also in Norfolk.

§ 143.   (4) The group wiu.

In Kentish, the otherwise usual change to *wu* does not occur, so that we get *weada, weotum*, instead of *wudu, wutum*. *Wudum* is found, however, in Bd. Gl.

The diphthongs *ı̃u, ěŏ* are not clearly and consistently distinguished in Kt. *ıŏ* is commoner in this dialect than *ēŏ* for earlier *eu*. For short *ěŏ* and *ıŏ* we find often *ia, io* by the side of *eo* : thus *seondan, siondon, weadu, gewriota, sioðǧan, niomanne*; *hiabanlic, begeotan, agiaban, -gecweodu*, etc.

§ 144.   Treatment of œ̄ (i-mutation of ō) in Kentish.

The ninth-century Charters consistently write *oe* for the *i*-mutation of *ō* of every origin—*foe* ' take ', *boeč, doeð, goes* ' geese ', *soečende, ǧerœfa*, ' reeve ', etc. The only exception seems to be *bledsung*. Surrey Charter (879–89) has *oe* once, but usually writes *eo—feo, ǧeforum* ' companions ' (W.S. *ǧefērum*), *seolest* ' best ', *rehtmeodrencynn*. In later Kentish *e* is the usual spelling—*ǧemete, gebetie, secende*, etc. (Psalm). The spelling *seočan*, however, occurs once in this text. The Late Kt. Glosses always write *ē*.

The spelling *eo*, occurring already in the latter half of the ninth century, seems to show that the traditional spelling *oe* was no longer felt as satisfactory, and may imply that the vowel was already but slightly rounded. It is curious that *eo* should crop up again in Late Kt. We can hardly take it to represent a rounded vowel, in the face of the far more numerous *ē*-spellings. The spelling *bœm* ' both ' Dat. Pl., which occurs in a Ch. of 831, compared with *bæm* in 805, shows clearly that even at this date *oe* could represent an unrounded vowel, and the spelling *hær* for *hēr* 'here' shows that *æ* could represent the mid-front vowel. It seems probable that by the year 831, the old vowel *ǣ* had already been unrounded in Kt. A form with slight rounding may have survived longer in Surrey.

§ 145. Summary of Chief Dialectal Characteristics in O.E.

It will be convenient to summarize briefly the principal features which distinguish the O.E. dialects. The following list includes only those which are of importance for the subsequent history of the language. A few examples are added to make the statement concrete.

(1) **Diphthonging after front consonants**: *sćeal, ġiefan, ćeaf, ġeat*, etc. (§ 115). In L.W.S. the *ēa* are monophthongized to *ĕ*: *sćel, ćef*, etc.

[This process of diphthonging is confined to W. Saxon.]

(2) **i- or j-Mutation of Diphthongs ēa, ēo, to ĭe** [only in W.S.] : *iermþu, hīerde* 'heard'; *ćīesþ* 'chooses', *wierþ* 'becomes'. In late W.S. these *ĭe* become *ȳ*: *yrmþu, hȳrde*, etc. (§§ 116–19).

(3) **Survival of Primitive O.E. ǣ** (W.Gmc. *ā*) [survives only in W.S.] : *sǣton, strǣt, dǣd*, etc., etc. (§ 120).

(4) **Survival of Primitive O.E. ǣ** [W.S. and Northumbrian, and part of Mercian area] : *glǣd, dǣġ, wǣs*, etc., etc. (§§ 97, 129, 137).

(5) **Change of ȳ (i-Mutation of ŭ) to ĕ** [Kentish, Essex (?), and S.E. Midl.] : *senn*, W.S. *synn*; *fēr* 'fire', W.S. *fȳr*, etc., etc. (§ 142).

(6) **Absence of Fracture of æ (ă) before ll or l + another consonant** [typically Anglian] : *all*, W.S. *eall*; *āld* 'old', W.S. *eald*; *cāld* 'cold', non-Angl. *ćeald*, etc., etc. (§ 126).

(7) **Smoothing of all Diphthongs before c, ć, g, ġ, h** [typically Anglian]: *hǣh*, W.S. *hēah*; *lēht* 'light', W.S. *lēoht* (§ 127).

(8) **Diphthonging of O.E. ǣ to eă by u-Mutation** [Mercian only] : *feadur, steaðelas* from *staðulas (§ 138).

(9) **Raising of Primitive ǣ (W.Gmc. ā) to ē** [all dialects except W.S.] : *sēton, strēt, dēd* (§ 123).

(10) **Raising of ǣ (i-Mutation of Pr. O.E. ā) to ē** [found chiefly in Kentish, but also in Suffolk texts] : *dēlan*, W.S. *dǣlan* (§ 140).

CHAPTER VI

HISTORY OF ENGLISH SOUNDS

II. The Middle English Period

§ **146.** THE number of literary works composed and written down during the M.E. period, that is, between, roughly, 1100 and 1450, is extremely large, and many of the individual works are of great length. M.E. literature is of the most varied character. Every kind of composition, in prose and verse, is represented; the religious treatise, the legal document, the lyric, the romance, history, serious narrative, satire, comedy, the sublime, the ridiculous, the grave, the gay; every note in the lyre of human passion is struck, every phase of human experience is portrayed. Almost every area, from Aberdeen to Sussex, except perhaps the Central Midlands, is represented by one or more works written in the local form of English.

Materials therefore are not lacking for the adequate study of our language, in all its forms, during the 350 years which begin within half a century of the Norman Conquest, and end fifty years after the death of Chaucer.

§ 147. The Norman Conquest.

This great event, while it undoubtedly marks a new departure in many ways in our social and political history, is by no means such a revolutionary factor in the history of our language as some writers would lead one to believe. Its main effects are seen in our vocabulary. While the M.E. period is characterized by far-reaching sound changes, which we think of as beginning soon after the Norman Conquest, there is every reason for believing that the germ of the tendencies which first find graphic expression at this time existed already long before, and that the linguistic phenomena which become noticeable in the texts of the twelfth and thirteenth centuries are the natural heritage of the past. In fact, there is no ground for assuming that the history of English sounds would have been other than we know it, had the Norman Conquest never taken place. The external form and the internal structure of English have undergone continuous, but gradual

G

change, from the earliest times to the present day. The Norman Conquest did not sever the continuity and begin a new era. We are to consider the changes in sounds and inflexions which we associate with the M.E. period, not as due in any way to the great historical cataclysm which befell in 1066, but as the natural outcome of forces that were at work long before Duke William was born, which can be traced to some extent in the texts of the late O.E. period.

§ 148. **Apparent increased rate of change in Early Transition English.**

If we examine the language of the latter parts of the Peterborough Chronicle which were written down about seventy to ninety years after the coming of the Normans, and compare it with that of the Charters written in the reign of Edward the Confessor (1043–66) or of William's English Charters, we are struck by certain obvious differences. The Charters are, to all intents and purposes, good Old English, showing to a superficial view but little difference from the language of Alfred, still less from that of Ælfric. The language of the Chronicle, during the last eighty or ninety years of the record, is something very different. Not only has the conventional O.E. spelling been largely given up in favour of what appear tentative efforts to express quite a different pronunciation, but the inflexions are greatly impaired; for instance, we get the indeclinable definite article, in such constructions as *of þe king*, we find a new personal pronoun *scæ*, the ancestor of the modern *she*, instead of *heo*, and the structure of the sentence is often very different from the old usage. As we note all the differences, we might be inclined to ask whether these considerable changes in the language, which have come about with such apparent suddenness, must not be attributed to some great event such as the Norman Conquest, which has upset society from top to bottom, and reacted upon the language. Why, it may reasonably be asked, has English suddenly changed more, in less than a hundred years, than it did during the three hundred and fifty years before 1066?

The answer is not far to seek. The Norman Conquest did not, indeed, produce a sudden change in the language itself, but it did cause the death, or nearly so, of literary prose tradition. The spoken language, we must suppose, had outgrown and gone beyond the written forms that we find in Ælfric and in the late charters. But the scribes were strongly conservative,

and adhered to the old methods of spelling which represented
approximately the facts of the language as pronounced,
perhaps, a hundred years earlier, but had long ceased to give
a true picture of contemporary speech. In the same way, the
style and structure of the sentence, in literary works, was
based upon the older models found in writings, and not upon
that of the colloquial language. We may assume, perhaps, that
in the latter respect the same kind of difference, only on a more
extensive scale, existed between the style of the written and
spoken language, in late O.E., as is seen at the present time,
when we write *is it not, will I not, were it not for that, the
Misses Smith*, whereas in ordinary colloquial speech we say
[*i*znt *i*t, wount *ai*, if *i*t wɔznt fə ðæt, ðə m*i*s sm*i*þ́s] and so on.
But soon after the Conquest, English learning sank to a very
low ebb. The great prelates, the Bishops and Abbots, were
Normans ; the language and literature of the English, regarded
as belonging to a rude and boorish race, were no longer objects
of solicitude for the learned. The art of writing, no doubt,
was hardly practised by Englishmen, or only by the more
aristocratic who had the opportunity of acquiring the language
of the dominant race. Documents were but rarely written
in English. The continuity of literary English prose style
was broken. When Englishmen again took up the pen, after
more than half a century of neglect, and attempted to set
down their thoughts on parchment, they had to create afresh
an English prose style. What models had they? The documents of the age which was gone, of the time when English
letters still flourished, were now hopelessly antiquated in style,
and too far removed from actual facts to serve as models.
The old traditional spelling, much behind the time even in
the days of Ælfric, was still less adapted to the requirements
of twelfth-century English. The only thing to do was to put
the thoughts, as far as possible, into the form of sentence used
in the ordinary spoken language, and to adapt, in some way
or other, what remained of a traditional mode of rendering
sounds to the changed conditions of pronunciation.

Such considerations as these enable us to understand that
the apparent gulf between pre-Conquest English and that of
the period immediately following that event is not a reality,
but that the appearance is a natural result of the conditions
inseparable from the graphic representation in the latter
period of a language whose literary cultivation had long been
neglected. It is perhaps worth while to point out here that
the documents of the Early Transition period probably
present a far more faithful picture of the spoken language of

the time, than do the writings of an age of highly developed
literary activity, based on a powerful tradition.

NOTE. On the other hand there is a remarkable continuity of poetical
diction and phrasing between Early M.E. and O.E., and this is preserved
in some of the fourteenth-century poetical Romances, at least to the
extent of employing certain conventional clichés which were used in O.E.

§ 149. Variety of Dialectal Types in M.E.

(1) It is constantly pointed out, and indeed it strikes at
once every student who makes the most superficial survey of
M.E. documents, that compared with the four or five well-
marked types of English which appear in the pre-Conquest
sources, there is an extraordinary richness of dialect types
preserved in M.E. It would be very wrong to draw the
inference from this fact, that the process of dialectal differentiation was more active after than before the Conquest, and
that a host of new varieties of English came into being in the
later periods.

The comparative uniformity of O.E. as we know it in the
written documents must be explained by the strength of
W. Saxon scribal tradition, which levelled many slightly
differing forms of speech under a single type for literary
purposes. No such check existed, for a long time, in the
M.E. period. Every writer was largely a law unto himself,
and while he no doubt owed something to the gradually
hardening tradition of spelling, he felt free to try experiments
of his own. The spelling of Orm (fl. 1200) is an example of
highly developed individualism, for which the whole of Old and
even of Middle English offers no parallel. The M.E. scribes do
full justice to the variety of regional dialects which undoubtedly
existed, but they also, by the individualism of their methods,
may occasionally suggest a variety greater than really existed.
We do not often find complete consistency in the spelling of a
single text, therefore when we compare that of several writers
of the same period, we may mistake for variety of dialect
what is really an experimental groping after the best way of
writing the same sound.

(2) But after all allowances are made for individual vagaries,
there are certain well-established modes of expressing sounds
which are fairly constant, and from which we may reasonably
infer a specific intention on the part of the scribes to express
a particular sound. If, for instance, one text has the spelling
erþe and another *urþe* for O.E. *eorþe*, and these spellings are
severally used with fair consistency in each text, for this and
other words which were written with *eo* in O.E., it is reasonable

to infer that two different pronunciations of the same original sound are thus expressed. In fact it is only from such differences of spelling that it is possible to arrive at those phonological differences which in M.E., as at the present day, form such important and characteristic indications of dialect variety.

Just as in O.E. we note that the same W.Gmc. sound develops differently in the speech of different areas, so in M.E. we observe similar differences in the treatment of O.E. sounds. These phonological idiosyncrasies are, together with certain others affecting grammatical forms or inflexions, the decisive tests of dialect identity.

In §§ 64, 65, the regularity of sound change in a given dialect was insisted upon as a necessary axiom of philological method. Now it will often appear, from the study of a M.E. text, that the same original O.E. sound is written sometimes in the same word, in two, or even three, different ways, so as to imply two or even three dialect types—e. g. *brigge, bregge, brugge,* for O.E. *bryċġ* ' bridge '. Are we bound in such a case to suppose that the text has been corrupted, and that it cannot represent a genuine ' pure ' dialect such as was actually spoken? Not necessarily. Before committing ourselves to such an opinion it is reasonable to inquire whether, as a matter of fact, there was an area within which these three types, or any two of them, as the case may be, were both or all in use at the time when our text was written.

It is possible that we may find several other texts, written by different scribes, which also exhibit a similar diversity. If this should be so, and if all the texts which we thus compare should prove to have the various types in *approximately the same proportions*, it would go far to establish the probability that the diversity was an actual fact in the speech of the area from which all the texts came.

The lesson of this, and it is a common experience in dealing with M.E. texts, is that the speech of a given region is not cut off from that of surrounding areas by impassable barriers, but may be influenced by the linguistic environment. We have only to look at a map of England to see how the boundaries of many counties bulge out here, retreat there, as neighbouring counties, in one area almost enclose a portion, in others, eat far into them. Note, for instance, how Oxfordshire in the N.E. has a tongue flanked to the E. by Northants, to the W. by Warwick; how in the S.E. it bites far into Berks., separated from the latter, it is true, by the Thames, while farther west, Berks., still bounded by the Thames, takes a great scoop out of Oxfordshire. Oxfordshire is on the whole typically W. Midl. in dialect, but we shall not expect to find that the dialect of the N.W. of the county, with its totally different linguistic environment, presents the same features in all respects as that of the S.W. area. We shall anticipate that usually the dialect of one area will pass by almost imperceptible gradations into that of another.

(3) Now the picture which is presented by the numerous M.E. texts, so far as we can piece together the evidence which they afford, is indeed something of this kind. We find not a series of entirely clear-cut, sharply distinguished dialect types, each of which is perfectly regular and ideally consistent in its character and constituent elements, but rather, as a rule, we get the impression of dialects which, as it were, dovetail one into the other, and each of which is, so to speak, shot and diversified by characteristics from others spoken in adjacent areas. The 'pure' dialect is hardly found, and even those texts which are regarded as exhibiting such 'purity' frequently present apparently incongruous features, while the great majority show a more or less variegated character, and represent in fact border dialects, types of speech belonging, evidently, to intermediate areas, lying between others of slightly different linguistic complexion, and partaking the characters of the surrounding dialects. Owing to the necessary lack of preciseness in our classification of the M.E. dialects and the vagueness and imperfections in our knowledge of the geographical diffusion of the principal characteristic dialect features, and especially of the ways in which these were combined and grouped in the speech of different areas, we have been inclined, in the past, to ignore the existence of border or intermediate dialects, and to attribute to various external corrupting influences what may well be a combination of features, really existing in a dialect actually spoken and faithfully reproduced in the suspected text.

A good example of a border dialect is that of London, as exhibited in the early sources, including the forms used by Chaucer and Caxton, and indeed the Standard English of speech and literature in the present day. This, which may be regarded as in origin a variety of Cent. Sthn. (§ 151 D.), presents, as is well known, a certain dialectal variety in its constituent elements. That this should be so in the Regional dialect of the London area was inevitable. The speech of the Middle Saxons, subject as it was to influence from Hertford to the N., Bucks. to the W., and from Essex to N. and E., could not but show some traces of all these types. But the same possibilities, or rather certainties, of influence and counter influence, exist in almost any area, and the more extensive an area, the greater the opportunities of environmental influence. The dialect of Kent in M.E., especially the type exhibited in Ayenbite, is singularly pure, and free from features not commonly accepted as belonging to this area. But if we consider the position of Canterbury, where the unique MS. of the text was written, this dialectal purity of the text does not appear surprising. Situated in the extreme E., in that part of Kent which juts into and is surrounded by the sea on three sides, with the great expanse of Kent stretching away behind it, Canterbury is completely isolated from direct contact with non-Kentish areas, and remote from the borders both of Sussex and of Surrey. Here, if anywhere, we should expect a ' pure ' dialect. In the same way, the consistent and uniform dialect character of Genesis and Exodus, and of the Bestiary, is intelligible if we are right in assigning these texts to the largely isolated county of Norfolk.

(4) The diffusion or distribution of a given dialect feature may vary from age to age; it may become more widespread, or its sphere may be contracted. This is another way of saying that the general dialect complexion of an area will not be the same at all periods. It may lose some of its original characters altogether, it may acquire others formerly alien to it. This variability in constituent elements is observable in the London dialect, and in all others whose history has been investigated throughout a period of several centuries.

§ 150. (1) **Problems and Methods of Investigation of M.E. Dialects.**

The age of a MS. can usually be decided by palaeographical experts to within a quarter of a century or less. It may usually be assumed that the language of a text represents, on the whole, that current at the time it was written. The M.E. scribe, even when he copies an earlier document, generally brings the language up to date, and those archaic forms which he reproduces are generally easily distinguishable from those which belong to his own speech. Exceptions to this exist in some deliberate attempts to write O.E. in the thirteenth century, when it was necessary to produce an ancient charter proving possessions or privileges long enjoyed by a monastery, etc. Certain Homilies (e. g. Holy Rd. Tree, Ed. Napier, c. 1175) are virtually faithful copies of L.O.E. with some occasional M.E. spellings introduced, but such do not concern us here. On the other hand, the English documents in Chertsey Chartulary (written c. 1275), see Kemble Cod. Dipl., although based on older documents are on the whole normal English of the day, with a very few archaisms.

To identify the regional dialect of a text is quite another matter. If we have the author's own MS., as in Ayenbite and Ormulum, one source of contamination is eliminated, and unless we are to believe that the author himself wrote a sham or artificial dialect, or that his own speech was an unreal, blended form of English, peculiar to himself, we must conclude that we have before us an example of a genuine, current dialect. If however our text is a copy, it is possible that the scribe may have introduced some forms from his own dialect here and there, while preserving, on the whole, the author's type; or he may reverse the process, and change the greater part of the text, only occasionally preserving the forms of his original. Again, several scribes may have made copies, and the text before us may be a copy of a copy and exhibit traces of both scribes as well as of the original author. In any of these cases we have a text which does not reproduce a genuine form of English, really spoken in a particular area, but a fortuitous mixture of dialect types. A further possibility, especially in the later fourteenth century, is that either author or scribe may introduce, side by side with the genuine forms of his own dialect, others quite foreign to it from the London type. These possibilities must be borne in mind by the student, but he must not forget the principles set forth in § 149. 2, 3, 4.

The question arises then : is the dialect of this or that text a genuine regional form of English, or is it not ? The answer to this involves a further question ; was there any area within which just such a collocation of dialect features as this text exhibits was in use in the M.E. period ? The only way to settle these points is to compare the doubtful text with one or more others, whose general complexion appears to resemble it. Should it appear, as it often happens, that several independent texts, written by different scribes, perhaps at slightly different periods, all show the same main features, and the same approximate combination of features, we may regard the question of genuineness answered in the affirmative. Further confirmation may be sought from a comparison with the forms of place-names recorded at the same date as the texts were written. See § 150. 2.

§ 150. (2) **Forms of Place-Names in M.E. as a guide to Phonology of Dialects.**

During the last dozen years it has been increasingly recognized by students of M.E. dialects that much light is

thrown on their special problems by a critical investigation of
the forms of English place-names as recorded in ancient
Charters, Rolls, Rentals, Inquisitions, Surveys, etc.   English
place-names, as is well known, are frequently compounds, and
contain in one or other element common words such as O.E.
hyll 'hill'; *hyrst* 'wood'; *neoþor* 'lower'; *hēah* 'high'; *lēah*
'field'; *stēpel* 'steeple', and others, which have a characteristic
dialect form in different areas.   These elements in M.E. place-
names exhibit the same varieties of form as they do when they
occur as independent words in prose or poetry of the same
period.   Provided therefore, that we have reasonable assurance
that the forms of place-names found in a given collection of
records were those in actual use in the area in which the places
are, at the date when the record was written, it is possible to
derive from them a more reliable notion of the phonological
features of the dialect of that area than from any other source,
except from a continuous English text whose precise date and
place of origin are known beyond any doubt.   Unfortunately
such texts are very few in number, and if we ignore the
testimony of place-names in the investigation of M.E. dialects,
we find ourselves in a vicious circle of doubt and difficulty.
A certain text, let us say, is believed for some reason or other
to be in the Dorsetshire dialect of the thirteenth century.   The
palaeographers can tell us the date of the handwriting within
a few decades, but how are we to test theories about the
dialect itself?   We do not know what were the precise
phonological features of the Dorsetshire dialect of the thirteenth
century, because we have no texts of which we dare affirm
positively that they represent that dialect.   But, failing such
direct information, we cannot recognize genuine Dorsetshire
texts when we see them, because we do not know what the
Dorsetshire dialect in M.E. was like.   Now although the fullest
collection of Dorsetshire place-names of the early periods,
selected from the most reliable documents we can find, may
not tell us everything we want to know about the dialect of
that county, we can learn a good deal from them which we
cannot discover at present from any other source.

We can at least lay the foundations of such knowledge as
will enable us to say whether the text whose dialect we are
trying to identify has such a combination of phonological
features as did actually exist in the dialect of Dorset at the
approximate date at which the text was written.

The use of place-names in the investigation of M.E. dialect
phonology has been exemplified by several valuable researches
published by Ekwall, Brandl, Heuser, Miss M. Serjeantson, and

Miss B. Mackenzie, also in some articles by the present writer. The value and reliability of this new instrument may be regarded as established, and it seems probable that, largely by its means, we shall before long reach something like clarity in our classification of M.E. dialects, together with a moderately complete picture of the essential features of the several regional types, and something like an exact account of the geographical distribution of each of the principal distinguishing dialectal features severally.

A few general principles of method in the use of place-names in dialect research may be formulated.

(1) The forms of place-names actually current in the speech of a given area will, as a rule, be most faithfully recorded in Charters, Wills, and other documents written locally. Preference should therefore be given as far as possible to the forms found in documents of this type. Records of a more public character such as Rolls and Inquisitions, though often surprisingly faithful to the genuine local type, may contain forms with a standardized spelling not strictly reproducing the local pronunciation.

(2) Although place-names throw light principally upon phonological characters, they may also occasionally reveal something concerning typical inflexional forms, especially those of the Present Participle.

(3) As mentioned in § 149. 4, the general character of a dialect may, and generally does, alter from age to age. This alteration may take the form, on the one hand, of the disappearance of a particular dialect feature from, or its extension into, the speech of an area ; on the other, when more than one type of pronunciation of a given original sound was in use, the relative frequency with which the types severally occur may differ at different times ; now this one, now that may preponderate. The relative frequency of the types should be noted.

(4) In comparing the phonological features exhibited by the place-names of a given area with those of a text, the most reliable results will be obtained by basing the comparison on forms of place-names written down at approximately the same period as the MS. of the text ; thirteenth-century texts should be compared with thirteenth-century place-name forms, fourteenth-century texts with fourteenth-century place-name forms, and so on. It may be very misleading, for instance, to deduce, as some have done, the distribution of dialect features in O.E. from the conditions revealed in M.E. place-names ; still more misleading to draw inferences respecting M.E. dialects from a survey of the rustic dialects of the present day.

(5) Conclusions regarding phonology, derived from place-name forms, should be based only upon those elements whose identity is established beyond all reasonable doubt. When possible, though this does not always happen, it is most satisfactory to compare a given element in a place-name with the same word occurring as an independent element of vocabulary in a text of the same date. If, for instance, in a fourteenth-century text O.E. *hēah* ' high ' invariably appears as *hyȝe*, whereas in the fourteenth-century forms of place-names of a given area this word never appears in any form but *heie*, we should hesitate to ascribe the origin of the text to this area.

§ 151. Classification of M.E. Dialects.

Owing to the reasons referred to in §§ 149, 150, a satisfactory scheme of classification of the M.E. dialects presents very great difficulties. We have still to be content with a rough general grouping into Northern, West and East Midland, and Southern. Within these divisions we recognize the further distinctions of N.- and S.-West Midl.; N.- and S.-East Midl.; S. Western, and S. Eastern. In Central Southern we include the later dialect of London as a whole, and in S. Eastern we include Kentish, and the Early City type. Kentish, because it is represented by several texts, especially by the Ayenbite (extant in the author's handwriting), exhibiting a very consistent form of language and known to have been written at Canterbury in 1340, has engaged a degree of attention which is perhaps rather out of proportion to its importance in relation to the S.E. type. Several dialect features, notably the occurrence of *ĕ* for original O.E. *ȳ*, have been labelled ' Kentish ', although they were by no means confined to the dialect of that county. Some of these features were current in the London dialect, where they have commonly been regarded as ' Kentish ' elements, although they more probably passed into London speech through the City type, from Essex.

The dialect areas of the Midlands and South may be tentatively sub-divided as follows.

1. West Midlands.

A. *N.-W. Midl.* Sth. Lancs., Chesh., W. Derbysh., Staffs, Nth. and Central Shropsh.

B. *Central W. Midl.* Heref., Worcs., W. Warwcs. (as far E. roughly, as Coventry and Stratford), and possibly S. Shropsh.

C. *S.-W. Midl.* Glos., W. Oxf. as far E. as Oxford itself.

2. CENTRAL MIDLANDS.

To the East of the large area occupied by the W. Midl. is a tract of country the dialect of which appears to form a speech unity of an intermediate character between West and East. This dialect area includes the Eastern part of Derbysh., Notts., Leics., Eastern part of Warwcs., Northants. (excluding the extreme N.E. area in which is Peterborough), N. Oxf., and N. Bucks. This dialect-unity, which naturally includes sub-areas, appears to be neither definitely W. nor definitely E. in character, and to have none of the features which are exclusively characteristic of, and peculiar to, either of these areas. According to Miss Serjeantson, the dialects of this central area, while they have both $\breve{\imath}$ and $\breve{u}$ for O.E. $\breve{y}$ (§ 158), show no traces of the characteristic S.E. and S.-E. Midl. $\breve{e}$; tense $\bar{e}$ for O.E. $\bar{æ}$ [2] (§ 162), which is found from Suffolk to Kent, and sporadically in later London, does not occur here; O.E. $e\breve{o}$ (§ 168) is always $\breve{e}$, never $\breve{u}$; such pronominal forms as *ho, hore, hom* are apparently foreign to these dialects, and so, apparently, is the Western *-on* for *-an*.

3. EAST MIDLANDS.

A. *N.-E. Midl.* All that part of Lincs. between the Humber and the Wash.

B. *Central E. Midl.* Rutland (?), Spalding division of Lincs., Nth. Beds., Hunts, N. Cambr., Norf., N. Suff.

C. *S.-E. Midl.* Herts, S. Cambr., Suffolk, and probably N. Essex (Saffron Walden), though the latter should perhaps be considered as a border area, the dialect of which had both Midl. and Sthn. features.

4. SOUTHERN DIALECTS.

A. *S. West.* (1) These include the speech of Devon, Somerset, Wilts., Dorset, Berks, Hants, Western Surrey, and that portion of S.-E. Oxf. which cuts into Berks, roughly from Dorchester to Caversham, and thence northwards to Henley.

(2) It is necessary to distinguish two areas of South Western: (*a*) the extreme west, including Devon, Dorset, Somers., and another, (*b*) comprising Wilts., Hants, Berks, S.-E. Oxf. It is proposed to call the former FURTHER, the latter NEARER, Wessex.

B. *Central Sthn.* To this area belongs primarily the greater part of Middlesex, as distinguished from the City of London, on which see C, below. The recent investigations of Miss

Mackenzie, based on the place-name forms of the thirteenth and fourteenth centuries, make it quite clear that the early dialect of the county of Middlesex differed in its most characteristic phonological features from that of the City (see §§ 158, 160, 167, 168, 207). The Middlesex dialect, in fact, was not South Eastern, but Central Southern, and had far more affinity with more westerly areas, specifically with those of Nearer Wessex. This type is pretty well represented in the Lamb. Homs. and in Henry III's Proclamation (1258). We should note that in the extreme S.W. of the county, a heart-shaped portion of Bucks, about 8 miles wide near Uxbridge, but narrowing to a point at Staines, is all that separates Middlesex from the Berks border, the most easterly outpost of the S.W. dialect area. From this area must have come the only trace of specifically S.W. character, y ($=i$) for O.E. $\check{e}a\text{-}i$, which exists in London documents, and that only in one or two forms in the earliest Ch. (See § 170.)

C. *South Eastern.* The whole of Essex exclusive of the district of Saffron Walden. Street, and other local names from the City of London, down at any rate to the middle of the fourteenth century, present some of the main phonological characters which distinguish the dialect of Essex. (Heuser: *Alt-London*, pp. 27, 28.) We must therefore regard the City of London as belonging to the South Eastern dialect area down to this period. After the middle of the fourteenth century, however, the specifically Essex character, even of the City, almost disappears (see §§ 167, 207). The dialect of Kent belongs to this area, but while it agrees with Essex in some particulars, e.g. $\check{e}$ for O.E. $\bar{y}$, it differs widely from this in many other important respects (§§ 202, 203). To this area also belong probably the eastern part of Surrey and part of Sussex. Concerning the dialect of the latter we have at present but scanty information.

D. *London Dialect.* We have seen (B and C, above) that in the earliest M.E. period the dialect of the City of London, so far as the evidence goes, was of quite a different type, at least in its phonological features, from that of the county of Middlesex. In the later periods these marked divergences seem to disappear, and the fourteenth-century forms of London street-names, etc., agree on the whole with the place-name forms of Middlesex. The phonology of both of these agrees, generally, with that of literary texts written in London at this period. In this more or less uniform dialect, however, the typical Essex $\check{e}$ for O.E. $\bar{y}$ survived to some extent. This is the feature formerly regarded as 'Kentish'. The dialect of Davy and Chaucer seems to be a natural development of the earlier Middlesex dialect. We find in the former, however, and still more in the latter, certain features (e.g. Pres. Plurals in *-en*), which occur, it is true, though to a less extent, already in Lamb. Homs. and Henry III's Proclamation. These and other features, which are usually associated with the East Midland, have by the fourteenth century become normal in the regional dialect of Middlesex. They may quite possibly have encroached gradually through Herts. The remarkable frequency of $\breve{e}$ for O.E. $\breve{y}$ shown in Chaucer's rhymes may perhaps be a personal characteristic, attributable to some extent to the poet's City origin, or to his later residence in Greenwich. We should in any case expect to find $\breve{e}$-forms in the City, and in those easterly parts of Middlesex which abut on Essex. We shall probably be nearer to the truth if we regard the dialect of London at the end of the fourteenth century as a naturally developed regional dialect, and inquire whether its characteristic combination of features may not be better explained by reference to those of the dialect areas immediately contiguous to it, rather than by the assumption that some of them have been imported from without, from regions with which London has no direct geographical contact. In the meantime it may be intimated that a study of the early dialect of Herts will probably throw new light on several problems which are now obscure. (See further, Heuser: *Alt-London*, pp. 45–56.)

A summary of the distinguishing features of the principal M.E. dialect types will be found on pp. 136–43 below, together with references to the sections where the points are specially treated.

§ 152.   M.E. Spelling and M.E. Sounds.

(1) It is essential to distinguish between the actual sounds of M.E. and the various methods of expressing these graphically. A change in spelling does not necessarily imply a change in pronunciation, though of course it sometimes may ; neither does the retention of an older spelling unaltered necessarily prove that the sound remains the same. The history of English spelling is one thing, and the history of English pronunciation is quite another. From the point of view of the former it is of importance to record that O.E. $\bar{u}$ in such words as *hūs*, *mūs*, etc., is written *ou* in M.E., owing to the habits of French scribes. But this fact is of no importance for the history of the sound, since this remained the same [ū] for centuries after the new spelling was introduced, and when, perhaps in the fourteenth century, this sound was diphthongized, no further change was made in the mode of representing it. On the other hand, in tracing the history of sounds it is vital to state that the O.E. diphthong $\bar{ea}$

in words like *deap, heap* 'crowd', etc., was monophthongized
to [æ] in most dialects before the end of the O.E. period
(§ 97. 3, Note), although the old spelling was often retained in
the Early Transition and later periods.

(2) It must not be supposed that the pronunciation of the
various vowels, when once the characteristic M.E. type peculiar to the several dialects was reached, remained unchanged
during the whole M.E. period.   Much work still remains to
be done in determining the path of change pursued by the
various vowels, and the approximate period at which each stage
was reached, but there are certain occasional spellings occurring
sporadically in M.E. texts which point to the probability that
in many cases something very like the Modern sound of the
vowels must have existed much earlier than was formerly
supposed.   This probability emerges from the evidence given
in chap. VII on the Modern Period.   If we are now compelled
to put back some of the typically 'Modern' changes to an
approximate date of a hundred or two hundred years earlier
than was assumed for them until recently, this fact must affect
our views of M.E. pronunciation, notably of that of Chaucer's
day. If, for instance, early M.E. *ā*, in *māken*, etc., had been fully
fronted by the first quarter of the fifteenth century, it is hardly
possible that Chaucer can have still pronounced a full back [*ā*].
At any rate, before he died, in 1400, he must at least have
heard the beginnings of something like the Modern type of
pronunciation from the younger generation.   We find such
occasional spellings as *sichen* for O.E. *sēcan* 'to seek' in the
earlier MS. of Laȝamon's *Brut* (early thirteenth century), and
ou is a frequent spelling for O.E. *ō* (*bouk* 'book' etc.) in widely
separated dialects during the fourteenth century.   These
spellings point to pronunciations closely resembling [*ī*, *ū*].
Now, if a pronunciation approaching the Modern type were
established for these two vowels in M.E., this would bring many
consequences, and would involve a re-statement of the whole
account usually given of M.E. vowel pronunciation. (See on this
point §§ 208, 213, below.)   In the meantime, until M.E. pronunciation has been further investigated, it is as well to be
cautious, and to continue to pronounce Chaucer as if his language were still pure M.E., that is, with so-called 'Continental'
vowels.   At the same time, the considerations just mentioned
must be borne in mind.   It must be remembered that to
change the pronunciation of one or two vowels may involve
changing all.   If Chaucer said [būk] he can no longer have
said [hūs] for 'house'; if he said [sīke] for *sēke* 'seek', he
cannot also have pronounced [ī] in *wīf* 'wife', and so on.

An important M.E. sound-change was the gradual and progressive un-rounding of the front rounded vowels representing O.E. *ў* and *ěŏ*. The former of these remained at first in Middlesex, and was gradually un-rounded to *ĭ*. The latter had become [*ø*], which is shown to have survived at first in the London area, west of the City, by not infrequent spellings such as *eo*, *o*, *u*. After the beginning of the fourteenth century there appears to be no trace of these spellings in the documents from this area, showing presumably that the un-rounding was complete.

§ 153. Changes in Spelling which are purely Graphic.

A. Vowels.

O.E. *ў*. The O.E. high-front-tense-round, so far as it survived in M.E. (cp. § 158 (*c*)), is never written *y* after the twelfth century, e. g. Holy Rd. Tree, but with the French symbol *u*: e.g. *sunn* 'sin', O.E. *synn*; *muchel* 'great', O.E. *mycel*. When long, it is frequently expressed by *ui*: *huiren* vb. 'hear', Late W.Sax. *hÿran*; *fuir* 'fire', O.E. *fÿr*.

The symbol *y* no longer expressed a rounded vowel, but simply [*ĭ*] in Early Transition. Thus in the latter part of Peterborough Chronicle, we may assume an un-rounded vowel in *yuel* 'evil', and *fylden* 'filled', for O.E. *y* had certainly long since been un-rounded in this E. Midl. dialect, and because this very text writes *y* for old *i*, as in *wrythen* 'twisted', Pret. Pl., O.E. *wriþon*; *gyuen* Inf. 'to give'; *myhtes* 'thou mightest'.

OE. *ū*. In order to distinguish this from old *ÿ*, now often spelt *u*, it is written habitually *ou* by French scribes, and later, by every one: e.g. *hous*, O.E. *hūs*; *bour* 'dwelling', O.E. *būr*.

O.E. *ŭ*. In the neighbourhood of the letters *v*, *u*, *w*, *n*, *m*, this sound, which remained unchanged, is often written *o*, purely for the sake of distinctness to the eye, e. g. *sone* 'son', O.E. *sunu*; *comen* P. P. 'come', O.E. *cumen*. In N.Fr. old *-on* had become [un] in pronunciation.

B. The Consonants.

O.E. *c* = back voiceless stop, generally preserved initially, before back vowels: *cot, comen* 'come', but written *k* before front vowels: *king, kēpen* 'keep'. Domesday Book, entirely the work of foreign scribes, constantly writes *ch* for initial *c* (k) in English names, e. g. *Chenulueslei*, O.E. *Cēnwulfeslēah* 'Knowsley'. *ch* in D.B. always stands for the back voiceless stop.

Medially, and finally, this sound is written *k*, *ck*, *c*.

The O.E. combination *cw* is written with the French symbol *q*+*u*, hence *queen*, O.E. *cwēn*, etc. *ku*, *cu*, etc., are also written.

O.E. *ċ*. As early as the twelfth century, some Sthn. texts write *ch* for this sound, in all positions—*chald* 'cold'; *sēchen* 'seek', O.E. *sēcan*; *ich* 'I', O.E. *iċ*. The earliest Transition texts still write *c*. In later M.E. *cch* and *tch* are written medially—*wretche*, *lacchen* 'catch'.

O.E. **ꞅ** or **ȝ**. These are the only forms of the letter used in O.E., but the latter part of the Peterborough Chronicle, written in the twelfth century, uses what is known as the Continental form of the letter, which is approximately that of our *g*. The Chronicle, and some other early Transition texts, e.g. Genesis and Exodus, use this symbol *g* exclusively for O.E. **ȝ** whether it expresses a back or front consonant, stop or open—so that we get even *gung* for O.E. *ȝeong*.

Later on, the more careful scribes use *g* and ȝ, a modified form of O.E. **ȝ**, and distinguish systematically between back and front sounds. The following are the typical M.E. ways of expressing the various sounds expressed by O.E. ȝ and *ċġ*:

(1) **Back-open-voiced** consonant (O.E. **ȝ**) is written *gh*, and ȝ*h*: *burgh*, O.E. *burg*; *laghe* 'law', O.E. *laȝu*, etc.

[This symbol (*gh*), as well as *h*, *hh*, is used also for the voiceless open sound.]

(2) **Back Stop** (O.E. **ȝ**) is written *g*: *gōd*, *god* 'good', 'God', etc.

Orm, who was a mediæval spelling reformer, invented a special symbol, ꝿ, for the stop, and uses it in words such as the above.

(3) **Front Stop** (O.E. *ċġ*). This only occurred medially and finally in O.E. words. In M.E. it is written *gg* by Orm and most other scribes, though sometimes *g* alone is written: *seggen* 'say', O.E. *seċġan*; *rugg*, O.E. *hryċġ* 'back'. In French words the sound occurred initially in such words as *juge* 'judge', and in these words the spelling *j* is generally retained, though *g* is occasionally written. When the sound occurs medially it was, in late M.E., not infrequently written *dg* as at the present day: *bridge*, etc.

(4) **Front-open-voiced** consonant (O.E. **ȝ**). The modified form ȝ of the O.E. symbol is used in a large number of texts quite systematically for this sound: *ȝer*, O.E. *ȝēr* 'year'; *ȝeuen*, O.E. *ȝefan* 'give', etc. Later M.E. texts use *y*—*yere*, etc.

H

O.E. f written v or u. This, as a systematic habit, was an innovation of the French scribes, though there are traces in some O.E. texts of *u* to express a voiced sound between vowels. In the Southern area of M.E. the O.E. *f* was voiced initially, and we consequently find such spellings as *vox, uox* 'fox', *vuir* 'fire', O.E. *fȳr*, with fair consistency. Medially, between vowels, the sound was voiced in all dialects, and we find therefore *uvel, ivel*, etc., O.E. *yfel* 'evil'; *ouer*, O.E. *ofer* 'over', etc. Since the forms of *u* and *v* were often confused, we constantly find such spellings as *vuel* 'evil' = [yvel] instead of *uvel*.

O.E. s written c. This is habitual in French words, and the usage is applied also to English words: *seldcene*, O.E. *seldsēne* 'rare'; *alce*, O.E. *alswa*.

O.E. voiced s written z. Spelling with initial *z* is typical of Kentish texts, in which dialect O.E. *s* must have been voiced in this position: *zayþ* 'says', O.E. *seg(e)þ*; *zoþe* 'true', O.E. *sōþ*; *zwete* 'sweet', O.E. *swete*, etc.

O.E. sċ is written sch, ss, sh: *schal, schencken* 'grant', *ssolde* 'should', *issote* 'shot', *shǣwenn*, etc.

The subject of M.E. spelling will be further considered later on, in dealing specifically with the sounds themselves and their changes.

§ 154. Illustrative Middle English Texts.

The following select list of M.E. texts will be found fairly representative of the various dialects and periods. Most of them are referred to in the account given below of the development of Sounds and Accidence in M.E. A useful illustrative selection of texts, dating from 1150 to 1390, is contained in Morris and Skeat's *Specimens of Early English*, Parts I and II, and others in MacLean's *Old and Middle English Reader*, Macmillan, 1893; of more recent collections we may note Emerson's *Middle English Reader*, Macmillan, 1909; Hall's *Early M.E. Reader*, 2 pts. Oxford, 1920; Sisam, *Fourteenth Century Verse and Prose*, Oxford, 1921; Carleton Brown's *English Lyrics of the Fourteenth Century*, Oxford, 1924. Scotch texts, though mainly of the Early Modern Period, are well illustrated in Gregory Smith's *Specimens of Middle Scots*, Blackwood, 1902. Valuable examples of Late M.E. and early Mod. texts (1384–1579) are to be found in Skeat's *Specimens of English Literature*.

Most of the texts enumerated below are published by the Early English Text Society; when this is not the case, it will be indicated. When selections occur in any of the above collections, this is also indicated. Several very important Early M.E. texts are contained in *An Old English Miscellany*, ed. R. Morris, E.E.T.S., 1872; and the chief groups of Early M.E. Homilies are to be found in two vols. known as *Old English Homilies*, 1st and 2nd Series, E.E.T.S., 1868 and 1873 respectively, by the same editor. The presence of a text in either of these collections is indicated by the words *O.E. Homs.* or *O.E. Misc.* placed after the name in the list.

I. M.E. Northern Texts.

Northern Legends. 1275. Ed. Horstmann, 1881.

Nthn. Metrical Psalter. Before 1300. Surtees Society, 1843-47. Extracts in Specimens.

Cursor Mundi. 1300. Extracts in Specimens, and MacLean's Reader.

Nthn. Metrical Homilies. 1330. Ed. Small, Edinburgh, 1862. Extracts in Specimens.

Richd. Rolle de Hampole's Pricke of Conscience. Before 1349. Ed. R. Morris, 1863. Extracts in Specimens, and Maetzner's ae. Sprachproben.

Minot's Songs. 1339-52. Ed. Scholle, Quellen und Forschungen, lii, 1884, and Hall, Oxford, 1887. Extracts in Specimens.

II. Scotch Texts.

Barbour's Bruce. 1375. Ed. Skeat, E.E.T.S., 1870. Extracts in Specimens, and MacLean. (The oldest MS., G. 23, St. John's Coll., Cambridge, was not written till 1487.)

Ratis Raving. First half of fifteenth century. Ed. Lumby, E.E.T.S., 1870.

The Taill of Rauf Coilyear. 1456-81. Ed. S. J. H. Herrtage, E.E.T.S., 1882.

III. Midland.

1. EAST MIDLAND.

A. *North East Midland.*

Peterborough Chronicle. 1121-54. (Laud MS.) Plummer, Two A.-S. Chronicles. Extracts in Specimens and Hall's Early M.E.

Ormulum. c. 1200. Ed. White, 1852, 2 vols., and Holt, 1878, 2 vols. Extracts in Specimens and Hall's Early M.E.

Bestiary. c. 1250. In O.E. Misc. Extracts in Specimens and Hall's Early M.E. (Norfolk.)

Genesis and Exodus. c. 1250. Ed. Morris, E.E.T.S. Revised 1873. Extracts in Specimens and Hall's Early M.E. (Norfolk.)

Havelok the Dane. 1300. Ed. Holthausen, Heidelberg, 1901 ; Skeat, Oxford, 1902. Extracts in Specimens. (Lincoln.)

Robt. of Brunne's Handlyng Synne. 1300–30. Ed. Furnivall, Roxburghe Club, 1862. Re-ed., Pt. I, 1901, Pt. II, 1903. Extracts in Specimens. (Lincoln.)

Norfolk Guilds. 1389. In English Guilds, ed. Lucy Toulmin Smith, E.E.T.S., 1870.

B. *South East Midland.*

Osbern Bokenam's Lives of Saints. Fl. 1370–1450. (MS. c. 1443.) Ed. Horstmann, Heilbronn, 1883. (Suffolk.)

2. CENTRAL MIDLAND.

A. *North Central Midland.*

Knyghton's Chronicle. 1381. English addresses in the Chronicon of Henry Knyghton of Leicester. Ed. Rolls Series 2, pp. 138, ff.

Parlement of the Three Ages. 15th c. Ed. Gollancz, Select Early English Poems, 1915.

Winner and Waster. 15th c. Ed. Gollancz, Select Early English Poems.

B. *South Central Midland.*

Earliest Complete English Prose Psalter. c. 1340. Ed. Bülbring, E.E.T.S., 97.

This text, hitherto claimed as exhibiting the W. Midl. dialect, has been shown by Miss Serjeantson to contain no typical W. Midl. features at all. A strong case has been made out by Miss Serjeantson for assigning it to Northants. See *English Studies*, 1924.

Coventry Leet Book. From 1421. Ed. Harris, E.E.T.S. 1901.

3. WEST MIDLAND.

A. *North West Midland.*

Compassio Mariae. c. 1250. Ed. Napier, E.E.T.S. 103. (? Cheshire.)

Wooing of our Lord. 1210. O.E. Homilies, I. Extracts in Specimens. (MS. Cot. Titus. D. 18.)

Sir Gawain and the Green Knight. 1350–1400. Re-ed. Gollancz, E.E.T.S. 1920, etc.; Tolkien and Gordon, Clarendon Press, 1925. The latter edition has a very full glossary and copious notes. (Generally assigned to Lancs., though there are grave reasons against this. See § 172 II.)

Alliterative Poems. 1350–1400. Ed. Morris (2nd Ed.) 1869.

Romances of the Ireland MS. c. 1400–13. Ed. Robson, Camden Soc. 1842. (Lancs.)

St. Erkenwald. 15th c. Ed. Gollancz, Select Early English Poems, 1922.

Lay Folks' Mass Book. c. 1440. (MS. Gonville and Caius Coll. Cbg. 84.) Ed. Simmons, E.E.T.S. 71, 1879.

Myrc's Instructions for Parish Priests. c. 1450. Ed. Peacock, E.E.T.S. (Revised) 1902. (Shropshire.)

John Audelay's Poems. c. 1426. Percy Society, vol. xiv, 1844. (Shropshire.)

William of Palerne. 1350. Ed. Skeat, E.E.T.S. (E.S.) 1867, 1. Usually regarded as W. Midl. (Possibly a North Centr. Midl. copy of a S.W. Midl. original.)

B. *Central West Midland.*

Worcester Fragments. c. 1180. In Hall's Early Middle English.

Laȝamon A. c. 1205. (MS. Cot. Calig. A. ix.) Ed. Madden, 1867. (N.W. Worcs.) See Hall, Early M.E. Vol. i.

For Laȝamon B. see C. below.

Ancren Riwle. c. 1230–50. (MS. Nero A. xiv.) Ed. Morton, Camden Soc. 1853.

The dialect of *Ancren Riwle* in MS. Cleopatra C. vi is practically identical with that of the Catherine Group (see I. Williams, Anglia 28), probably that of North Herefordshire; that of MS. Nero A. xiv, on the other hand, is in many respects different, and may probably be assigned to S. Worcs. A.R. was long considered as Sthrn., chiefly, probably, on account of *u* for O.E. *y* (*ŭ–i*). This feature is now known to be also West and Central Midland. Cp. § 158. (c).

God Ureisun. c. 1230–50. O.E. Homs. I. Extracts in Specimens.

Catherine Group. c. 1230–50. (Legends of St. Juliana, ed. Cockayne, E.E.T.S., 1872; St. Margaret, ed. Cockayne, E.E.T.S. 1866; St. Catherine, ed. E. Einenkel, E.E.T.S., 1884.) (Heref.)

Sawles Ward. c. 1230–50. O.E. Homs. I. Hall, Early M.E. (Heref.)

English Poems of MS. Harley 2253. 1310. Ed. Böddeker, Altenglische Dichtungen, Berlin, 1878. (Heref.)

Poems of William Herbert. c. 1333. In Carleton Brown, Religious Lyrics of the 14th century, Oxford, 1924. (Heref.)

Joseph of Arimathie. 1350. Ed. Skeat, E.E.T.S., 1871.

C. *South West Midland.*

Laȝamon B. c. 1250. (MS. Cot. Otho C. xiii.) Ed. Madden, 1867. See Hall, Early M.E. (S. Glos.)

Southern Legendary. c. 1280–90. (MS. Laud 108.) Ed. Horstmann, E.E.T.S. 87. (? N.W. Wilts.)

St. Brandan. c. 1300. (MS. Harley 2277.) Ed. Wright, Percy Soc., 1844.

Life of Thomas Beket. c. 1300. (MS. Harl. 2277.) Ed. Black, Percy Soc., 1845.

St. Juliana. (Metrical.) c. 1300. (MS. Ashmole 43.) Ed. Cockayne, E.E.T.S., 51, 1872.

Robert of Gloucester. (Metrical Chronicle.) c. 1320–30. Ed. Wright, Rolls Series, 1887. 2 vols. Extracts in Specimens.

Trevisa. (Translation of Higden's *Polychronicon.*) 1387. Ed. Babington (vols. i and ii), and Lumby (vols. iii–ix), Rolls Series, 1865–86. Extracts in Specimens.

IV. Southern

1. SOUTH EASTERN.

A. *Kent and East Surrey.*

Kentish Gospels. 1150. In Skeat's Gospels in Anglo-Saxon.

Kentish Homilies. 1150. (MS. Vespasian A. 22.) O.E. Homs. I. 217–43. Extracts in Specimens.

Kentish Sermons. Before 1250. (MS. Laud 471.) O.E. Misc. 20–36.

William of Shoreham's Poems. 1307. Ed. Conrath, E.E.T.S., 1902. Extracts in Specimens.

Aȝenbite of Inwyt. 1340. Ed. Morris, E.E.T.S., 1866. Extracts in Specimens.

B. *Essex and City of London.*

Vices and Virtues. c. 1200. Ed. Holthausen, E.E.T.S., 1888. May with great probability be assigned to N.E. Essex, to the neighbourhood of Saffron Walden.

Place-Names, Street-Names, etc., in early City Documents (see Heuser, *Alt. London*, and Mackenzie, *Early London Dial.*). ? Original text of *King Horn.* (Essex?) Ed. Hall, Clarendon Press, 1901.

2. Central Southern.

A. *London including Westminster and Middlesex.*

Charter of London, by the King William the Conqueror (1066). In Liebermann, Gesetze d. Angelsachsen, i. 486.

Proclamation of Henry III. 1258. In Ellis's Early English Pronunciation, Pt. II, pp. 501, etc. Emerson, M.E. Reader, p. 226.

Adam Davie's Five Dreams. c. 1307–27. Ed. Furnivall, E.E.T.S., 1878.

London English, 1384–1425. Ed. R. W. Chambers and M. Daunt, *in the press.* (A collection of original documents.)

London Charters and Documents (1). From 1384–c. 1450. See account given in Morsbach, Englische Schriftsprache, 1888.

London Charters and Documents (2). From 1430–1500. See account in Lekebusch, Londoner Urkundensprache, 1906.

History of St. Bartholomew's Church. MS. c. 1400. Ed. Sir Norman Moore, E.E.T.S. 1923.

B. *Middlesex with appreciable influence of City type.*

Trinity (Cambridge) *Homilies.* Before 1200. O.E. Homs. II. Ed. Morris, E.E.T.S., 1873. Extracts in Specimens and Hall's Early M.E.

Lambeth Homilies. Before 1200. O.E. Homs. I, 1–182. Ed. Morris, E.E.T.S., 1868. Extracts in Specimens and Hall's Early M.E.

On the dialect of the Lambeth and Trinity Homilies, see Wyld, Essays and Studies, vi, pp. 136–39.

Westminster Charters. (*a*) MS. Cott. Faustina A. iii (early thirteenth century), and (*b*) various MSS. c. 1100 ; (*a*) in Kemble, Codex Dipl., nearly all in vol. iv ; one in vol. v, and, together with (*b*) in Neufeldt, Z. Spr. d. Urkundenb. v. Westminster ; Berlin, 1907.

3. SOUTH WESTERN.

History of Holy Rood Tree. 1170. Ed. Napier, E.E.T.S., 1894.

Moral Ode or *Poema Morale.* (Egerton MS.) c. 1200. Other versions, from Trinity, Lambeth, and Jesus MSS. in O.E. Misc. and Specimens. Egerton MS. printed in MacLean, O.E. Homs. I, and Hall, Early M.E. (Lamb. and Trinity also in the last.) Critical text by Lewin, Halle, 1881.

Owl and Nightingale. (Surrey.) 1246–50. O.E. Misc. Extracts in Specimens and Hall's Early M.E. Ed. Wells, Belles Lettres Series, 1909 (revised).

Chertsey Cartulary. (Surrey.) Written c. 1259–80. (MS. Cot. Vitellius A. xiii.) In Kemble's Codex Dipl. Nos. 151, 222 (vol. i), 812, 844, 848, 849, 850, 856 (vol. iv), 986, 987, 988 (vol. v). Nos. 844, 848, 849, 850 are in English. No. 987, in Latin but with boundaries in English, is the most important. The documents are copies of earlier charters, but the language is on the whole that of the time the MS. was written.

Proverbs of Alfred. 1250. O.E. Misc. 102–38. Extracts in Specimens, and Hall's Early M.E. Ed. Skeat, Oxford, 1907, and Borgström, Lund, 1908.

Winchester Usages. 14th c. In English Guilds, ed. Lucy Toulmin Smith, E.E.T.S., 1870.

St Editha. 1420. (Wiltshire.) Ed. Horstmann, Heilbronn, 1883.

V. Literary English.

Chaucer's Works, Ed. Skeat, Complete Works, in 6 vols., also in one vol. Oxford.

Gower's Confessio Amantis. Ed. Macaulay, in Complete Works, Oxford ; and Selections from C.A. Oxford, 1903. (Has marked Kentish features.)

Hoccleve. 1400. Minor Poems, ed. F. Furnivall, E.E.T.S., 1892 ; Regiment of Princes, Furnivall, E.E.T.S., 1899. Short Extracts in Skeat's Specimens of Engl. Lit.

Lydgate. c. 1420. Troy Book, ed. Bergen, E.E.T.S., I and II, 1906 ; III, 1908 ; IV, V, 1910 ; Temple of Glass, ed. J. Schick, E.E.T.S., 1891 ; London Lickpenny, and Extracts from Storie of Thebes in Skeat's Specimens. Shows marked Suffolk characteristics.

John Capgrave's Chronicle. Ed. F. C. Hingeston, Rolls Series, 1858.

Caxton, Historyes of Troye. Extracts in Skeat's Specimens, III.

§ 155. The Treatment of O.E. Sounds in M.E.

The changes which befell the old vowel sounds in M.E. fall under the two main heads—*Quantitative*, and *Qualitative*. The former class of changes involves the lengthening of original short vowels, and the shortening of vowels originally long, under conditions which it will be our business to describe. The latter category of changes involves an alteration of the actual nature and quality of the vowel sound without any change of quantity.

The *Quantitative* changes are as important as the *Qualitative*, and their results in the subsequent history of English are far-reaching.

Our ideas concerning the nature and quality of M.E. sounds are based (1) upon the spelling in the various texts; (2) upon comparison (*a*) with O.E., (*b*) with Mod. Engl., (*c*) with other forms of Germanic speech; (3) upon the character of Rhymes in M.E.; (4) upon occasional phonetic spellings in M.E., and upon still more of these in the fifteenth century; (5) upon the contemporary descriptions of the pronunciation of English in the sixteenth century, when many M.E. vowel quantities, though not the sounds themselves, still remained unaltered; (6) upon the spelling adopted by Orm, which throws great light on M.E. quantity. Orm systematically writes a consonant single after a long vowel, and doubles it after a short—*child, chilldre*, etc. He also sometimes marks short vowels—*gŏd*, etc.

Qualitative Vowel Changes in M.E. Simple Vowels.

§ 156. The Rounding of O.E. ā to ō.

This change is shown by the spellings *o* and occasionally *oa*, later on, to have taken place in some dialects at least as early as the middle of the twelfth century, since there are examples of *ō* spellings already in the Peterborough Chronicle. The rounding of *ā* ultimately involved all the dialects of the *South and Midlands*, but it is pretty certain that it did not begin everywhere at the same time.

Since the Norman-French loan-words in M.E. retain their long *ā* unchanged, e.g. *dāme, fāme, grāve*, it is clear that the O.E. *ā* in *hām, stān, hlāf* 'loaf', etc., etc., must have undergone some slight rounding before these foreign words got into the language; otherwise, had the process begun later, it must have involved them as well.

The Peterborough Chronicle (E. Midland 1154) has the form *mōre*, O.E. *māra* (four times) ; the Kt. Homilies (Vesp. A. 22) before 1150 have a few *ō* forms, *ōʒe*, and *ōʒen*, but *a* enormously preponderates.　The Holy Rood Tree (1170), Trinity Homilies (before 1200), Lambeth Homilies (before 1200), Prose Life of St. Juliana (1210), Wooing of our Lord (1210), all Southern texts, have no *o*-spellings.　Other Southern or S. Midl. texts of about the same date have *o*, either occasionally or exclusively.　Poema Morale (Egerton MS. before 1200)—*ōre* 'grace', O.E. *ār* ; *lōre, mōre, wōt* 'knows', O.E. *wāt*, etc., but also many *ā*-spellings—*āre, māre, wāt*, etc. ; Gōd Ureisun of ure lauerd (1212)—*hōlie, ōne* ; Ancren Riwle (1225), Metrical Life of St. Juliana (1300) have *ō* throughout.

Of the other earliest Midland texts, the East Midland Ormulum (1200) has *a* throughout, while the S.W. Midland Laʒamon has even in the early MS. (c. 1205) occasional *o*, and the later (1250) has generally *o* ; Genesis and Exodus, and Bestiary (E. Midl. 1250) both have regularly *o*.

These statistics show that the change must have begun at least well before the middle of the twelfth century, though its results were not consistently nor universally expressed by the spelling before the first quarter of the thirteenth century.　The two forms in the Chronicle can hardly be accidental, but it is rather remarkable that the later E. Midl. Ormulum, so careful in its spelling, should give no indications of it.　The Southern texts mentioned, except the Vespasian Homilies, which are Kentish, are all from the South-West, and they appear to be slightly behind the former in writing *o*.　It may perhaps be argued that the rounding began slightly earlier in the Sth.-East than elsewhere.

Under the rounding of O.E. *ā* we must include that of *ā* in the Anglian combination -*āld*, in *āld, cāld, hāldan, bāld*.　The forms *ōld, cōld, hōlden, bōld*, appear in Midland and even in some Sthn. texts in the middle of the twelfth century.　They soon oust the typical native forms in the Sth.-Western dialects and even gain a footing in Kentish.　(See §§ 165–6.)

§ 157.　O.E. ā in the Northern Dialects.

In the Northern Dialects of England, and in Scotch English, no rounding takes place.　Many texts preserve the symbol *a* unaltered in the M.E. period—*ham, stan*, etc. ; others, especially in the fourteenth century, write *ai* in words of this class.　As regards the sound, this must have been advanced, and fronted to [æ] pretty early, and this was subsequently raised to [ē̜] and [ē]. Modern North English and Scotch dialects have [ē] or [ī] as a representative of O.E. ā.

It is impossible to say with anything like certainty when the fronting process began. For one thing, our Northern texts only begin with the end of the thirteenth century or the beginning of the fourteenth. The rhymes of the fourteenth-century Scotch texts, however, make it certain that by that period the fronting was complete, and probable that the vowel had already been raised to a mid-front. It further is apparent from the earliest M.E. Northern texts that O.E. ā and Norman-French ã, and O.E. ă in open syllables were levelled under the same sound. The Scotch texts from Barbour onwards constantly write *ai, ay*, e.g. *fayis* 'foes', *tais* 'toes', *raid*, O.E. *rād* 'rode'.

(*a*) Rhymes of O.E. *ā* with O.E. lengthened *ă*: **Metr. Ps.,** 1300: *mare—ouerfare*; **Sunday Homilies in Verse,** 1300: *schāthe—lāthe*; Hampole, 1340: *wāte* (pl. vb.)—*late*; *bāre* (adj.) —*sāre*; **Barbour's Bruce** (1375): *hāle* 'whole' rhymes with *douglasdale, braid* 'broad' rhymes with *maid* 'made'.

(*b*) Rhymes of O.E. *ā* with Fr. *ā*: Bruce rhymes *blāme* with *schame* (O.E. *ă-*) and the latter with *hame* 'home'.

(*c*) Rhymes which show the fronting of O.E. *ā*: Hampole: *māre—ware*, O.E. *wēre* 'were' subj.; Bruce: *gais* 'goes'— *wes* 'was'; *mair*, O.E. *mār—thair*, O.E. *þēr*.

NOTE. Chaucer, *Reeve's Tale*, 158, puts *geen*, P.P. (O.E. *ȝegān*), into the mouth of Alleyn the Scottish scholar.

§ **158. The Treatment of O.E. ȳ (i-Mutation of ŭ, §§ 108-9).**

(*a*) In the North, including Yorks., and in the East Midlands, including Lincoln, Hunts., Norf., and part of Suff., O.E. ȳ is unrounded, probably in the late O.E. period. M.E. texts from these areas write *i*, or *y*, for the original [ȳ] sound, e.g. Orm, and Gen. and Ex.

(*b*) In the O.E. period, O.E. ȳ had become ĕ in Kent and Suffolk (cf. § 142). In S.E. and S.E. Midl. texts of the M.E. period these sounds continue, and are written in the old way. The evidence of Pl. Ns., however, of the thirteenth, fourteenth, and fifteenth centuries shows that by this time the *e*-forms were the prevailing ones in Essex no less than in Kent, and they are found also in varying degrees of frequency in Sussex and Suffolk, in the Lynn area in extreme East of Norf. (Guild of S. Thomas of Lynn), and Pl. Ns. fr. this area (Mackenzie, *Lond. Dial.*, § 365 (*a*)), and to some slight extent in Cambridgeshire also. There are traces of these forms in texts from S. Lincs.

(R. of Brunne), Northants (Peterb. Chron.), Suffolk (Bokenam and Bury Wills). The early Nth. Essex text, Vices and Virtues, has *e* as the prevailing form, by the side of several *i*-forms and a few *u*, while the fifteenth-century Palladius, also Essex, though influenced by London English, has some traces of *e*-forms.

(*c*) In by far the greater part of England, that is to say in the whole of the West Midlands, and Central Midlands, south of Yorkshire, and in all the Southern Counties apart from those mentioned under (*b*) above, and with the qualification stated below, O.E. *ȳ* remains with, approximately, its original sound, at any rate well into the fifteenth century. From a very early period, at least as early as 1170 or so, the French spelling *u* is used for the old sound, and later, this, with occasional *o*, becomes the exclusive mode of representing it when short. When long it is frequently written *ui, uy*.

(*d*) From the forms of Pl. Ns. containing such elements as O.E. *hyll, byrig, pytt, lȳtel*, etc., etc., it would seem that there was also an area in the extreme South-West, starting probably in Devon, where isolative unrounding of O.E. *ȳ* took place in the M.E. period, if not before.

(*e*) **The London area.** The early street and other names from the City of London (1200–1350) agree with the Essex type in having *e* as the characteristic form ; Westm. Ch. have *i* (sometimes written *y*) as the prevailing form, but have a few written *u, geburaþ, furmest, munstre*, in both texts ; the only trace of *e* seems to be *gripbreche* in the later text.

In Lamb. Hom. *u* distinctly predominates but there are a few *i*-forms—*unafillendliche, pinchep, kinesetle*, etc. ; in Trin. Hom. *i* and *u* appear to be pretty equally divided, and there are a few *e*-forms—*senne, kenne, werse, werchende* ; the Procl. of Hen. III has only one example of O.E. *y*, and that is spelt *u*—*kuneriche* ; Davy writes only *y*, or *i* ; Chaucer's rhymes show a larger proportion of *e*-forms than is usual in London documents of his period, which may be due either to a survival in his speech of the older City type, or to his later residence in Kent ; it is impossible to be sure whether, apart from the *e*-forms, Chaucer favoured the *i*-, or the rounded type ; Petition of Folk in Mercery has very few words of this class : *hidynges, hidde*, but *lust* vb. ; Hoccleve has *i* as the predominating form, with a few *e*- and a few *u*- spellings—*velthy, mery, beriad, thēmel*, etc. ; *suche, burdon, cusse* 'kiss', n., on anal. of vb. The Hist. of S. Bartholm. Church (1400) generally writes *i*, or *y*, but has a few *e*-spellings, *kechyn, mery, sterid, schete*, etc., and an almost negligible number of *u*'s, e.g. *sundry*.

The Pl. Ns. of the County of Middlesex have predominating *i*, side by side with a few *u*-spellings, but no *e*-forms, during the same periods in which the latter appear to be the leading type in the City documents. The central and more westerly areas of Middlesex appear to have unrounded O.E. *ȳ* by the early thirteenth century, and the Herts. border as far as S. Albans seems to have shared this early unrounding process. Other areas of Herts., according to Miss Mackenzie, retained the old round vowel, and the rounded type penetrated later to the southern border, and across this into Middlesex. This is probably the explanation of the not infrequent *u*-spellings in some of the later London documents, some of which survive to the present-day standard. See Mackenzie, *Lond. Dial.*, §§ 322-7.

To sum up, the *e*-forms which occur in the later literary and standard spoken dialect may be regarded as survivals of the City type, which was virtually identical with the Essex dialect. Thus, in this respect Chaucer, to judge by his rhymes, distinctly favours the City type.

(*f*) The process of unrounding *ȳ* before front consonants (*ċ, ċġ, sċ*), which took place in O.E. (cp. § 122 above), can be clearly traced in M.E., especially in Pl. N. forms. From these sources it is possible to localize the process more definitely than was possible in O.E. texts. The words *myċel, bryċġ, rysċ*, etc., appear as *michel, brigge, rissche*, etc., with the greatest frequency, especially in the *u*-areas of the S.-West, Devonshire, Dorset, Wilts., Somerset; with less frequency in Hants, and hardly at all in Glos. and Surrey. In the latter areas, *muchel, brugge*, etc., are the prevailing forms, and this is true also of the *u*-areas in the Midlands.

NOTE. The view of Kluge (Paul's *Grundr.*[2] i, p. 1046) that at a certain period, in an area not clearly defined, O.E. *ȳ* was retracted before front cons. [tʃ, dž, ʃ] to the corresponding back vowel, should be mentioned. In this way Kluge explains the mod. forms *cudgel, rush*, etc., which, according to hitherto received views, should be **kidgel, *rish*, etc. He calls the process ' *Rückumlaut*'.

§ 159. The occurrence of both *i*- and *u*- spellings, often for the same word, in the same text, and in Pl. N. forms of the same area, may best be explained by assuming a progressive unrounding of O.E. *ȳ*, a process which started in the East and gradually spread Westwards till the tendency apparently died out. Perhaps the E. border of Berks., i.e. Surrey and E. Hants, may be regarded as the westward limit of the unrounding. Westward and Sth. of this, it looks as if we had a genuine *u*-area, in which rounding persisted, till we reach the *i*-area in

the extreme W. To the N. we have a broad Central and
W.Midl. belt of *u*-area which includes the N. part of Herts.
In most of the old *u*-areas proper, the *i*-type later on ousted
the native forms. This tendency of gradual unrounding probably ceased altogether before the end of the fifteenth century.
After that, *i*- forms may penetrate from other areas, but are
no longer developed by the natural process. The sporadic
u- spellings in thirteenth and early fourteenth century London
and Middles. may imply that the existence of slightly different
degrees of unrounding among different speakers, at the same
time, led to a hesitation among the scribes in writing the
partially rounded vowel. I now agree with Heuser therefore,
in accepting the view of progressive unrounding of O.E. *ȳ* in
certain areas, including London and Middles., but apparently
still differ from him, in holding to the existence of other
'genuine' *u*-areas, in which I think unrounding did not occur
at all. The gradual unrounding of *y* is in my view comparable
to that of the other M.E. front round vowel, *ø*, from O.E. *ĕŏ*,
see § 168. On the distribution of the various types of O.E. *y*
in M.E. see Wyld, *Essays and Studies*, VI, pp. 112, etc.;
Luick, *Hist. Gr.*, § 183, Anm. 2; Heuser, *Alt-London*, p. 50,
etc.; and Brandl, *Z. Geogr. d. Altengl. Dialekte*; and above
all, now, Mackenzie, *Lond. Dial.*, §§ 355–8.

§ 160. Treatment of O.E. *æ̆*.

(1) In O.E. it will be remembered that *æ* remains in spelling,
and perhaps to a great extent also in pronunciation, in W.S.
and Northumbrian consistently, also in part of the Mercian
area, while it is raised to *ĕ* already in Early Kentish, and in
the Mercian dialect represented by the Vesp. Ps. (cp. § 137).
The Early Transition texts of the Sth.-West, on the whole,
preserve a front vowel, variously written *e*, *æ*, and (occasionally)
ea. [Cp. §§ 97, Note, and 120, Note, concerning probable
raising of *æ̇* in L.W.S.]. The Midland texts of the same date
invariably have *a*, showing that *æ* was retracted to a back
vowel. The E. Midl. Peterb. Chron. writes *æ*, and *e*, but is
still much influenced by the earlier spelling; *a*, nevertheless,
is frequent in the later parts of this text; Orm, however, and
the E. Midl. Bestiary, and Gen. and Ex. have *a* throughout.
The early thirteenth-century Wooing of our Lord (Sthn.) has
a throughout, and this feature has presumably come in from
the Midl. type. After the beginning of the fourteenth century,
pure Sthn. texts have *a*, which can hardly be a true phonetic
development from *e*, but must indicate that the Midland type
has spread over the Sthn. area as well, to the extinction of the

true Sthn. type.   A few statistics of the spellings of the Sthn.
texts are desirable.   H. Rd. Tree (circa 1170) generally writes
æ, occasionally *e*, and once *ea*: *bead*, O.E. *bæd*, and, after *w*, *a*:
water; God Ureisun (1210), *e*: *gled, efter*, etc.; Poema Morale
(Egerton MS. circa 1200), *e*: *wetere, hedde*, O.E. *hæfde, hwet*,
also *æfter*; Ancren Riwle (1225), generally *e*: *efter, feder*
'father', *et* 'at', *þet, epple* 'apple', etc., but also *blăc, bac, hwat*,
etc.   Owl and Nightingale (W. Surrey, c. 1270) and Chertsey
Ch. of about same date, both have usually *a*, but retain a few
e-spellings. The Metrical Version of the Life of St. Juliana (1300)
has *a* throughout: *wat, quaþ, ʒaf, was, glade*, etc.; Trevisa (1387)
almost always writes *a*: *þat, blak, gladlych, schal*, etc., but
creftes; St. Editha (c. 1420) has always *a*.   The Essex Vices
and Virtues (c. 1200) has only *a*: *fader, after, scal, cwað,
smac*, etc.

The Catherine Group, Centr. W. Midl., have *e* frequently.

(2) In the London area we find two quite different types in the
early M.E. period, the Eastern or City type which agrees with
that of Essex, and the more central and westerly dialect which
originally had *e*.   Thus in the early City names, as in Essex,
we get only *a*, with, apparently, no trace of *e*; in Westm. Ch.,
according to Miss Mackenzie (*Lond. Dial.*, § 30), about three-
quarters of the entire number of O.E. *æ*-words in the text have
a, and the remaining quarter *e* (also written *æ*), this minority
including *biqueð, hebbe, ðes*; the Middles. Pl. Ns. are rather
inconclusive, but *e*-spellings occur down to the middle of the
twelfth century—e. g. *et grenanforde* in a Ch. dated 845,
Birch. II, p. 29; *Heselingfeld* (near Stepney, Ch. of Hen. II in
Dugd. ii. 85; Mackenzie, § 36); *Exeforde* Inq. P.M., vol. III, p. 60
(1293), Mod. *Ashford*, nr. Staines; Trin. Hom. has at least
twice as many *a*- as *e*-forms; while Lamb. Hom. has at least
twice as many *e*-forms as *a*-forms.   In the fourteenth century
there appear to be no *e*-spellings in any London or Middles.
document; the City or Eastern type has won the day.

We may sum up the history of O.E. *ǽ* in M.E. as follows.
It was retracted to *ă* in Essex and in the Midlands and North
quite early, perhaps in Late O.E. itself.   In the Sthn. dialects,
other than Kentish, where the raising took place in the ninth
century, *ǽ* was raised to *ĕ* (mid-front-slack) in Early Transition
English, or before, and remained, in this speech-area, until it
gave place to the Midland or Essex *ă* late in the thirteenth
century.

(3) In Kentish the O.E. *ĕ*-type survives longer, though
even here we find a few *ă*-forms in the middle of the twelfth
century: thus *fader, hwat, þat*, alongside of more frequent

ĕ-forms : *ƿet, wes, efter*, etc., in Kt. Hom., Vesp. A. 22 (1150). The Laud. Sermons (before 1250) have more *ă*- than *ĕ*-forms, but still retain *ƿet, efter, wet*, etc. ; in Aȝenbite (1340) the *e*-forms are more frequent : *eppel, gled, gles, ssel* 'shall', *weter*, etc., but occasional *ă*, cp. *smak, uader*. W. of Shoreham (1307) has predominating *e, schel, wet, creft, wesschere, heƿ, hedde, wetere*, etc., but also *a* in *wat, schal, water, glass, wasscheƿ*, etc.

The Northern and Midland *ă*-type becomes the predominant, and finally the sole type, apparently throughout the whole country, as is shown by the testimony of the Modern Dialects. In the Standard Dialect, *a* has come in from the old City-Essex type.

§ 161. The Combinations *-an-, -am-* in M.E.

(1) In London and the Easterly areas, apart from Lamb. Hom. which has *ƿonkien, con*, and Trin. Homs. *ƿonke*, there appears to be no evidence before the middle of the thirteenth century of any other type than *-an-, -am-* in *man, can, ƿank, name*, etc. But there are slight indications of the use of forms with rounding after 1250 or so, in parts of the East. Fl. and Blancheflour (Suffolk ?) has *mon* (rhymes *on*, and *anon*); *bigon* Pret. 5, rh. *anon* ; *con*, rh. *ston* ; Octov. has *con, bigon, thonkede* ; S. Patr. Purg. *mon* ; in the fourteenth century Rich. C. de L. has *I con*, and *mon* ; the Lynne Guilds (Norf.) *mon*. In the fifteenth century Lydgate has *I konne* rh. *bigon* ; Pallad. *mon, thonk* ; Cely P. *con* (George C.) ; *con, connot* (Rich. C. the younger); Gregory has *thonke* passim ; Chron. of Engl., Herts., *shonkel*. Therefore the existence of these forms, to some slight extent, in Suff. and Ess. seems certain. None of the later London texts and docs. have any trace of *-on-*, nor have the Pl. Ns., neither here nor in the eastern counties. (Mackenzie.) Otherwise, only *-an-* in Orm, Peterb. Chron., Bestiary, Gen. and Ex., King Horn, Havelok, R. of Brunne, Norf. Guilds, etc. In the W. Midl., we find *an* in the Sthn. portion of the area, but *on* as the characteristic type in the Central and Nthn. parts of the area. The dialect of the large region lying between the W. and E. Midl., the so-called Central Midl., had apparently *-an-* in agreement with the Eastern type.

(2) **i-mutation of *-an-*.** It is characteristic of the Early Dialects of Essex and of London City that they have *-an-* instead of *-en-* as in other M.E. dialects, derived from earlier *-æn-* (see § 109, Note) with retraction of O.E. *æ* as shown in § 160 (2). Thus in V. and V. we get *ande* 'end', *utsanden* 'send', *angel*, O.E. *engel, wandende*, O.E. *wendan*, etc., etc. ;

in Essex Pl. Ns., *Dane-*, *Fan-* ('fen'); City Ns., *Fancherch*, *Thamis*, etc.   Even in Westm. Ch. we find a slight trace, *awanded*, due to City influence. The normal form in Middle as in Later London is *-en-*. Texts such as Arth. and Merl., and K. Alisaund., which show other Essex features, have *-an-* occasionally, in spelling and in rhymes. South of the Thames, the Surrey Pl. N. form *Wandlesurth* 'Wandsworth' must owe its *-an-* to the influence of City dialect.

§ 162. O.E. ǣ in M.E.

(1) It will be convenient to distinguish the two origins of this sound as $\bar{æ}^1$ and $\bar{æ}^2$. The former represents Prim. O.E. $\bar{æ}$, W. Gmc. $\bar{a}$, as in W.S. *dǣd* 'deed', *sǣd* 'seed', *sp(r)ǣċe*, etc., the latter, the result of the *i*-mutation of O.E. $\bar{a}$, W.Gmc. *ai*, as in *dǣl* 'part', *hǣlu* 'health', etc., *tǣċ(e)an* 'teach', etc.   It will be remembered that in all the non-W. or Central Sax. dialects $\bar{æ}^1$ was raised to $\bar{e}$ early in the O.E. period (§ 123), while $\bar{æ}^2$ remained everywhere, except in a limited eastern area (§ 140). W.S. therefore had $\bar{æ}$ in words of both classes, Kentish had $\bar{e}$ in both, the Anglian dialects had $\bar{e}$ for $\bar{æ}^1$, and retained $\bar{æ}^2$.

It seems probable that in Late O.E. or Early Transition, O.E. $\bar{æ}$ wherever it existed, except in the area referred to in § 162 (3), and no matter what its origin, was raised to [ē̜] mid-front-slack.   Since Kt. had not this sound (O.E. $\bar{æ}$) at all, we may dismiss this dialect at once.

Midland and Northern dialects distinguish $\bar{æ}^1 = $ [ē̜] tense from $\bar{æ}^2 = $ [ɛ̄] slack during the whole M.E. period, as is shown by the rhymes in careful poets, and by the descriptions of the two sounds by sixteenth-century writers on pronunciation.

The dialects of the W. and Central Sax. areas, and some dialects north of the Thames, preserve the equivalent of $\bar{æ}^1$ and $\bar{æ}^2$ as [ɛ̄], and careful scribes often distinguish this sound in the spelling from the tense $\bar{e}$ in *dēman*, *grēne*, etc., derived from O.E. $\bar{e}$ (*i*-mutation of $\bar{o}$). The least satisfactory spelling is *e, ee*, the most unambiguous are *æ, ea*. *æ* is found comparatively rarely after the thirteenth century, and probably not at all after the beginning of the fourteenth.

It should be noted that Orm's spellings with *æ* for $\bar{æ}^1$ are remarkable, for though he occasionally writes *e*, the former is his favourite symbol.   It is hardly conceivable that an E. Midl. dialect can really have pronounced the slack sound here, and the occurrence of the *æ*-spellings must probably be attributed to the domination and persistence of the classical W.Sax. mode of writing among learned persons like Orm.   It is difficult otherwise to account for his forms *spæche*, *spæken* (pret. pl.), *forȝæfe*; *ēvenn*, O.E. *ǣfen*, l. 1105, is, as we should suppose, the type normal to his dialect.

Examples of O.E. *ǣ* in Southern texts are: (i) *ǣ*[1] : Rd. Tree—*spǣce* and *spēce* (*æ* predominates for both *ǣ*-sounds in this text, with some *e*-spellings, and a few *ea*); P. M., *e* chiefly—*wēre, drēden*; Gōd Ur.—*misdēden, grēden*; Lambeth Hom.—*nēddren, wēren*; A. R.—*weaden*, O.E. *ġewǣde*; *read*, O.E. *rǣd*; *meal*, O.E. *mǣl* 'time'; *heren* 'hairs'; Metr. St. Jul.—*strēte, brēþ*; Trevisa—*weete* (sb.) 'wet'.

(ii) *ǣ*[2] : Rd. Tree—*dēl, deales, aleaden, nēfre* (*æ* predominates); P. M.—*sǣlþe, sēlþe, unhēlþe, þǣre, ǣuerich, lǣden* (vb.); Gōd Ur.—*cleane, todealen, heale, leafdi*, but *tēchen*; Lambeth Hom.—*sea* 'the sea', *clēnesse*; A. R.—*leafdi, dealen*, and *delen* 'parts', *geat* 'goats', *leareð* 'teaches', *heale, arearen*; Metr. St. Jul.—*sē* 'sea', *brēde, lēuedi*.

It appears from these examples that *ea* is written with far greater consistency for *ǣ*[2] than for *ǣ*[1], but the identity of the sounds is proved by the fact that *e, ea, æ* are written indifferently for both, and further from such rhymes as *þǣre—wēre, drēden —lǣden* (P. M., Egerton MS.); *brēde—sprēde—dēde* 'dead' (St. Jul.). The Kentish type with [ē] in this class of words certainly survived in M.E. The Kentishman Gower, who habitually uses *ie* for the tense vowel, writes *cliene, diel*, O.E. (Kt.) *clēne, dēl*.

(2) The precise geographical extent of the *ǣ*[1]-area is very difficult to establish. Was it co-extensive with the W. Sax. sphere of speech influence, and if so, how far did this extend? Some authorities believe that the *ǣ*-area was considerable in extent. See the important article by Pogatscher in *Anglia* xxiii, and 'Mittelenglische Mundarten' by Jordan *G.R.M.*, ii, p. 124, etc.

The London dialect was originally within the area. The earliest London Charters and Davie have [ē], and even in Chaucer, who often uses the Anglian *ē*-forms, as is shown by his rhymes, the W.S. [ē]-type still predominates in the poetry. It is practically impossible to trace the survival of the W.S. *ǣ*-type beyond the fourteenth century. It was apparently ousted by the increasing predominance of the non-Sax. form. The most certain test of a M.E. slack [ē] in a word containing originally O.E. *ǣ*[1] is the survival of the sound as a mid-front in Early Mod. Engl. By the early fifteenth century all M.E. tense *ē*-sounds were raised to [ī] unless previously shortened; cp. § 229 below.

It is indeed highly probable that in some dialects this change was far earlier than is commonly supposed, as shown by such

occasional spellings as those of Laȝamon MS. Calig. (c. 1200)
spiche 'speech,' 1, 141. 12 ; *sichinde* 'seeking', 1. 310. 15 ;
and *bediemde* 'judged, declared ', 1. 367. 20 ; *siche* 'to seek',
Beket 1. 60 (Percy Soc.) (c. 1300) ; *wyping* 'weeping', Harley
Lyrics (1310) Geistl. Lieder XI 3 ; *hyde* 'heed', Trevisa, Polychr.
MS. Tib. D. vii, Pfeffer, pp. 107², 121, 124 ; *myde* 'meed',
pp. 109, 137, *spyde* 'speed', pp. 121, 140 ; *hy* p. 110.   These
spellings are very numerous in this MS.   See Pfeffer, p. 15.

NOTE. Pogatscher, in the article mentioned, on the evidence of the
forms of Pl. Names beginning with *strat-* (O.E. *strǣt-*, shortened to *strĕt-*,
and retracted to *străt-*), tries to show that the æ-area included the following counties : Cornwall, Somerset, Dorset, Wilts., Hants, Gloucestershire, Oxfordshire, southern part of Northants which borders on Bucks.,
Bucks. itself, Bedfordshire, Middlesex, Suffolk, Norfolk.   In Essex and
Warwickshire both *stret-* (= O.E. *strēt-*, non-W. Sax.) and *strat-* occur.
The rest of England belonged to the *ē*-area.   These results are, however,
somewhat dubious, as Pogatscher relies only upon the Modern forms of
the names.   Cp. the criticism by O. Ritter in *Anglia*, N.F. xxv, p. 269, etc.
Cp. now on this question Heuser, *Alt-London*, 1914, and Brandl, *Z. Geogr.*
etc., 1915.

(3) Area in which O.E. ǣ¹ and ǣ² become *ā* in M.E.

In a restricted area in the East, the spelling *ā* is fairly
regular for O.E. *ǣ* of both origins.   In Essex Pl.-Ns. this
predominates from beginning of thirteenth into the fourteenth
century, and the *ā*-forms are found as late as the fifteenth
century, the elements *mād(e)* 'meadow', *strāt(e)* 'street',
also *hāth(e)* 'heath ', *clāne* 'clean ', *wāte* 'wheat.'   In Vices and
Virtues *ā* is very common, but *æ* and *e* are also written.

Ā is also the prevailing spelling in City of London documents
in the twelfth and thirteenth centuries, and the *ā*-type is found,
though in smaller numbers, in the fourteenth century.   Heuser,
loc. cit., lays stress on the occurrence of this type in London, but
Miss Mackenzie (*Lond. Dial.*, §§ 93, 94, 249, 251) gives more
precise statistics.   She finds, in twelfth century 8 *ā*, and no *ē* ;
in thirteenth century 116 *ā* and 70 *ē*, of which latter, only 14
are found before 1270; in fourteenth century, on the other
hand, she has counted 250 *ē* forms to 40 *ā* ; in fifteenth century
she finds no *ā* spellings at all in City documents.   It appears
therefore that this characteristic Essex feature gives way before
the Middles. type and disappears altogether from the City
dialect.   In Westm. Ch. (Faustina MS.) which is strongly tinged
by City dialect influence, though in many respects resembling
the more westerly Middles. type, Miss Mackenzie calculates
that the *ā*-spellings are four times as numerous as *æ*, or *e*, in
strāte, māde, lāse (O.E. *lǣs*), *sālþe, hāþe*, &c. (§§ 101-2, 122).
In Middles. Pl.-Ns. Miss M. has only noted 5 *ā* forms (-*mād*,

-*strāte*) down to end of thirteenth century, all of which occur in places along the Essex border, *ē* being the normal type in the county (*Lond. Dial.*, § 110). In Trin. Homs. *ē* largely predominates, but scattered forms such as *dāde* ' deed ', *adrāde*, inf., *sād* 'seed,' *grādi, forlāten, rāde* vb.; Lamb. Homs. has hardly any *ā*'s, but *rāde* vb. ; Hen. III Procl. has only *ǣ* or *ē*, and *ā*-spellings are unknown in any later London texts of any kind.

There is a group of M.E. texts whose area of origin is rather uncertain, but which have many points in common with Essex, which not infrequently write *ā* for O.E. *ǣ*. These include all those mentioned in § 164. 4. as having [ē] for O.E. *ēā*, *except* Octovian, and Floris and Blancheflour. That these spellings represent a real pronunciation with [*ā*] is, I think, proved both by their frequency and their systematic employment in well-defined areas, and also by the fact that words so spelt rhyme with M.E. *ā* of other origins, e.g. *rāde* (O.E. *rǣd*), —*māde* vb., *sāde* ' seed '—*māde*, Arth. and Merl.; *strētis* (for *strātis*),—*gātis, drēde* (for *drāde*),—*māde* K. Alisaunder ; *slāpe*, n.—*knāpe*, Seven Sages, &c. The Cambr. MS. of King Horn has traces of these rhymes—*lāte* vb.—*gāte*, which suggests that the original was in the dialect of the *ā*-area. On the Pl.-N. evidence Miss Mackenzie, *Lond. Dial.*, § 350, defines the area in which O.E. *ǣ* became *ā*, as Hertford, Beds, Hunts, as well as Essex and London City, thus agreeing in the main with Heuser, who however does not distinguish the City from Middles. Miss Mackenzie points out a few *ā*-spellings in Pl.-Ns. south of the Thames in the neighbourhood of Rotherhithe— *Weststrāte* (1170), and *mādbroke* (1314) (*Lond. Dial.* 354). This area must be regarded as an outlying portion of the City in respect of its dialect. Chertsey Ch. has a few *ā*-spellings which must surely be scribal, since Surrey Pl.-names with which the dialect of Chertsey otherwise agrees, show no traces of these forms.

The development of O.E. *ǣ* is, as we see, largely parallel with that of *ǎ*. In O.E. *ǣ* is differentiated into (1) *ǣ*, and (2) *ē* ; *ē* remains as [ē] in M.E., but the *ǣ* types are further differentiated in M.E. ; in some areas the sound is raised to [ē], in others it is retracted to [*ā*], the type we have just considered. Before the end of the M.E. period this type was completely superseded by the [ē] type in some areas, in others by [ē].

§ 163. Treatment of O.E. ō in M.E.

O.E. *ō* was a mid-back-tense vowel, and in the South and Midlands, and in Kent, was preserved as such in Early Transition and Middle English. During the M.E. period, this sound, in both English and Norse words as well as in those of French origin, gradually underwent a process of *over-rounding* (see § 49 above) and was subsequently raised to a high-back-tense [ū], which stage it had reached in Late Middle English. Although there is nothing in normal M.E. spelling to indicate that this process was going on, it is clear from the rhymes that original *ō* was quite distinct in sound from the other *ō* which developed during the M.E. period and was a long slack vowel. See §§ 165, 173 (*c*) below. There is further a fair sprinkling of occasional spellings with *ou* in texts from various parts of the South and Midlands, which tends to show that O.E. *ō* was gradually moving towards [ū] even if it did not actually reach this precise stage during the earlier M.E. period : e. g. Handlyng Sinne (1303) *þe touþer* 'other' 406, *doun* 'do' 1101; Will. of Shoreham (c. 1320) *roude* 'rood', 25. 685; *douþ* 'they do' 53. 1471 ; *bloude* 'blood' 60. 1701 ; *loukeþ* 'looketh' 75. 2142, etc.; Feudal Aids (c. 1370) *Bouc*—O.E. *bōc*, *-brouc*, O.E. *brōc* 'brook',—*poule*, O.E. *pōl* 'pool', etc., and in MS. Tib. of Trevisa (before 14th. c.) *touk, forsouk, foul* 'fool,' etc.; Allit. P. (c. 1350) *goud* 'good' Patience 336, Pearl 33, etc. These spellings, and subsequent developments (cp. § 236) establish a strong probability that by the end of the fourteenth century the [ū] stage was fully attained.

In the North of England, on the other hand, and in Scotland, original long *ō* underwent an entirely different development, evidence of which is afforded by the spelling, by rhymes, and by the pronunciation in the Mod. dialects of these areas. In Scotland, at any rate, it was gradually advanced to a sound which, in the fourteenth century, was identified with Fr. *u*=[ȳ]. Cursor Mundi (1320) and Nthn. Homilies (1330) still appear to write only *o*—*tōk, bōk, gōd, mōd, dō*, etc. ; Hampole (1340) writes *o*, but also *u*—*bukes, gudes*. It should be remembered that *u* at this period generally stands for [y̆], [ū] being usually written *ou*—*hous*, etc. The approximation of O.E. *ō* to [ȳ] in sound is made certain by the fact that it rhymes with this ; thus Hampole has *sone* rhyming to *fortōne*. The symbol *o* is used indifferently with *u* for the French sound. Minot (1352) has *suth*, O.E. *sōþ* 'true', *flude, gude*, but also *loke, stode*, etc. Barbour's Bruce (1375), written in Scotland in a language still undistinguishable from that of Nth. Engl., writes *o* and *u*, also *oy*—*soyne* 'soon', *doyne* 'done', and rhymes O.E. *ō* and Fr. *ū* [ȳ] *aventure*—*forfure*, O.E. *-fōr* 'departed'. The later Sc. Schir W. Wallace rhymes *blud*—*rude*; and *fude, blude, gud*, all with *conclud*, and so on.

Gavin Douglas (c. 1525) commonly writes *ui* as *buik*, *fluid*, etc., and this remained as the conventional Scots spelling for this sound.

§ 164. Disappearance of the O.E. Diphthongs in M.E.

(1) O.E. *ĕă.* We have already seen (§ 97. 3, Note) that in Late O.E. there are many examples of *æ*-spellings for *ēa*. Although *ea* is often written in M.E. in words where it would normally occur in O.E., there is no doubt that, in the former, it represents the sound [ẽ] and not a diphthong. From the moment that the old *ĕă* was simplified to [ắ], later [ẽ], it was natural that *ea* should be used to represent these sounds, since the symbol *æ* gradually fell into desuetude, and *e* was ambiguous. The commonest source of *ĕă* in L.O.E. was Fracture (§ 102). In W.S. the *ĕă* which resulted from *æ* preceded by a front consonant was monophthongized in L.O.E. itself, and became *e—ĉef*, etc. That from Fracture was also simplified, as is shown by Ælfric's *swælt*, *swært*, etc. (§ 102, Note 1).

(2) Before the *l*-combinations Anglian had no fracture—*căld*, etc., and in W.S. *eall*, *ĉeald*, *healf*, etc., must have become *æll*, *ĉæld*, *hælf* in the late period. This form, or the development of it with [ẽ], is found in the South, generally written *ea*, sometimes *æ*, and *e*, in Early Transition: e.g. *heald, anwealde*, but *hældan* in H. Rd. Tree ; *wealdes*, in Wohunge ; *eald, fealde, healden, wealden*, but *wælde*, in Poema Morale. The Essex Vices and Virtues preserves the front vowel before *-ld*, *ēld*, adj., *wealden, wēlden, ihēlden, sealde, ǣldmone* ; but where there is no lengthening, *æ*, as elsewhere in this district, is retracted to *a—alle, half, halp*, etc. We may assume that *ea* here represents the mid-front-slack vowel, and that, before *-ld*, this was lengthened to [ẽ] (§ 114 above).

(3) The Kt. texts, by the side of *ea*, for O.E. *ēa* often write *ia, ya*, e.g. Laud. Homs. *diath* 'death', *diadlich* 'deadly', *beliaue* 'faith' ; W. of Shoreham, *lias*, O.E. *lēas* Pret. 'lost', etc. ; Ayenb. *dyaf* 'deaf', *lyaf* 'leaf', *dyaþ* and *dyeaþ* 'death', *dyead* 'dead', etc. These spellings have been taken to indicate that Kt., unlike all other M.E. dialects, preserved some kind of diphthong for O.E. *ēa*. This however is by no means certain. It is possible that the spellings indicate no more than [jẽ] or even merely [ẽ]. See remarks in § 166.

(4) In most dialects, *ēa* in O.E. *dēaþ*, etc., was simplified to *ǣ* (and levelled with O.E. *ǣ*[2] and in some cases also with *ǣ*[1], see § 162 (1. 2.)) whence we get [ẽ] in M.E. There appears, however, to have been an area in the East where *ēa* was monophthongized to [ẽ] without passing through [ǣ] at all

Thus in the Essex Vices and Virtues where $\bar{æ}^1$ and $\bar{æ}^2$ commonly appear as $\bar{a}$, see § 162 (3), O.E. $\bar{ea}$ is never so written, but always either *e*, or *ea*, while the latter spelling is not used for O.E. $\bar{æ}$. In several later texts which present other characteristics of Essex or neighbouring dialects, the vowel from O.E. $\bar{ea}$ rhymes with undoubted tense $\bar{e}$.

Miss Mackenzie has noted these rhymes in the following texts:—Octovian, Floris and Blauncheflour, Arthur and Merlin, K. Alis., Seven Sages, Religious Lyrics (late thirteenth century Ed. Jacobi), S. Alexius, S. Patrick's Purgatory, Rich. Coeur de Lion. In the fifteenth century they are frequent in Lydgate (of Bury), Palladius (Colchester), and Stephen Hawes (Suff.). It is significant that there are no examples of these rhymes in Chaucer, nor in Lydgate's contemporary Hoccleve. The spelling *lipe*, O.E. *hlēapan*, is found in the S. Albans book of Hunting (1486), which would be a very early example of raising, if the vowel represented a M.E. [ē]. See on this point Mackenzie, E. Stud. 61. 1927, and *Lond. Dial.*, § 359. We are forced to suppose an early monophthonging to [ē] which must have become partly tense before the lengthening of the $\breve{e}$ in open sylls. (§ 173 and Note 1). None of the above texts rhyme lengthened $\breve{e}$ with undoubted tense $\bar{e}$. The dialect area in which O.E. $\bar{ea}$ became M.E. tense $\bar{e}$ seems to have included Essex—the starting point—part of Suffolk, and later, part of Herts. (Mackenzie, *Lond. Dial.* 360.)

§ 165.   Ousting of W.S. type before -ll, -ld, etc.

It is remarkable that the W.S. $\bar{e}$-type was, quite early, completely ousted by the Anglian type—*all*, *āld*, instead of *eall* or *æll*=[ɛll, ɛld], etc. We find this beginning in the late twelfth century in H. Rd. Tree, which Napier says has *all* fifty times; Wohunge has such forms as *halde, balde, caldliche*; Soules Warde has *halden*; A. R. has *ōld, tōlde, ihōlden, cōld*; Prov. of Alfr. (Jesus MS., 1246–50) has also the Anglian *cōld, hōlde, alre*, but preserves the Sax. type in the solitary forms *wēlde* 'wield', *wēldest*. See however § 166, Note.

Thus the native Southern type is early—one might almost say, suddenly—superseded and ousted by alien forms, in the Saxon area, both in words with lengthening such as *cōld*, instead of the normal descendant *che(a)ld*, of W.S. *ċeald*, L. W.S. *ċæld*, and in words without lengthening such as *all, half*, etc.

Such forms as *hōlde, old, cōld* from Anglian *hāldan, āld*, etc. fall of course under the ordinary rounding of O.E. $\bar{a}$, § 156.

The London Area undoubtedly had fracture originally before -*l* + cons. and the approximate date at which the

unfractured forms gain the upper hand varies in different parts
of the area. The old City names agree with Essex in having *ēld*,
etc.:—*Eldenes Lane* (1257), *Eldefishstrate*, *Eldemariecherch*
(Heuser 22–32), and these forms occur in late fourteenth
century, e. g. *Eldene lane* (1391) and *Eld ynne* = ' Old Inn' in
fifteenth century, cp. Mackenzie, § 246. Westm. Ch. writes *æld*,
eald, *elden* dat. pl.: *ald* being rare, also *ysēld*, *gehēlde*, and
beholde; Hen. III Procl. *eald* and *ald*; Trin. Homs. *eld*, *eald*,
and a few *ald*, *old*; Lamb. Homs. on the other hand has chiefly
āld, *ōld*, and a few such forms as *ealde*, *ēld*, *wēldende*. In the
fourteenth century *ōld*, *hōlden*, etc. are the regular forms in the
London dialect of Chaucer, Petition of Folk in Mercery, etc.,
and the only ones in Hist. of S. Bartholomew's Church (1400)
and later texts. Chaucer has a few examples, confirmed by
rhymes, of the old City and Middles. type—*hēlde*, *bihēlde* (inf.),
hēlde (Pres. Pl.), *wēlde* (inf.). These may well be due to
Chaucer's early connexion with the City, and need not
necessarily be explained as new formations from analogy of
the old 2nd and 3rd Pers. Sing. Pres.

The ousting of the old London type may be due to the influence of the neighbouring Bucks dialect. The Pl. Ns. of this
county show that it belonged to the non-fracture area, except for
a small portion in the S.E. which, according to Mawer, Bucks
Pl. Ns., p. xiv., was early settled by Middle Saxons; otherwise
we find *Caldecote* (1199), *Calverstone* (1182); *Aldemede* (temp.
Rich. 1), etc. See Mackenzie, §§ 300–2.

In *l*-combinations where no lengthening took place we find
in different parts of the London area, either the Essex type
al- with retraction, from *æl-*, or *el-*, with raising. The latter
appears to have been the characteristic original regional type,
though the *al*-type later becomes the sole form in use. F. of
F. 1196 has *chelchuð*. The City docs. have *Āldredesgate*
(1196), and *Āldemanberi* (1202), both with shortening; Mackenzie, § 10; Westm. Ch. by the side of -*al-*, has such remarkable
forms as *stellere*, *ellswa*; further *Elfward*, and *Chilchelle*, for
Chelk- (Mackenzie); Trin. Homs. *half*, *halle*, *bifallen*, *salt*, *alle*,
but *ealse*, *sealmboc*; Lamb. Homs. generally -*al-*, but a fair
number of the other type;—*help* Pret. Sing., *abelh*, -*bealh*,
swealh, *swealte*, *ealle* (Mackenzie 60); Procl. and the later
docs. have -*al-* only.

§ 166. O.E. ċeald, half, etc., in Kentish.

It seems possible that in Kt. the O.E. diphthongs survived
in some forms as diphthongs into the M.E. period, O.E. *éa*
probably becoming a 'rising diphthong' and passing through

[*eá, iá*] to [já] or [jǽ, jé]. The Aȝenbite (1340) exhibits the characteristic Kt. state of affairs more consistently, in the spelling, than the earlier texts in the same dialect. Thus Aȝenbite writes *yalde, ealde* 'old'; *ofhyealde, yhyealde* p. p. O.E. *ǧe-healden*; *by-wealde, chealde, chald*, and *bēld*, O.E. *beald*. These spellings are by some authorities supposed to indicate such a pronunciation as [tʃǣld, tʃēld, ihjǣlde, ihjēlde] or something of the kind. Such spellings as *hald* 'holds', *chald* 'cold', in this text may be attempts to express [jǣ] or [jē]. No doubt after *ch* [tʃ] the [j]-sound was lost. Of earlier Kt. texts, the Vespas. Homilies write *manifeald*, but also *manifald, unitald*; the Laud. Homilies have the Kt. spelling *ihialde*, the ambiguous *chald*, the Anglian *i-told*, and the hybrid *chōld*. All Kt. texts in M.E. have such forms as *alle, falle, half*, which we may regard either as Anglian importations, which here, as in the West and Central Sthn., have ousted the native forms; or merely as showing retraction of *æ* in *ċealf* < *ċælf* < *chalf*.

NOTE. In Mod. English *weald* n. and *wield* vb. seem to be the sole survivors of the old *ea*, M.E. *ǣ*, [ē]-type, and even here the noun has the alternative Anglian form *wold*.

§ 167.   O.E. ĕa followed by r + consonant.

O.E. *hearm, eart, earm* 'arm' (L. O.E. *hærm*, etc.) are written *herm, ert, erm* in thirteenth-century texts in the West and Central South. The combination -*er*- seems generally to become -*ar*- later. In the Midlands and Essex, *harm, art*, etc., are the prevailing types already in Early Transition, and appear to show retraction of *æ*. The same forms in the Nth. represent the un-fractured type.

§ 168.   O.E. ĕŏ monophthongized to ĕ, or becomes a rounded vowel.

There were apparently three possibilities in regard to this diphthong. (*a*) In one area, in Essex and Suffolk, and perhaps elsewhere in the extreme East, it was monophthongized to *ĕ* before the end of the O.E. period. As early as the tenth and eleventh century Suff. Charters write *werþ*, etc., and in the middle of the twelfth century Peterborough Chron. has *e*, though *eo* is also frequently written.

(*b*) In another area, including the whole of the S.W., the West Midl., Central Midl. and also, in the East, apparently including London and some adjacent counties, exclusive of Kt, the first element of *ĕŏ* was rounded, giving [øo], and this was monophthongized to [ø]. This stage is found in the earliest M.E. (twelfth and early thirteenth centuries). The earliest

Lond. Ch., write *eorl, þeof*, etc. The Lambeth Homs. (1200) probably from Sth. Middlesex, by the side of *e*, write also *eoden* ; *heorte, orþe* ' earth ', etc. ; Trin. Homs. (N.E. Middles. ?) have slight traces, *storre* ' star ', *trowen* ' trees.'

(*c*) During the thirteenth century a process of un-rounding affected this vowel, and it became *ĕ* everywhere East of a line which will be defined hereafter. Henceforth we have, excluding Kt. for the moment, two types of dialectal development in words containing the old diphthongs : (1) *ĕ*, which is now found in the old *ĕ*-area ((*a*) above), as well as in that part of the country where un-rounding of [ø] took place ; (2) a rounded vowel which survives in the extreme S.W. and perhaps further Nth., as late as the middle of the fifteenth century. This vowel which at first was [ø] was gradually raised to [y̆] and was thus levelled with Fr. [y] and with the same sound, when it survived, from O.E. This rounded vowel continues to be written, for some time, with the traditional spelling *eo*, but the typical M.E. spellings are *ue, oe, u, ui, uy, o, u*, the last being the most frequent. Rhymes point to the early development of [y] ; thus Laȝamon rhymes *neode* ' need ' with *hude* ' to hide ' (though rhymes in this text must be received with caution), and Sthn. Leg. *duyre* ' dear ', with *huyre* ' to hire '. This *u*-area, as we may call it, includes, as Miss Serjeantson, basing her results on an extended survey of Pl. N. forms, suggests tentatively, all the English dialects west of a line drawn from Dorking to Birmingham, and thence perhaps to Derby. Rounded forms occur in all the S. and S.W. texts ; *sulve* ' self ', *heonne* ' hence ' rh. *moncunne*, Owl and Nightingale ; *duere* ' dearly ', *suelfer* ' silver ', O.E. *seolfor*, in Moral Ode (Egerton MS. Hants) ; *furþe* ' fourth ', in Us. of Win., *Dupe*-' deep ', *Nuther*- O.E. *neoþor*, in fourteenth century Hants Pl. Ns. fr. Hund. Rlls. ; *clupeþ* ' calls ', *lume* ' limbs ', *brŭst* ' breast ', etc. R. of Glos. ; Trevisa for *eŏ* always has *e* unless when the vowel is lengthened, but then writes *eo, eu, u* ; once *ue* ; *ēo* written *e*, but usually *eo, u, ue*; see Pfeffer, pp. 21-2 ; 27-9 ; *vrthe* ' earth ', *dure* ' dear ', etc. S. Editha. *Dure* occurs in Shillingford's Letters (Exeter 1447-50). Similar forms with *eo, u, ue*, etc. occur in the early S.W. Midl.—Laȝamon, Ancr. Riwle (Morton), the Catherine group, in the fourteenth century Harley Lyrics (Heref.), in Jos. of Ar., Audelay's Poems, Allit. P., and Sir Gawayne, all W. Midl. (See Serjeantson.)

None of the Eastern dialects, after the middle of the thirteenth century, show any traces of a rounded vowel, either in texts or in Pl. Ns. London documents write nothing but *e* after this period. The earliest charters have *eo*, and so have

the early thirteenth century Homs., see above. Westm. Ch.
has a trace of the rounded vowel *ðōf* 'thief'; Procl. of Hen. III
has *Hurtford, eorl, beon*. Among early Pl. N. forms from
Middles., Miss Mackenzie has noted (§ 182) *Sovenhacres*
'Sevenacres', near Shoreditch (temp. Hen. III); *Mosewella*
'Muswell' (1152); *Prostmād* (thirteenth century). This
occurrence of a rounded vowel in Middles. is one of the features
which distinguish this dialect from that of the City of London
and the Essex type. The typical Eastern sound is *ẹ̆*, which,
when from old long *ēo*, is tense. Peterborough Chron. writes
heom, eorl, heolden, deoflen; but also *erthe, sterres, hēlden, dēr,
undēp*, etc., and that *eo* does not denote a rounded vowel here is
made certain by its use in *ċeose* 'cheese', for *cēse*. Vices and
Virtues (Nth. Essex) writes *ierðe, erðe, liernen, lemen* 'limbs',
lief, diepliche, dieuel, pieues, etc., *ie* being the regular symbol of
this scribe for tense [ē]. The occurrence of *e*, or *eo, u*, etc. in
a text is a valuable dialect test in discriminating between East
and West.

§ 169.   O.E. ēo in Kentish.

The Kentish texts frequently write *ie, io, ye*, for these diphthongs, especially for the long, though not with perfect consistency. Vespasian Homs. (1150), write *hierte, sielfe*, but also
eorðe, ærlen 'earls', *nemen* 'take'; but for the long, *chiesen* inf.
O.E. *cēosan, dier(cynne), diofles, þiode, þiesternesse, þesternesse*;
Laud. Homs. (1250) *erþe*, and *yerþe, herle, sterre*; *dieules, liese*
inf. O.E. *-lēosan*; *bien* inf., but also *dēvel, frēnd, prēst, helden*,
Pret. Pl., etc.; W. of Shoreham (Nth. W. Kt. 1320) writes *e, ee*;
Aȝenbite (Canterbury, 1340) is the most consistent in writing
-ye- for the long: *þyēf, dyēuel, byēp, dyēp*, etc.; *lyerny* 'to learn',
yerþe, but more commonly *e—sterve* O.E. *steorfan* 'die', *erl*,
erþe, herte, heuene, etc. It has been held that the *ie, ye* spellings
represent diphthongal pronunciation, but this seems extremely
doubtful, especially for the short, and is not very probable
for the long, since *ie* is a recognized symbol for tense *ẹ̆* (Laud.
Homs. write *hieren* = *hēren*), and is consistently used for this
in the Essex Vices and Virtues, and much later by the Kentishman Gower, who however does not write it for *ẹ̆* from *ēo*. In
yerþe, by the side of *erþe*, the *y* may represent a tendency to
develop an initial front cons. before *e-*.

§ 170.   O.E. ĭe (ӯ̆) in M.E.

Since *ĭe* is purely W. Sax., its representative is only found
in the Saxon area in M.E. Already in O.E. in one part of the
area *ĭe* was apparently levelled under *ĭ*, which sound survives

unaltered in M.E. In another part this diphthong, whether long or short, became $\bar{y}$ in L.W.S. (cp. § 119 above). This is preserved in M.E. but always written *u*, or (when long) also *ui*, *uy—hurde* 'shepherd', *huiren* 'hear', etc.

Unlike the other O.E. $\bar{y}$ (from $\breve{u}$-*i*, cp. § 108) which was universal in O.E., and which survived widely in M.E. (§ 158), the sound we are considering is confined to part of the South.

The original Saxon character of the London Dialect is shown by the occurrence of $\breve{i}$, $\bar{y}$ in the earliest Charters and Procl. *yrfnume*, *alȳsednesse*, etc.; after the beginning of the fourteenth century, however, non-Saxon *ē*-forms are alone found—Davie, *hēre* 'hear', *stēl* 'steel.'

§ 171. Development of New Diphthongs in M.E.

Numerous diphthongs arose in M.E. through the development of glide-sounds between vowels and the following [j], [h̨], [h] and [ʒ]. The glide took the form, in the former cases, of the vowel *i*, in the latter, of *u*. The diphthongs are written *ai, ay, ei, ey, au, aw, ou, ow*, etc.

(1) M.E. *ai*—O.E. *æġ* becomes M.E. *æi, ai*; O.E. *dæġ*, M.E. *dæi, dai*.

(2) M.E. *ei*—(*a*) O.E. *eġ* becomes M.E. *ei*; O.E. *weġ*, M.E. *wei*; O.E, *legde*, M.E. *leide*.

(*b*) Late O.E. *æ̆h̨* from *eah̨* becomes M.E. *ei*: *æhta*, 'eight', M.E. *ehte, eihte*, etc.

(3) M.E. *ēi*—(*a*) O.E. *ǣġ* becomes M.E. *ēi*; O.E. *ǣġ* 'egg', M.E. *ēi*.

(*b*) Late O.E. *ǣ* from *ēa+ġ*, *h̨*, which is subsequently fronted, becomes M.E. *ēi*: O.E. *ēage*, later *ǣge* 'eye', M.E. *ēyē*. This is subsequently raised.

(4) M.E. *eu*—O.E. and M.E. *ef-* +consonant becomes *ew* in Late M.E. : O.E. *efete, ev(e)te, ewte* 'newt'.

(5) M.E. *ēu* [ɛ̄u]—O.E. *ēaw, ǣw* becomes M.E. *ēu* : O.E. *dēaw* 'dew', M.E. *dēū*; O.E. *scēawian*, M.E. *schēwen* 'show'.

(6) M.E. *ēu* [ēu]—O.E. *ēow* becomes M.E. *ēu*: O.E. *trēowe*, M.E. *trēue* 'true'; O.E. *blēow* 'blew', M.E. *blēu*.

(7) M.E. *au* has several origins—(*a*) O.E. *ag-* followed by a back vowel: O.E. *sagu*, M.E. *sāwe*; O.E. *slagen*, M.E. *slāwen*.

(*b*) *af-* followed by a vowel becomes *av, aw, au*: O.E. *hafoc* 'hawk', M.E. *havek, hāwek, hauk*.

(*c*) O.Fr. *au* : *faute* 'fault'.

(*d*) O.Fr. nasalized *ā* followed by *n*: M.E. *daunten* 'daunt'.

(8) M.E. *ǭu*—O.E. *āw* becomes M.E. *ōu, ōw*: O.E. *cnāwan*, M.E. *knōwen*.

O.E. *āg-* becomes *ōw* between vowels: O.E. *āgan*, M.E. *ōwen*.

O.E. *ŏ* in an open syllable followed by *g* in the next is lengthened; *g* becomes *w* as in O.E. *bŏga* 'bow', M.E. *bōue*, *bōwe*.

NOTE. It is rather doubtful whether *ōu, ōw* in these words is really to be regarded as a diphthong at all. The subsequent history of the sound is that of ordinary M.E. *ō* [ɔ̄]. See §§ 156 above, and 173 (*c*) below.

(9) M.E. *ōu*. O.E. *ōg, ōh*, M.E. *ōȝ, ōh*, seem first of all to have been diphthongized to *ōuw, ōuwh*, and then the *ō* assimilates to the second element of the diphthong which disappears so that *ūw, ūh* result: O.E. *plōh*, M.E. *plōuh, plūh*; O.E. *ġenōh*, M.E. *inōuh, inūh*. The inflected cases of these words have in O.E. (gen.) *plōges*, M.E. *plōuwes, plūwes*; *ġenōges*, M.E. *inōuwes*, *inūwes*, etc.

NOTE. The combinations [aʃ, antʃ, andž] in some dialects (Sth.-Western?) often becomes diphthongal in M.E. *aisschen* 'ask', *chaynge*.

The O.E. combination *-enċt* becomes *-eint*, chiefly in S.W.: O.E. *drenċte*, M.E. *dreinte*; O E. *blenċte*, M.E. *bleinte*, etc.

§ 172. Monophthongizing and later alteration of M.E. Diphthongs.

(1) Diphthongs in *-u*.

(*a*) Diphthongs whose second element is *-u* lose this element in M.E. and lengthen the first element before lip-consonants: *chāmber* from *chaumber*; *sāve, sāfe* from *sauve, saufe*; M.E. *rēme* (Trevisa) by side of *rewme* 'kingdom'; Mod. Engl. *jeopardy* [džepədi], in spite of its spelling, implies M.E. *jēpardi*; *people, feoff* [pīpl, fīf] are also probably examples of this influence of the lip-consonant. The name *Beaumont*, now usually [boumənt], owes its pronunciation to French influence, but the variant *Beamont* [bīmənt] is a case in point (cp. Luick, *Anglia*, xvi, pp. 485, 499, 500, 503). Luick rightly conjectures the existence of [bīmənt] *Beamont*, although he is unacquainted with it. Further, the name *Belvoir* [bīvə] from *Beuveir* < *Bēveir* (also *Belveire*), and *Bevis* [bīvis] from *Beufitz* are good examples. *Beaufort*, now [boufət], is no doubt to be explained like *Beaumont*. The spelling *Buforde* (Duke of) in the *Wentworth Papers* (1710) points to [bjū-] and must be due to association with the first syll. of *beau*tiful. On the other hand, *Beaulieu* = [bjūli] is normal. Cp. §§ 198, 265.

(*b*) The second element of -*u* diphthongs is also lost in M.E. before [ʃ, tʃ, dž] and the first element lengthened. Examples: M.E. *āge* from *auge*; *ānge* from *aunge*; *chivachie* from *chivau-chie*; *Beauchamp* [bītʃəm], M.E. *Bēchamp (Luick, *Anglia*, xvi, pp. 503, etc.).

(2) O.E. -*ēah*, *ēag* become *ī*.

By far the most usual way of writing the O.E. words *ēage*, 'eye', *hēah* 'high', *lēag* 'field' in M.E., is *ēye*, *ēʒe*, *hēih*, *hēʒ*, *lēih*, *lēʒ*, etc.; there are many variants, but the vowel appears either as *ēi* or *ē*. This is equally true of the spellings in both texts and Pl.-Ns. From about the middle of the thirteenth century, however, spellings with *y* and *i* appear occasionally in the documents of some areas. The scribes appear to have avoided these latter spellings, and even in texts and Pl.-Ns. in which they do occur they are far less frequent than the other spellings, and indeed when the rhyme shows that the pronunciation [ī] was intended, the scribe often still adheres to *ei*, *ey*, etc. So infrequent are the *y*, *i*, spellings that even the slightest trace of them in a document may be significant of the new pronunciation in the dialect of the area whence it comes, or at least in that of the scribe. In most M.E. texts, and in the elements of Pl. Ns. from the greater part of the counties, the *y*, *i* spellings are not found at all.

From the evidence of the Pl. N. forms, Miss Serjeantson considers that -*īʒ* had developed in the first half of the thirteenth century in the dialects of part of the West Midl., in the Central Midl., and the central area of Nearer Wessex (see § 151, IV. A 2.), that is in Derby, Notts., Staffs., Leics., Warwcs., Northants, Oxfords., Berks., Wilts., Hants, Surrey, and Sussex; probably also in Herts. and Bucks. ; possibly in Shrops., Heref., and Worcs. In the fourteenth century the *i*- forms appear in Hunts. records, and in Lincs. texts. There appears to be no trace of them down to this point in Cambs., Norf., Suff., Essex, and Kent.

London texts and Pl. Ns. appear to contain no *i*- *ʒ*- spellings, and Chaucer's scribes write *eye*, etc., though in all cases where the word occurs in rhyme, the sound [ī] is indicated. See Wild, *Chaucer's Handschriften*, pp. 180–84.

The N.W. Midl. dialects of Lancs. and Cheshire show no traces of *y*- forms in the texts or Pl. Ns., the former presenting not one such spelling out of over 900 examples of names containing *hēah*, *lēah*. The *y*- spellings are absent also from the Pl. Ns. of the S.W., Glos., Somers., Devon., and Dorset.

Where it is possible to compare statistics taken from texts of known origin with those from Pl. N. forms of the same period, there is found substantial agreement regarding the presence or absence of the *y*- spellings. This is especially the case in Wilts. whose Pl. Ns. show more of these spellings than those of any other county. The early fifteenth-century Wilts. text S. Editha has twenty such spellings, and in eight other instances *heyʒe* and *neyʒe* (so spelt) rhyme with *envye*, and *by* respectively. See Serjeantson, J. E. G. Phil. 1927.

The complete absence of the *i-* spellings from London documents of all kinds before the fifteenth century is puzzling in view of Chaucer's rhymes, and of the fact that the *y*-spellings are frequently found in Hist. of S. Bartholomew's Ch. (1400)—*nygh* adv.; *an hye place*; *highnesse*; *yie* 'eye'; *thyis* 'thighs', etc., and that this form is the ancestor of the later Received Standard. There are indications of the survival of the other type, from M.E. *ēʒ*, etc., as late as the eighteenth century. See § 254, Note 3.

The treatment of O.E. *ēah*, etc. in M.E. is therefore an important dialect test, when taken in conjunction with other features.

Quantitative Changes in M.E.

[See very full treatment of the quantity of M.E. vowels in Morsbach's *M.E. Gr.*, pp. 65–117, and the article of Luick cited below.]

§ 173. Lengthening of O.E. Short Vowels.

(1) Already in Late O.E. short vowels were lengthened before the consonantal combinations *nd, mb, ld, ng*; cp. § 114 above.

(2) When either of the vowels *a, e, o*, occurred in a word of two syllables, with only one consonant following it, e.g. *bla-ke* 'black', the consonant belonged to the second syllable, and the vowel of the first syllable which was thus 'Open', that is not ending in a consonant, was lengthened.

(*a*) O.E. *fæder*, M.E. *fāder*; O.E. *măcian*, M.E. *mākien, māken*; O.E. *săcu* 'dispute', etc., M.E. *sāke* 'crime', etc.; O.E. *hăra* 'hare', M.E. *hāre*.

(*b*) O.E. *běran*, M.E. *bēren* 'bear'; O.E. *mĕte* 'food', M.E. *mēte*; O.E. *mĕre* 'lake', M.E. *mēre*; O.E. *stĕlan* 'steal', M.E. *stēlen*.

(*c*) O.E. (*ġe*)*bŏren* 'born', M.E. *bōren*; O.E. *smŏca* 'smoke', M.E. *smōke*; O.E. *hŏpa* 'hope', M.E. *hōpe*.

NOTE 1. The *ē* and *ō* due to lengthening of old short vowels in open syllables are slack vowels [ē, ō] respectively.

NOTE 2. Many words in O.E., which in the Nom. Sing. ended in a consonant, appear in M.E. with a vowel ending in all cases. Such words undergo lengthening : O.E. *hŏl* 'hole', 'cave', M.E. *hōle*, from an inflected form. In fact the forms of nouns in M.E., and still more in Mod. Engl., very commonly point to their derivation from an O.E. or M.E. oblique case with an inflexion. On the other hand, doublets often arise in M.E.—a form with a long vowel from an inflected case, and one with a short vowel from an uninflected case : O.E. *blǣc* adj. ' black', with inflected forms *blaca*, etc., gives two M.E. forms, *blǎk* from *blǣc*, and *blāke* from *blǎca*. In Mod. Engl. one or both forms may survive, in different dialects, or in the same dialect with specialized meaning : Mod. *black*, beside the Family Name *Blake*. See 214, p. 156.

NOTE 3. It is easy to see how a final -*e* came later to be considered as a sign of length. The stressed vowels in L. M.E. *thrōte*, *hōpe*, *blāke*, etc., were necessarily long, and when later the -*e* ceased to be pronounced as a separate syllable, the preceding vowel of course kept its length, and the traditional -*e* in the spelling was associated with this, in distinction from *hŏp*, *blǎk*, etc.

NOTE 4. Examples of rhymes from early (thirteenth century) texts, which show that lengthening in open syllables had already taken place :— *dēle—wēle* 'property'; *ephĕte—swēte*, *bēte* ; *strēte, unimēte—biʒēte* (Sinners Beware); *unhēle—wele* ; *lēten—onmēte* ' meet' (Moral Ode); *On slāpe* . . . *yschape* (K. Horn).

§ 174. Lengthening of ĭ and ŭ in Open Syllables in M.E.

It is now pretty generally accepted that, as stated by Luick (*Untersuchungen z. engl. Lautgesch.*, 1896 ; *Studien z. engl. Lautgesch.*, 1903), *ĭ* and *ŭ* in open syllables were lengthened, lowered, and made tense, before the beginning of the fourteenth century, so that *ĭ* in this situation became *ē*, and *ŭ* became *ō*. The examples in Mod. Standard English are not very frequent, as in various cases analogies of doublets without lengthening have preserved the short forms with *i* and *u*. In M.E. the examples are more numerous.

O.E. *wicu* 'week', M.E. *wēke* ; O.E. *bitul*, M.E. *bētel* ; O.E. *wifol*, M.E. *wēvel* 'weevil' ; M.E. *ēuel* is explained by Luick as due to earlier M.E. *iuel* from O.E. *yfel*.

O.E. *wudu*, M.E. *wōde* 'wood' ; O.E. *duru* 'door', M.E. *dōre* ; O.E. *lufu* 'love', M.E. *lōve* ; O.E. *sumu*, etc., M.E. *sōme* 'some'.

NOTE. Nearly all the forms in M.E. and Mod. Engl., explained by Luick by his law of lengthening *i* and *u* were formerly explained in other ways. Thus *bētel* was said to represent an O.E. (non-W.S.) *beotul*, *eo* becoming *e* and being lengthened in the open syllable ; *wēke* was derived from Early M.E. *wĕke*, O.E. *wĕcu*, with Anglian Smoothing from **weocu* (cp. § 127).

ēuel was supposed to have ' Kentish ' *e* for *y*, with lengthening in an open syllable. Against this is the fact that the *ē* from the above sources was slack [ĕ] in M.E., whereas the *ē* in these words must have been tense since it was raised to [ī] among the first changes of Early Mod. Engl. (cp. § 229, Note 1).

The *o* in M.E. *love*, etc., is still said by some to represent a short vowel, and that *ŭ*, the *o* being merely graphic before *u, v*. In this case the word in M.E. was [lŭve]. This lengthening is established from the evidence of spellings and rhymes in M.E., and from the Mod. Dial. forms, for the North and Midl. The spellings *-woude* ' wood ', Cockersand Chartul. 1365, are clear indications of a long vowel. The exact area over which this lengthening obtained is uncertain. The forms in Standard Engl. may be importations from another dialect.

§ 175.   Shortening of O.E. Long Vowels in M.E.

(a) *Effect of Consonant Groups.*

Before certain groups of two consonants, other than *ld, nd*, etc., and before long consonants, long vowels are shortened. The shortening takes place also before *ld*, etc., when a third consonant follows.

(1) *Before long or double stops* : O.E. *hȳdde* (pret. of *hȳdan* ' hide '), M.E. *hĭdde* ; O.E. *lǣdde* ' led ', M.E. *lĕdde*.

(2) *Before stop + stop :* O.E. *cēpte* (pret. of *cēpan*), M.E. *kĕpte* ; M.E. *wĕpte*, pret. of *wēpen* ' weep '.

(3) *Before open consonant + stop* : *wĭsdom*, cp. *wīs* ; *fĭftēne*, cp. *fīve* ; O.E. *sōfte*, M.E. *sŏfte*.

(4) *Before stop + open consonant* : *dĕpthe*, cp. *dēpe* ' deep ' ; *Ĕdward*, O.E. *Ēadweard* = L. O.E. *Ǣdward*.

(5) *Before open consonant + m, l* : O.E. *wīfman*, M.E. *wĭmman* ; M.E. *gŏsling*, cp. *gōs* ; M.E. *dĕvles*, Pl. of *dēvel*.

(6) *Before open consonant + open consonant* : O.E. *hūswīf*, M.E. *hŭswĭf*.

(7) *Before ld, mb, nd + another consonant* : O.E. *cīld*, Pl. *cĭldru*, M.E. *chīld, chĭldre* ; O.E. *lāmbru*, Pl. of *lāmb*, M.E. *lōmb, lămbre* (Orm. *chilldre, lammbre*) ; O.E. *frēōndscipe*, M.E. *frĕndschip*.

NOTE. The shortenings very commonly occur in compounds, as seen above, among which Pl. Ns. often exhibit good instances. Cp. such names as *Bradley*, where the first element is O.E. *brād* ' broad ', *Deptford, Depden* where the first element is O.E. *dēop*, M.E. *dēpe*, etc.

(8) Shortening before *st* and *sch* seems to have been normal. Mod. Engl. has, it is true, mostly long forms before *-st* : *ghost*, O.E. *gāst*, M.E. *gōst* ; *Christ*, M.E. *Crīst* ; *priest*, M.E. *prēst*. The M.E. long vowels in this position may be explained from the inflected forms : *prēstes, gōstes* (syllable division *prē-stes, gō-stes*), etc.   Before *sch* [ʃ] : *wĭschen*, side by side with O.E.

K

wȳscan; *flĕsch*, O.E. *flǣsc*; we get also *flǣsch*, *flēsch*, which must be explained on the analogy of the inflected *flē-sches*, etc.

§ 176. (*b*) Shortening of Long Vowels in Words of Three Syllables.

In three-syllabled words, the vowel of the first syllable, if long, is shortened ; if short, is not lengthened, even though it stand in an open syllable (Luick, *Anglia*, xx).

These three-syllabled words occur chiefly in compounds such as Pl. Names, and otherwise as the inflected forms of words of two syllables.

M.E. *hōli* 'holy', but *hŏliday*; *Whĭtăker*, Pl. N. in Lancs., etc., of which first element is O.E. *hwīt* 'white'. Mod. *utter*, O.E. *ūterra*, shows this shortening.

NOTE. In M.E. there are many doublets, due to different conditions as to the number of syllables, in inflected and uninflected forms of Nouns and Adjectives. In Nouns which end in *-er, -el, -en, -y*, the inflected forms often lose the syllable before the *r, l, n,* thus *fāder*, but *fădres*, etc., *sādel* 'saddle', but *sădles*, etc., *boodi* 'body', but *bŏddyes*, whence Mod. [bɔ́di], etc. In these forms the shortening, or absence of lengthening, is due to the combinations *-dr-, -dl-*, etc.

On the other hand, in forms without syncope, such as *făderes*, etc., according to the principle formulated by Luick, the first syllable would remain short, although in an open syllable. Thus we may say that *fāder* and many other M.E. words normally had a long vowel in the Nom. and Acc. Sing., but a short vowel in the other cases. The result was, as a rule, that either a long or a short vowel was generalized, for all cases, Sing. and Pl. Thus we get two types—*fāder* and *făder*. The form in Mod. Standard Engl. is derived from the *fāder* type, the Dialectal [fēðə(r)] from M.E. *făder* (see §§ 220, 225 Note, below). In the same way *boddi(y)es* retained *ŏ* in first syllable.

§ 177. Shortening of Long Vowels in Unstressed Syllables.

Long vowels, whether in prefixes such as O.E. *ā-*, or, as is more frequent, in final syllables of compounds, are shortened in M.E. Thus O.E. *ārĭsan* is M.E. *ărĭsen*. So too O.E. *ān*, when used as an indefinite article, and therefore unstressed in the sentence, is shortened to *ăn, ă*, whereas when it stands for the numeral it remains long, as appears, e. g., in Chaucer, either as *ō*, or *ōn(e)*.

Shortened forms *hăve, ăre, yŭ, yŭre, mĭ, mĭn, thĭ, thĭn, tĕ*, etc., occurred in unstressed positions, by the side of the stressed *hāve, āre, mī(n), thī(n), tō*. See § 222.

Most of these shortenings, however, occur in the second elements of compounds, in which the secondary stress of O.E. was further reduced in M.E.

O.E. *cyngestŭn* 'Kingston', M.E. *Kingestŭn* ; M.E. *hus(w)ĭf*, O.E. *wīf*; the Mod. Engl. Family Name *Wodehouse* = [wudəs] shows this shortening of O.E. *hūs* in the second element; M.E. *stĭrŏp* 'stirrup', in which the second element is O.E. *rāp* 'rope'.

§ 178. Treatment of Vowels in Scandinavian Loan-words in M.E.

This whole subject has been elaborately treated by Björkman, *Scandinavian Loan-words in Middle English*, Pt. I, 1900; Pt. II, 1902.

We are obliged here to state the main facts as simply and briefly as possible.

Scandinavian vowels were not on the whole very different from those of O.E., and in M.E. the majority of them undergo the same changes as those in native words. Scandinavian *ă*, *ĕ, ĭ, ў, ŭ, ŏ* are treated in the same way as the same vowels in native English words.

The chief sounds deserving notice are the diphthongs *ai, ei*, and *au*, which did not occur in O.E. in native words.

§ 179.   *O. Scand. ai* in some cases was Englished to *ā* (the historically equivalent sound) in O.E. itself: O.E. *hāmsōcn* 'attacking an enemy in his house', O.Sc. *heim-*.

In O.West Scand. *ai* was preserved much longer than in East Scand., in fact it still survives in some Swed. Dialects at the present time.

In O.Danish. *ai* became *ei* which was simplified to *ē* in the pre-literary period.

Both *ai, ei*, and *ē* are found in M.E. loan-words: *baite* 'bait, food', *blayke* 'pale' (cp. the native M.E. form *blōke* from O.E. *blāc*), *wayke* 'weak' (O.E. *wāc*, M.E. *wōke*), *heil* 'hale, healthy', *reisen* 'raise' (cp. O.E. *rǣran* 'rear'), *þei, þeir* 'they, their', etc.

The Danish type probably occurs in M.E. *wēke* 'weak'.

§ 180.   *O. Scand. au*. This diphthong appears in M.E. in the three forms *au, ou, ō*. M.E. *gauk, gowk, gōke* 'cuckoo', 'fool', also as a man's name, cp. Lanc. *Gawthorpe*, M.E. *Gaukethorp*; M.E. *windoge* 'window', O.West Scand. *vindauga*; M.E. *coupe* 'pay for, buy', O.W. Scand. *kaupa*; also in M.E. Lancs. Pl. N. *Coupmoneswra*, Mod. *Capernwray*.

In Old Scandinavian *au* before *h* was early monophthongized to *ō*, hence M.E. *þōh, þōgh, þough*, etc. 'though' is from Scand. *þōh*, earlier **þauh*, compared with O.E. *þēah* which gives M.E. *þēih*, etc.

NOTE. M.E. *þauh* probably represents O.E. *þēah*, later *þǣh*, shortened to *þǎh*, in unstressed positions, and retracted to *ǎ*, whence *au* developed before *h*. Cp. § 171.

The Treatment of Vowels in French Loan-words.

(See Jespersen, *Mod. Engl. Gr.*, pp. 130–45, etc., etc.; Kaluza, *Hist. Gr. d. engl. Spr.*, ii, pp. 45–72.)

§ 181. Norman-French, or as they are also called, Anglo-Norman, words passed into English speech for the most part with approximately the same sounds which they already had. We may say that very few new vowel sounds were added to the language from this source. The nasalized vowels which stood before *n, m*, lost their nasalization, with the exception of *ã*, which retained its quality, at any rate, in the speech of the upper classes. On the peculiar development of N.Fr. *ã*, see below, §§ 183, 184. Another new sound was the diphthong *oi*; see § 200.

§ 182. *N.F. ǎ* (1) remains: *balle* 'ball', *part, chartre, cacchen* 'catch'.

(2) Is lengthened in open syllables in the same way as O.E. *ǎ*, § 173. 2 (*a*): *plǎce, cǎge, rǎge, corǎge, fǎme, ǎble*, etc.

(3) Lengthened before *st*: *chǎste, hǎste*, etc.

(4) Lengthened before a final single consonant: *estǎt, debǎt, cǎs*, etc.

§ 183. *N.F. ãn, ãm*. The nasalization is kept in the first instance, and the combinations *ãn, ãm* develop a diphthong *au* from the nasal vowel: *chaumbre, chaunticleer, graunten, chaunce, chaunge, daunce, auncient, exaumple, aunt*, etc.

§ 184. By the side of the *au*-spellings, we frequently find *an, am* in M.E. The diphthongized forms have another development in Mod. Engl. from those without a diphthong: thus M.E. *haunten* yields Mod. [hɔnt], whereas *hanten* yields [hãnt]; cp. § 259 below. These double types are very common in Mod. Engl. and prove the existence of the un-diphthongized forms in M.E. if we were inclined to believe that the distinction was merely a matter of spelling. Jespersen (*Mod. Engl. Gr.*, pp. 110, 111) explains the undiphthongized forms as due to the influence of Continental French, where the diphthongization did not occur, in the M.E. period.

This would hardly account for all the forms, as we cannot suppose a widespread or universal knowledge of Continental French, whereas the words in question, having come in from Norman-French, were well established in the language. I am inclined to suggest that the distinction is due to social causes. The upper classes, in the Early M.E. period, knew and spoke Norman-French, and the sound of the nasal vowel was natural to them. It was different with the lower sort of people, who did not speak French from the cradle. They would hardly pronounce loan-words with a sound that was quite unknown in their own English speech. Thus it seems probable that apart from Court circles *dăncen, ănt* 'aunt' were pronounced simply *dăncen, ănt,* etc., and these forms underwent no diphthongization. Both types got into popular use, and appear to have been equally current in Early Modern.

NOTE. Before *-ge a* seems to have been lengthened in M.E. in the undiphthongized forms; the form *straange* (Trevisa) may be the direct ancestor of the Mod. form. Cp. § 225 below. See §§ 171 (9), Note, and 172 (*b*) above for *chaynge*, etc.

§ 185. N.F. ĕ is preserved in M.E. in close syllables: *dĕtte, lĕttre, sĕrchen* ; lengthened before *-st* : *fēst, bēst* ' beast '.

§ 186. N.F. ē, M.E. *ē*: *degrēé, pouertēé, deintēé* ' dignity value ', *profēte, clēre, frēre* ' brother '.

§ 187. N.F. ī (*i* in open syllable), M.E. *ī*, *mercīé, folīé, vīce, īle, sīre, bībel.*

§ 188. N.F. e, ē from O.Fr. ie, M.E. e. In close syllables : *aleggen, cerge* ' candle '. Lengthened in open syllables : *grēuen* ' grieve ', *pēce* ' piece ', *sēge, manēre, chēre* ' face, appearance ' ; also before a single final consonant : *greef, breef, squiĕr.* This *ē* is often written *ie*; see § 162, p. 114 above.

§ 189. N.F. ŏ preserved in close syllables : *propre, cofre, force,* etc. Lengthened in open syllables = [ɔ] : *cōte* ' coat ', *suppósen, nōble, rōse* ; also before *st* : *hōst, rōst.*

§ 190. N.F. ŭ, ū = [ŭ] remains or becomes short in M.E. before several consonants : *court, purse, turnen.*

ŭ in open syllables and before a single final consonant becomes *ū* in N.F. and remains as such in M.E. : *vou* ' vow ', *goute, spouse, flour* ' flower ', *labour, culour.*

§ 191. N.F. ŭ = M.E. *ū*: *mount, croune, ounce, countre.*

§ 192. N.F. [ø] eo, ue, from O.Fr. ue. Variously written *oe, ue, e* as in *poeple, people, peple, preef* ' proof ', *boef, beef,* etc. It seems likely that these words had the sound [ø] (§ 168), which either survived as a rounded vowel, or, in other dialects, was unrounded to [ē]. This would explain the variations in spelling *pēple, people. eo* no doubt represented [ø]. We have retained this spelling in the last word and in *jeopardy*, which is also written *juparti, juperdi* in M.E. where *u* = [ȳ].

§ 193. **N.F. u, ū** = [y̆] **in M.E.** This sound remains in M.E. and the great majority of words containing it are of Fr. origin. How far it differed, or in what way, from the O.E. ȳ̆ (§§ 108, 109, 119), also written *u* in M.E., it is difficult to determine. Since, however, the sound in Fr. words does not undergo the fluctuations in time and place which characterize the sound in Native words, it is fair to suppose that there was some difference between them. Possibly the Fr. [y] was tenser and higher than the English sound.

Examples of short *ŭ* [y] in M.E.: *just, juge, sepulcre,* etc. Lengthened in stressed open syllables: *pursúen, rúde, súre, natúre, creatúre, vertúe, vertew.*

§ 194. **N.F. üi** [ȳi] becomes simply [ȳ], generally written *ui, uy,* in M.E.: *fruit, nuisance.*

§ 195. **N.F. Diphthongs in M.E.**

N.F. ai remains in M.E.: *gai, deldi, tráitre, grain, chapelain, batáile, vitáiles.*

N.F. *ai,* when it does not bear the chief accent, is generally monophthongized to *e* in M.E.: *resóun, sesóun, tresóun;* but *raisoun,* etc., also occurs.

§ 196. **N.F. au remains in M.E.:** *faute, cause, baume, sauf* 'safe', *auter* 'altar', *sauváge, laundere* from *lavendere* 'washer-woman'.

NOTE. Before lip-consonants *au* becomes *ā* already in M.E. in some cases: *saaf* (Wycl.). Cp. § 172 (*a*).

§ 197. **N.F. ei remains in M.E.:** *palefréi, monéie, feiþ, faiþ* 'faith', *lei* 'law', *streit* 'narrow', *burgeis.*

In Central Fr., O.Fr. *ei* becomes *oi,* and M.E. *exploit, coi* are from this source.

§ 198. **N.F. eau** from earlier *eal* + consonant becomes *eu* in M.E.; *beutée, beautée.*

§ 199. **N.F. eu, ieu, remains as eu in M.E.:**—*Jew, reule.* [The last word may also represent O.E. *regol,* M.E. *rewel.*]

§ 200. **N.F. oi remains in M.E.:** *joie, cloistre, vois, chois, destroien, point, boilen.*

§ 201. **Table of Late M.E. Vowels, and their Sources.**

M.E. ă, O.E. *ă, ắ,* as in *căt, băk,* § 160.

M.E. e $\begin{cases} \text{O.E. } e, \text{ as in } bed, setten. \\ \text{O.E. } \breve{e}o, \text{ as in } h\breve{e}rte, erpe, \text{ etc., } \S 168. \\ \text{O.E. } \breve{e}a, \text{ as in } herm, \text{ etc., } \S 167. \end{cases}$

M.E. ĭ $\begin{cases} \text{O.E. } \breve{\imath}, \text{ as in } s\breve{\imath}tten, ch\breve{\imath}ldre, \text{ etc.} \\ \text{O.E. } \breve{y} \text{ (in Nth., E.Midl. and in S.W. before front} \\ \text{consonant), as in } hill, pit, brigge, \S 158 (f). \end{cases}$

M.E. ŏ $\begin{cases} \text{O.E. } \breve{o}, \text{ as in } fl\breve{o}k, G\breve{o}dd, \text{ etc.} \\ \text{O.E. } \bar{o} \text{ shortened, as in } g\breve{o}sling, bl\breve{o}sme, \text{ etc.,} \\ \S 175 (5). \end{cases}$

M.E. ŭ, O.E. *ŭ*, as in *sŭne* (*sŏne*).

M.E. [ў] (written *u*) O.E. *ў*: *hull, rugge* (in W. and Central Midlands and Sth.-West), § 158 (*c*) ; O.Fr. *ü*, as in *juge*, etc., § 193.

M.E. ā $\begin{cases} \text{O.E. } \breve{a} \text{ in open syllables, as in } m\bar{a}ken, f\bar{a}der, \text{ etc.,} \\ \S 173 (2). \\ \text{O.E. } \bar{\textit{æ}}^1 \text{ and } \bar{\textit{æ}}^2 \text{ (in Essex ; City of London to } 1350 \\ \text{or so ; parts of Herts., Beds., Hunts., } \S 162 (3). \\ \text{O.Fr. } \bar{a}, \text{ as in } f\bar{a}me, d\bar{a}me, \text{ etc., } \S 182 (2). \end{cases}$

M.E. ē (1) = [ē] $\begin{cases} \text{O.E. } \bar{e}, \text{ as in } sw\bar{e}te, h\bar{e}, h\bar{e}ren, \text{ etc.} \\ \text{O.E. } \bar{e} \text{ from } \bar{\textit{æ}}^1 \text{ (non-W.S.), as in } d\bar{e}d \\ \text{ 'deed', } w\bar{e}ren, \text{ etc., } \S 162. \\ \text{O.E. } \bar{e}o, \text{ as in } feend, h\bar{e}ld, \S 168 \text{ (a).} \\ \text{O.E. } \breve{\imath} \text{ in open syllables, as in } w\bar{e}ke, \S 174. \\ \text{O.E. } \bar{e} \text{ (S.E.Midl., S.E. and Kentish),} \\ \text{ earlier } \bar{y}, \S 158 (b). \\ \text{O.E. } \bar{e} \text{ (S.E.Midl., S.E. and Kentish)} \\ \text{ from } \bar{a}-i, \S 162. \\ \text{O.E. } \bar{e}a \text{ as in } d\bar{e}the \text{ 'death', etc. (Ess. and} \\ \text{ Suff.), } \S 164 (4). \end{cases}$

M.E. ē (2) = [ɛ̄] $\begin{cases} \text{O.E. } \bar{\textit{æ}}^2, \text{ as in } d\bar{e}len, cl\bar{e}ne, \text{ etc., } \S 162. \\ \text{O.E. } \bar{\textit{æ}}^1 \text{ (only in Sthn. forms), as in } d\bar{e}de, \\ st\bar{\imath}\bar{e}te, \text{ etc., } \S 162. \\ \text{O.E. } \bar{e}a, \text{ as in } r\bar{e}de \text{ (}reade\text{) 'red', } d\bar{e}pe \\ \text{ (}deape\text{), etc., } \S 164. \\ \text{O.E. } \breve{e} \text{ in open syllables, as in } m\bar{e}te, \\ b\bar{e}ren, \text{ etc., } \S 173 (b) \text{ and Notes.} \\ \text{O.E. } \breve{e} \text{ (Kt. fr. } y\text{) in open sylls. as in } \bar{e}uel, \\ \S 174, \text{ Note.} \end{cases}$

M.E. ī, O.E. *ī*, as in *wīne, wīfe, chīld,* etc. ; Earlier M.E. *ēġ, ēḣ* : *ȳe* 'eye', *hīē* 'high', *nīh* 'nigh', § 172. ii.

M.E. ō (1) = [ōʷ] $\begin{cases} \text{O.E. } \bar{o}, \text{ as in } g\bar{o}de, c\bar{o}l, \S 163. \\ \text{O.E. } \breve{u} \text{ in open syllables, as in } w\bar{o}de \\ \text{ 'wood', etc., } \S 174. \\ \text{O.Fr. } \bar{o}, \text{ as in } f\bar{o}le, \text{ 'fool'.} \end{cases}$

M.E. ō (2) = [ŏ]
{
O.E. ā, as in *hōm, stōn, cōld*, etc., § 156.
O.E. ŏ in open syllables, as in *bŏren, hŏpe*, etc., § 173 (c) and Notes.
O.Fr. ŏ in open syllables, as in *cōte* 'coat', § 189.
}

M.E. ū (written *ou*, etc.)
{
O.E. ū, as in *house, foul, nou, young*, etc., § 152.
O.E. ōȝ, ōh, as in *plou, inou*, etc., § 171 (9).
O.Fr. ū, as in *floure, doute, courte*, § 190.
}

M.E. [ȳ]
(written *u, ui*)
{
O.E. ȳ (in W. and Central Midl. and S.W.), as in *huithe* 'landing-place', *bruisen, huiren*, 'hear', §§ 158 (c), 170.
O.E. ēō (in W.Midl. and S.W.), as in *lud* 'people', *dure* 'dear', *hulden* pret. pl. 'held', § 168.
O.Fr. ū, as in *fruit, suit*, etc.
}

Diphthongs.

M.E. ai, O.E. ǣġ, as in *dai*, § 171 (1).

M.E. ei, O.E. ěġ, as in *wěi, leide*, § 171 (2).

M.E. oi, O.Fr. *oi*, as in *joie, oystre*, § 200.

M.E. au
{
O.E. -ǎġ, as in *drawen, lawe*, § 171 (7 a).
O.Fr. *au*, as in *faute*, § 196.
O.Fr. *au*, as in *haunten, daunten*, § 183.
}

M.E. ŏu, O.E. -og-, ŏh, as in *dŏuhter*.

M.E. ēi
{
O.E. ǣġ, as in *ēi* 'egg', § 171 (3 a).
O.E. ēag (ǣg), as in *ēye* 'eye', § 171 (3 b).
}

M.E. ēu
{
O.E. ēaw, as in *dēu, schewen*, § 171 (5).
O.E. ēow, as in *blēw, trēwe*, § 171 (6).
O.Fr. *eau*, as in *bēutēe*, § 198.
}

M.E. ōu, O.E. -oga, as in *bōuwe*, O.E. *bŏga* 'bow', § 171 (8).

Summary of the chief characteristics of the M.E. Dialect Groups.

SOUTH-EASTERN : KENTISH ESSEX AND LONDON CITY

§ 202.   KENTISH

A. Sounds.

(1) *e* written for O.E. *æ*; this is later displaced by Midl. *a*: O.E. *eald*, Late O.E. *æld* appears as *ēld*.

(2) *ye, ie* for O.E. *ĕŏ*: *yerþe, chiese, chyese*, etc.

(3) *ya, ia* for O.E. *ĕā*: *hyalde, dyaþ*.

(4) (*a*) *ē* = [ē] for O.E. *ǣ* from *ā—i*: *dēl, clēne*; (*b*) [ē] for Pr. O.E. *ǣ*: *dēd* (as in Nthmb. and Merc.).

(5) *ĕ* for O.E. *ȳ* from *ŭ—i* (*ĕ* in Lt. O.Kt.): *velle* 'fill', *hēþ* 'landing-place', *uēr* 'fire'.

(6) *z-* for *s-*: *zēche* 'seek'.

(7) *u-, v-* for *f-*: *uless* 'flesh', *uox* 'fox'.

B. Accidence.

(8) Retention of *y-* in P. P.
(9) Dropping of *-n* in P. P. and Inf.
(10) Pres. Part. in *-inde*.   As in W. and
(11) 3rd P. Pres. Sing.   Central Sthn.
(12) Pl. Pres.   in *-eþ*.
(13) Pl. Imperat.

(14) *she*, etc., unknown in Fem. Pers. Pron.; usual form *hi*.

(15) *their, them, they*, unknown; only *here, hem, hi*, etc.

(16) The curious form *his* Acc. Pl. 3rd Pers. Also elsewhere in S.E. and S.E. Midl.

§ 203. Kentish compared with Essex and London

A. Sounds.	Kent.	Essex.	London, etc. City.	Middles. and L. London.
(1) O.E. *ǣ*	e	a	a	e-a
(2) O.E. *ăn-i*	-en	-an	-an	-en
(3) (*a*) O.E. *ea* (un- lengthened)	a	a	a	e (later *a*)
(*b*) O.E. *ea* (length- ened) etc.	-ēld,	-ēld	-ōld	-ēld (later *-ōld*)
(4) O.E. *ǣ*[1]	ĕ	ā	ā	ē (ē)
(5) O.E. *ǣ*[2]	ē	ā	ā	ē (ē)
(6) O.E. *ȳ* (*ŭ-i*)	ĕ	ĕ	ĕ	early *ŭ, ĭ* (later *i* (*ü*) (*ĕ*))
(7) O.E. *ĕŏ*	ye, ie	ĕ	ĕ	early round vowel writ- ten *eo, u, o*, later un- rounded to *ĕ*
(8) O.E. *ĕā-i*	ĕ	ĕ	ĕ	traces of *i, u*, in early texts; later only *ē*
(9) O.E. *ēġ, ēh*[1]	*ēy* (*ȳ*)	*ēy*, (*ȳ*)		*ēy*; later rh. w. *ī*.
(10) O.E. *sel-, siel*, etc.		sel-	sel-	traces of sil- and sul-

[1] In the tables the variants of each form are placed in order of the relative frequency in which each occurs. Brackets indicate that the forms which they enclose are very rare.

London, etc.

B. Accidence.	*Kent.*	*Essex.*	*City.*	*Middles. and L. London.*
(11) 3rd Pres. Sing. Pres. Indic.	-eþ	-eþ	-eþ	-þ, -t, -eþ
(12) Pl. Pres. Indic	-eþ	-eþ		early -eþ (-*en*) ; later chiefly -*en* (-*eþ*)
(13) Pres. Part.	*-inde*	-inde, -ende		-inde -ende
(14) P. P.	*i-; -e*	i-; -en, -e		ġe-, i- -en, later -*en*, -*e*
(15) 3rd Pers. Pron. Pl.	hi, hir, hem	hi, her, hem		hi, hij ; later *thei, her, hem*
(16) Acc. Pl. 3rd Pers. Pron.	his	his		his, is, in early texts ; later only *hem*

§ 204.   SOUTH-WEST

A. Sounds.

(1) O.E. *ǣ* (W.Gmc. *ā*) becomes *ē* [ɛ̄] ; *dēd* = [dɛ̄d]. (Also in early London Dialect.)

(2) *ŭ* [*ў*] for O.E. *ȳ* except before front consonant. There appears to have been a large area in which progressive unrounding to *ĭ* took place. On the other hand, in another part of S.W. not yet precisely determined, the rounded vowel seems to have remained until ousted by the other type from surrounding areas. (As in W. and Central Midl. except that unrounding before front consonant is less consistently carried out here than in Sthn.)

(3) O.E. *ǣ* remains as *e* [ɛ̆] in Early texts ; this type, however, replaced by Angl. *ǎ* earlier than in Kentish.

(4) O.E. *ā* becomes [ɔ̄], written *o, oa,* etc. (as in Kent and Midl.).

(5) W.S. *ĭe* (*i*-mutation of *ĕā*), Late W.S. *ў*, retained at first, and written *u*, or often *ui* when long, but soon ousted by non-Sax. *ē*-type.

(6) O.E. initial *f*- written *u, v* (as in Kentish).

B. Accidence.

The principal features are the same as those noted for Kentish.

The forms of Fem. Pers. Pron. Nom. are *heo, hue, he, ha.*
The Pret. of Str. Vbs. formed according to P. P. type.

§ 205.   MIDLAND (See opposite page.)

COMPARATIVE TABLE OF THE MIDLAND DIALECTS

A. *Phonol.*		EAST MIDL.	CENTRAL MIDL.		WEST MIDL.	
	N.E.	*S.E.*		*N.W. Midl.*	*S.W. Midl.*	*Centr. W. Midl.*
(1) O.E. æ	a	early e, a; later an (on) [a only er; ar	an	early e; later a on ar; al	ǎ an a	e, later a on al-; -ar
(2) O.E. *an*	an	an			an a	
(3) O.E. *ea* (unlength.)	-er-, -ar-					
O.E. *ea* (lengthened)	-ōld, (ēld)	-ēld; later *ōld*, and a few survivals of -*ēld*		-old	-ōld	-ōld
(4) O.E. ǣ¹	[ē]	[ē] ([ē])	ē Sth.; ē Nth.	[ē]	[ē]	[ē] rarely [ē]
(5) O.E. ǣ²	[ē] and [ē]	[ē]; rarely [ē] except in Suff.	[ē]	[ē]	[ē]	[ē]
(6) O.E. ў̆	i, e	i, e; no *e* in Norf. till 14th c., then only in W.Norf.	i, and u	u; later *i*	*u* before -*ch, gg* i only before *n*	u; i+n
(7) O.E. ĕŏ	æ̆ĕ	æ̆ [forms	e; no rounded	e (u)	early eo, u, o; later e; e+rk,*u*	e, u; e+back cons.
(8) O.E. ĕā-i	e	e	ē; -el	ē (ēa-i); al (al-i) ēy in West; ī in [East of area	ē, (u); el ēgh, ēy (to end of [14th c.]	ē; al-, later el ēgh, ēy
(9) O.E. *ēag-*						
(10) O.E. *sel-*						
B. *Accidence.*						
(11) 3rd Sing. Pres. Ind.	-es, -ys ; eð	-eð, ið; -es, -is freq. in 14th c.	eþ Sth.; -es Nth.	-es	-eð	-eð
(12) Pres. Pl. Ind.	-en, -yn ; -ys, -s and(e), -ende; -yng	-en, -yn -ende; ande No i-; -en (-e)	-eþ; -es, -en Nth. -ind Sth.; -and [Nth.	-en; -es -and No i-; -en þey; hore; hom	-eð -inde; (-iende) i-; -e	-eð -inde; (-iende) i- early; -en, -e hi; heo; heore; heom
(13) Pres. Part.	No i-; -en, -e					
(14) P.P.						
(15) 3rd Pers. Pron. N.G.D. Pl.	he, later þey; here; þeir; hem, þam	he, later þey, etc.; here; hem (pers.)		Never his, etc.	hi	Never his, etc.
(16) Acc. Pl. 3rd Pers. Pron.	his, es, 13th c.	his, is, es in 13th c.			is occasionally	
(17) Fem. Pron. N. Sing.	she, sche, sho; later she only	scæ (Ld. Chr.); she, sge (Gen. and Ex.)		ho; later *scho* also; (*sche*)	early 14th c. heo; hue	heo, hue, ha
(18) Pres. Pl. of *Be*	bēn, are	bēn; aren, arn, ern		bēn; aren	bēoþ, būiþ, bēþ	bēoþ, būth, bēþ

§ 206.   NORTHERN

A. Sounds.

(1) O.E. *ā* not rounded as in Midl. and Sth. but fronted to
[æ], etc. The spelling *a* remains, but later the fronted vowel
is often written *ai*.

(2) O.E. *y̆* unrounded to *ĭ*. (As in E.Midl.)

(3) O.E. *ō* becomes a sound identical with that of Fr. *ü*,
with which it rhymes: e.g. *sone—fortone*. This Nthn. sound
is written *o, oi, oy, u, ui*.

B. Accidence.

2nd and 3rd Pers. Pres. Sing. -*s*.

Pl. Pres. ends in -*s*.

Pres. Part. ends in -*and*.

Pret. Pl. of Strong Vbs. formed on type of Sing.

Fem. Pers. Pron. *scho*, etc.

Pron. of 3rd Pers. Pl.: *þai, þair, þaim*, etc.; no *h*-forms.

Loss of suffix syllable of Inf.

§ 207. SUMMARY OF THE HISTORY OF THE DIALECT OF
LONDON TO BEGINNING OF THE FIFTEENTH CENTURY

The accompanying table gives the chief phonological features
and the characteristic points of accidence of a number of texts,
written in London or the surrounding areas. As a basis of
comparison, the features, on the one hand, of Vices and Virtues,
which all recent students of the subject agree to regard as
exhibiting the Essex dialect, and those of Essex Pl. Ns. are
added, and, on the other, the phonological features of Middles.
Pl. Ns.

It will be seen that the phonological character of the old
City of London names is, as Heuser pointed out, practically
identical with that of Essex, although in Nos. 6, 9, and 10 the
influence of the Middles. dialect is observable.

The principal features which distinguish this (Essex and
City) dialect type from that of Middles. of the same period
are No. (1), *a* where early Middles., both in texts and Pl. Ns.,
has *e*; No. (2), Ess. *al*, Middles. *el*; No. (4), Ess. *an*, Middles.
en; Nos. (5) and (6), Ess. *ā*, Middles. *ē* = [ē]; Nos. (7) and
(8), where Ess. has no trace of a rounded vowel, whereas
Middles. Pl. Ns. and the texts have very definite traces
of this in the early period; Nos. (9) and (10), Ess. and City
prevailing *e*, contrasted with typical Middles. *i* or *u*; No. (11),
where Ess. has only *ĕ* whereas the early Middles. or London
texts have occasional *i* and *u*; No. (12), where Ess. has only
sel- whereas early Middles. has occasional *sil-, syl-*.

TABLE showing main typical features of London-Middlesex Dialect, contrasted with that of Essex and the City of London.

	V. and V. Ess. Pl. Ns.	City N's.	Westm. Ch.	Lamb. Homs.	Trin. Homs.	Procl. Hen. III.	Davy.	Chaucer.	Hoccl.	Hist. S. Barthol.	Middles. Pl. Ns. West of Westm. (1150–1300).
(1) O.E. æ	a	a	æ, e; a	e; (a)	a; (e) er (ar)	a, e	a	a	a	a	et, Hesel
(2) { O.E. -ear + Cons -ar- } { O.E. -eall, and -alf, } eal + Cons.	-ar- all, -alf,	al-	-er ell, all	all	alf, etc.	all	-all,	-ar er	ar; er all	-al	-el early; al later
(3) O.E. -eald	-ēld	-ēld	ēld, eald, ǣld; (ōld)	eald, ǣld; (ald)	eald, ēld (-old;ald)	-eald, -āld	-en	ōld; (hōlde Inf.)	ōld	-oold, -old	-ēld, later -ōld
(4) O.E. -en (> an -ĭ)	-an (-æn)	-an-	-en, -an	-en	en; -en	en; -en	-en	-en		-en-	-en, an on Ess. border Daneland
(5) O.E. ǣ¹	ā (æ, e)	ā	ā; ǣ, ē	e	æ, ea	æ, e	[ɛ; ē]	[ɛ; ē]	[ɛ̄, ē, ɛ̆]	e	-ā; a few ā on Ess. border
(6) O.E. ǣ²	ā (ǣ, ē)	ā (e)	ā; ē e; eo	ē; ea eo, o; e	æ, ea e; (eo, u)	æ, e eo, u	e	[ɛ; (ē)] e	[ɛ̄, (ē)] ĕ	e e	-ā̆ e; but trace of rounded form soven = '7'
(7) O.E. ēo	e	e	e; eo, o	e; eo	ie; (eo)	eo	ē	ē	ē	e	
(8) O.E. ēo	ē	ē	ī	eo			ē	ē	ī (ē)	y, i	ē; traces of u and o spellings
(9) O.E. ȳ	e	e (ī, ū)	i, (u); (e) i; e	u	ī, (u, ui); (ie)	u, i (e)	i e	i, u; ē e	ī, e, (u) ē	i; (e) ē	u and i; e only on Ess. border or near City
(10) O.E. y̆	e	e e		u, i	i, w; (e)						i, u generally long i; but Rislip̄e; short e
(11) O.E. ēa -i	e			ē; (schup-pend)	e; gist shippend						
(12) O.E. sel-	sel-		sil-, syl; (sel)	sel-; sul-	sel-	sel-		sel-			
(13) 3rd Pers. Pron. Pl. N.G.D.	hie (hi, he); here; hem		hi, hy; here; heom hi (his)	he; hem, hie, he ham; hire, here	hie, he (þei)		hij; her	thei; her; hem	they; hire; hem	thei; them; ther them	
(14) 3rd Pers. Pron. Acc. Pl.	his, is, hes			hes	hes, is		no his	no his, etc.	[-t; (s)]		
(15) 3rd Pres. Sing.	-eð		-t, -ð -eð	-eð	-eð	-en; eð	-eþ	-eth, -ith	-eth; -th	-ith	
(16) Pl. Pres.	-eð; (en)		-eð, -að, -að; (-en)	-eð, -en, (e)	-en; eð		-eþ	-en, -e -inge	-en, -e -ing, -ynge	-eð, -yð; -yn; -e	
(17) Pres. Part.	-inde; -ende		ge-	-inde; -ende	-inde; -ende	-inde	-ing				
(18) Str. P.P. (a) prefix	i-, ʒe-	ge-		i-	i-; no pref.	i-	i-	i- freq.	i- freq.	i- often	
(b) ending	-en; -e	-en	-en	-en; -e	-en; (-e)	-en; -en -e	-e; -en	-e; -en	en; -e	-en; -e	

It is thus evident that the City dialect was S.E. of the Ess. type, whereas that of the county itself was quite different, and belonged to a more westerly type. The early Westm. Ch. in respect of dialect is a kind of intermediate link between the City and county types; it shows the influence of the former, notably in points 1, 4, 5, 6, but it belongs more closely to Middles. proper; note points 1, (occasional *e*); 2, (*er, el*); 4, *-en* as prevailing form; the rounded vowels in 7 and 8; the almost complete absence of *e*-forms in 9 and 10. Of the two early collections of Homilies, Trinity is rather nearer to the City type than Lambeth, but agrees far more closely with the Middles. Pl. Ns. and with the later dialect of London. The traces of City dialect are: prevailing *ă* for *ĕ* in 1; *-alf-* and occasional *-ar-* in 2; the rare *e* in 9 and 10; the rare *-an-* in 4. Of the characteristic City and Essex feature *ā* in 5 and 6 there appears to be no trace. Still more purely Middles. in phonology are the Lamb. Homs. This is particularly observable in 1, 4, 5, 6, 7, 8, 9, 10, 11, where the prevailing forms are clearly distinguished from those of the City and Essex. It is interesting to note that Lamb., Trin., and Westm. Ch. all agree with Ess. in using the form *hes*, *is*, in the Acc. Pl. of the Pron. of the 3rd Pers. Pl. This feature, which is found also in early S.E. Midl. texts, and in Kt. as late as the fourteenth century, may well have been general in the early Middles. dialect. The Procl. of Hen. III is very meagre in its evidence, and is obviously deliberately following as far as possible the conventional O.E. spelling. As far as it goes it agrees pretty closely with the phonology of Middles. Pl. Ns., and has none of the features characteristic of the City dialect, except the solitary *e* in 10. The later texts agree pretty closely among themselves in phonology and accidence, and exhibit on the whole that peculiar combination of features which, from the fourteenth century onwards, we recognize as the normal dialect of London, a type which early in the following century we begin to think of as the standard for official and literary English. Chaucer's frequent use of *ĕ* for O.E. *ў̆*, which is alien to the Middles. dialect proper, has already been discussed, § 151 (4) above.

Now if we compare the London English from Davy onwards, with that of the early City type on the one hand, and with that of the early texts and Pl. Ns. of London and Middlesex on the other, we find that it presents a considerable contrast to both in several respects.

We may enumerate the chief points of difference between the earlier and later forms of London and Middlesex dialect:

	Earlier Middles.	*Later Middles. and London.* (14th c. and later.)
(1) O.E. ǣ	chiefly *e*	*a* as sole form. (Probably influence of City type.)
(2) O.E. *eal*+f; *eall-* etc. *-eard-* etc.	*-elf*; *-el*, etc. *-erd*	*-alf*, *-all* etc. ⎫ (Probably *-ard* ⎭ City influence.)
(3) O.E. *-eald-* etc.	*-ēld*	*-ōld* practically the only form; rare survivals *hēlden* (P.P. etc.) in Chaucer (new form possibly from Bucks. dialect)
(4) O.E. *ĕŏ*	rounded vowel survives to some extent; un-rounding not complete.	no trace of rounded vowel; *ĕ* sole forms; (due to gradual un-rounding process).
(5) O.E. *y̆*	*i* prevailing form; *u* often written; varying degrees of un-rounding existing among differ-ent speakers; *e*-type very rare and found only on Ess. border, or in neighbourhood of City	(*a*) un-rounding complete; *i* the usual form (*b*) some forms with rounding re-introduced in 14th and 15th c.'s; probably from Herts. (*c*) *e*- forms far more frequent; introduced from City type
(6) O.E. *an-i* (*sendan* etc.)	City *an*-type fairly com-mon in easterly areas of county (Westm.), and occasional in county farther west; *-en* the chief type	*-en* the only type; *an*- type disappears even in City, and on Ess. border
(7) O.E. *ǣ*[1] and *ǣ*[2]	City *ā* type spread to Westm.; found in other parts of county on Ess. borders. Prevailing type [ɛ̄]	*ā*- type completely vanished from London area and Middlesex; (*a*) *ǣ*[1] evidently [ɛ̄] as pre-vailing type; occasional [ē] in rhymes (*b*) *ǣ*[2] [ɛ̄] practically uni-versal; rare [ē] in rhymes

It appears, then, that in the earliest M.E. period there were in London and Middlesex two very distinct dialectal types : (1) the CITY TYPE, practically identical with that of Essex ; and (2) the Middles. county type which we have called CENTRAL SOUTHERN. Westminster Chartulary exhibits an intermediate variety possessing several characteristic features from both of its neighbours, east and west.

The fourteenth century London dialect is a development of that of the Middles. county type, but by this time it has lost some of its earlier features, these having been ousted in favour of others, penetrating, whether from the City, whether from Herts., whether from such a westerly area as Bucks.

NOTE. The chief peculiarities of the Accidence of the various texts are dealt with in Chapter IX below.

CHAPTER VII

HISTORY OF ENGLISH SOUNDS

III. THE MODERN PERIOD

§ 208. WE have seen in the preceding chapter that there occurs sporadically, in the MSS. of the period covered by the 12th, 13th, and 14th centuries, direct evidence that some of the vowel sounds are being altered from their original or earlier pronunciation, and are apparently tending towards one nearer to that of the present day. But what is direct evidence of change in one vowel sound may be at the same time indirect evidence that a change must have occurred in other sounds also. For if we are satisfied that the *ou* spellings for O.E. *ō* (§ 163) in *bouk*, *touk*, etc. imply that a stage resembling [ū] has been reached, we are bound to infer also that, before this stage was actually attained, O.E. *ū* in *hous*, etc. had been altered, to some extent at least, from its original sound, though it need by no means have reached its present [*au*] stage. It is clear that if old *ō* had ever caught up old *ū*, so that there was a time when they were pronounced exactly alike, the subsequent history of the two sounds, now become one, must have been identical, and if the tendency which has made old *ū* into [*au*] had started *after* the new [ū] had developed from *ō*, it must have affected all the words containing this old *ō* as much as those containing original [ū], and we should now pronounce [*bauk*, *tauk*] for O.E. *bōc*, *tōc*, etc. We may say, then, that evidence, direct or indirect, exists, which proves that the tendencies which have made our present vowel sounds such as they are, were operative during the M.E. period.

When the moment arrives at which these tendencies culminate and when a considerable number of vowel sounds have been so far altered that they are either identical with the sounds of the present day, or so closely approximated to them that they resemble these far more nearly than they resemble the old so-called 'continental' sounds, then the age of whose speech this can be asserted must be claimed as part of the modern period.

To refuse to designate as modern what is characteristically so in a dozen ways is to rob the term of all meaning as applied to the history of English. From a body of evidence which appears to admit of no other interpretation, we conclude that by the first third, at latest, of the fifteenth century, over the greater part of England, the typical M.E. pronunciation had passed away, and that the greater number of the characteristic modern sounds were already developed, while the rest were far on the way to being so. By the beginning of the sixteenth century the actual vowel sounds of Standard English were practically those of to-day. The evidence for these statements will be given when we come to deal with the vowels in detail.

It is not asserted that the exact shade of sound now heard in Standard English had developed, in each case, in the corresponding form of English in the fifteenth century. But the following changes had certainly come about: (1) M.E. $\bar{a}$ had been fronted; (2) M.E. $\bar{e}^1$ had become [ī]; (3) M.E. $\bar{e}^2$ had become [ē], and in some dialects had probably already been raised to [ī]; (4) M.E. $\bar{\imath}$ had been diphthongized, probably to [əi]; (5) M.E. tense $\bar{o}$ had become $\bar{u}$, and the first shortening had already taken place, to [u], in some dialects; (6) M.E. $\breve{u}$ in *run, bud*, etc. had been un-rounded in many dialects, to something like [a], and since this change involves also the shortened $\breve{u}$ from new $\bar{u}$ (as in No. 5), cp. present-day *glove, blood*, etc., it follows that this shortening preceded the un-rounding process; (7) M.E. $\bar{u}$ had been diphthongized, and had probably reached the [ɔu] stage, though in some dialects the first element had apparently been un-rounded, giving something very like our present [au] in *south*, etc.; (8) M.E. and Early Mod. *au* had been monophthongized to [ɔ], e. g. in *taught, all*, etc.; (9) M.E. $\bar{e}u$, *iu* had either been monophthongized to [ȳ] or still remained at the [iy] stage; in any case they rhymed with M.E. [ȳ] from Fr. sources, and the spellings *eu, ew, u* are interchangeable—*dewke* 'duke', *dew* 'due' and *hue* for M.E. $h\bar{e}u$, O.E. $h\bar{e}ow$ 'hewed', etc.; (10) M.E. *ai* had become a monophthong, probably [ē] by the end of the century; (11) M.E. [ȳ] as in *just, judge*, etc., had been un-fronted, or retracted to [$\breve{u}$] in time to undergo un-rounding together with the [$\breve{u}$] mentioned in No. 6, and that in No. 5, so that early in the sixteenth century *just* rhymes with *must*; (12) M.E. $\breve{a}$, in *began, back*, etc. had apparently become a front vowel [æ] in some dialects of English, although it would appear that the fronted type did not penetrate into Standard English for another century at least. Such a combination of differences from the typical M.E. vowel system, all of which can be proved to have existed in the fifteenth century, warrants us, for the moment, in placing the beginning of the Modern period in

L

that century; subsequent investigations may compel us to put it earlier still.

§ 209. Special Problems of the Modern Period.

The study of the written documents of the fifteenth century tends to be concentrated rather upon questions concerning chronological developments in the language than upon those varieties of dialect which are so striking a feature in M.E. writings.   During the fifteenth century Regional dialect gradually disappears from written English, not only in works which have some pretensions to be called literature, but also from written documents of a private character.   What is usually called London English, for this type first grew up in the Metropolis (§ 207), becomes more and more the predominating form, and is used before the end of the century, for all purposes, by persons from all parts of the country, so soon as they wish to communicate their thoughts in writing.   This widespread use of London English has often been attributed to, or even dated from, the introduction of printing.   But while undoubtedly the dissemination of works which every one could read helped to hasten the process, it had begun before Caxton's labours started, and the letters of John Shillingford, Mayor of Exeter (1447–50), and the Governance of England by Sir John Fortescue (1471–6), also a Devonian, are on the whole very fair representatives of the London English of the day, although the former contains a few unmistakable South Westernisms, while the latter appears to show no traces of provincialism.   Indeed Gower, in the previous century, although a Kentishman, has but few marked provincialisms in his English writings.   It seems probable, therefore, that if printing had never been invented at all, the London type would, from the pressure of social and political causes, and owing to the prestige, among writers, of that form of English used by Chaucer, have ultimately become the dominant dialect, the vehicle of literature, and the recognized medium for all writing. To ascribe the predominance of this dialect to Caxton is to misrepresent the facts.   His labours promoted, but could not start, what had already begun.

But while provincial dialects become henceforth very unimportant, they did not die out simply because they were no longer used in writing.   As we know, they flourish to-day as the normal means of verbal communication among thousands of our countrymen, sadly battered and mutilated it is true, and considerably modified by Standard English, but still preserving much that is strange in vocabulary, and even a few genuine traces of their ancient phonological character. In the fifteenth century, however, the Regional Dialects of English, especially in districts remote from London, while sharing in those chronological changes which affected the language generally, still retained in the main their old typical regional character. Men continued, for several centuries longer, to speak the dialect natural to their native province, although the higher ranks, and others who had occasion to move about the country, acquired also, as a rule, the type of English employed in the metropolis, which was now gaining increasing currency as a spoken form, all over the country. The letters of Shillingford have been already referred to, as exhibiting traces of provincial influence, and the same is true of the private letters of the Paston's, the Cely's, and others of the fifteenth century. Much later, in the sixteenth and even in the seventeenth century, there are occasional traces of provincialism, in isolated forms, in private and in published writings, and in the rhymes of poets.

§ 210. The Spoken Standard.

It is difficult to prove, though we may surmise, the existence, during the fifteenth century, of a keen sense that one type of spoken English was 'good', the 'right' one to use, and that other types were vulgar. During the sixteenth century, the remarks of professional and other writers on pronunciation, a passage in Puttenham's *Arte of English Poesie* (1580), and scattered remarks occurring both in letters and published works, during this century, leave no doubt that a standard of speech was perfectly recognized, namely that of the Court, and of the upper classes who frequented it. Among others, Sir Thomas Elyot writes, in the *Gouernour*, of the sons of noblemen and gentlemen learning a 'corrupt and foul pronunciation' from their 'nourishes' and other 'folisshe women'. It is not to be supposed that the Standard at that time was anything like so definite and settled in its character as at present. Much greater latitude was permitted, than at present, in the use of variants in pronunciation and in grammatical forms. To speak with the accent of a rural district, even at Court, was not derogatory to the character and prestige of a gentleman, who might be supposed to speak the dialect in vogue on his own estate. Sir Walter Raleigh, in spite of his experience of the Court and of the world, and notwithstanding his many graces and accomplishments, never lost the accent of his native Devon. What was not tolerated, was to speak like a tradesman. And this brings us to an important point.

§ 211. Two Kinds of Dialect.

(1) The dialects, in the old sense of the term, the only one we need take account of in dealing with M.E., that is forms of speech associated with specific geographical areas, have passed out of literature, except as quaint and eccentric revivals. They have also largely perished in their native habitats, and are constantly losing ground even among the inhabitants of remote country villages. The schools, the parsons, and other founts of light, are gradually, sometimes deliberately, sometimes unconsciously, contributing to oust the native local speech, by precept and example. The place of the old local form is being taken by what is still called by some 'Standard English', and certainly it may be supposed to aim at reproducing that more current form which is known as 'good, educated,' English. The English now spoken by the more sophisticated villagers certainly differs from the pure old local dialect, but is it identical with the English heard, let us say, in an Oxford Common Room, or in an Officers' Mess? We should probably say that it was not.

(2) In large towns there are perhaps tens, or even hundreds, of thousands of persons who have never themselves spoken, nor heard their usual associates speak, a country dialect ; whose parents and forbears for several generations have never spoken a rustic dialect. These persons, representing various occupations, and positions in life—errand-boys, shop-boys, mechanics, shop-keepers, clerks of various grades, and so on, have often what is called a 'vulgar' accent. Their speech is not a provincial dialect, and again it is certainly not that of the politest circles. What is it? It is evident that there are forms of English which are neither pure local dialect nor pure Standard English, although they may perhaps resemble the latter more than the former. Both the sophisticated rustic and the town vulgarian speak a form of the standard language, yet one far removed from the most refined and most graceful type.

We have to recognize the existence of two kinds of dialect, which owe their several origins to different circumstances.

The old provincial or local dialects, which it is convenient to call *Regional Dialects*, owe their long-standing differences to the factors of geographical isolation (see §§ 66, etc.). The other kind of dialects, which owe their variations from each other primarily to social causes, we may for convenience call *Class Dialects*.

Every one who does not speak a Regional dialect, speaks a Class dialect. Chief among the latter we must reckon what

is usually called *Standard English,* that is, the best and most
refined type of English, that which in one form or another has
long been usurping the place of the old Regional dialects.
This Standard is, in origin, as we have seen, the speech of
London, and the best type of it was formerly held to be that
which grew up at the King's Court. But it would be misleading
now, to speak of this as London English, since it is no longer
confined to London, but is spoken all over the country among
those who do not speak Regional Dialect. But since there are
many types of pronunciation among these speakers, many
varieties, that is, of Standard, some further definition is required.
It is proposed to use the term *Received Standard* for that form
which all would probably agree in considering the best, that
form which has the widest currency and is heard with practically no variation among speakers of the better class all over
the country. This type might be called Public School
English. It is proposed to call the vulgar English of the
Towns, and the English of the Villager who has abandoned
his native Regional Dialect, *Modified Standard.* That is, it is
Standard English, modified, altered, differentiated, by various
influences, regional and social. Modified Standard varies from
class to class, and from locality to locality ; it has no uniformity,
and no single form of it is heard outside a particular class or
a particular area.

These facts are so patent that they have merely to be stated
to command assent by all who consider questions of this kind.

The existence of Modified Standard is not only a reality,
but it has an important bearing on the history of English.
For while Received Standard is also a reality, it is a variable
one, and changes from age to age, so that what in one age is
elegant, polite, and fashionable in speech, is held, within a few
generations, to be old-fashioned, and may thence come to be
considered vulgar. Conversely, what the Received Standard
of one age considers vulgar, affected, absurd, may gradually
pass into the Received Standard of a later day, and become
fully accepted, and current among the best speakers. These
changes in taste, and in the standards of 'correctness' and
propriety, in speech, are due to that shifting of the social
structure which, without violent cataclysms, has been constantly taking place, from economic and political causes, during
the last two or three centuries. The result of this has been
that the old upper classes, whose speech was the Received
Standard when this first emerged from the chaos of uncouth
provincialism, have been slowly mingled with the classes from
below, who brought with them not only their ruder manners,

and new and strange tricks, of coarseness on one hand, and of squeamishness on the other, but also their various types of Modified Standard. The new men, it is true, learned the speech of the class they entered, but they put, and left, their own characteristic marks upon it. The changes which, as we shall have occasion to note later on, have befallen Received Standard since the time of Elizabeth, are very largely, as it appears, due to the influence, continuously exerted from age to age, of Modified Standard in one form or another. For the last three or four hundred years, the influence of Regional Dialect upon the main current of English speech appears to have been almost nil, at any rate as concerns pronunciation and grammar. Some trifling influence on the vocabulary may perhaps be discernible from this source.

§ 212. Changes in Received Standard during the Modern Period.

To make the bearing of the above general remarks clearer, and their application more concrete, it is desirable, even at this stage, to go into a little more detail as to the precise nature of those changes, or shiftings, in the standard, which are alluded to. Speaking generally, we may say that in the actual sounds of English speech, there has been comparatively little change since perhaps the middle of the sixteenth century. Yet much has happened, not only in respect of the idioms, and the grammatical forms used, but also in the pronunciation. What has happened is that although, in the main, the stock of sounds is the same, or nearly so, as it was at the beginning of Elizabeth's reign, the *distribution* of them is different. This means that we now use in many cases, in a given word, not a type of pronunciation which has developed by the ordinary processes of sound change from that which was current in Elizabeth's time, but a different type altogether, a type which certainly existed in the sixteenth century, but which, so far as our evidence goes, was not the current type in use among the best speakers, but was perhaps then confined to a comparatively small group. It is certain that in the sixteenth century, and far on into the eighteenth century, words which in M.E. contained $\bar{e}^2$, e.g. *stream, dream, heat, meat, sea,* and dozens more, were pronounced with a mid-front vowel, probably tense [ē], and that the above words rhymed, and were used by the poets as rhyming, with such words as *name, fate, away* respectively. We now pronounce all the words of the first group with [ī]. But nothing could be more mistaken than to suppose that in this case [ē] has become [ī] since the early eighteenth century, by a phonetic change parallel to that which long before had made M.E. [ē] into [ī]. If such a late change had taken place, it must have involved also words containing M.E. ā, and the second group of words above would now be [nīm, fīt], etc. No; the change of M.E. ē² to [ī] did indeed take place, but in the fifteenth century, and it did not, apparently, affect the London dialect. This new type of pronunciation, though it occasionally appears in a very few words of the *stream* class as early as the sixteenth century, was evidently not the type current among either the courtiers or the poets. The change must have been confined to a small group of speakers, the majority, including speakers of the Received Standard of the day, long adhering to the other type. During the latter part of the eighteenth century it is evident that gradually, word after word containing M.E. ē² came to be pronounced according to the [ī] type. Now, we pronounce in this way all words of this class, except *break*, *great*, and *steak*. What has happened is that for some reason or other one type has been gradually abandoned, and another gradually adopted. See § 232.

Again, during the eighteenth century we notice a gradual giving up of the type with -ar- in M.E. words which had -er-. Thus *learn, servant, service, heard, sermon, divert, diversion*, etc., etc. appear to be pronounced according to the fashion in which we now pronounce them, by an increasing number of speakers, after the middle of the eighteenth century, whereas they were formerly pronounced [lān, sāvənt, hād, dɪvāʃən], etc., or at any rate according to the type which at the present time would be pronounced in this way had it survived, as indeed it has in other words, such as *hart, heart, hearth, Derby*, etc.

Here again, one type has been given up among the best speakers, and another adopted. The same thing has happened in the pronunciation of dozens of isolated words. For instance, *Rome, gold, oblige, yellow, farthing, Edward* were pronounced by polite speakers [rūm, gūld, oʊblīdʒ, jælə, fā(r)dɪn, ɛdə(r)d], and some of these pronunciations were still heard within living memory, though they are now all passed away except among the vulgar.

There are other isolated words whose pronunciation has been changed during the lifetime of those who are now but middle-aged, of which the older and the newer types are still both current. Thus *humour, waistcoat, forehead, landscape, often, neighbourhood, handkerchief*, until a few years ago were universally pronounced by good speakers, as [jūmə, wɛskət, fɔrɪd, lænskɪp, ɔfn, ɔfn, néɪbrʊd, hænkətʃɪf] respectively; now, even otherwise good speakers are sometimes heard to say [hjūmə, wéɪstkoʊt, fɔ̄hɛd, lǽndskeɪp, ɔ̄ftən, hǽnkətʃɪf], while [néɪbəhʊd] is now almost universal. Yet within the memory of the present writer, all the pronunciations indicated in the second group were considered hopelessly vulgar, and indeed are still felt to be so by many, though they are gradually getting a footing in Received Standard, and in a generation or so will no doubt be fully established there. There is small doubt that all these alterations in the older Received Standard came originally from below, and represent attempts at greater correctness and refinement on the part of persons who lacked the tradition of the old established polite usage. The latest innovations cited above are the result of the same process, and come ultimately from the same source as the older substitutions. They are, in fact, all examples of the influence of Modified Standard. Enough has perhaps been said to indicate that no student of the history of English can afford to ignore this factor. It may be added that whatever influence is now exerted by the Regional Dialects, upon Received Standard, generally comes through the medium of some form of Modified Standard.

Some fairly categorical statements have been made in the preceding paragraphs, about the pronunciation of English, during the fifteenth and following centuries, and we cannot with propriety delay any longer a statement of the grounds on which these were made, and a description of the kind of evidence available.

This may be grouped under four main heads :—(1) Spellings in such documents as are not written purely according to scribal tradition, and which are not characterized by a rigid adherence to the rules of 'correct' spelling; (2) Rhymes of poets; (3) General considerations of the whole history of English; (4) Statements by writers on pronunciation, and grammarians, concerning the English of their own day; this source is not available until the end of the first third of the sixteenth century. We proceed to deal with these points in order.

SOURCES OF INFORMATION CONCERNING THE HISTORY OF
ENGLISH PRONUNCIATION SINCE CHAUCER

§ 213.   (1) SPELLINGS

It was formerly held that soon after the close of the fourteenth century, and especially after the introduction of printing, English spelling had become so fixed and conventional that little or nothing could be learnt from it. Scribes, it was said, and still more printers, no longer altered the spelling to suit a changing pronunciation. The amount of obvious truth in this statement was just sufficient to prevent people from recognizing the still greater amount of misapprehension which it gave birth to, and the unfortunate error which it suggested. It is true that in the fifteenth century, no less than in the fourteenth, or earlier, the most careful scribes spell according to a traditional plan. They take no account, except now and then, when the human machine fails for a moment, of the facts of pronunciation, so far as these were the result of changes arising naturally in the course of time, though, fortunately, they do record dialectal variants. It almost seems, indeed, as if the scribes were determined that the truth should not leak out through any act of theirs. It is also true that Caxton and the other early printers, instead of bringing English spelling up to date, as had long been desirable, simply took over the methods of the most 'correct' and conventional scribes they could find, and they may be said to have stereotyped English spelling for ever, in all its essential features. But even Caxton and his immediate followers do occasionally, though rarely, depart from convention, and lapse for a moment into a phonetic spelling. We may note in passing that these occasional phonetic spellings continue to occur in a sporadic way in printed books for several centuries. Thus those who know what to look for, though they do not always perhaps include those who know most of textual criticism, may find very informing spellings in the early Folios and Quartos of Shakespeare. There is, however, another, and by no means uninteresting class of writing, much of which has now been printed, which yields information of great value for our purpose. While in the fourteenth century there are but few private letters in English written by the hands of their real authors, from early in the fifteenth century onwards, private persons wrote their letters more and more in English, and with their own hands. Fortunately many collections of these have been preserved. Now the importance of the private, often unlearned person, compared with the professional scribe, is that the former, no matter how lofty his station in life, very often cared but little for scribal tradition, constantly forgot it, and therefore drifted unconsciously into a spelling which expressed, more or less faithfully, his pronunciation. The list of collections of letters and diaries, given on p. 13 above, represents only a small portion of this kind of material which has been already printed, but as a glance shows, even this short list includes documents ranging from the first quarter of the fifteenth century to about the same part of the eighteenth. It is difficult to over-rate the importance of the evidence which these writings afford. Many of them are so natural, unstudied, and artless, that in reading them we almost feel that we are overhearing conversation.

When we find a certain kind of spelling which differs from that of M.E. tradition, occurring, whether in the same word, or in a whole class of words all containing the same sound, independently, in document after document throughout several centuries, this in itself establishes a strong presumption that such a departure from tradition has a meaning, and that it expresses some reality in the speech of those who make it. When further it turns out that these occasional spellings, as it is convenient to call them, point in the direction of changes which, as we know from other sources, have actually taken place in English; when we have ourselves heard the pronunciations which the spellings suggest; when even the Grammarians indicate the same pronunciations, sometimes both by description and by a simple phonetic spelling, identical with that into which the letter-writers, etc., have naturally and unconsciously lapsed in their hasty, unstudied writing; when the pronunciation thus suggested is already implied also by the poets in their rhymes, it would be rash indeed to refuse to credit the evidence thus afforded. The fact is, that so far from the spelling of the fifteenth century being valueless as a guide to the pronunciation of the day, it is actually more conclusive and enlightening, if only we study it in the right kind of documents, than is the spelling of most documents written from the beginning of the thirteenth to the end of the fourteenth century. If these facts were not fully recognized until quite lately, this is simply because the rich treasury of information about spoken English which exists in the numerous collections of private papers of all kinds, has been for a long time neglected and unexplored by students of our language. A vast mine of valuable ore, still almost unquarried by English philologists, awaits investigation, in the many volumes of State Papers, and in the publications of the Surtees and Camden Societies, to mention no more. And these by-ways of literature will supply us with information, not merely on the pronunciation of the past, but on the grammatical forms, the current vocabulary of everyday life, and on colloquial idiom as well. In fact the attentive perusal of such collections as the Paston Letters, the Cely Papers, Gabriel Harvey's Letters, those of Lady Hungerford, of Queen Elizabeth and the Verneys, brings the reader into a more intimate touch with the spoken language, and gives a clearer view of some aspects of the genius and spirit of the centuries to which they belong, than can be gained from the study of the great works of literature alone.

The credit of first pointing out, in a conclusive manner, the value of the occasional spellings as throwing light on pronunciation, must be given to Professor Zachrisson of Upsala, who, in his very important work *The Pronunciation of English Vowels from 1400–1700* (see Bibliogr., p. 11), brought together a considerable number of these spellings from documents written in the fifteenth and sixteenth centuries, and proved by his acute interpretation of this new evidence, that the chronology of the Modern English sound changes, as commonly accepted, must be reconsidered, and that it should be dated much earlier than students of the subject had hitherto believed.

Subsequent and more extended investigations on the same lines have confirmed Professor Zachrisson's views in all vital points, and we may now perhaps, with some confidence, feel justified in going even farther than he was inclined to go in 1912, in putting the origin of the principal characteristic Modern features of English back into the past. (See also § 152.) It certainly does not follow that because the first spelling actually noted, which indicates a 'new' pronunciation, occurs, let us say, in a document written in 1430, that this is the earliest date at which the change in question was fully accomplished. We may be quite right in saying that it *was* accomplished at latest by then, but we are not bound to any particular earlier limit. This must always be a matter of speculation so long as the evidence is defective. Caution is necessary in all investigation, but while we must guard against rashness, we must also beware of undue timidity.

§ 214. (2) WHAT CAN BE LEARNT FROM THE RHYMES OF POETS

The study of rhymes may throw most useful light on our problems, but the limitations of this source of information must be faced, and we must not base too much upon rhymes alone, unsupported by other evidence. In the first place it is clear, that supposing we are persuaded that our rhymes are really sound and reliable, all they can establish, in a given case, is that two words have a common sound, but the rhyme by itself cannot inform us what the precise character of that sound was. To determine this we must invoke help from an independent quarter. Thus, if we find the word *sea* rhyming

in a whole series of poets, within a given period, with such
words as *obey*, *play*, *sway*, *away*, etc., there is a probability
that the vowel in *sea* was pronounced in the same way as that in
the other words, but we must ascertain by further inquiries what
that common sound was. Such a rhyme as *care—were*, occurring
as it does in 1420, arrests attention. We know that the older
poets, even in the fourteenth century, would not habitually
rhyme these two words. We know also that the vowel in
were was never anything but a front vowel, generally [ē], in a
stressed position, and that *care* has *ā* in M.E. Now [ā, ē] are
so different in sound that it seems highly improbable that
even the worst poet should rhyme them together. The inference is that M.E. *ā* had already been fronted, and that the
rhyme intended was [kēr—wēr]. Is there any reason why this
change should not have taken place as early as 1420? We
may further ask why should the rhymester have departed
from M.E. tradition at all, unless his rhyme were a good one.
But if the rhyme were not good, that is, if M.E. *ā* had not
been fronted, and assimilated in sound to M.E. *ē²*, how came
he to anticipate a sound change which certainly did take place
at one time or another, since our present-day pronunciation,
in which *were—care* do rhyme, is the result of it, unless it had
already taken place in the form of English with which he was
familiar? Here, by applying a little elementary historical
knowledge, and using ordinary common sense, we reach the view
that this rhyme establishes a strong probability that M.E. *ā*
had become a front vowel as early as 1420.

Again, we know that in M.E., *ă* and other short vowels were
lengthened in open syllables, and therefore that such a word
as *blăc* 'black', must have had inflected forms such as *blāke*,
and *smăl*, inflected forms *smāle*, as in Chaucer's *smāle foules*,
etc. These doublets have now disappeared, but they survive
in the surnames *Blake* and *Smale*, and they may well long
have survived as variants, by the side of the originally short
forms *black* and *small*. The history of the language teaches
us how these forms arose, and we are therefore not surprised to
find them in the rhymes of sixteenth-century poets, e. g. in
Sackville's rhyme *black—lake*, and Surrey's *smale* (here the
actual spelling is retained) with *tale*, *pale*, *bale*, etc. Such
a rhyme as Milton's *end—fiend* would be surprising from the
present point of view, but the history of English informs us
that vowels were lengthened before *-nd*, and that *eend* is not an
uncommon M.E. spelling; further, the survival of this type is
confirmed by Cooper (1685), who writes *eend* to express the
pronunciation of the word. A careful survey of the rhymes

of several of the principal poets of the sixteenth and seventeenth centuries, if checked by the application of critical tests such as the occurrence of occasional spellings which point to a type of pronunciation identical with that demanded in order to constitute a good rhyme, and an appeal to the testimony of contemporary writers on English pronunciation, establishes the fact that although, here and there, out-and-out bad rhymes do occur, even in the best poets, these writers present on the whole a singularly faithful mirror of the speech of their time. Again and again some rhyme which appears freakish is shown to be consistent with a type of pronunciation actually current when the rhyme in question was made. This is a valuable piece of information, which has its interest also for the student of our older literature, and entitles us to urge the importance of rhymes as contributory to, and confirmatory of, other kinds of evidence.

It must be borne in mind, however, that poets are usually conservative in their use of language, and that they follow a tradition set by their great predecessors. This may lead them, basing their usage upon the authority of earlier poets, to use rhymes which are no longer perfect, though they once were so. These purely traditional rhymes are usually of the class known as eye-rhymes, such as *wood—flood, love—prove*, etc., which survive to the present day. Such rhymes need to be tested in order to discover, from other sources, whether the two words thus linked together really had the same vowel in the current pronunciation of a given age.

A few instances may be given in which rhymes apparently faulty are fully vindicated as good and perfect during the sixteenth and seventeenth centuries. The Earl of Surrey rhymes the Past Participle *swollen* with *bemoan*, clearly implying that no *l*- sound was pronounced in the former word. We might hesitate to accept this as proved merely on account of this rhyme, were the existence of this very form not confirmed by the spelling *swone* in Machyn's Diary about 1550.

Such rhymes as *sweat—heat, heath—breath*, which are common in the sixteenth century, may certainly be accepted as genuine, since we know that the vowel was long in all these words in M.E., and these rhymes may be taken as indicating that the old quantity still survived in the sixteenth century. Rhymes may further supply evidence of the currency of a provincial type in certain words, as when Waller rhymes *build* with *field*, and Dryden with *yield* and *field*. There is independent confirmation of the use of '*beeld*' a S.E. form in London in the sixteenth century.

Shakespeare rhymes *dally—folly*, which an ill-informed reader might take for a 'poetic licence'; but it is proved a perfect rhyme from three different sources : (1) the unrounding of M.E. *ŏ* is a well-known process, and had taken place in the Western dialects at least as early as the first quarter of the fifteenth century; (2) the spellings show that this type of pronunciation had penetrated into London English among high and low (e. g. Q. Eliz., and Machyn); (3) the Grammarians of the sixteenth and seventeenth centuries recognize the type, and late in the seventeenth century Vanbrugh burlesques it as a fashionable trick of speech. See § 244 (2).

§ 215   (3) HISTORICAL CONSIDERATIONS

Since our whole inquiry is of an historical character, it would seem just that every problem which arises in connexion with it should be judged in the light of our general and particular knowledge concerning the history of English. Success in the interpretation of the various kinds of evidence from which we construct our picture of English between the period say of Chaucer and that of Johnson, depends principally upon the judicious use of philological knowledge in a wide sense. It is necessary on the one hand to bear in mind the antecedents of any given form, in M.E., and on the other to consider what its subsequent development has been down to the present day. Further, the student must never lose sight of the existence of variant forms, whether of dialectal origin, or arising within any dialect owing to combinative changes. These may vary in the same word according to different phonetic conditions produced severally, in inflected or uninflected forms, or from alterations in the incidence of stress in the word or sentence. It must be remembered that a given pronunciation in the sixteenth, seventeenth, or any other century, necessarily implies a certain ancestral type in M.E., and a certain development at the present day. If, therefore, we are led, by evidence of any kind, to reconstruct for the sixteenth or seventeenth century, a form which does not square with known facts concerning the language before and after this period, due allowances being made for variants of different kinds, then we must conclude either that our interpretation of the evidence is at fault, or that the particular piece of evidence on which we are relying is untrustworthy. Several instances of the importance of applying the historical test to rhymes have been given in the preceding section, but one or two more may be cited. Our purpose for the moment, it must be remembered, is not primarily to show that good poets generally employ genuine rhymes, but to discover whether a particular type of pronunciation was in vogue at a given time. The spelling *gretter* for the Comparative of *great* is used by Palladius, Shillingford, Fortescue, Gregory, and many others in the fifteenth century. A century later, Spenser rhymes *get her—greater*. In spite of the spelling of the last word, it appears that the rhyme necessitates a short vowel here, the same in fact as seems to be suggested by the fifteenth-century spelling just quoted. A reference to M.E. Gr. at once informs us that *grĕttre* was a normal M.E. form as the Comparative of *grēte*, and further, that the vowel shortening is due to a regular process which took place before the consonantal combination *t+r-*. Here a reference to earlier stages of the language establishes the ancient existence of this type of Comparative with a short vowel, historical phonology explains the reason for the shortening, the fifteenth-century spellings show the persistence of the type far into that century, and in the light of all this, we are justified in taking Spenser's rhyme to prove that the form was in use for at least another century.

Milton rhymes *God* with *abode*, and *load*, Dryden with *abode*, Pope with *road*, Gray with *abode*. Are we justified in assuming that a form [gōd] really existed in the seventeenth and eighteenth centuries? Price (1668) definitely states that *God* and *goad* were pronounced alike. Even this might not be conclusive unless we are assured that such a form as [gōd] could really exist. The word has a short vowel now, and was short in O.E. But we remember that vowels were lengthened in open syllables in M.E. and that this process, which produced M.E. *prōte* from O.E. *prŏta* 'throat', would also produce *Gōdes*, *Gōde* in the inflected syllables. We know that a type so derived was often transferred to the uninflected cases, as in *yoke* from O.E. *geŏc*, M.E. *зŏk* (N. and Acc.) but *зōke* (Dat.), etc. whence the modern form. Having established that *Gōd* might have existed, and might have survived into the seventeenth and eighteenth centuries, it is not unreasonable to believe that Price was telling the truth when he says that it *did* survive, and further that in the cases cited above, the poets were making use of this type. It is certainly open to question whether Gray, and perhaps even Pope, were not merely following tradition, but by an appeal to the history of the form we can see how the tradition arose, and what it was based on. Only historical considerations again can help us to put in its proper place another variant pronunciation of *God* [gɔ̄d], which survives to-day as a vulgarism or provincialism. This type may with considerable certainty be surmised as underlying another rhyme of Pope's, of this word with *unawed,* and is indicated earlier still in the spelling *Gaud* in Otway's play, *The Soldier's Fortune* (1681).

That this is not the same type with the lengthened vowel that has just been discussed, is shown by the equation of the latter with *goad,* which has now become [gou*d*], and it cannot be from a form with M.E. lengthening, because M.E. *ō²*, as we see, has not developed into [ō], but into [o*u*] at the present time. The vowel in [gōd] is rather to be regarded as a late lengthening from M.E. *Gŏd,* which took place perhaps as late as the seventeenth century in certain Regional or Social dialects, some forms from which, this being formerly one, got a footing in Standard English. We may compare the vowel in *cost, soft, froth,* and many other words ending in -*s,* -*f,* -*th,* often pronounced by speakers of Received Standard as [kōst, sōft, frōþ], which must also be due to a late lengthening. It is possible that *broad* [brōd] from M.E. *brōde* may be derived from a shortened *brŏd,* subsequently lengthened in the same way as M.E. *Gŏd, frŏth, cŏst,* etc. The pronunciation of *broad* in present-day Received Standard is one of the minor puzzles, for the form we should expect is [brou*d*]. It has been suggested that the [ō] is derived from some Regional dialect which has developed M.E. *ō²* in this way, but the above explanation seems quite as likely to be right.

Enough has been said here and in other sections to show the importance of applying the test of known philological facts to whatever conclusions we may feel inclined to draw from any kind of evidence. We may include under this head the line of argument pursued in § 208 above in regard to the relative chronology of sound changes, and the use of the direct evidence that one change has taken place, as indirect evidence for the start, or completion, of another.

§ 216. (4) THE EARLY WRITERS ON PRONUNCIATION

A short list of books on English Pronunciation is given above, p. 12. There are many dozens of books of this kind, and for full lists of them, and some account of the various writers, the reader must be referred to Ellis's *Early English Pronunciation,* Sweet's *History of English Sounds,* Jespersen's *Modern English Grammar,* pt. i, and Zachrisson's *Pronunciation of English Vowels.* We can give here only a very brief and general account. Most of these writers are Englishmen, but some are foreigners. The latter describe English pronunciation for the benefit of those of their own countrymen who wish to learn our language. The former have various objects in view—to settle how English *ought* to be pronounced ; to improve the current pronunciation of their time by pointing out common errors, vulgarisms, etc. ; to reform English spelling.

These authors vary greatly in intellectual calibre. There are distinguished scholars among them, and bishops, and there are country clergymen of no particular attainments ; some appear to be mere cranks. For many years now, students of English here, in Germany, in Scandinavia, and in America, have devoted much patient ingenuity to the scrutiny of these varied dissertations, to comparing one statement with another, and endeavouring to extract a meaning from material much of which is obscure and unsatisfactory. The chief criticism that must be directed against these writers is that very few of them, before the middle of the seventeenth century, have an adequate knowledge of speech sounds. They are bad observers, and they do not know how to describe intelligibly what they do observe. Further, their method is faulty, and they are obsessed by the 'letters'. They invariably start from the written symbols, and attempt to give an account of the 'powers' of these. They are disinclined to admit the existence of vowel sounds which do not fit into the system of the classical languages, and of the chief European tongues. The English writers of the sixteenth century, for instance, are very loath to admit that the symbol *a* in English expresses sounds quite different from those expressed by it in Latin and Greek. The French writers of this period, it is true, are less prejudiced, and do not mind telling us that the long vowel sound expressed by *a* in English is that of French *ai*, or *ê*.

A very unsatisfactory feature in these descriptions of sounds is that most of the writers, before Wallis and Cooper, do not appear to understand what a diphthong is, from the point of view of a phonetician, and it is generally doubtful whether they grasp that a sound expressed by two letters may be a monophthong, and that, on the other hand, a single letter may, in the conventional spelling, express a genuine diphthongal sound. It may be doubted whether our Grammarians would have recognized a diphthong in *how, out*, etc., had the sound not been written with two vowel symbols. The early descriptions of the sounds spelt *au, aw*, and *ai*, give rise to the gravest suspicions of their adequacy and accuracy.

In the latter part of the seventeenth century Wallis (1643) and Cooper (1685) mark the beginning of a new era in knowledge of the nature of speech sounds, and in the power to describe them, no less than in acuteness and honesty of observation. In the next century much may be learnt from Jones (1701), Baker (1724), Elphinston (1765–87), and Walker (1785–1801). It is best not to trust the Grammarians before Wallis as to the character of the vowel in a given word or group of words, unless their statements are confirmed by the occasional spellings; it is not always safe to trust the later ones, when they tell us that such and such a pronunciation is ʻbarbarousʼ. If we have evidence that the mode of speech which the Grammarians condemn was in vogue among wits, and courtiers, and poets, we shall hesitate to accept the former's strictures as final. But, in spite of their many limitations, it would be very unwise to ignore even the sixteenth-century Grammarians altogether. We may often believe them as to the quantity of a vowel, though they may give quite a false impression, or none at all, of its quality. We may trust them when they put a number of words together as being all pronounced with the same vowel, or when they bracket two, or sometimes three, words together as being pronounced alike, or ʻnearly alikeʼ. These things can often be tested by the usage of the poets in their rhymes, and as we cannot suspect poets and pedants of being in collusion to deceive posterity, we may assume that agreement between them implies the truth. Lastly, the Grammarians are often peculiarly instructive when they warn their readers against some form of speech. We may take it for granted that these writers will not invent a pronunciation which no one uses, merely for the sake of deriding it, and therefore that what they condemn had an actual existence.

The Grammarians sometimes employ a rough and ready phonetic spelling to drive home their meaning, and curiously enough this is often identical with that into which the careless letter-writers slide, quite naturally and unconsciously, to express what is clearly the same sound. Thus, when Gill (1621) writes *skallers* ʻscholarsʼ to illustrate a type of pronunciation which he despises, he is merely expressing the unrounding of M.E. *ŏ* of which we have evidence from the same kind of spelling (*a* instead of *o*) just 200 years earlier, and, nearer to his time, from precisely the same spellings, in Machyn, and in Q. Elizabeth when she wrote *stap* for *stop*; a type of pronunciation also which Shakespeare had in his mind when he rhymed *dally* and *folly*. When Gill writes *liv* for *leave*, we see that he refers to the change of M.E. [ē] to [ī], a type of pronunciation abominable in his eyes, which, though not yet widespread, we know, both from much older spellings with *i* and from the rhymes of Sackville, Spenser, and Shakespeare, was in occasional use, even by Q. Elizabeth herself, during the sixteenth century, and which was destined, 150 years later, to become the sole type used in Received Standard.

We have now indicated some of the chief principles of method applicable to the problems which confront us, have emphasized some of the more important considerations which the student should bear in mind in attempting to grapple with them, and have briefly surveyed the main sources from which information is to be derived.

In this, as in other investigations, it is wise to seek light from every available source, and to compare the results which each yields with those derived from the other channels of information. When several, or all, of the avenues of approach converge on a single point, we may feel some confidence in the final result.

THE VOWELS IN DETAIL

§ 217. M.E. ă (cp. § 160) is fronted to [æ].

So far as the testimony of the Grammarians goes, the old back sound remained in the 'best English' throughout the sixteenth century. Early in the next century, however, there are indications of fronting in their descriptions, but it is not till Cooper (1685) that we have a definite description of a low front. It is certain, however, that the sound had developed long before this. Already in the sixteenth century Palsgrave indeed hints, with disapproval, at the existence of another sound than [a]. A front pronunciation is pretty certain from Shakespeare's rhymes *scratch—wretch* (Viëtor, *Sh. Pr.*, p. 208), *neck—back* (Horn, § 40), both from *Venus and Adonis*.[1] The following occasional spellings suggest a much earlier existence of the fronted vowel:—*thenking* 'thanking' Dk. of Buckingham, P. Letters i, p. 61, 1442–55 ; Bokenam, *venyschyd*, Agn. 603, *wecheman* ib. 295, 1443 ; Gregory, *becheler* 203, *jesper* 209, *fethem* 'fathom' 213, before 1467 ; Thos. Pery, Ellis 2. 2. *Jenewery*, p. 142, 1539 ; *Crenmer*, Machyn, p. 57, 1547–50 ; 'if you *hed* him', Alleyne, p. 32, 1593 ; *settisfie* Mrs. Basire, p. 135, 1655.

In some parts of the country, then, the fronting appears to have begun in the fifteenth century and been completed by the end of that century; the fronted type seems to have been introduced slowly into the Standard Language, and was

---

[1] As a result of an examination of the MSS., Zachrisson now vouches for *e* in the following forms—*rensackyd*, Marg. Paston (1450) ; *fend*, M.E. *fand* 'found', Pref., M. Paston (1450); *begen* 'began', a servant in Past. Letts. (1457). See *Engl. Pronunc. taught by Wm. Bullokar*, pp. 139-40.

perhaps not fully accepted until towards the end of the six-teenth century. It took the Grammarians some time longer to recognize, and to find means of describing, the new sound. Once established, [æ] has remained unchanged.

Combinative developments of M.E. ă in the Modern Period.

§ 218. The combination al becomes [*aul*].

This process is very similar to that described in §§ 171. 7 (*a*), 196, 183 above, or to the O.E. Fracture. It took place primarily in stressed syllables, when -*al* was final, as in *all, small, fall,* etc., also when *al* is followed by another consonant—*salt, malt, talk, bald, half, calf.* When a vowel follows the *l,* no diphthongization occurred—*hallow, fallow, valley,* etc.

The diphthong, or some later development of this, is fully established at least as early as the third quarter of the fifteenth century, as is shown by the spellings in the Cely Papers (1473–88), e.g. *Tawbot,* p. 46, *aull* 'all' passim ; *schawl* be, which is from the old stressed type. The earliest Gram-marians all describe a diphthong in these and other similar words, but no weight can be attached to their statements on this head. This [*au*] like the older M.E. *au* (§§ 171. 7 (*a*), 196, 183) very early became [ɔ̄] except before lip-cons. Its history will, however, be discussed under M.E. *au.* See § 260 below.

The pronunciation [ɔl] at the present day always implies an earlier [*aul*].

NOTE. *Shall* = [ʃæl] is derived from Early Mod. *shăl* without diph-thongization. This is the unstressed form. *Shăl* would also occur in the breath-group *shăl I.* On the other hand, the strong form *shaul* is recorded by the early Grammarians, and its descendant [ʃɔl] is heard to-day in some dialects.

§ 219. M.E. ă before [s, f, þ].

In M.E. words like *ăske, grăs, păssen,* etc. ; *chăf, stăf, crăft, ăfter,* etc.; *băþ, păþ,* etc., the vowel was first fronted in the usual way, giving [tʃæf, græs, pæþ] and so on, and then lengthened to [tʃæf, græs, pæþ], etc. This [æ] was again retracted to [ā] giving the present-day [tʃāf, grās, pāþ]. The early Grammarians appear to differ in their pronunciation of these groups of words, just as we differ to some extent nowa-days. It is difficult to fix the date of this lengthening, but such spellings as *crooft* 'croft' Coventry Leet Bk., pp. 43 and 46, 1420 and 1443 ; *geests* 'guests', ib. p. 29 ; also *gueast* Roister Doister ; *toossed* 'tossed' Euphues 208 ; and *moathes* 'moths' ib., p. 34 ; Cely Papers *marster* (= ǣ)? ; Palladius, 1420, *graas* 4. 1080, seem to indicate that it was very early, since, apart

from the two last forms, there is no reason for supposing that
ă would escape a process which lengthened ĕ and ŏ. The
period when [ǣ] was retracted to [ā] is also uncertain. Cooper,
1685, still gives [ǣ] in *cast, past, path, carp, grant,* etc. Other
late seventeenth-century writers appear to describe [ā] in these
and similar words, but they and the eighteenth-century writers
are very ambiguous. We must remember that [æ, ǣ] are
sounds which only persons with some phonetic training can
either recognize properly or describe. Almost all stages
[ă, æ, ǣ, ā] exist to-day in different Regional and Class
Dialects. In spite of Zachrisson's disbelief in variant developments, I cannot escape the conviction that they are recorded
by the early Grammarians in the above as in other classes of
words, and I attribute them largely to Class Dialect.

NOTE I. Jespersen, *Mod. E. G.*, i, pp. 304-310, rejects the ordinary
view of the development of [ā] in present-day English, and believes that
it is of L. M.E. or Early Mod. origin, and has been retained unaltered.
The difficulty of believing in the application of his complicated theory of
'preservative analogy' here appears very great.

NOTE 2. Present-day [hæþ, hæst] instead of [hāþ, hāst] are due to the
analogy of [hæv], q. v., § 225, Note.

§ 220. The words *father, rather* fall under the above statement. They are developed out of the M.E. short forms
făther, răther (cp. § 176, Note), the series being [fáðer < fæ̃ðər <
fǣðər < fāðər]. Provincial [gāðər] has had the same development.

§ 221. The present pronunciation of *laugh* [lāf] must go
back to [laf] from **lauf*, a (M.E. ?) variant of *lauh*, with loss of
u before *f* (cp. §§ 172. 1, and 260) ; *to laffe* occurs in a letter of
Barnabe Googe, 1563, Arber's Reprint p. 12, this can apparently
only represent M.E. *lăf*. The present pronunciation of *calf, half*
must go back to M.E. *hăf, *căf*; the former actually occurs
in the fourteenth century, in Aȝenbite, p. 190, and Bp. Bekinton's
Letters, 1442, have *behaf*. These spellings show that *l* was lost,
in some dialects, very early before *f*. In dialects where *l* in this
position survived longer, the preceding *a* was diphthongized,
hence the fifteenth-century spellings *haulf, caulf,* etc. This
type would produce [hɔf, kɔf] as in some Mod. Engl. dialects,
and has no relation to the forms of the standard language.

§ 222. The M.E. combination ·ar.

M.E. ăr became [ær] and this was lengthened to [ǣr] in
the first instance before another consonant—[hærd, pært], but
still [ær, fær], etc. (Sweet, *H. E. S.*, § 780). This is seventeenth

century, but before the end of the century the lengthening seems to have involved those words also in which no consonant followed the *r*. This [ǣ] developed to [ā] like that in § 219.

Such is the origin of our present-day [ā] in *car, are, card, heart hard*, etc., etc. In fact [ā] in present-day English always goes back to M.E. and Early Mod. *ă* with subsequent fronting and lengthening as described above.

Are [ā] is not from the M.E. *āre(n)* type, which produced the now obsolete [ēr, ɛər] that used to be written 'air' by comic writers, but from the M.E. variant *ăre* which occurred in unstressed positions. Cp. § 177. (2).

Present-day *clerk, Berks., Bertie, Berkley, hearth, Derby* [klāk, bāks, bāti, hāp, bākli, dābi], in spite of the spelling, are derived from a M.E. *clărk, Bărks(chire), Dărbi, Bărklei*, etc. Concerning the history of M.E. *-ĕr*, the type represented by the spelling in above forms, see § 228.

NOTE. The [ar] type of original *er*-words was very usual in eighteenth-century Received Standard. Lady Wentworth regularly writes *sarve, sarvents, Jarmany, sartainly, hard* 'heard', *parson* 'person', etc., etc. Cp. *Wentw. Papers*, passim. *Vardy* 'verdict, opinion', occurs in Swift's *Polite Conversations*.

§ 223. M.E. wă-, quă-.

These combinations appear in present-day English with a rounded vowel: *wash, wan, swallow, swan, watch, wasp, quality, quantity, squash*, etc. [wɔʃ, wɔn, swɔloᵘ, swɔn, wɔtʃ, kwɔntiti, wɔsp, kwɔliti, skwɔʃ], etc. There is some slight evidence, even in M.E., for the rounding of *ă* after *w*- when followed by *l*: *swolwe-bridde* E. E. Pr. Psalter, 1350, p. 180; *swolʒ* 'swallow' the bird, Allit. Poems (Patience) 250; Chaucer rhymes *swallow* vb. with *holowe* H. of F. 1035. Zachrisson, p. 62, cites *Wolsyngham*, Paston Letters, *whor* 'war', and the inverted spelling *what* for *wot* vb. from Cely Papers, and also *reword* 'reward' from Paston Letters, in the sixteenth century. Machyn (1547–50) writes *wosse* 'wash', but the spellings with *o* are rare. In the latter half of the seventeenth century we find *wore* 'war' 1644, *Worik* 'Warwick' 1658, *quorill* 1674, *quollity* 1683, and a few more, in the Verney Mem. The Grammarians make no mention of the rounded forms till Daines (1640), who says that *au*,= [ɔ] is heard in *quart, wart*, and a few others, before *-r*; Cooper (1685) recognizes a rounded vowel in the words where we now have it. The poets, down to Dryden, appear never to rhyme *wa*- with anything but *-a*-, but Dryden has *wallow—follow, war—abhor*; Swift has quite a number of such rhymes as *morals—quarrels, short—quart, warning—morning, quarter—mortar, warm'd—perform'd*, etc. The above evidence seems to show that although the rounding process was an early one in some dialects, the rounded forms were not established in polite speech, at Court, nor favoured by the poets till far on in the seventeenth century.

There seems to have been two periods of this rounding in different speech communities, one before and one after the fronting of old ă. Thus the above early spellings seem to show that L. M.E. *wa* became *wo* direct. On the other hand, some of the seventeenth-century Grammarians give forms like [wæz, swæn, kwæl*it*i], which show that *w* did not hinder the fronting, and that [w*a*] did become [wæ]. In this case, the series must have been [sw*ă*n, swæn] or [sw*ă*n sw*ɔ*n], respectively.

In the dialect of some classes, the rounding did not involve all words, for [kwæliti, kwæntiti] were well-used eighteenth-century forms, and have been heard in the last century by old people still living. Leigh Hunt, Autobiogr., p. 180, mentions that John Kemble the actor (1757–1823) always said [kwæ-l*it*i.]

The form *swam* [swæm] instead of [sw*ɔ*m] may be explained from the analogy of *ran, began*, etc.

Before back consonants the rounding did not as a rule take place among standard speakers; cp. *wag, quack, wax*, etc. On the other hand, [kw*ɔ*g] instead of [kwæg] in *quagmire* may be occasionally heard.

§ 224. When *r* follows, whether as a final sound or succeeded by another consonant, the rounded vowel just described is lengthened, and appears now as [ɔ̄], thus *war, warm, warp, warn, swarm*, etc.=[w*ɔ̄*, w*ɔ̄*m, w*ɔ̄*p, w*ɔ̄*n, sw*ɔ̄*m]. The history of *ăr*, § 222 above, shows that this lengthening is due to the *r* itself, and not to the later loss of this sound.

The lengthening did not take place when the *r* was followed by a vowel—*warrior, warren, quarrel*=[w*ɔ*ri*ə*, w*ɔ*rin, kw*ɔ*r*ə*l].

It may be noted that certain groups of young speakers at the present time show a tendency to drop intervocalic -*r*-, and in this case the preceding vowel *does* appear to be lengthened; either [w*ɔ*j*ə*, kw*ɔ*r*ə*l], etc., or [w*ɔ̄*j*ə*, kw*ɔ̄*r*ə*l]. On loss of *r* see § 284. (4).

M.E. ā.

§ 225. **Independent Development.**

ā fronted to [æ] which is raised to [ē̜] and then made tense: [ē].

As early as the thirteenth century MS. Egerton 613 has the spelling *mēden* 'made', O.E. Misc. 198. 33. The doggerel Siege of Rouen, c. 1420, rhymes *care—were* vb., Bokenam, c. 1443, writes *credyll* M.E. *crādel*, 'cradle' S. Cecil. 80, and the inverted spelling *bare* for 'bier', O.E. *bǣr*, which in Suffolk would almost certainly have [ē]; Cely Papers have *ceme* 'came', p. 46, and Zachrisson notes *meke* 'make', John Paston 1469, P. L. II., p. 392; the inverted spelling *maid* 'made', Cov. Leet Bk., p. 24, 1421, shows that M.E. *ā* had by this time been levelled under M.E. *ai*, and the sound of this we have reason to believe was [ē] or at least [ɛ̄], see § 268. In 1528, *declare* rhymes with *theare* 'there', and with *weare* vb., and *spare* with *wheare*. French writers on English pronunciation from 1529 onwards indicate that English *ā* has the sound of French *e*, or *ai*. The English Grammarians of the sixteenth century are, as usual, utterly ambiguous on the quality of *ā*, but throughout the century poets rhyme it with M.E. *ē*[2]; *betake— break, speake—make*, Sackville; *feature—nature, states—seates*, Spenser; *nature—defeature*, Shakespeare. This evidence is enough to establish that *ā* was fronted long before the period of the earliest English Grammarians, so that Gill (1621), who insists on the old back [ā] as the proper pronunciation, and only admits the existence of a front pronunciation in order to censure it, cannot be taken seriously. Such a reliable observer as Cooper (1685) recognizes the complete identity of the vowel in *meat* and *mate*.

Examples are: *ale, name, dame, cape, flake, gate, lane, behave, make, take*, etc., etc.

The words *danger, grange, safe* (§§ 171. (9), Note, 184, Note, 196), in so far as they go back to M.E. *ā* and not to *ai*, belong to this group.

The present-day diphthong [ei] in [neim], etc., is first recorded by Bachelor in 1809.

NOTE. The provincial [reiðər, feiðər] are from M.E. *rāðer, fāðer*. This type is probably indicated by Lady Wentworth's spelling *rether* (1708). Cf. *Wentw. Papers*, p. 64. *Have* [hæv], as distinct from [biheiv], goes back to M.E. *hăv* with shortening, or absence of lengthening, in an unstressed position (§ 177), but the long *hāve* is also found in M.E., cp. Chaucer's rhyme with *grāve*, etc., and the poets of the sixteenth and seventeenth centuries recognize this type in their rhymes. Later than this, Pope, etc., rhymes *have* with *save, crave*, etc., which may well be mere traditional usage. For [hæst, hæþ], see § 219, Note 2.

M.E. ā + r.

§ 226. In the combination *ār*, M.E. *ā* developed, according to § 225, to [æ, ɛ̄] and remained at this stage. Then a parasitic [ə] developed between the vowel and the -r, and the latter was lost, in Standard English, early in nineteenth century. See § 284. (4) *b* and *c* below.

Thus M.E. *hāre* 'hare' had the following series of changes: [hār < hǣr < hēr < hě̄ər < heə] and so with the words, *care, dare, bare, snare*, etc. It will be seen that in the [ēr] stage original *ār* was completely levelled under M.E. *ē²r* (§ 233), and M.E. *air, eir* (§ 269).

Development of M.E. ě.

§ 227. Independent Treatment.

M.E. *ě* remains as [ɛ]: *set, read* (Pret. M.E. *rědde*), *men, tell, well* (adv.), *kept, get, help*, etc., etc.

The vowel in *fledge, left* (hand), *knell* is M.E. and O.E. *ě* from earlier *ỹ*, according to the Essex or 'Kentish' type. See § 158 (*b, e*).

§ 228. Combinative Treatment. M.E. ěr-.

In so far as this combination did not become *ǎr* in M.E., it remained till the Early Mod. period, and was then apparently made into a flat vowel [ə]. With the weakening of the [r], this vowel was lengthened, and lowered, and made tense, becoming present-day [ʌ̄]. Examples: *earth, earn, churl, heard* (Late M.E. *hěrde*), *fern, learn, servant*, etc.

The vowel in *kernel* is the Essex or 'Kentish' form of O.E. *ỹ*, W.S., etc., *cyrnel* (§ 142).

Herd, in shep*herd, herds*man, etc., is from the O.E. Merc. *heorde*, M.E. *heorde, herde*, W.S. *hierde* (§§ 117, 119, 139).

In sixteenth-century literary English the type *yearth* 'earth' is much used, e. g. in Edw. VI's First Prayer Book. This is probably from the M.E. Kentish type *yerþe* as found in Aȝenbite (§ 169).

Clerk, Berks., etc., whose spelling shows that they represent M.E. *ěr*, are yet pronounced according to the M.E. *ar*-type (§ 222).

For other sources of [ʌ̄] see §§ 239, 252, 256.

NOTE. When a vowel follows -er- [ɛ] remains: *verity*, etc.

M.E. ē¹ (tense; see sources under § 201).

§ 229. Independent Development [ē < ī].

There are numerous spellings with *y* and *i* in M.E. (see § 162. (2)), and still more in the fifteenth century, and in the sixteenth, which leave no doubt that the present sound was fully developed in the pronunciation of the writers. All the Grammarians, even those of the sixteenth century, agree also in describing the sound [ī] in words which had *ē* in M.E. Examples: *hyre* 'hear' S. of Rouen (1420); *besychen* 'beseech' Bokenam, S. Marg. 925 (1443); *myte* 'meet' Shillingford, p. 6, *dyme* 'deem' ib., p. 13 (1447–50); *symed* 'seemed' Marg. Paston (1440–70), P.L. 2. 186, *spyde* 'speed' ib. 2. 188, *shype* 'sheep' ib. 2. 196; Anne Boleyn, Ellis, I. 1. 306 and 307, *besyche* (1528); Ascham, *style* 'steel' Toxophilus 112 (1545); Q. Eliz. Letters to James VI (1582–1608), *Kiping* 'keeping', p. 23, *nideful* 'need-' 27, *besiche* 53, *spidye* 53 'speedy', etc.; *dides* 'deeds' Ellis I. 2. 147 (1549). The inverted spelling *Mons. de Guees*, 'Guise', Cavendish, Life of Wolsey, p. 76 (1577) is interesting.

It is quite possible, however, that in some dialects, the raising of [ē] to [ī] was well on its way, if not completed, in the M.E. period. See § 162. This [ī] has so far remained in Standard English. Examples of the various groups are: *seek, sweet, feet, green*; *believe, steel, steeple*; *he, we, me*; *shield, wield, field*; *deed, seed*; *freeze, bee, deep, see*; *beetle, evil, weevil.* Norman-French words: *beef, chief, grief, piece.*

NOTE 1. *Evil*, O.E. (W.S.) *ȳfel*, was formerly explained as a 'Kentish' form, but as Luick has pointed out (*Untersuchungen*, p. 281), M.E. *ē* lengthened from *ĕ* in an open syllable was slack, whereas the tenseness of *ē* in the ancestor of *evil* is proved by the sixteenth-century Grammarians, who record this word with [ī]. The frequent early spelling *ivel, yvel*, may represent our type, or may be E.Midl. type without lengthening. The word must therefore be explained together with *beetle* and *weevil*, according to § 174.

NOTE 2. The fact that *deed* is recorded as containing [ī] and is spelt with *i* already in the sixteenth century, as well as the present spelling of this word, and of *seed*, shows that these forms are derived from the non-W.S. *dēd*, etc., which of course had [ē] in M.E. Chaucer often uses the Anglian forms of these words in his rhymes, but has a preponderance of rhymes with undoubted M.E. [ē] (§§ 162, 207).

§ 230. M.E. ē¹ before ·r.

Before *-r* a parasitic vowel developed after M.E. *ē*, Mod. [ī]: *here, hear, dear*, etc.=[hiə, diə]. The diphthong [iə] is heard at the present time, both when final *r* is lost as in the above words, and when it has been retained before a vowel as in [hiəriŋ], etc.

NOTE. *Hear* from Anglian *hēran*, § 124; *fear* from Anglian *fēr*, § 124; and *year* from Anglian *gēr*, § 123 (but cp. § 115, Note), are all normal in having [iə]. For the [ɛə] in *there, were, hair*, cp. § 233.

§ 231. Shortening of Mod. [ī] from M.E. ē¹.

Shortening, comparable to that of [ɛ̄] (§ 235), has taken place in *breeches* [britʃiz], (hay)*rick*—though [rīk] survives in the dialects—*riddle*, O.E. (Anglian) *rēdels*; *sick, silly*, etc. This can hardly be the result of a direct shortening of [ē] as is sometimes suggested, but must surely imply a previous raising to [ī]. See § 229.

M.E. ē² (slack [ē̞], § 162. 1. and 2.

§ 232. Independent Treatment.

Examples of words containing M.E. [ē̞] are: *beam, dream, beat, east, leap*; *clean, deal* (vb. and n.), *heat, heath, teach*; *breathe, eat, speak, steal*; French words: *beast, feast, veal.*

This sound was kept quite distinct from M.E. [ē] far into the Modern period. On the spelling *ea*, see § 212. All words of this group except those which have been shortened in the Modern period (such as *dead, death, sweat, threat, thread*, etc., etc.) on which see § 235 below, are now pronounced with [ī] in Received Standard, except *break, steak, great*, and are therefore indistinguishable from those containing M.E. *ē¹* (§ 229) in respect of their vowel. In the fifteenth, sixteenth, seventeenth, and part of the eighteenth century, however, no less than in M.E., *ē²* was kept distinct from *ē¹*. During this period, the difference is shown (*a*) by the retention, as an almost universal rule, of the spelling *e* for *ē²*, among those who constantly write *i, y,* for *ē¹*; (*b*) by the rhyming of *ē²* with M.E. *ā*, as *care—there, states—seates, speake—make*, etc. (see § 225); (*c*) by occasional spellings with *a*, as *retrate*, Spenser, *spake*, Verney Memoirs; (*d*) by the definite statement of seventeenth- and eighteenth-century Grammarians, e. g. Cooper, who equates *meat* and *mate*, besides describing quite unambiguously a mid-front vowel as the sound pronounced in a long list of typical *ē²* words.

It is open to discussion whether this E. Mod. vowel was tense or slack, [ē] or [ē̞]. It seems probable that when *ē¹* became [ī], *ē²* very soon took its place and was made tense (see (2) below). After M.E. *ā* had been fronted it appears soon to have been completely levelled under the sound of *ē²* (§ 225), and the same is true of M.E. *ai, ei* (§ 268), and we therefore find *ē²* words rhyming with words originally containing both these other sounds, right down to the time of Pope. Examples of rhymes showing the identity of the three originally distinct vowels are:—Surrey, *please—days*; Sackville, *breake—betake, speake—make*; Spenser, *uncleane—mayntayne*; Drayton, *dreams—Thames, mead—braid, maids—beads*; Suckling, *clean—Seine*; Waller, *sea—way, make—snake—speake*; Cowley, *play—sea*; Dryden, *dream—shame, obey—sea, seas—sways*; Pope, *weak—take, eat—gate, eat—state, speak—take, great—*

state, shade—dead, etc. ; Swift, perhaps owing to his Irish connexions, has a larger number of these rhymes than any
other poet : *meat—say't, yeast—haste, seat—weight, dreams—
streams, dream—name, cheap—rape, veal—ale*, etc., etc. The
fact that such rhymes are not even more plentiful than they are,
must be ascribed to the well-known tendency of poets to avoid
rhymes which do not appeal to the eye as well as to the ear.

(2) The other type.

Although, down to the middle, at least, of the eighteenth
century, the usually accepted pronunciation of $\bar{e}^2$ appears to
have been [ē], there is evidence of the early existence of
another pronunciation, [ī], and this in words which had [ɛ̄] in
all M.E. dialects, namely, those with O.E. *ĕ* lengthened, as
well as those with ē from O.E. $\bar{æ}^1$ and $\bar{æ}^2$ (§§ 162 (1, 2); 173) of
which tense types existed in O.E. and M.E. by the side of the
slack.

As early as Gregory (before 1467) M.E. *hēlen* ' conceal ' is
written *hylen* (p. 146); Machyn has *prych* ' preach ', p. 13,
bryking 109, *brykefast* 199, *spyking* 35 ; Ascham has *lipe*
' leap ', Toxophilus 89 ; Gabr. Harvey, Letters (1573-80), *birive*
' bereave ', p. 53 ; Q. Eliz. Transl. *bequived* ' bequeathed ', p. 140.
The Queen has also *spich* ' speech ' (O.E. $\bar{æ}^1$). Of the rhymes
which indicate [ī] some are open to question as being from O.E.
$\bar{æ}^1$ and $\bar{æ}^2$, which, though the slack type is the more usual in
London English, and though these very words usually show
the slack type, were also pronounced tense, even according to
Chaucer's rhymes : Rede me and be not wrothe (1528) *sleane—
bene* ; Surrey, *reach—beseech, grene—clene*, Tottel, p. 3 ;
Skelton, *stepe* ' steep '—*lepe* ' leap ', Ph. Sparow 111-15 ; Wyatt,
beseech—reach ; Spenser, *seas—these, streame—seeme, uncleane
—weene* ; Marston, *sweetness—greatness* ; Drayton, *beat—fleet,
these—seas* ; Waller, *sea—she—be* ; Milton, *sea—thee, seas—
these, seize—please*; Cowley, *sea—be,—he,—thee*; Dryden, *see—
free, meet—seat, bread—feed* ; Swift, *cheat—meat, seas—these,
great—meet* ; Pope, *seat—fleet, queens—means, sea—flea*, etc.
Gill (1621) mentions this type of pronunciation in *leave* and
meat, which he transliterates *liv, mit*, respectively, as occurring
in his day among certain classes of speakers whom he speaks
of with derision and contempt. It appears from all this that
the raising of the vowel to [ī] in some areas or classes was
very early, that some words were pronounced according to
this type by the good speakers (e. g. Q. Eliz.) as early as the
sixteenth century, and that the poets knew, and occasionally
used this type. On the other hand it was not widely current,

and may have been regarded as a vulgarism, until the second half of the eighteenth century.

(3) **Introduction of [ī] type as usual form in Received Standard.**

Our present pronunciation of the $\bar{e}^2$ words is the result of the gradual abandonment of one type, and the adoption, universally, of another. The process involved one word after another, and went on slowly during the seventeenth, more quickly in the following century. Jones, the authority on pronunciation, writing in 1701, mentions *steam, team, beam, yeast,* as having the [ī] sound. In 1747, Dr. Johnson, perplexed what pronunciation to recommend in certain cases, quotes, in his *Plan of a Dictionary,* Rowe's couplet:

'As if misfortune made the throne her seat,
And none could be unhappy but the great'

as evidence for the pronunciation [grīt], which shows that Johnson himself took [sīt] for granted, but by no means proves that Rowe (1673–1718) pronounced in this way; in fact, the latter almost certainly still said [sēt].

Johnson further quotes Pope's

'For Swift and him despised the farce of state,
The sober follies of the wise and great,'

as authority for the other type [grēt], which shows that in Johnson's day this word was pronounced by some as [grīt], otherwise it would not have been necessary to discuss it. Cowper, in the hymn 'God moves in a mysterious way', rhymes the last word with *sea.* The old pronunciation lingered on in some words, and perhaps especially in the provinces, for a long time. Charles Lloyd, the Birmingham Quaker banker (1748–1828), who translated Homer and Horace, rhymed *steal* with *prevail,* saying that whatever Londoners may do, 'we pronounce it *stale*', when Christopher Wordsworth took exception to the rhyme.

NOTE. Present-day [greit], M.E. *grēte,* may be due to a doublet in M.E. formed on the analogy of the Comp. *grёttre,* which survived in Caxton's English. If this survived after [grēt] had become [grēt], a form [grēt], whence later [grēt], might arise again with the vowel *quality* of the Comp., but the *quantity* of the Positive. See Jespersen, p. 338, who, however, explains the form rather differently by his principle of 'preservative analogy'. *Steak* and *break* may owe their vowel to a S.W. dialect type, and this explanation would of course account for *great* also. But all three may be chance survivals of the old type. [grīt, brīk] certainly existed, see above, but for some reason did not become current in Received Standard along with the other words of this class and type.

M.E. [ēr].

§ **233.** It appears that in Standard English the vowel in this group did not normally undergo raising to [ī] as in the independent position, and in the group M.E. [ēr] (§ 230).

Examples are : *bear* vb., and the name of the animal, *swear, wear, ere. There, where, were, hair* must contain M.E. [ē] from O.E. (Saxon) type *ǣ.* Cp., on the other hand, *fear,* § 230, Note.

§ **234.** There is, however, another group of M.E. [ē] words which have [iə] at the present day, and where the pronunciation [īr] is recorded in Early Mod. : *ear, spear, rear* (vb.), *beard, shear, smear, tear* (from the eye). *Ear* may possibly owe its vowel to association with *hear,* but the others must come from a dialect where the change of M.E. [ēr] to [īr] was normal, presumably by virtue of the same tendency which raised this sound to [ī] as stated in preceding § 232. (2).

Great divergency exists among the seventeenth century Grammarians as to the pronunciation of these words, some giving [ēr], others [īr] in the same words. The same difference occurs in the rhymes of sixteenth and seventeenth century poets. Pronunciations, though differing from our own, which are suggested by the rhymes, and confirmed by the Grammarians, may be regarded as genuine. Practically all words with *-ear-, -eer-,* appear to have been pronounced according to both types. The fact is probably that there was one type of pronunciation which made M.E. *ē¹r* into [īr] but kept M.E. *ē²r* as [ēr]. When in the speech of this group, we find [īr] as in *fear, rear,* (O.E. *fǣr, ǣ¹,* and *rǣran, ǣ²*), we must assume that [fiə, riə] descend from the tense types, and represent M.E. [ēr]. But in another Regional or Class Dialect M.E. [ē] (from O.E. *ĕ* in open syllables or from O.E. *ēa*) unless previously shortened, became [ī] before *-r* as elsewhere, and to this we owe our present pronunciation of *spear, ear, shear, tear* (in the eye), as well as that represented in the rhymes *bear* (vb.)—*hear,* Wyatt; *swear—appear,* Suckling; *appear—bear* vb., *dear—wear* vb., Milton ; *here—bear, bears—peers,* Waller, etc., etc. See Wyld, *Studies in Engl. Rhymes,* pp. 63–67.

NOTE. *Beard* = [biəd] presupposes earlier [bērd], but another pronunciation [bērd], which develops into [bᴧrd], is also recorded. Walker states that this persisted on the stage in late eighteenth century, and it may still be heard in Ireland.

§ 235. Shortening of M.E. [ē] in Modern Period.

A large number of words which appear still to have retained the old long vowel in M.E. are now pronounced with a short vowel: *breath, dread, spread, wet, sweat, shed* vb., *bread, thread, threat, dead, death, head, deaf, red, fret, get, stead, heaven, heavy, tread* vb. Many of these still retained their length in sixteenth and seventeenth centuries, and even later, as appears from occasional spellings, rhymes, and Grammarians' statements. Spellings :—*beheeddyd* ' beheaded ', Berners' Froissart, 1. p. 34; *threed,* ' thread ', Euphues, p. 157 ; *havey* ' heavy ', Lady Hobart, Verney Mem. (1679). Rhymes which imply long vowels where we have short : Wyatt, *eaten—threaten, freat,* ' fret '—*great, sweate* vb.—*heate, drede—spede—drede* (*speed* has ē[1]) ; Spenser, *breath—beneath—death, intreate—heate—sweate* ; Shakespeare, *entreats—frets, heat—get, sweat—heat, heaven—even, dread—mead, heavy—leafy* (=[hēvi-lēvi], cp. Lady Hobart's *havey* above) ; Drayton, *wreath—breath* ; Habington, *lead* vb.—*tread, dead*; Milton, *spreads—meads* ; Dryden, *bread—feed* (the latter from M.E. ē[1]) ; Pope, *dead—shade.* Evidence of Grammarians : Wharton (1654) gives *bread* as having the long sound of which that in *tread* is the short; Cooper (1685) includes *sweat* vb. in the same list with *seat* (' long *ea* ') ; Baker (1725) says the vowels in *deaf, breath, sweat, threat* are all long.

On the other hand, in spite of the above, the shortening process is old, and many traces of this occur in the rhymes of the same poets who in other words retain the ancient quantity. Indeed the rhymes indicate a shortening in some cases where we have kept the un-shortened form : Wyatt, *repeat—set*; Sackville, *depth—leapeth* (=[lɛpþ], *ykept—reapt* ; Shakespeare, *steps—leaps* vb., *confesse—decesse*—(so in Quarto's 1–4) *decrease* ; Drayton's *east—possessed, beat*(prep.)—*set*; Pope *beat*(P.P.)—*set.* Shortened *lĕp* is vouched for by Hodges and Price (1643, and 1668), who equate *leaper* and *leper* ; it is still often used of a horse at the present time. The P.P. and Pret. *bet* indicated above is perhaps on analogy of *met* from *meet.* The occasional spellings also point to the existence of shortened forms : Marg. Paston, *dedde* ' dead ', P. Letters ii. 372 (1469) ; Elyot's Gouernour (1531) *hedde* ' head ', Berners' Froissart (1529), *presst* ' priest ' ; Machyn (1547–50), *mett* ' meat ', *swett* ' sweat ', *heddes* ; Cavendish (1577), *strett* ' street '. The whole question of these shortenings is obscure, and deserves special investigation. The long and short types have long existed side by side.

M.E. ō¹ (tense).—Independent Treatment.

§ 236.   M.E. ō¹ (tense) becomes [ū].

(1) The two M.E. ō-sounds, that from O.E. and O.Fr. ō (ō¹), and that from O.E. ā, or from lengthening of ŏ (ō²) are kept distinct in rhyme in M.E.

(2) The process of change from M.E. ō¹ [ō] to [ū] was that of a gradual increase of rounding accompanied by raising of the tongue position.   The stage reached in the early fourteenth century may well have been that of the present Swed. ō in *bo*, etc.

The process must have begun pretty early, since there are numerous occasional spellings with *ou* in M.E., by the side of the orthodox *o*, or *oo* ; see § 163.   During the fifteenth century *ou* and *u* spellings for M.E. ō¹ are common, and are found in S. Editha (1420), Palladius (1420), Bokenam (1443), Pecok (1449), Cely Papers, and Paston Letters, to mention no more. It is impossible to say exactly when the absolute [ū] stage was reached, but this much may be said at once, that the new [ū] must not only have been fully developed, but, in some words, was also shortened to [ŭ] in time to undergo the un-rounding process which overtook original short *ŭ*, and produced the vowel now heard in *cut, run, bud*, etc.   (See on this un-rounding, § 250).

The *ou* and *u* spellings occur constantly throughout the sixteenth century, not only in private letters, etc., but also in printed books, *floud* and *bloud* being used, for instance, in the First and Second Prayer Books of Edward VI, *it buted not* in Ascham's Toxophilus, *houke* in Q. Elizabeth's letters, and so on.   The earliest Grammarians admit [ū] in words of the class we are considering.

(3) Of the words containing M.E. ō¹, we now distinguish three groups :—

(*a*) those pronounced with Late M.E. [ū] unchanged—*moon, spoon, rood, soon, brood, tooth, stool, food, goose, hoof* ;

(*b*) those pronounced with an entirely different vowel, [a]— *blood, flood, glove, must, done, month, Monday, mother, brother* ;

(*c*) those pronounced with short, slack [*u*] —*good, hood, stood, foot, soot, shook, cook, rook, look, took.*

Of these groups (*b*) is the most interesting.   From the moment that the new [ū] was shortened, it was completely levelled under the other short ŭ-sound, of various origin, already in existence, and shared its fate.   The reasons for the shortening are not, apparently, to be found in the phonetic conditions existing in the words themselves, since other words preserve the long type although the same consonants follow the vowel as in group (*b*).   The explanation must most probably be sought, as in so many cases in Received Standard, in an old diversity of dialect, Class or Regional.

Group (*c*) is the result of a comparatively recent shortening which apparently always affects the vowel before -*k*, though it is impossible to say why it should take place in *good* but not in *food*, in *foot*, but not in *root*, or *boot* ' profit, bargain '.   Here again dialect variety must probably be assumed.

There is plenty of evidence of short forms of many of the words in each of the three groups, in the sixteenth and seventeenth centuries, but they probably represent the early shortening (*b*) in all cases.   Lord Berners has *fludde* (three times at least in Froissart, vol. I) ; Edward VI's First P. B. has *fluddes* and *bludd* ; Gabr. Harvey, Letters, has *blud*, *futt*, and *whudd* ' hood ', rhyming with *budd* in the Letter Bk. ; Sackville rhymes *done* with *run* ; Gill (1621) gives *blood*, *glove*, *good*, *brother*, *done*, *does* vb., *mother*, *other*, as short ; Butler (1634) *gud*, *blud* ; Sir Edm. Verney (1639) writes *bludd*, *bluddynose*, Papers, 212 ; the Verney's bailiff (1653) writes *tuck* ' took ' ; Sir R. Verney (1686) writes *sutt* ' soot ', V. Mem. iv. 358 ; Cooper's list of words includes *flood*, *hood*, *other*, *soot*, *stood*, as having the sound of ' *oo* shortened ', which should mean [*u*], but gives *fut* as a ' barbarous form '.   Does this imply [a] ?   He appears to recognize [u, ū] as well as [a] in *foot*, *forsooth*, *good*, *hood*, *look*, -*sook*, *took*.   Jones (1701) gives a list of these words with [*ŭ*] which corresponds to our present usage except as regards *forsooth*, now [sūþ].

It is open to question whether all these, except Cooper's and Jones's lists, do not imply [a], though in the latter two we have apparently our present type with the late shortening.

§ 237. Distribution of the Types from M.E. ō¹.

This is pretty definitely fixed in present-day Received Standard, but there was great diversity in this respect formerly among good speakers.   *Soot* was pronounced [sat] among good speakers within living memory, though regarded as old-fashioned for the last fifty years or so.   (Cp. Sir R. Verney's spelling, and Cooper's view of this type in preceding § 236.) There was considerable diversity among good speakers in the sixteenth and seventeenth centuries, and much difference between them and ourselves, in the distribution of types.   In the fifteenth century there was probably at first only one type, [ū]; later two types [ū, ŭ]; still later the latter became [a], and these two [ū, a] remained the only types till towards the end of the seventeenth century, when, apparently, the third, [ŭ] developed, by a later shortening of [ū]. It is highly probable that every word was by some group of speakers pronounced according to any of the existing types. Thus Salesbury (1547) and Smith (1568) represent the vowel in *good* as being either long or short, Gill (1621) as being short; Salesbury describes *flood* with a long, Bullokar (1580) and Gill, with a short; *good* according to Price (1668) had [a] as in *cut*; according to Jones (1701) it had both this and [ŭ]; *foot* for Price had a long vowel, for Cooper either short [u] which was the best pronunciation, and [a] which was 'barbarous'; Price affirms that *soot* had [ū], Cooper and Jones that it had [ŭ], and also a pronunciation [a] which was not so good.

The early poets, as at present, rhyme all words with M.E. ō¹ indiscriminately, which most likely reflects the fact that all might be, and were, pronounced according to either type. The modern practice in this respect is based on old tradition.

Examples from the older poets which appear to indicate the use of a different type from that current to-day are :—Spenser, *buds—woods*; Drayton, *woo'd—stood, took—luck*; Suckling, *look—struck*; Dryden, *flood—mood—good*, etc.

NOTE 1. If we accept Luick's interpretation of M.E. *wode* 'wood', *above, love*, § 174, we must assume Late M.E. [wūd, abūv, lūv], and they will fall under § 236, group (2) with *hood*, etc., or under (3) with *blood*.

NOTE 2. M.E. *gōld*, with lengthening before *ld* (§ 114), normally became [gūld], and this was the fashionable Received Standard form well into the nineteenth century. By the side of M.E. *gōld*, however, *gŏld* also existed, due probably to the analogy of the adj. *gŏldene, gŏldne* (§§ 175. (7), 176), and this later became [gōld] long after the old long form had become [gūld]. (See § 242 for *ŏl*+cons.) This late form has completely ousted the old [gūld], which survives, however, in the family name *Gould* by the side of *Gold*.

NOTE 3. Our present pronunciation of *Rome* [roum] is not the traditional English type, but derived either from French or Italian. Hodges, Cooper, Jones all assert that the word was pronounced with '*oo*' long, i. e. [ū]. Shakespeare rhymes the word with *doom, groom*; Donne with *roome* and *come* [kūm]; Pope with *doom*; Swift with *gloom*. Cowley and Dryden have already adopted the newfangled form, and rhyme it with *home*.

§ 238. Combinative Treatment of M.E. ō¹+r.

In M.E. *flōr, swōr, mōr, pōre, hōre*, 'floor', 'swore', 'moor', 'poor', 'whore'; in M.E. *dōre* 'door' (§ 174); in *bōrd* 'board' *hōrd* (§ 114), etc., *ō* was not raised to [ū], but seems to have become [ō] in part of Early Standard. Some early writers

however, have [mūr, pūr, būrd], etc. At the present time
both types survive among different speakers, in some words.
Thus [puə, pɔ̄, muə, mɔ̄]. As a rule, in Received Standard,
apart from *poor, moor, boor*, only [ɔ̄] obtains in words containing M.E. *ōr.* In the dialects, however, we may hear [būərd,
flūər, būər], etc.

Luick, *Anglia*, xvi, p. 461, assumes the series [ōr, ūr, ôr, ɔ̄r].
There is no reason, however, why [ɔ̄(ə)] should not have come
straight from [ŭə].   Dr. Watts rhymes *door* with *to her*,
= [dŭə]; note also the fluctuation in the present day between
[pjuə-pjɔ̄, ʃuə-ʃɔ̄], and we even get [fjɔ̄, brɔ̄] for *fewer, brewer.*

Mutschmann, *Beibl. z. Anglia*, June, 1908, suggests the
influence of the preceding lip-consonants to account for [puə,
muə, buə, muən].

§ 239. *Word, worthy*, which now have [ʌ̄], may have had
ō[1] in M.E. In this case, they had [ū] in Early Mod., a view
supported by such spellings as *woord, woorthie* in *Edw. VI
First P. B.* The development from Early Mod. would be
[wūrd, wurd, ward, wǎrd, wʌ̄d], etc.

M.E. ō[2] (slack).

§ 240. Independent Development.

M.E. *ō*[2], whatever its origin (§ 201, p. 135), was probably
a long mid-back-slack-round [ɔ̄]. This sound seems to have
remained until well into the sixteenth century and then to
have been made tense [ō]. The latter sound was, much later,
diphthongized to the present [ou].

Examples : *stone, bone, loaf, on*ly, al-*one*, etc. ; *hope, throat*;
coat, rose, pole.

NOTE 1. *Broad* [brɔ̄d] instead of [broud], and *groat*, now [grout] from
the spelling, but formerly [grɔ̄t, grŏt], have been explained as derived from
a dialectal type in the S.-West of England, where this development is
normal. Sweet's explanation (*H. E. S.*, § 841) that the lowering is due to
the influence of *r* can hardly hold good in the face of *grove, grope*; see
Horn, *Hist. ne. Gr.*, p. 84.

NOTE 2. Present-day *one* [wan] shows a different vowel development
from *on*-ly, al-*one*, which have a normal sound from O.E. *ān*, M.E. *ōn*.
[wan] seems to presuppose an earlier [wun], like [wats] ' oats ', earlier
[wuts], now dialectal or vulgar. So many widely separated dialects now
have [úəts, wáts ; úən, wán] that it is difficult to decide from which area
this type passed into Standard English. The spelling *wonlyche* occurs
as early as 1421 (*St. Editha*, 3529). A fair number of examples of this
spelling are found in the sixteenth century: *Such a wone* (Latimer's
Sermons, 1549) ; the spelling *won(e)* is also found in letters of Henry VIII,
Queen Elizabeth's Translations, Machyn's Diary, Latimer's Sermons, in
letters in the Verney Memoirs, and the Wentworth Papers. But the

older type [ōn] long survived. Hodges gives *owne* and *one* as 'near alike', Price as identical in sound; Wallis says that *one* and *none* have 'ô rotundum', which is the sound attributed to the *o* in *pole, boat, oat*, etc.; Cooper couples *own* and *one* as pronounced alike, and includes *wuts* 'oats' in his list of dialect forms; the *Writing Scholar's Companion* (1695) actually represents '*wun*' as being a vulgar pronunciation! The poets rhyme according to the old type :—Sackville, *one—stone*; Shake-speare, *one—gone* [gōn], also with *bone*; Cowley, *grown—one*; Dryden, *one —thrown;* Pope, *one—undone* which shows our present type. It seems evident from the spelling that in Early Standard *one* had the same vowel as *on*-ly, *al*-one, etc., and that the other type gradually got a footing later from a lower Class Dialect. It is suggested by some that old [ōn] survives in '*un—a good 'un, a wrong 'un*, etc.; but this may equally well represent [wan] with loss of initial [w] in an unstressed syllable.

The process was [ōən-, ŏn-, ōən-, úən, uə́n, wan] or something of the sort. *Whome* 'home' is used by Tyndale (1528), and *whoale* 'whole', *wholy* for *holy*, forms similar to *wone*, occur, the latter several times, in *Rede me and be not wrothe* (1528); *wholy* in Sir T. More, by side of *holy* and *hole*.

NOTE 3. A similar tendency to develop [w] may be noted before old tense *ō* which had become [ū]. The spelling *wother* 'other' occurs on p. 117 of the *Shillingford Letters* (1447-50, Camden Soc., 1871).

Combinative Treatment of M.E. ō².

§ 241. **M.E. ō²+r.**

Before *r* M.E. slack *ō* seems to have become tense, as else-where, and then lowered to [ɔ̄]: *roar, boar, born,* for *lorn, glory, hoarse, sore,* etc. All these from earlier [rōr, bōr, glōri], etc. The tense [ō] or sometimes [ōə, ouə] still survives in the Northern and North Midland Dialects, and is heard also in the various forms of Vulgar Modified Standard in Liverpool.

§ 242. **M.E. ō²+l.**

It seems certain from the statements of the Grammarians, and from occasional spellings, some of which survived pretty late, that in the above combination a parasitic [u] developed, at least as early as the late fifteenth century—*owld, could,* etc., 'old, cold,' etc. This diphthong was subsequently contracted to [ō] and had the same history as independent *ō²* (§ 240).

§ 243. **Shortening of M.E. ō².**

Our present *hot*, M.E. *hō(a)te*, O.E. *hāt*, is a result of this. Spellings indicating shortened forms occur from fifteenth century: *hottest*, Palladius 64, 275; *whott* 'hot' Lord Burghley, Ellis 2, 3, 99, (1582); *hotte* Euphues 41; by the side of *hoate* Latimer, Sermons 293, etc. Other shortenings of this vowel are indicated in Lord Berners, Froissart: *loffe* 'loaf' 1, 52, *bottes* 'boats', *rodde* 'rode' 1 350. This is presumably

part of the same process as that involving the shortening of
M.E. $\bar{e}^1$ and $\bar{e}^2$, §§ 231, 235, and of [ū] from $\bar{o}^1$, § 236.

M.E. ŏ.

§ 244. Independent Treatment.

(1) M.E. ŏ remains unaltered, so far as we can tell, far into
the Modern Period. It was probably *mid-back-slack-round* [ŏ].
It cannot be determined precisely when it was lowered to its
present sound [ɔ]. Examples : *cot, rot, ox, long,* etc., etc.

(2) Un-rounding of ŏ.

Very few traces of this now remain in Received Standard,
but the un-rounded forms once existed in fashionable speech.
The doublets *chap-chop, strap-strop, Gad, egad-God*; *plat* (of
ground, Authorized Version, and Milton) for *plot* are nearly all
the survivors. The un-rounding of ŏ is typical of many Regional
Dialects of the West of England to-day, and this pronunciation
is very prevalent in many districts of U.S.A.   Early examples
are *starme* 'storm', rhymes *harm*, St. Editha 932 (1420); *afte-
tymes,* 'oft', Shillingford 53 (1447–50); *last* 'lost' Pret. Subjunct.
Marg. Paston (1469) P. Letters 2, 373.   During the sixteenth
century a few forms of this type penetrate into London English;
apart from Lord Berners *yander* 'yonder', Froissart 1, 205,
Machyn (1547–50) has *hars* 'horses' 12, *marrow* 'morrow' 47,
Dasset 'Dorset' 48, 57, *caffen* 'coffin' 120 ; Q. Eliz. *stap*
'stop' Letters 64. Lady Hungerford (c. 1569) has *swarn*
'sworn' Letters 256, but this may be regarded as a frank
Westernism.   A fair sprinkling of these forms occur in the
Verney Letters, *sassages* II. 318 (1648) ; *faly* 'folly' (1647) II.
380, etc.; Mrs. Basire writes *Gearge* (1655) Corresp. 139.
The type was apparently adopted on a large scale by fops, cp.
Lord Foppington in Vanbrugh's *Relapse* who is made to sub-
stitute *a* in every word where ŏ normally occurs : amongst
other forms he agrees with Q. Elizabeth in saying *stap* for *stop*.
In the early eighteenth century Lady Wentworth has *beyand*,
Anslow (Onslow). The un-rounded forms are not much represented in the rhymes, but *plot—that*, Spenser ; Shakespeare's
dally—folly (cp. *faly* above) in R. of Lucr., and Swift's *yonder—
salamander* are of interest. This process of un-rounding must
have been earlier than the rounding of M.E. ă after *w*.

§ 245. Lengthening of ŏ.

Before [s, f, þ] M.E. ŏ appears in Present-day English,
though not among all speakers, as [ɔ̄] as in *cost, soft, froth,* etc.

This is due probably to a late lengthening. Cp. the parallel lengthening of [æ], § 219.

M.E. ū.

§ 246. Independent Treatment: *ū* becomes [*au*].

The statements of sixteenth century Grammarians that this sound, in their day, was a diphthong, composed of *o* and *u*, do not in themselves inspire much confidence, since from what we know of these writers, this is just the way we should expect them to describe a sound which was normally spelt *ou*. At the same time it is most probable that [ou] was a stage in the development from [ū] to [*au*]. Cooper (1685) analyses the diphthong as consisting of [au], which again is one of the later stages, shortly before the present sound was reached. Zachrisson cites the fifteenth century spellings *abaught* 'about', *faunde* 'found', *withaught*, all from Paston Letters; *aur* from Cely Papers 20, and *sauth* 'south' from Godstow Register. It may perhaps be considered an open question whether these really are phonetic spellings at all. Why should *au* occur to the writers as a natural way of expressing a diphthong, at a time when this combination of letters was coming to be regarded as a way of representing [ɔ]? [1] It will not do to build too much on these spellings. The essential thing is that the old *ū* had certainly been differentiated from the old sound before the new [ū] had fully developed, and this latter process was probably complete round about 1400 at latest (§ 236). The series of changes from the old long vowel to the diphthong was probably [ū < ūᵘ < ou < au < *au*], but our present knowledge does not allow us to fix with any confidence the approximate chronology of the various stages.

Examples are: *how, house, mouse, bow* (vb.), *mouth, foul, ground, plough*; *crown, power, flower, count*, etc. *Drought* (drɑut) is from M.E. *drŭht < drŭ(h)t*.

NOTE I. In *country, plum, rough, southern, thumb*, *ū* was shortened to *ŭ* before the diphthongization began, and the vowel shares the history of other M.E. *ŭ*-words (§§ 236. (3); 250).

NOTE 2. *Youth* [jūþ] may be a Northern loan (*ū* remains in the North), or it might owe its vowel to association with a short M.E. *young* (jŭŋg], giving an early [jŭþ], which later underwent lengthening. Cp. similar lengthenings in §§ 219, 245. It is possible there may have been an O.E. mutated *ġȳġþ*, since [jȳþ] seems to have existed in Early Mod.

---

[1] As a result of careful scrutiny of passages in fifteenth-century MSS. in which *au* or *eu* for M.E. *ū* were supposed to occur, Zachrisson now finds only two absolutely certain instances—*aur* 'our' (1480) in Cely Pprs, and *hew* 'how' (1484) also in Cely P. See *Engl. Pronunciation at Shakespeare's Time*, pp. 134-5. Z. interprets *hew* as [həu], *aur* as [aur].

(Luick, *Anglia*, xiv, p. 291, cit. Horn, p. 92). *Uncouth* [ankúþ] must be a Northern form.

NOTE 3.   Modern [kjūkambə] is a spelling pronunciation for *cu-* from earlier [kū-], which gives normally [kaʊkambə], now obsolete or vulgar.

Combinative Treatment.

§ 247.   **M.E. ū before r + consonant is not diphthongized.**

Examples: *court, source, course*, etc.   [ū] is still recorded in these words in the sixteenth and seventeenth centuries.   In the eighteenth century the vowel was lowered to [ō], whence by further lowering we get the present [ɔ] in these words. (Luick, *Anglia*, xvi, pp. 455–61 ; cp. also remarks in § 241 above on the slackening of [ō] in eighteenth century.)

§ 248.   **ME. ū before lip-consonants, not diphthongized.**

In this position the sound of M.E. *ū* remained unaltered. (See Luick, *Anglia*, xvi, p. 501.)

Examples: *droop, loop, stoop, room, tomb, Cowper* [kūpə], etc.

§ 249.   **M.E. wū- remains.**

The vowel in *wound* (subst.), to *wound*, M.E. *wūnd, wūnd(en)*, has been preserved owing to the influence of *w-*. The pronunciation [waʊnd], which formerly existed, is probably influenced by the spelling.   The pret. of to *wind* is still [waʊnd], and this may be explained by the analogy of *found*, which belongs to the same class.

M.E. and Early Modern ŭ.

§ 250.   **Independent Treatment : ŭ becomes [a].**

The earliest English Grammarians, hide-bound as they are by the spelling, leave it doubtful whether they are aware of any other sound than [ŭ] in words *buck, cut, but*, etc.   Most of them down to the middle of the seventeenth century are evidently describing the old [ŭ] pure and simple.   Hodges, in 1644, is the first English writer to recognize the existence of the new sound, and most old short *ŭ*-words have this sound in his pronunciation (Zachrisson, p. 211).   Wallis however (1653) definitely refers to the 'obscure' sound of *ŭ*, and Cooper (1685) very explicitly distinguishes 'guttural *ŭ*', in *nut*, which he describes as pronounced in the throat with the lips retracted; and further states that if while *o* is being uttered, the lips are drawn back, this guttural *u* results.   The sound, he says, resembles that which a man makes when groaning from sickness or pain.   We can hardly doubt that the sound [a] is

meant. On the other hand, the Frenchman Bellot as early as
1580, while stating that *Buck* and *Book* are both pronounced
with French *ou* (= [ŭ]), says that the sound of French *o* is
heard in the first syllable of *upon* (Spira, *Englische Lautentwickelung*, p. 52). Mason (a French merchant), 1622, says
that French *o* is heard in *upon* and *hungrie* (Spira, p. 67).
A work called *Alphabet anglois*, 1625, describes *o* as occurring
in *up, butter, sunder, curse*, etc. This identification of the
sound of English *u* with French *o* is significant when we
remember such Modern French spellings and pronunciations
as that of *tôb*, English *tub*. The occasional spellings, however,
point to the un-rounding being considerably older : [1] Marg.
Paston *gannes* 'guns' (twice) P.L. ii. 372 (1469); Fortescue,
Governance of England, 126, *sadanly* (1471–6); Cely Papers
camyth 146, and perhaps *warsse, wars = wurse* (?) 146; Machyn
(1547–50), *Samerset* 182, *Chamley* 38 (= *Chumley*, pronounced
as now [tʃámli]) *Cholmondely*. These spellings would scarcely
be possible for speakers who still pronounced [ŭ]. What
degree of un-rounding they express, and whether this was
complete, is another question. It is enough that they show
that the process had started. Its effects may not have been
equally strong in all dialects, and the London dialect may
have been slightly behind Norfolk and Essex in this respect.
The statements of the Frenchmen just quoted need certainly
not be taken literally, and they would be consistent with
a fully un-rounded [a], but for the present, and pending fresh
light, it is better to be cautious and conservative. The present-
day Lancashire vowel in *bush, bull*, etc., which is mid-back-tense,
slightly rounded, might easily sound as a kind of [ŏ] to unaccustomed ears, and this may well represent approximately
the stage reached by the last quarter of the sixteenth century,
and lasting beyond the first quarter of the century following.

This unrounding process involved all the words containing
[ŭ] no matter what the origin, the main groups being : (*a*) O.E.
and M.E. *ŭ* as in *run, cut, bud, honey, nut, rust, son, summer,
won, wonder*, etc., etc., [ran, kat, bad, hani, nat], etc.; (*b*)
O.E. and M.E. *ō*, Early Mod. [ū] with early shortening, as in
blood, flood, etc. [blad, flad], cp. § 236. 3 ; (*c*) words with Early
Mod. *u* from earlier [y], as in *cudgel, drudge, rush*, etc. [kadʒəl,

---

[1] Zachrisson has now shown that of the fifteenth-century forms here
cited as containing *a*, those from M. Past. have certainly *o* in the MS.,
and that *camyth* fr. Cely P. probably has *o*, though the letter much
resembles *a* ; Fortescue's form should perhaps not be accepted as having
a without further examination of the MS. Machyn's forms have undoubted *a*. See *Engl. Pron. in Shakespeare's Time*, pp. 125–30.

dradž, raʃ]; (*d*) Early *ŭ* from M.E *ü* in French words, as *judge*, *just*, etc. (See § 253, M.E. *ü*, for the sound in this group of words.)

Combinative Treatment of M.E. ŭ.

§ 251. Influence of Initial Lip-consonant: [u] restored.

The sound in *put, bull, bush, full, pull, wolf, wool*, which goes back to earlier *ŭ*, was apparently unrounded to start with, but later, the influence of the initial lip-consonant restored [ŭ]. It looks as if this tendency existed only among certain classes of speakers, and as if the above were survivals of their dialect, while on the other hand in *mud, bud, but, fun*, etc., we have forms from another type of speech, in which the later rounding did not take place.

NOTE. Modern *come* [kam] apparently represents M.E. *cumen* (often written *comen*) and not M.E. *cōmen* with lengthening of *ŭ* (§ 174), to judge by such spellings in E.Mod. as *cummeth*, etc., *Edw. VI's First P.B.*

§ 252. M.E. ŭ before r or r + consonant: becomes [a], which becomes [ā].

The vowel in *burn, cur, murder, purse, worm* became [a], giving [barn, kar, mardər, pars, warm], etc., as in Modern Scotch; as the [r] sound weakened the vowel was lengthened, and ultimately made into a flat vowel, fully lengthened, giving present-day [ā]. For other sources of this sound see §§ 228, 239, 256.

NOTE. When a vowel follows the combination -*ur*-, this becomes [a], and the [r] being retained, no lengthening or other change of the vowel occurs: *flourish, nourish, Surrey*, etc. = [flariʃ, nariʃ, sari], etc.

M.E. ŭ = O.E. ў; O.Fr. u.

§ 253. (See § 158 for O.E. *ў* in M.E.)

The [ў] sound, whether of English or French origin, was simply retracted to the corresponding high-back vowel [ŭ] (in Late M.E. ?), and this sound underwent the subsequent lowering and unrounding which overtook the other [ŭ] sounds no matter what their origin, and developed into present-day [a]. See § 250.

Examples: (*a*) English words: *bundle, blush, thrush, much, such, drudge, clutch, cudgel, rush* (the plant); (*b*) French words: *just, judge, humble, study, public*. The distribution of the three types in English words was rather different in the fifteenth and sixteenth centuries from that of Received Standard at the present time.

NOTE 1. *Busy*, now [b*i*z*i*] (§ 158 (a, e)), and *Bury* [b*e*r*i*] (vb. and n.) represent the M.E. *ü*-type in spelling, but the former shows the unrounded M.E. type, the latter the Essex-London City type, in pronunciation. The survival in pronunciation of the old [y]-type in *bury* is recorded in the seventeenth and eighteenth centuries. The spelling *buiryed* (1710, *Wentw. Papers*, p. 122) almost certainly implies [bjūrjəd]. (See also *E. St.* 47, pp. 165–6.) Earlier non-dialectal writers have the *u*-type in several words beside those where we have it : *furst* 'first', in Lydgate; Cr. Knt. of Bath 389; Machyn ; Sir Thomas Smith, etc., etc. ; *burthe* 'birth', Caxton; *thursteth*, Hoccleve; *thurst, thursty*, Sir Thos. Elyot ; *sturre* 'stir', Bp. Fisher; *sturred, sturrs*, Latimer; Q. Eliz.

NOTE 2. In a large number of words of English origin, O.E. *ȳ* occurs in Standard Engl. with the M.E. (Middlesex) *i*-type—*hill, wish, sin, fill, thin*, etc., and these words therefore fall under M.E. *i* (§ 255). *i*-forms occur in fifteenth and sixteenth century writers where we now have other types :—*lyfte, lift* 'left hand', Gregory; Cr. Knt. of Bath ; *syche*, etc. 'such', Gregory; Bk. of Quintessence; John Mason (1533); Sir Thos. Smith (*suich*); *schytte, shitte* 'shut', Pret., Gregory; Caxton; Ld. Berners ; *biriede* 'buried', Bk. of Quint.

NOTE 3. In a certain number of words, the O. and M.E. S. Eastern (or London City) *e*-type survives in Standard Engl., e.g. *fledge, kernel, merry, knell, left* (hand), etc. These, therefore, fall under M.E. *e* (§§ 227, 228). This type was formerly much used in earlier London speech, and that among persons of the better class : *sterr*- vb. 'stir', Lydgate; Gregory ; Bk. of Quint.; Ld. Berners ; Sir Edw. Howard (1513); Sir Thos. Elyot; Latimer; Cavendish; *shette* 'shut' Pret., R. Sustr. Men. ; Caxton; Cavendish; *knett(ed)*, etc. 'knit', Caxton ; Rede me ; *kechen, ketchyn*, etc.' kitchen', Sir Thos. Elyot ; Machyn; *weshing* 'wishing', Q. Eliz. (O.E. *wȳscan*).

NOTE 4. *Church*, O.E. *ċyrċe, ċirċe*, is found in M.E. spelt with *u, i, e*. Its origin is, however, doubtful. The initial *ch*- cannot easily be accounted for if we assume original *y* (from *u-i*, § 109) ; the *e* and *u*-spellings are difficult, if we assume that the vowel was originally *i*.

§ 254. M.E. ī becomes [ai].

Under this sound we may include original O.E. *ī* in *write*, etc., French *ī*, and the *ī* which developed before [x̣] in *light*, etc., probably in the late M.E. period in some dialects. [x̣] seems to have lingered on into the seventeenth century among some speakers (§ 284. (7)). The preceding vowel may have been lengthened just before the total disappearance of the front consonant.

The diphthongizing process probably began by a slackening of the latter part of *ī*, thus [*ī* < *i*ⁱ]. The first portion was then further differentiated to [e]. This mid-front vowel was then made into a flat vowel, and then retracted to [a], giving [ai]. When once the diphthongization starts, by the differentiation of the first and latter part of [*ī*] it is possible to suggest various paths of development, none of which can be proved beyond a doubt to be the one followed. The above series, however, seems to square with what is known. From [ai] the development to the present [*ai*] is simple and is merely a question of slackening.

There is little doubt that the [ei] stage was reached pretty early in the fifteenth century if the fairly frequent spelling *ey* in *St. Editha* (1421) means anything: *bleynd, myeld, feyr,* ' blind, mild, fire ', etc. The beginnings may have been in the preceding century (Dibelius, *Anglia*, xxiii, pp. 349, 352). The question as to what the precise stages were, and when they were reached, is very difficult. See on these points Zachrisson, pp. 73-6. The development was not uniform all over the country. Some of the sixteenth-century English Grammarians still insist on a pronunciation [*ī*], but this is no doubt due to the domination of the spelling (Zachrisson, p. 205). It seems probable that the [a*i*] stage was reached before the end of the fifteenth century, as is shown by the inverted spellings *defoyled* ' defiled ', Mnk. of Evesham (1482) ; and those cit. Jespersen Mod.E. Gr. 320, *joyst* (1494) for *jiste* and *boyle* (on the body) for *bile* (1529) ; cp. also *defoylyng*, Rede me, etc. (1529). At this point old [*ī*] is levelled under *oi*. The rhyme *tryall— disloyal* occurs in Marston's *Insatiate Countess*, iv (1613). Cp. also the spelling *voiolence*, *Wentw. Papers*, p. 280 (1712). (See § 270 for the history of *oi*.) Many dialects still remain approximately at this stage, the best known being Irish English, whose sound is usually, but inaccurately, rendered *oi* by popular writers of to-day.

Examples of present-day [*ai*] from earlier [ī] are : *life, ride, my, I, bite, blind,* etc., *knight, night, light,* etc. *Eye, high, nigh* of course go back to M.E. *ī*-forms, for which see § 172. (2).

NOTE I. *Oblige* was pronounced [oblídž] in the seventeenth and eighteenth centuries, a fashionable habit due to French influence. The spellings *obleged, obleginge, obleg, disablegin* are frequent in the Verney Memoirs between 1647 and 1666, and a search would probably reveal this before and after these dates. Pope, as is well known, rhymes *obliged* with *besieged* (Epist. to Arbuthnot, 207-8) and *oblige ye* with *besiege ye* (Imitations of Horace, Bk. I, Epist. vii, 29-30). It has been said that this pronunciation was killed by Lord Chesterfield in a letter written in 1749 in which he is supposed to refer to it as a pronunciation of ' the vulgar man', which ' carries the mark of the beast along with it '. Any one reading the passage will see that on the contrary [oblídž] is the pronunciation insisted upon as proper, and that it is [oblaidž] which is referred to as vulgar. Coleridge (*Table Talk*, Dec. 29, 1822) repeats a story told by George IV to Charles Mathews about Kemble the actor, who, a great precisian in speech, actually corrected the King, then Prince of Wales, for saying '*obleege*', with the reproof ' it would become your royal mouth better to say oblige'. George IV may have retained the fashionable pronunciation of a former day which had been abandoned by actors, but it is recorded that Wilkie Collins (1824–89) still retained the old type (*Book-man*, May 1907, op. cit., Jespersen, Mod. Engl. Gr. 8. 3).

NOTE 2. [ĭ] is preserved in words of late French origin, *machine, invalid*, etc. In unstressed positions [ɩ̆] or [ə] is normal, the shortening being far earlier than the diphthongization, e.g. *housewife* = [hazĭf], *Berkshire* = [bāɑkʃə], the artificial [-ʃaɪə] in the names of counties being due to the spelling or the influence of the stressed *shire*. Walker (1801) recommends [mĭ] in unstressed positions, but the strong [maɪ] is largely used now in such phrases as [aɪv lɔ̄st maɪ weɪ], etc. The otherwise obsolete [mɪn] may sometimes be heard on the stage—I have heard Sir Frank Benson say [ou mɪ̆ proʃɛtɪ̆k soul, mɪ naŋkl].

NOTE 3. The words *high, nigh, eye*, etc., represent the M.E. *ī*-type, from O.E. -*ēah, -ēag-*, see § 172. The other M.E. type -*ei*- also survived in some of these words as late as the eighteenth century. Price (1668) gives *high* and *hay* as having the same sound ; Cooper (1688) says the same sound is heard in *height* and *convey* ; Baker (1725) says that *height* is pronounced both as ' hate ' and ' hĭte '. Waller rhymes this word with *strait*, Dryden with *fate*. We preserve this type in *neighbour*, contrasted with *nigh*.

M.E. ĭ.

§ 255. Independent Treatment.

This sound remains unchanged, so far as can be discovered, except that the ordinary sound in Received Standard is not a pure *high front*, but a *high flat*, slack [ꟿ] : *bid, spring, sit, ship, dish*, etc., etc.

Ridge, bridge, thin, hill, midge, fist, etc., are from the M.E. *ĭ*-type from O.E. *ў* (§ 158 (*a*) and (*e*), 253 (Note 2)). This form is typical of the Middles. dialect from the fourteenth century at least.

An apparent lowering of *i* to *e* [ɛ] is so common among all classes from the fifteenth to the eighteenth centuries that it must be noted. Only a few of the dozens of examples which occur can be given ; the following do not include spellings from persons who show definite traces of Regional influence ; Fortescue, *contenually, lemited, deficult* ; Caxton, *shellyngs* : Ld. Berners, *mengled* ; Sir Thos. Seymour, *fessher men, Prem-rose, begennyng* ; Latimer, *sence* ' since ' ; Ascham, *splettyd* ; Q. Eliz., *bellowes* ' billows ', *rechis* ' riches ' ; Machyn, *deleverd, chelderyn, essue, red* ' rid ' Pret. of *ride, denner, ennes of the court* ; various writers in Verney Mem., *fefty, strept* ' stripped ', *cheldren, sence, stell* ' still ', *untel, shelings, pell* ' pill ', *bet* ' bit ', *consedowring, speriets* ; Mrs. Basire, *sens* ' since ', *Prence, cheldren* ; Lady Wentworth, *tel* ' till ', *senc, spetting*, etc., etc. That these spellings represent a current pronunciation is, apart from their recurrence through the centuries, confirmed by the poets' rhymes : *sperit—merit*, Spenser, Drayton, Waller, Swift,

Pope; *prince—sense, thence, pretence,* etc., Dryden; *wit—coquet, gift—theft,* Lady Mary Montague.

NOTE 1. *Chill,* O.E. (W.S.) *ćielu,* is one of the few words of definitely W. or Middle Sax. type in Mod. Standard English. The non-W.S. form was O.E. *ćelu,* M.E. *chēle,* which would have given Mod. **cheal* [tʃīl].

NOTE 2. *The form Bushop.* Such spellings as *bushop, busshop* for *bishop* are common from the fifteenth century to the eighteenth. They are found in Marg. Paston (1469); Ld. Berners' Froissart; a letter of Archbp. Cranmer (1537) Ellis 3. 3. 23 (at least nineteen times!); Ascham, Scholem. 127 ; Roper's Life of Sir T. More ; Dr. Denton in Verney Mem. (1688). Cooper (1685) includes *Bushop* among pronunciations to be avoided, as peculiar to a 'barbarous dialect' (a phrase hardly applicable to that of his contemporary Dr. Denton); Jones (1701) says that the word is 'sounded *Booshop* by some'. There is no doubt therefore that the spellings represent a genuine pronunciation, which perhaps arose from rounding of *i* to [y] after *b-* then retracting to [ŭ] which appears to have remained. The form is apparently quite extinct now.

Combinative Treatment.

§ 256. i + r, or r + consonant.

In such words as *sir, bird, first,* etc., *i* seems to have been considerably modified, perhaps during the sixteenth century. The first stage may have been a raising of the back of the tongue, thus giving a high-flat vowel. This then became a pure back vowel, through the abandonment of the front action of the tongue. The high-back thus produced was levelled under the same sound from old *ŭ* (§ 250) and became [a]. [bard, farst], etc. survive in Scotch. In English, the vowel was gradually lengthened as [r] was weakened, and finally lowered to a low-flat vowel [ʌ]. See history of *ur* in § 252. The combination *ir* is therefore a fruitful source of Modern [ʌ]. See also §§ 228, 239, and 252.

§ 257. When *-ir-* is followed by a vowel, it remains unaltered : *spirit, stirrup, squirrel,* etc.

§ 258. The *i* in *England* [iŋglənd], *singe, hinge, wing, string* is M.E. *i* from earlier *e,* before [ŋ, ndž]. Quite apart from Northern influence, the spellings from fifteenth century onwards indicate the *i* type : *Ingland, Yngland,* Gregory; Fortescue, Wm. Paston (Judge) ; Cr. Knt. of Bath ; Letters of Thos. Pery, Ellis, 2. 2. 146 (1539); Letter J. Mason, Ellis, 2. 2. 56 (1523) ; Ld. Berners, passim, etc., etc. *Kynges Bynche,* Gregory 149; Short Eng. Chron. 68, etc. ; Machyn 195 (twice) ; *wrynchynge* Ascham, Toxophilus 145. Scattered spellings with *i* for *e* before *-n + d, t, s*: *Gintleman,* Laneham's Letter 40 (1575); *repint,* Verney Mem. ii. 56 (1645);

rintes ' rents ', ibid. ii. 84 (1642) ; *attinding* ibid. iv. 113 (1665) ; *sincible* Wentworth Papers 211 (1711).

M.E. and Early Modern au.

§ 259. Independent development—[*a*u] < [5].

The English Grammarians of the sixteenth and some of the seventeenth century are open to the gravest suspicion when they deal with the old diphthongs. Having their attention rivetted on the spelling, it is enough that a sound should be spelt with two letters for them to describe two vowel sounds. The French writers, being more independent, are able, even in the sixteenth century, to indicate that *au* or *aw* expresses a single vowel. Wallis (1653) and Cooper (1685) attribute to these symbols a monophthong which must be approximately our present sound. The series of changes whereby this was reached from the M.E. sound were [*au < ou < ǫu < ɔ̆ᵘ < 5*], the first step being the rounding of the first element by the influence of the second ; and the last stage, the loss of the weakened *u.* Before the last stage was reached, old *au* was levelled under old *ou*, with the result that we now have the same sound in *taught* and *daughter* (earlier *douhter*, etc., see § 264). Surrey's spelling *tought* 'taught', and the rhyming of this with *y-wrought*, show that the levelling has taken place. Occasional spellings in the sixteenth century point to monophthongal pronunciation : Zachrisson (E. Stud., vol. 53, pp. 313–14) cites *oll, defolte, ofull* (' awful '), all from Suffolk Wills, c. 1500-15 ; one or two may be quoted from Machyn : *hopene* 'halfpenny', *solmon* ' salmon' 170, *ontt* ' aunt' 64, *a nobe* = ' an aulb ', ' alb ' 62. The inverted spellings *caumplet* Machyn 12, and *clausset* ' closet' Latimer, Seven Serm. 38, tell the same tale. There are a certain number of occasional spellings from fifteenth century documents which are illuminative, such as *y-fole* ' fallen ', St. Editha 522 (1420), and several others cited by [1] Zachrisson, especially *beholue* ' behalf ' = *behaulve*, from Rolls of Parliament, cited from Morsbach, Schriftspr. 50. It is probable that monophthongization of *au* was complete before M.E. *ū* reached the [ou] stage (§ 246).

Examples of M.E. *au*, present-day [5], are : *claw, draw, law, hawk* ; *naught, slaughter, taught* ; *cause, fault* ; fifteenth century *au* (§ 218) occurred in *call, malt, chalk*, etc., etc. (On the loss of *l* in *chalk*, etc., cp. § 284. (3).)

[1] Zachrisson now (*Engl. Pron. in Shakespeare's Time*, pp. 37–8) shows the inverted spelling *auffer* ' offer ', from Cely P., previously quoted by him, and seriously questioned by Ekwall, Engl. Stud. 49, 279, &c., to be absolutely reliable.

Further, from M.E. *aŭn* in French words we have *daunt, haunt, launch, laundress, taunt,* etc., in so far as these have the pronunciation [dɔnt], etc.

NOTE. As regards the pronunciation [ā] which exists also in these words, as well as exclusively in *aunt*, the least unsatisfactory explanation seems to be that it goes back to a M.E. variant with *ă*. The same applies to *branch, chance, dance, chant, grant,* etc., whose vowel interchanges with [æ]. The difficulty is to account for the lengthening to eighteenth-century [æ] in [ænt], etc., which form is a necessary precursor of the present one. *Branch,* etc., have [ɔ] forms recorded by the early writers, and these also exist in the Mod. Dialects.

Combinative treatment of au.

NOTE. The following account of the combinative treatment of *au* in Mod. Engl. follows the ingenious and plausible article of Luick, *Anglia,* xvi, pp. 462–97. These views are very widely accepted, and appear to settle many difficulties. On the other hand, they raise others. The whole question cannot be regarded as finally settled.

§ 260.   au before lip-consonants becomes [ā].

The words *calf, calve, half, halve, balm, salve, laugh,* etc., are shown both by occasional early spellings and by the accounts of Grammarians to have had *au* at one time (cf. § 218). They now have [ā] in Standard English. It is suggested that shortly after *al* in these words became [aul], the *u* was lost before the following lip-consonant, and the *ă* underwent compensatory lengthening to [ā]. This *ā* was then fronted to [æ] at the same time that short [ă] was fronted. This [æ] then became [ā] again in the late eighteenth century. Thus the career of the vowel in *calf* was, after a certain point, identical with that in *chaff,* thus :

$$\text{[tʃăf—tʃæf—tʃǣf—tʃāf}$$
$$\text{kau(l)f—kāf—kǣf—kāf]}$$

and so on with the other words of this group. Luick admits that the [kāf] stage, which he has to assume for Early Modern, is not vouched for by any of the writers. He assumes that this development took place in the speech of the lower orders, which did not come within the Grammarians' province.

As regards *laugh, laughter, draught,* where the *au* developed in M.E. before a back consonant which subsequently became *f* (§ 282); Luick assumes the series [lauχʷ < lauf < lāf < læf < lāf], etc.

NOTE. The disappearance of the *u* in *laugh* depends in Luick's scheme upon the development of the old [χʷ] into [f]. In dialects where [χ] remained, the diphthong also remained and became [ɔ]; cp. [lɔh] in Scotch. Luick rightly says, p. 496, that there were two different developments in M.E., which led, one to [f], the other to [χ].

The starting-point is a back open cons. [χ] with lip-modification. In one type of speech the lip element is increased and the back weakened, and this ultimately results in [f] as in [lɑ̃ftə]. In the other, the lip element is weak and the back element strong, and no [f] arises, but [χ] remains, and is subsequently lost as in [slɔ̃tə]. The weak point in Luick's scheme, it seems to me, is the assumption of the form [lauf] at all. There is, so far as I know, no evidence that it ever existed. (I am bound, however, to make him a present of *loffe*, Shakespeare, *Midsummer N. D.*, First Fol. I. I, which looks like [lʌf] from [lɔ̃f] from [lauf]. It is capable of another interpretation nevertheless.) [lauχ], which gave [lɔ̃χ], we are certain of. It seems much simpler to assume that the type which developed [f] was never diphthongized at all, but passed from [lɑ̆χ^w] to [lɑ̆f] in M.E. Cp. the 1563 spelling *laffe* cit. § 221. If we take the two words *slaughter* and *laughter* we can compare and contrast the development [slɑ̆χtər < slauχtər < slouχtər < sloutər > slɔutər < slɔ̃tər ; lɑ̆χ^wtər < lɑ̃ftər < læftər < lǣftər < lɑ̃ftər]. Luick's scheme necessitates [lɑ̆χ^wtər < lauχ^wtər < lɑ̃uftər < lɑ̃ftər < lǣftər], etc. It is ingenious, but assumes too much, besides being, as it appears, unnecessary. Again, as regards the suggested history of present-day [kɑ̃f], it is not proved that diphthongization before *l* was universal. What if there were M.E. dialects in which *l* was lost quite early before *f*? This might result in *hăf, căf*, which would do away with difficulties involved in Luick's view. As a matter of fact *haf* 'half' occurs in Ayenbite, see §221. On loss of *l*, see § 284. (3) below. Luick's theory assumes that the form [kaulf], whence [kauf], arose only to be monophthongized the next moment to the dubious early [kɑ̃f]. The evidence of the Modern Dialects, among which [æ, ɑ̃, ɔ̃] forms are found for all the -*al*- words, even where *l* remains, seems to point to there being two types in E. Mod.—[ɑ̆l-], which became [ɑ̃(l)], and [aul], which became [ɔ̃(l)].

§ **261.** Present-day *safe, save, chamber* [seif, seiv, tʃeimbə] presuppose a M.E. *ā* (§ 225). Although these words occur with *au* in M.E., they are also found written *saaf*, etc. (§ 196). This monophthongization of an earlier *au* is due to the following lip-consonant, and took place, in some dialects, as early as the thirteenth century (Luick, *Anglia*, xvi. 503).

§ **262.** au before [dž, ndž].

Before these sounds, *au* loses the second element and becomes *ā*, whence Present-day [ei]: *gage* or *gauge*, M.E. *gage* and *gauge, danger* earlier *daunger, angel* earlier *aunge(l), strange* earlier *straunge, change* earlier *chaunge*, etc.

We have seen (§ 184) that in M.E. *an* and *aun* spellings both occur in these and other French words, and also that there is M.E. evidence for *ā* in such words. This will account for the present pronunciation. We assume therefore M.E. *straunge* < *strănge*, etc.

§ **263.** Another tendency in M.E. (§ 171, final Note) is the diphthongization of *a* to *ai* before [dž, tʃ, ʃ], and the sixteenth-century Grammarians give some evidence of the existence of this. It is therefore possible to explain *danger*, etc., either from M.E. *daunger* < *dānger*, or from M.E. *dainger*.

See on these points Luick, *Anglia*, xvi. 485.

§ 264. M.E. ou.

This diphthong went through the stages [*ou*, ɔ̄ᵘ, ɔ̄] and was therefore levelled under old *au* (§ 259). The spelling *tought*, Tottel's Misc., p. 7, which rhymes in Surrey's poem with *ywrought*, together with Sackville's rhyme *wrought—caught*, Compl. D. of Buckingham 125, and *draught—thought*, ib. 127, show that the levelling has already taken place. Examples: *daughter, brought, sought, wrought*, M.E. *douhter, brouhte*, etc.

NOTE. Undiphthongized forms, in which old [χ] had become [f], are also recorded in Standard Engl. as late as eighteenth century—[brɔ̄ft, dɔ̄ftər] (cp. Horn, *Hist. ne. Gr.*, p. 195), and such pronunciations survive in the Mod. Dialects (cp. Wright, *E. D. Gr.*, § 359). In Early Standard the two types must have coexisted—*douhter, dofter*, and the former won the place. The rhyme *after—daughter* [dæftər] occurs in Marston's *Eastward Hoe*, v. 1 (1605). On the unrounding of M.E. *ŏ* cp. § 244 (2).

§ 265. M.E. ēu, īu, ū̆ [ēu, īu, ȳ].

There are several classes of words included here, some of native English, some of N. French origin: *Tuesday, steward, true, knew, brew*; *rule, Jew*; *due, sure*; *rude, use, pure, duke, Luke*; *fruit, suit, pew, tune*, etc., etc. It is quite simple to state that all these words, whether they had [ēu, īu, *or* ȳ] in M.E., now have either [jū], as [nyū, djū], etc., or [ū] after [r, dž, tʃ] and sometimes after [l], as [brū, rūl, tʃū, džū, lūk], etc.

¹ The difficulty begins when we ask, what were the intervening stages, and at what point the old diphthongs were levelled under old [ȳ]. (1) The process seems to have been that *ēu* and *īu* were first both levelled under *iu̇*, which became [iẏ, jȳ]; this was caught up by old *ū̇*, which also became [jȳ], thus giving at one and the same time [stjȳərd, knjȳ, djȳk, jȳz], etc.

¹ An elaborate discussion of this matter by Luick will be found in *Anglia* 45, pp. 132–181 (1920), and another has just been published by Zachrisson, *Shakespeare Pronunc.* (1927) pp. 79–95. Both of these writers review all the evidence with great care and minuteness, but reach different conclusions. Luick interprets the seventeenth century *you*-spellings as indicating [jȳ], Zachrisson agrees with me that they mean [jū]. On the other hand, Zachrisson disbelieves in the prolonged survival of the French [ȳ] at all, in England, and thinks that [jū] was very early substituted for it by English speakers, a process which is common at the present day, statements to the contrary by the Grammarians being due to a faulty analysis of the French sound. I do not know whether Professor Zachrisson will dismiss the very specific statement of Voltaire (see next page) as a Frenchman's error, nor whether Professor Luick will find in it, as I do, support for the view that the [ȳ] sound was retained—at least among some speakers.

O

From the fifteenth century at any rate, this sound, no matter which of the above sources it came from, is spelt indifferently *ue, eu, ew*: *blwe* 'blew' Pret. St. Editha; *hue* 'hewed', and *slew*, Robt. the Devil 922; *greu* 'grew', O.E. *grēōw*, rhymes *vertú*, Bokenam Pr. Marg. 159, and with *issew, pursew*, Bokenam Hom. 261; *nyew* 'new', R. Sustr. Men. 96. 25; *sewer* 'sure', Cely Papers 77, *Dewke*, and *dew* 'due', ib. 112, *continew* 78; Gabr. Harvey Letters, *blue* 14. 4; *nu* 'new', 14; *shued* 'showed', Verney Mem, iv. 107 (1665); *hewmor*, ibid. ii. 392 (1648). The levelling under a single sound is apparently quite early. (2) The next question is how long did the [ȳ] sound remain in use? when was it retracted to [ū]? This point has been much discussed, and opinions are still divided upon it, especially among those who rely chiefly on the old Grammarians. The facts are these: in the seventeenth century some Grammarians assert, as clearly and positively as they assert anything, that [ȳ] still exists; others are as positive that it does not, Bp. Wilkins (1688) going so far as to maintain that Englishmen cannot pronounce this 'whistling letter', as he calls it, at all. Unless we are going to reject the Grammarians altogether, for which there is perhaps something to be said, it seems reasonable to believe that both groups are right, and that some speakers said [djȳk, bljȳ, frjȳt], etc., and others [djūk, bljū, frjūt], etc. The two usages may have belonged to different social dialects. The occasional spellings seem to prove at any rate that [ū] existed as early as the middle of the sixteenth century: A. Boorde c. 1535, Ellis' Letters III. ii. 303, *yowse* 'use'; Lady Hungerford, *youes* 'use' vb., Letters (c. 1569); Mary Verney's Will, *youst* 'used' (1639), V. Mem. ii. 17; Verney Mem. have also *yous*, ii. 380 (1647); *youseg* iii. 214 (1655); Wentw. Papers, *youmore* 'humour' 320, etc.; Mrs. Basire, *ashoure* 'assure' Correspond. 112 (1653); Mrs. B.'s *quewre, quewored* 'cure, cured', p. 112, may imply either [kjȳə(r)d] or [kjūə(r)d]. The *ou* spellings can surely only imply [ū]. On the other hand Voltaire, who knew English well, and was in England from c. 1725 to 1728, states that in spite of the corruption of Engl. vowels, *u* retains the sound which it has in Fr., *true* being *tru*, not *trou*. See Dictionnaire Philosophique, article *Langage*. (3) The other point, when [jū] became [ū], is of secondary importance. [jū] is retained by most speakers of Received Standard, except after *r-* [rūl, rūd, frūt], etc. and also, as a rule, after *l-*, though usage still fluctuates here, the same speaker sometimes saying [lūk] and [ljūt]. When another cons. precedes *l-* [ū] is usual, [bljū, fljū], etc. being now felt as old-fashioned or provincial. After *d-, t-*, [jū] is now universal among good speakers, and the once fashionable [dūk, tūzd$i$] are now confined to vulgar speakers. Note that the pronunciation [ʃugɔ, ʃuə] presupposes [sjū-]. See § 283. (2).

§ 266. M.E. [ēu].

This diphthong was levelled under old [ēu], and like this, developed first to [jȳ] then to [jū]. See § 265.

Examples: *dew* < M.E. *dēu*, O.E. *dēāw*; *few*, M.E. *fēwe*, O.E. *fēāw*.

§ 267. M.E. ü [ȳ] in Native English Words.

The only word in which the M.E. rounded type survives is *bruise*, and it is disputed whether this really represents O.E. *brȳsan*, or rather an Old French *bruiser*. *Build* preserves in its spelling the old *ü*-type from O.E. *bȳldan*, but not in pronunciation; the pronunciation [byld] is, however, recorded in the seventeenth century.

We have seen that O.E. *ȳ* became *ē* in the O.E. period in Kent, the S.E., and part of the E. Midland (§ 158 (*b*)). This O. and M.E. *ē* regularly becomes [$ī$]; see § 229 (*b*).

In the North, in an area of E. Midl., and in Middles., O.E. *ȳ* was unrounded to [ī] in Early M.E.; see § 158 (*a*). This type is found in *bride, fire, hide, mice, lice, kine*, M.E. *brīd, fīr, hīden, mīs, līs, kīne*, O.E. *brȳd*, etc. They have the normal development of M.E. ī (§ 254).

NOTE. This South Eastern ē- type, with Mod. [ī] from O.E. *ē*, earlier *ȳ*, occurs in some Modern Dialects [mīs, līs], etc., in Kt. and E. Midl. Similar forms in the South and S. West cannot, as sometimes stated, be so explained, but must be from M.E. unrounded forms *mīs, kīn* 'kine', etc., which were lowered to *kēn*, etc. in L. M.E. and then normally became [mīs, kīn], etc. in Mod. Engl. The West Country *-beere*, etc., in Pl. Ns. is of this origin, and represents M.E. *bīr*, O.E. *bȳre* 'byre'. See Wyld, *E. St.* 47, p. 166. The form *heered* 'hired', *Wentw. Papers*, p. 65 (1708) = O.E. *hȳran*, may represent the S. Eastern type.

M.E. ai and ei.

§ 268. Independent Treatment: [*ai* < *æi* < *ǣ* < *ē̆* < *ē* < *ei*].

The old diphthongs *ai, ei*, were levelled under one sound [*ai*] in the M.E. period (Chaucer), though the traditional distinction survived in the spelling. Evidence of the levelling of this M.E. *ai* under M.E. *ā*, the new sound being at first either [ǣ] or [ē̆], exists from the fifteenth century onwards.

(1) Duke of Buckingham, *fethful*, Past. Letters i. 62 (1442–5); Shillingford, *feale* 'fail', p. 19; Mary Beaufort (1442–1509) *sa* 'say', Ellis i. 1. 47; Anne Boleyn, *panes* 'pains', Ellis i. 1.

3c6 (1528) ; Q. Eliz., *agane*, Ellis, II. ii. 213, (1553) ; *pade* 'paid ', and *wate* 'wait', Verney Mem. ii. 103 (1642).

(2) Inverted spellings of *ai* for M.E. *ā* : *maide* ' made', Cov. Leet Bk. 1. 24 (1421) ; *trayvell*, Ld. Berners, Froissart 1. 222 (1533) ; Thos. Pery (1539) Ellis, *spayke* 2. 2. 141 ; *bayde* ' bade', *tayking*, ib. 146, etc.

(3) Rhymes : Surrey, *please—days* ; Sackville, *dispair—fear*, etc. See § 225 on M.E. *ā*, and § 232 on M.E. *ē²*. It appears from above, and from the discussion on M.E. *ā* and *ē²*, that these two vowels and M.E. *ai* had all the same sound from the fifteenth century. In addition to the use of *ai* for *ā* just cited, the spelling *ey* for M.E. *ē²* in St. Editha may be mentioned ; *deythe* ' death' 445 ; *meyte* ' meat' 1001 ; *eyer* 'ere', etc. It is hardly conceivable that this should have been written, as in these instances, to express length, if *ey* had still represented a diphthongal pronunciation in those words where it belonged historically. The Fr. Grammarians of the sixteenth century identify Eng. *ai* with Fr. *ai* and *ê*. English writers in this and the following century still insist that it represents *a+i* ; Gill (1621) admits the existence of a monophthong in *ai* words in affected speech, but represents diphthongal pronunciation to be the normal mode. Even Cooper clings to this, but admits that when speaking ' negligently' people pronounce simple *a* as in *cane*. A fresh diphthongization occurred in the nineteenth century, and in the East Midland and Cockney dialects this has become [*ai*]. In many rural dialects at the present day, e. g. Oxfordshire and Berkshire, the full M.E. [*ai*] remains, and these dialects distinguish absolutely between this and the sound in old *ā* words—*name*, *pale*, etc., which remains as [ɛ̄] or [ē] ; they also distinguish the old *ai* from the diphthong derived from old *ī*, which has become [*ai*]. See §§ 254, 270.

On the other hand, it is argued by Jespersen, *Hart's Pronunciation of English*, pp. 33-42 ; *New Engl. Gr.*, pp. 323-8, that the old diphthongs were never monophthongized at all in Standard English, and consequently that the levelling of these with M.E. *ā* did not take place till the [ē] which arose from this was diphthongized. Zachrisson (pp. 196, etc.) thinks that ' much speaks in favour of Jespersen's theory'. These different views depend upon the interpretation placed on the statements of the early Grammarians. The most careful survey and weighing of these frequently leads to very different conclusions in different minds.

Examples : *clay*, *day*, *way*, *eight*, *rain*, *pray*, *sail*; *vein*, *pain*, *reign*, *dainty*, *saint*, etc.

NOTE. *Key* [kī] is abnormal, and probably owes its form to rural dialect.

Combinative Treatment of M.E. ai.

§ 269. M.E. ai + r becomes [ɛə].

Just as M.E. *ār* did not pass beyond the [ēr] stage, so M.E. *air* remained at this point of development : *fair* became [fæir, fær, fēr, fɛə]. The M.E. pronunciation [fair] still survives in Oxfordshire.

Other examples are: *chair, heir, prayer* (French) ; *stair, lair* ; *their* (Scandinavian).

§ 270. M.E. oi.

This sound appears at the present time as [ɔ*i*], but there is no doubt that this pronunciation is due to the spelling. In order to understand the problems connected with the history of this diphthong in the Mod. period we have to consider (1) the spellings ; (2) the rhymes ; (3) the statements of the more careful observers among the Grammarians.

(1) and (2) seem to establish quite conclusively an identity of pronunciation between the old *oi*, and that of the diphthong developed from M.E. *ī* § 254 : St. Editha spells *anynted* for 'anointed' 376 ; Gregory, *dystryde* 'destroyed', p. 59 ; *pyson* 'poison', p. 161 ; Verney Mem., *gine* 'join', iii. 433 (1656) ; *byled* 'boiled', iv. 223 (1670) ; *implyment* 'employment', iv. 276 (1686) ; Mrs. Basire, *regis* 'rejoice', Corresp. 137 (1654). For use of spelling *oy* to express the diphthong from old *ī* see § 254. Such rhymes as *toyle—compile—awhile—assoile*, Spenser ; *smile —coil*, Suckling ; *toil—isle*, Waller ; *reviles—spoils*, Denham ; *entwin'd—joyned*, Cowley ; *refines—joins—lines*, Dryden ; *surprise on—poison*, Swift ; *toil—pile, join—divine—line*, Pope, etc., etc. point in the same direction as the occasional spellings. The stage at which the old diphthong was levelled under the new was probably [ai], a common diphthong used both in *isle* and *oil* at the present time in Berks. and Oxfordshire.

In the sixteenth century Mulcaster (Elementarie 1582) appears to distinguish two types among the *oi* words : [ɔi] in *boy, enjoy, joy, annoy, toy* ; and [ŭi] in *anoint, appoint, foil*. The former of these was probably a spelling pronunciation. Wallis (1653) gives [ɔi] in *noise, boys, toil, oil*, but says that some pronounce either [ui] or [ai] in certain words, e. g. '*tūyl, ūyl*' by the side of *toil*, etc. Cooper (1685) gives (1) *wines, blind, wind* on one hand, and *injoin, broil, ointment*, etc. as having [ai]; (2) *joy, coy, coif* as having [ɔi] ; and (3) *boil, moil, point, poison* as having [ui]. We may take the 'oi' pronunciation to be due to the spelling as at present; the [ai] as the normal survival of the type represented by the above rhymes and spellings; and [ui] as due to a rounding after lip consonants, of the first element. This type is comparable to the rounding of the vowel in *put* (§ 251) and evidently was not a universal development, and soon disappeared as a pronunciation of the *oi* diphthong.

The normal phonetic development of earlier [ai] in Received Standard would have been to [*ai*], a type which survives in vulgar speech and in many Regional dialects at the present day. This type disappeared gradually from polite use, as may be gathered from the statements of late eighteenth-century orthoëpists. Kenrick (1773), cit. Ellis, p. 1052, and Jespersen, *New Engl. Gr.*, p. 329, declares that it is an affectation to pronounce *boil, join*, otherwise than as *bile, jine*, and yet it is 'a vicious custom in common conversation' to use this sound in *oil, toil*, which thereby 'are frequently pronounced exactly like *isle, tile*'. This shows that the new pronunciation [*ɔi*] had not yet been extended to all words.

NOTE. In *joist, boil* (on the body), *groin*, which go back to forms with *ī*, the [ɔi] is generally explained as due to the artificial restoring tendency being carried too far, by including some of the wrong words. Jespersen, *New Engl. Gr.*, p. 320, objects to this on the ground that *oi* spellings of some of these words occur very early—*boyle* 1529, *joyst* 1494, *groin* Shakespeare's *Ven. and Ad.* rhyming with *swine*. J. suggests that [ɔi] in *groin* may be due to the influence of *loin*, but offers no suggestions for the other words. It seems preferable to regard all these as survivals of the kind of spelling discussed, § 254.

§ 271. Table showing the M.E. origin of Modern English Vowel Sounds.

Present-day Sound.	M.E. Vowel.	Present-day Examples.	Reference to §
[e*i*]	(1) *ā*	name	§ 225
	(2) *ai, ei*	day, way	§ 268
[*ai*]	(1) *ī*	wife	§ 254
	(2) *ih*	night	§ 254
[*oi*]	*oi*	joy	§ 270
[*au*]	*ū*	house	§ 246
[o*u*]	(1) *ọ̄²*	bone, throat	§ 240
	(2) *ōu*	bow (noun)	§§ 171.(8), 242
[*iə*]	*ēr*	fear	§ 230
	(1) *ār*	bare	§ 226
[ɛə]	(2) *air*	fair	§ 269
	(3) *ɛ̄r*	bear	§ 233
[ī]	(1) *ẹ̄¹*	see	§ 229
	(2) *ẹ̄²*	sea	§ 232
[ū]	(1) *ọ̄¹*	moon	§ 236
	(2) *ǖ*	brute	§ 265

Present-day Sound.	M.E. Vowel.	Present-day Examples.	Reference to §
[jū]	(1) *ū*	tune	§ 265
	(2) *ēu*	blew	265
	(3) *ɛ̄u*	dew	265
[ā]	(1) *ăr*	hard	§ 222
	(2) *auf*, or *ăf*	half	§§ 218, 221, 260
	(3) *ăs*	pass	§ 219
	(4) *ăþ*	path	219
[ɔ]	(1) *au*	cause	259
	(2) *aul*	all	218
	(3) *or*	cord	241
	(4) *oþ, of, os*	froth, lost, off	245
[ʌ]	(1) *ur*	curse	252
	(2) *or*	word	239
	(3) *er*	earth	228
	(4) *ir*	bird	256
[a]	(1) *ŭ*	nut	250
	(2) *ō¹* (with Early Mod. shortening of [ū] to [ŭ])	blood	§ 236. (3)
[ŭ]	(1) *ŭ* after lip cons.	put	§ 251
	(2) *ō¹* (with late shortening of Early Mod. [ū])	good	§ 236. (2)
[æ]	(1) *ă*	back	§ 217
	(2) *ă* from *ŏ*	strap	244. (2)
[ɔ̆]	(1) *ŏ*	cot	244
	(2) *ō²* (with Mod. shortening)	hot	243
	(3) *wa, qua*	wan, quantity	223
[ɛ]	(1) *ĕ*	well	227
	(2) *ē²* (with late shortening)	breath	235
[i]	(1) *i*	sit	255
	(2) *eng, engʒ*, etc.	England, hinge	§ 258
	(3) *ē¹* Early Mod. shortening	breeches	231
[ə]	Back vowels in unstressed sylls.		§ 272

§ 272. The Vowels in Unstressed Syllables.

The tendency to shorten, reduce, or eliminate vowels in syllables that are weakly stressed, or totally devoid of stress, is common to all Germanic languages, and is traceable in English throughout its entire history. We see the effects of this tendency in the confusion of vowels in suffixes in Late O.E., and in M.E. the process has gone farther, with the result, for instance, that the old *a, u, e* in suffixes are no longer kept distinct, but for the most part merged in a sound which is written *e*. From the fifteenth century onwards the frequent occasional spellings make it clear that a wholesale system of reduction of unstressed vowels, in words of English, Scandinavian, and French origin, has long been established in the habitual pronunciation, the results of which are, so far as we can see, practically identical with what occurs in ordinary, unstudied, natural pronunciation at the present day. It is evident that this is no sudden innovation, but must have been long preparing, and it is only because of the relatively close adherence to tradition by the professed scribes in M.E. that the reduction of unstressed vowels on a large scale cannot be traced much earlier.

There has been a counteracting tendency at work now for some centuries which aims at deliberately 'restoring' what is supposed to be the original sound, and this artificial attempt has been to some extent successful inasmuch that in many words a vowel may now be heard in an unstressed syllable which has been introduced from a desire to approximate to the spelling, where formerly a quite different sound was pronounced. In innumerable cases these artificial forms have become traditional, and must be regarded as more or less fixed, unless indeed, in the course of time, some fresh and irresistible tendency to reduce or eliminate shall sweep them away. Such a vowel is the *o* in *obey*, formerly [əbéi], now universally [oubéi] except in very rapid speech. In other words the restoration is a matter of individual preference, and such pronunciations as [tótɔiz, pópɔiz, místʃíf, pénsil] and so on, instead of the normal [tótəs, pópəs, místʃif, pénsl] must be regarded as solitary flowers of utterance, cultivated by those who wish to impart what they take to be some special grace and beauty to their speech.

It is sometimes said that Shakespeare, or Milton, or Dryden, if they could revisit this transitory life, would be shocked and distressed to hear their lines rendered by modern lips, and that they would be more particularly disturbed by the 'slurring' of the unaccented vowels. It is pretty certain that these great poets would feel some surprise, and perhaps some disapproval, could they hear our present-day speech, but it would not be of the kind, nor would it arise from the cause, that some anticipate. Our speech would in all probability strike them as highly artificial, affected, finicky, and over-precise.

The only source of our information concerning the pronunciation of unstressed syllables before the late seventeenth century is the occasional spelling. The earliest Grammarians are dumb on the subject; even Cooper gives us but scanty information, and that only about a few words. More can be gathered from Jones (1701) and from some of the later writers, but in order to obtain anything like a comprehensive picture there is nothing for it but to collect laboriously a mass of illustrative material from the private letters of the fifteenth and following centuries. Even the official records of the fifteenth century throw considerable light upon forms of the grammatical suffixes, and occasionally upon other points, but documents of this character will not serve us much for the sixteenth, and not at all for the later centuries.

The occasional spellings, upon which we attempt to form our views regarding the pronunciation of unaccented vowels a few centuries back, may either (*a*) merely indicate indecision on the part of the writer, how to express a sound no longer adequately represented by the conventional spelling, as when we find the second syllable of *staple* written *-el*, *-al*, *-ul*, *-yl*, or (*b*) these spellings may point definitely to a specific sound, as when we find *biskitt, sartyn, sesyn*, etc. for *biscuit, certain, season*. These spellings sometimes indicate the existence of more than one type of pronunciation, the result of different tendencies, as *fortin, fortewn*, etc.

Speaking generally, the characteristic changes of the modern period may be summarized as follows :

Front Vowels [æ] from earlier *ă* becomes *e* [ε] which is levelled under original *e* which becomes *i* [*i*].

Rounded Vowels are unrounded : *o* and *u* are apparently levelled under a single sound, probably [a], whence [ə] ;

French *u* [y] becomes *i* [*i*].

Diphthongs are monophthongized :	*oi* becomes [*i*] written *e, i* ; *ai, ei* become *e*, later *i*, written *e, i*; *ou, au* become *o*, which unrounded to [a] written *a*; this sometimes remains, sometimes is fronted and written *e, i*, or *y*.

At the present time we may say that in Received Standard, old back (rounded) vowels, and the old diphthongs *au, ou*, tend to be pronounced [ə] in unstressed syllables, while old front vowels, and the old diphthong *ai*, are pronounced [*i*], always supposing the pronunciation has not been influenced by the spelling. The old diphthong *oi*, in unstressed positions, is now very commonly ' restored '. On the other hand, some Regional and Class Dialects often tend to level all unstressed vowels under [ə], others, though these are now probably rarer, seem to prefer [*i*], whence such pronunciations as the vulgar [mat*i*n] for *mutton*, now perhaps but rarely heard. We shall see in the early spellings what appear to be the predecessors of both types. For a fuller treatment of the problems and more copious illustrations the reader is referred to my *History of Colloquial English*, chap. vii.

UNACCENTED VOWELS IN DETAIL

§ **273. M.E. e in Unstressed Syllables.** These suffixes by the side of the conventional *-es*, *-εth*, *-ed* spellings, appear frequently as *-is -ys*, *-ith -yth*, *-id*, *-yd*, in private letters and public documents from the fifteenth century onwards. By this time the *-i-* spellings can no longer be regarded as Regional. This type, which is now the established in Received Standard, becomes increasingly common in London documents by the end of the fifteenth century, and, to judge by the spellings, was that henceforth in use among the best speakers; it will suffice to mention that *-yd*, *-ys*, *-yth*, *-id*, *-is*, *-ith* spellings are found in the letters of Sir Thos. More, Sir Thos. Smith, Gabriel Harvey, Q. Eliz., the Verneys, and Lady Wentworth.

-est (2nd Pers. Sing.) ; Superl.; nouns (*harvest*, etc.) : *clepyst* vb. Bokenam ; *eldyst*, *-ist*, Gregory, etc. ; *harvist* 'harvest', Sir T. Elyot, Gabr. Harvey ; *honist*, *dearist*, Gabr. Harvey ; *largist*, *hottist*, Q. Eliz.; *honist*, Alleyne Papers; *sadist* 'saddest', *greatist*, Verney Mem. ; *dearist*, *modist*, Lady Wentworth.

NOTE. *intrust* 'interest', Mary Verney's Will (1639), corresponds to type [*intrəst*] still sometimes heard.

-en appears very frequently as *-yn*, etc., and *-en*, corresponding to present [*-in*], also less frequently as *-on*, probably corresponding to present [*-(ə)n*]: *opynly*, *erthin*, adj., Bury Wills ; *kechyn* 'kitchen', Lincs. Will (1451); *lynyn* 'linen', Cely Papers; *carpynter*, Cely Papers ; *opyn*, Ld. Berners ; *kytchyn*, Lincs. Inventory (1527) ; *hevyn* 'heaven', Sir Thos. More, Letters ; *chykynnes*, Thos. Lever's Sermons ; *chickins*, Gabr. Harvey ; *heavin* 'heaven', Q. Eliz. ; *childrin*, *wimin*, pl., Verney Mem. ; *kitching*, Lady Strafford, Wentw. Papers; *sentimint*, *conshince*, so pronounced by John Kemble, according to Leigh Hunt. The other type is represented by: *ywryton*, P. P. St. Editha ; *aunsion* 'ancient', Shillingford ; *opunli* R. Sustr. Men.; *writun*, *gotun*, Fortescue; *hofton* 'often', Cely Papers; *burdon* 'burden', Sir Edw. Howard, Ellis ii. 1. 216 (1513).

-er, often written *-yr* in fifteenth century, by the side of *-ar*, *-or*, *-ur*, *-r*; these may all mean the same thing, as it is doubtful how long English really tolerated a clear '*i*' before *-r*; the latter group presumably imply [ər] or simply syllabic [r]: *aftyr*, Bokenam, Bury Wills, Fortescue; *ovyr*, Bury Wills, Gregory, Cely Papers ; *fadir*, *modir*, Bury Wills; *bettyr*, Bury Wills, Cely Papers. The other type occurs in: *wondurful*, Bokenam; *remembr*, Marg. Paston and Fortescue ; *soupar*, Bury Wills; *murdre*, *watre*, *undre*, Caxton ; *mannor* 'manner',

annsor 'answer', *octobor*, *finar* 'finer', *brocur* 'broker', Cely
Papers; *sistar, bettar, murdar*, Q. Eliz. Note *-ir-* in middle of
word, *misirable*, Verney Mem.

-el, written *-yl, -il*, as well as *-ul, -le*, etc. : *appyltre*, Bokenam ;
unkyll 'uncle', Marg. Paston ; *bokyl* 'buckle', *litil, candylstikke,
pepil, stepyll, ladyll, archangill*, Bury Wills ; *litil, sadyl*, Caxton ;
saddyl, stapyll, craddyl, Cely Papers; *startyl, sparkyll, devyll*, etc.,
Skelton ; *postyll*, Machyn ; *evangill*, Sir Thos. Smith ; *cruilty*,
Verney Mem.(1644); spellings implying [(ə)l]: *double* R. Sustr.
Men. ; *nobole, noble*, Caxton ; *stabul*, Lincs. Wills (1451 and
1465) ; *stapal, stapul*, Cely Papers.

-less : *harmlys*, Marg. Paston (1465) ; **-mest** (*-most*): *utmyst*
'utmost', Shillingford (1447-50).

-ness : *kindnis, happinis, darknis, businis*, Q. Eliz. ; *bisnis*,
Verney Mem. (1665).

-ess : *mistriss*, Shakespeare First Fol. passim ; Habington's
Castara (1630-40) ; Jones (1701) ; *dutchis*, Lady Wentworth.

-lege (= *-leche, -lege*) *knowlych*, Marg. Paston ; Shillingford ;
acknowliges, Verney Mem. (1661) ; *collidg*, Gabr. Harvey ;
collage, Bury Wills (1480).

-et: *markyt*, Cely Papers; *interprit*, Gabr. Harvey ; *interprett*,
Lady Lambton, Basire Corresp. (1649) ; *bullits, blanckitt*,
Wentworth Papers.

Initial e- : *astate*, Bokenam, Fortescue, Gregory, Elyot,
passim, Lord Berners, passim ; *alectyd*, Cely Papers ; *ascapyn*
'they escape', Bokenam ; *ascaped*, Lord Berners ; *aronyous*
'erroneous', Machyn.

§ 274. **-a + consonants in unstressed syllables.**

-ac : *stomechere*, Paston Letters ; *stummock*, Gabr. Harvey ;
stomichers, Verney Mem. (1647) ; *stomick*, Baker (1724) ;
almyneke, Cely Papers ; *obsticle*, Verney Mem. (1647) ; *carictor*,
Verney Mem., *carecter*, Wentworth Papers.

-age (later *-ange*) : *mesynger(s)* S. of Rouen (1420), Gregory,
St. Papers Hen. VIII, Bucks Will (1534).

-age : *longege* 'language', Gregory ; *marieges*, Archbp. Cranmer, Letter, Ellis (1533); *marriges*, Roper's Life of More, Alleyn
Papers 1593; *vicaridge*, Alleyne Mem. (1605), Dr. Basire (1673).

-mas : *Cryustynmus*, Machyn ; *crismus*, Verney Mem. (1639
and 1656).

-as : *purchisse*, vb., Gabr. Harvey ; *Sir tomis chike*, Verney
Mem. (1643) ; but *Sir tomos*, Verney Mem. (1642).

-ave : *Saynt Oleffes*, Paston Letters (1462), *St. Olive*, Jones (1701).

-an : *compeny*, Machyn, *compiny*, Verney Mem. (1642).

-ate : *pryvit*, Wentworth Papers (1709); *chockolet*, ibid. (1711).

-dale : *Dugdel's Baronage*, Wentworth Papers (1709).

§ 275.   -o- in unstressed syllables.

-on (M.E. *-oun = -ŭn*); shortened to *-ŭn* when stress was shifted to preceding syllable. *sesyn* 'season', Marg. Paston ; *resenably*, Cely Papers ; *reasyn* 'reason', Dr. Knight (1512); *burgine*, vb., Sir T. Elyot ; *mutten* 'mutton', *Rede me*, etc. (1529); *dungen*, Bp. Latimer ; *dungin*, Baker (1724); *Devynshyre*, Gregory ; *commyshin*, Thos. Pery (1539) ; *duggin* 'dudgeon', Gabr. Harvey ; *posshene* 'portion', Alleyne Papers ; *fashin'd*, Chapman (1605) ; *fashing*, Verney Mem. (1664) ; *sturgin* 'sturgeon', *punchin* 'puncheon', *flaggin* 'flagon', Baker (1724); *surgin* 'surgeon' (1657), *ribins* 'ribbons' (1664), *prisiner* (1647).

-o⊥ : *dysabey*, Marg. Paston ; *abedyensses*, Cely Papers ; *abay*, Mrs. Basire (1654) ; *apinions*, Machyn.

§ 276.   French ü [y] in unstressed syllables.

-une : *commyne* 'common', *comynlaw*, Shillingford ; *comyners*, Gregory ; *comyngasion* 'communication,' Wolsey to Hen. VIII; *mysseforten*, Machyn, *misfortin*, Verney Mem. (1642) ; *fortin(e)*, Verney Mem. (1644, 1645, 1664, 1663) ; *unfortinate*, Verney Mem. (1659) ; *fortin*, Tony Lumpkin in *She Stoops to Conquer*.

-ure : *to paster*, vb., St. Editha ; *moister*, Palladius ; *aventer*, *venter*, Cely Papers, *venterous*, Machyn, Lily's Euphues, Verney Mem. (1642) ; *venter*, ibid. (1643, 1657) ; *unscripterlye*, Bp. Latimer ; *jointer*, E. of Bath, Ellis Letters (1553) ; Roper's Life of More; *gointer* 'jointure', Alleyne Papers (1593) ; *jointer*, Verney Mem. (1643, 1657) ; *picture* said by Cooper (1685) to be pronounced like ' pick't her ' = [pɪktə] ; *mánnering the ground*, Wilson, Arte of Rhet.

-ut : *savecondyte*, Cely Papers ; *condytte* 'conduit', Gregory ; *byskitt*, Cely Papers ; *minite* 'a note', Letters and Papers (1501).

-u⊥ : *repetation*, Marg. Paston ; *menishone*, ' munition', Verney Mem. (1642).

⊥u- : *argament*, Shillingford ; *newys* 'nephews', Machyn ; *neuie* 'nephew', Mrs. Basire (1655) ; *valy* 'value', vb., Verney Mem. (1642), *Debity*, ibid. (1662); *vallyed*, Wentw. Papers.

NOTE. Forms like *fortin, moister, byskitt*, etc., above, show the normal treatment of Fr. *ū* in unstressed syllables, and go back to types accentuated on the first syllable, M.E. *fórtune, móisture*, etc. The forms of *fortune, moisture, pasture, nature*, etc., now used in Received Standard presuppose a different M.E. type, accentuated on the second syllable, *fortúne, moistúre, natúre*, etc. This stressed form of *-túne, -túre* develops in the way described § 283. (1) to [-tjȳ<-tjȳ̆<-tʃȳ<tʃū] so that the normal forms of this type in the above words, would be [nətʃúə, fətʃűn], etc. Our forms [néɪtʃə, fɔ́tʃən], etc. are a kind of compromise, which may be accounted for by a late alteration of the place of stress after the [fortʃűn] stage had been reached, producing first [fɔ́tʃūn] then with shortening of *ū* and subsequent unrounding of the resulting *u* [fɔ́tʃun<fɔ́tʃən}. We find in M.E. both types *natúre* and *nátúre* indicated by metrical usage. The latter, with the English mode of accentuation produced sixteenth century, etc. [nétə(r) ; the former, with French accentuation, would produce [nætjȳr<nætjȳ̆r<nætʃȳr<nætʃűr], from which last, by a new shifting of the stress, we get our present [néɪtʃə].

§ 277. Unrounding of Back-round vowels in unstressed syllables.

ŭ⌐ : *apon*, Shillingford, Fortescue, Gregory (thrice), Cely Papers (four times), Machyn ; *anethe* 'scarcely ', O.E. *unéþes*, Bokenam.

-our (*ūr*): *faveryng*, Gregory ; *faverabull*, Cely Papers ; *faver*, Verney Mem. (1647) ; *unsavery*, Ascham, Tox. ; *semer* 'Seymour ', Machyn.

§ 278. Shortening of Long Vowels in Unstressed Syllables.

-ite: *Muscovitts* rhymes *wittes*, Shakespeare L.L.L. ; *infenit*, Lady Wentworth.

-ile : *fertill*, Cavendish, L. of Wolsey ; *stirrell* 'sterile', Shakesp. (First Fol.) Hen. IV. pt. I.

-meal: *oatmell* 'oatmeal ', Verney Mem. (1657) ; Baker 1723 gives *otmell* as the pronunciation.

-night : *senet* 'se'nnight', Verney Mem. (1656), *sennet*, Roger L'Estrange (1681) ; *fortnet* 'fortnight' (1681).

§ 279. M.E. *ai, ei* in Unstressed Syllables.

ain, ein: *výleny*, St. Editha ; *villens*, Sir Thos. Smith ; *villin*, Verney Mem. (1655) ; *vilanous*, Q. Eliz. Letters, and Transl. ; *cértyn*, Shillingford ; Cavendish L. of Wolsey ; *sartinly*, Verney Mem. (1642).

-ain⌐: *synt Stevyn, sent Paul*, Shillingford ; *syn Lenard, syn John*, Gregory.

⌐ail : *counselle, counsyler*, St. Editha, *counselle*, Lord Berners, Capgrave's Chron.; *travell*, n., Lord Berners, Cavendish, vb., *travills*, Autograph Letter from Isaac Walton in Aubrey's Lives.

⌐eis-: *curtessy*, Shillingford, Lord Berners ; *courtisie*, Sir Thos. Smith.

⌐ai : *Mundy*, Gabr. Harvey, Verney Mem. 1647 ; *Fridy*, ibid. (1642).

N.B.—*the* 'they' is used in unstressed positions by Shillingford, Gregory, Q. Eliz. ; *ther* 'their' by Gregory, Ordinances of Worcester, State Papers (1515), Skelton (*thyr*), Q. Eliz., Cavendish L. of Wolsey ; *them* (by the side of *thaim, theyme,* etc.) in Hoccleve, Marg. Paston, Gregory, Sir Thos. More, Elyot, Latimer, Cavendish, etc. All these writers use *theim*, etc. also ; *them*, which after the middle of the sixteenth century soon becomes the sole form, may have been influenced by *hem*, which survived by the side of the *th-* forms.

§ 280. M.E. *oi* in Unstressed Syllables.

⌐ois: *Porpys*, Gregory, Marston (*porpice*); Sir Thos. Browne's Vulgar Errors, *porposes* = [pɔ́rpəsiz]; *toorkes*, Bury Wills (1500); *turkis*, Milton, Sabrina's Song, Comus ; but *turkas*, Cavendish, *turcasse*, Thos. Wilson ; *Shammee Gloves*, Sir R. Verney (1685), *shammy breeches*, Mrs. Aphra Behn, *Lucky Chance* (1686).

⌐oin : 'Mr. George *Gaskin*', Spenser ; *Borgin* = Burgoyne, Verney Mem. (1642).

CHAPTER VIII

THE PRONUNCIATION OF CONSONANTS IN THE MODERN PERIOD

§ **281.** It is impossible to form an adequate idea of the pronunciation of an age unless, in addition to an approximate knowledge of the sounds of the vowels, stressed and unstressed, we are also able to gather some notions of the pronunciation of consonants, especially as this is affected by other sounds occurring in close juxtaposition, and sometimes, also, by absence of stress. These consonantal pronunciations are markedly characteristic ; any deviation from the usage to which we are accustomed is apt to produce an effect of strangeness. In the examples which follow, there is unquestionable evidence of the respectable antiquity of many of our present-day pronunciations, and also of the existence, in earlier centuries, of others which have now been altogether abandoned in Received Standard, and of yet others which are being gradually eliminated in the speech of many of the younger generation. There can be no doubt that could we hear the pronunciation of the politest circles in the age of Elizabeth, of the Charleses, or of Anne, this would strike us as careless, slipshod, and ' incorrect ' in respect of the consonants, just as the distribution of vowel sounds then current would produce on us the effect of rudeness and provincialism. As we have before had occasion to note, Received Standard has been much affected, during the last hundred-and-fifty years or so, by the tendency to regard approximation to the spelling as the test of elegance and correctness in speech. The result has been that many ancient and traditional pronunciations have been swept away by the schoolmaster, and many others will hardly survive more than a few generations longer.

The phenomena to be dealt with fall under the following heads :

A. Isolative Changes without either Loss or Addition.

B. Combinative Changes involving neither Loss nor Addition.

C. Loss of Consonants.

D. Addition of Consonants.

E. Voicing of Voiceless Consonants.

As a rule it has only been possible here to give a comparatively few examples of each pronunciation, though, as far as practicable, an attempt is made to illustrate the occurrence of each over a wide period of time. Some of the phenomena are probably far older than the date of the earliest example given, but the greater adherence to traditional spelling by the M.E. scribes, compared with the habits in this respect of fifteenth-century and later writers of letters, etc., has here, as with the vowel changes, made it difficult to discover what were the conditions in earlier centuries. Doubtless a careful search in some of the by-ways of fourteenth-century written records would reveal much that at present can only be surmised.

For a fuller discussion and further illustrations see Chap. VIII of my *History of Modern Colloquial English.*

§ 282.   A. Isolative Changes without Loss or Addition.

(1) (*a*) *M.E. -(g)h becomes f.*

At the end of a syllable, or before *t*, this sound [χ] either disappears as a consonant, or, if it remains, is lip-modified, and finally becomes [*f*]. In the south it probably disappeared early in most dialects; such a spelling as *Edinburth* (Lord Berners) for *Edinburgh*, which indicates a mere substitution of one sound for another, shows that the voiceless back open cons. was an unfamiliar sound. Cp. the similar substitution in [kíþli] for *Keighley*, instead of [kíχli].

f- spellings:—*thorf*, Marg. Paston (1465); *troff* 'trough', Leics. Will (1553); *to laffe*, Barnabe Googe (1563) and Gabr. Harvey Letters (1573–80); *chuffes*, Shakesp. Hen. IV, First Fol.; Butler (1643) gives *f* as the final sound in *laugh, cough, tough, enough.*

(*b*) M.E. -(*g*)*ht* becomes *-ft-*, Gregory, *unsoffethe* 'unsought' = [ansᴐft]; Marston (1604) rhymes *after—daughter*; Butler (1634) gives *dafter* as the usual form of *daughter*, and *dafter* occurs several times in Verney Mem. (1645–55); Jones (1701) gives *f* in *daughter, bought, nought, taught,* etc.; a waiting-woman in Tom Jones writes *soft* for *sought*; Baker (1723) gives *slafter* as the pronunciation of *slaughter.*

Except in *laughter* we no longer use the types with *-f-*.

NOTE. The rhyme *softe—dohter* (MS. Harl.), = 'softly, daughter' *-douter* (MS. Laud.), K. Horn, 391–2, points to a very early change of *-ht-* to *-ft-*.

(2) *Substitution of -in for -ing in unstressed positions.* (Popularly and inaccurately called 'dropping the 'g'.')

Holdyn, drynkyn, Norf. Guilds (1389): such Pres. Part. forms occur throughout the fifteenth century in Paston Letters, Gregory, Exeter Tailors' Guild, etc. ; in the sixteenth in Letters of Sir R. Graham (1520), Q. Eliz., *besichen*, and they are fairly numerous in Machyn's Diary ; in the seventeenth *missin, bein, comin, disoblegin, lodgins*, etc., etc., are frequent in Verney Mem.; Cooper (1685) states that *coughing* and *coffin, coming* and *cummin*, are pronounced alike ; Lady Wentworth has a large number— *ingagin, mornin, fardin, writin*, etc.; in the late eighteenth century Walker actually recommends *-in* when the first syllable of the word contains *-ing*, thus *flingin, singin*, etc. ; he tolerates *-in* in other words also.   Poets of the eighteenth, and those born early in the nineteenth century, constantly rhyme *ruin—viewing*, etc.   At the present time thousands of the best speakers still use *-in* forms, but it seems that since the thirties of the last century this was one of the ' mistakes ' against which governesses and schoolmasters successfully waged war, and the result has been a widespread adoption of *-ing* [*iŋ*] to agree with the spelling.

(3) *Substitution of f for th* [*þ*] *and v for* [*ð*] *in all Positions.*

erf ' earth ', Bk. of Quint. (1460-70) ; *Lambeffe*, Gregory; *frust* ' thrust '; *Frogmorton* for Thr-, Machyn ; *bequived* ' bequeathed ', Q. Eliz. Transl. ; *helfe* ' health ', Alleyne Papers (1593) ; *kiff nor kin*, Middleton, Chaste Maid in Cheapside (1630) ; Elphinston (1787) speaks of a tendency of the ' low English ' to say *Redriph* for ' Rotherhithe ', and *loph* for ' loath '; *lofte* for ' loathe ' occurs in Verney Mem. (1645).   At the present time this substitution seems to be rather a personal idiosyncrasy than a dialect feature, though it does appear to be frequent in a very low type of Cockney English.   Lady Wentworth writes *threvoles* ' frivolous ', which may imply that she attributed the sound *v* to the symbol *th*.

(4) *sh* [*ʃ*] *for final and medial s.*

Reioshe ' rejoice ', R. of Brunne (1303), cp. Bokenam's *reioy-shyng* (1443) and *dysshese* ; *blesshyng*, Oseney Register (1460); *vesshell* ' vessell ', Marg. Paston 1461; *kysshed* ' kissed ', Caxton Jason (1477); *prynche*, Machyn ; *burgishes* ' burgesses ', Verney Mem. (1645); *parshalles* ' parcels ', Mrs. Basire (1653); *winch'd*, Congreve (1693) ; Elphinston notes *cutlash, nonplush, frontish-piece* as vulgar.   The spelling *Porchmouth*, where the implied change is perhaps combinative, occurs three times in a letter of Sir T. Seymour, St. Papers Hen. VIII (1544); Verney Mem. (1665 and 1693-1780) ; and the slightly altered *Poarchmouth* is used by Elphinston to express what he regards as a vulgarism.

P

These forms appear to be used in the following rhymes, e. g. *prince—ynch*, Rede me, etc. (1529) and Crashaw (1612-49), *wishes—blisses—kisses* ; *this is—wishes—kisses*.

(5) *Interchange of v- and w.*

(1) *v- for w-*, Bokenam, *valkyng* 'walking'; *avayte* 'await', Marg. Paston (1465) ; *Prynce of Valys* 'Wales', Gregory (1450-70) ; Machyn the Londoner has *vomen* (twice), *Vestmynster*, etc., etc.; Elphinston notes the confusion of *v* and *w* as characteristic of Londoners, and Walker mentions it with strong disapproval.

(2) *w- for v-*. Bokenam, *wyse* 'vice'; Gregory, *wery* 'very'; Cely Papers, *wase* ; Machyn, *welvet* 'velvet', *woyce* 'voice', *wetelle* 'victuals', *wergers* 'vergers', etc., etc. These vulgarisms, so typical of Mr. Weller, appear to have died out.

§ 283. B. Combinative Changes without Loss or Addition.

(1) *-si-, -ti-*, that is [-sj-, -tj-], become [ʃ] ; *su-* [sjū-] becomes [ʃū-] through intermediate [-s̮j-, -tj̮-].

Marg. Paston, *conschens* 'conscience' (twice, 1469) ; Cely Papers, *partyschon* 'partition' ; *restytuschon, oblygaschons*, etc., etc. ; Thos. Pery (1539) *commyshins* ; Sir Thomas Seymour (1544) *instrocshens* ; Gabr. Harvey Letters (1573-80) *ishu* ; Verney Mem., *indescreshons* (1647) ; *suspishiously* (1646) ; *fondashon* ; *adishon* (1650) ; *condishon* (1655), etc., etc. Cooper (1685) indicates *-sh-* as the sound of *-ci-, -ti-*, etc.

(2) Initial *su-*, = [sjū-] or [sjȳ-] (cp. § 265), becomes [ʃū-].

Alleyne Papers, *sheute* 'suit' (1593), *shuite*, Verney Mem. (1653) ; *shewtid*, Verney Mem. (1653), and *shut*, Mrs. Basire (1650) ; *shuer, shur* 'sure', Verney Mem. (1642), *shewer*, ibid. (1657) ; Mrs. Basire, *ashoure* 'assure' (1653) ; Cooper (1685) mentions the pronunciations *shure, shugar* ; Jones (1701) says that *sh-* is heard in *assume, assure, consume, ensue, suet, sugar*, etc. In all these except *sure, sugar, assure*, present-day Received Standard has 'restored' [sjū-].

(3) *-di-, -du-* = [-dj-, -djŭ] becomes [-dž-, džu].

In some words such as *grandeur* [grændžə], *soldier* [souldžə], the old pronunciations still survive among most good speakers, but a more 'careful' pronunciation prevails in *India, Indian, idiot, hideous, tedious, educate*, etc., where [ídžət, índžə, hídžəs, tídžəs, édžukeɪt] are hardly heard now except among rather old-fashioned speakers.

Machyn writes *sawgears*, Verney Mem. *sogers* (1642), Lady Wentworth, *sogar* 'soldier'; Verney Mem., *teges* = [tídžis]

(1647). Jones (1701) spells *contages, soger, injan* to express the pronunciation; Bertram (1753), transliterating for Danes, writes *soldjer, indsjan, kudsju*, etc., which certainly means [sóldžə, índžən, kúdžu] 'could you', etc. Walker (1801) says good speakers pronounce *edjucate, verchew, verdjure*, and that they ought to say *ojeous, insidjeous, Injean*. Leigh Hunt (Autobiog.) records that John Kemble said '*ojus*', '*hijjus*', '*perfijjus*'.

NOTE. [zj] becomes [ž] in *pleasure, measure, brasier*, etc. Verney Mem. has *plesshur, plesshar* (1642), and Jones indicates 'sh', clearly [ž], in these words.

§ 284. C. Loss of Consonants.

(N.B. It is convenient to classify under this head one or two phenomena which from a strictly phonetic point of view do not involve a real loss; e. g. ' dropping the h ', which is a mere change in the incidence of stress, and the omission of a final -*d* after *n*- as in *poun* for ' pound ', which results from failure to denasalize.)

(1) *Loss of Initial Aspirate.*

In considering this process, a distinction must be made between words of pure English origin and those from French. It is doubtful whether the latter were originally pronounced with *h-*. Even in respect of genuine English words, a Norman, French-speaking scribe often omits initial *h-* in the M.E. period, but it would be rash to assume, on that account, that among English speakers the aspirate was already lost. Again, the particular point now to be considered only arises in regard to stressed syllables. The loss of an aspirate at the beginning of unstressed syllables is an old habit, certainly belonging to the M.E. period, as we see from the spellings of forms of personal pronouns in unstressed positions (§§ 301, 305, 306), and of the auxiliary *have*, and of the second elements of old compounds, etc.

The spelling *alf a pound* Norf. Guilds (1389) appears to be a genuine early example of the loss in a stressed syllable. The Celys, who often insert an unnecessary *h-*, do not appear to omit it where it probably belongs. The following are apparently genuine: *Owsold* 'household' Lincs. Will (1451); *astely* 'hastily', Marg. Paston (1463); *ede* 'head', *alff*, 'half', *ard* ' hard ', *elmet* 'helmet', all in Machyn. Cooper does not mention the ' dropping of *h-* ' among his ' barbarisms '. There seems to be no example in the Verney Memoirs. Fielding makes a lady's maid in Tom Jones omit *h-* in *ave, as, ad*, though these are bad examples, since only the last occurs in a stressed position. This person also writes *at ome*, but this is not a vulgarism, [ətóᵤm] being frequently heard now from excellent speakers, and *atóm* is actually found in Layamon (c. 1200).

In a letter by Mr. Jackson's fiancée in Roderick Random (ch. xvi), which contains many vulgarisms and examples of illiteracy, *h-* is never omitted, though it is several times put in where it has no business.

On the other hand, Elphinston (1787), Walker (1801), and Bachelor (1809) refer to the omission of initial *h-* among Londoners, the first-mentioned saying that 'many Ladies, Gentlemen, and others have totally discarded it'. The evidence is too scanty to enable us to judge when the habit became widespread, and at what period it came to be regarded as a vulgarism. It is now universal in Regional Dialects until we reach the North Country, and among many classes of persons who speak Modified Standard.

(2) *Loss of w.*

(*a*) *Initially before rounded vowels.* *sor* 'swore', Agnes Paston, Past. Letters (1451); *sord* 'sword', Alleyn Papers (1593) ; *sourd*, Sir R. Verney (1641), and Verney Mem. (1685) *sord*. Daines (1640) and Cooper (1685) agree in stating that *w* is ' quiescent' in this word, the former adding also *swore* and *swound* 'swoon', the latter *sworn*, and *quote* (= 'coat' in sound). *Swollen* is written *sowlen* in a sonnet by Thos. Watson (1593) ; Jones writes *sord, solen, sorn*.

(*b*) *Loss of w- at the beginning of unstressed syllables.* This is normal, and a very old process, cp. *uppard* 'upward', Trinity Homs. (c. 1200) ; *hammard* 'homeward', in St. Editha several times. Mrs. Basire writes *forard* ' forward' (1654), now confined to nautical language ; Mrs. Aphra Behn, *aukard*; *Eddard* is recorded as the pronunciation of Lady Lucy Pusey, who died in the middle of the last century. Except in Pl. Names such as *Norwich, Southwark*, etc., *w* is usually ' restored' in Received Standard.

(3) *Loss of -l- before consonants.*

In Received Standard *-l-* is normally lost in pronunciation before lip consonants and *-k*; otherwise, except in *Colne*, it is retained in stressed syllables. *Should* and *Would* lost the *-l-* in unstressed positions ; *Could*, which originally owed its spelling, and later its pronunciation, with *-l-*, to the analogy of these words, also lost it in unstressed positions, if, indeed, it was ever pronounced there.

Apart from *haf* 'half' (see § 221) found in the fourteenth century, the earliest examples of *l*-less spellings date from the fifteenth century: Bp. Bekinton has *behaf* 'behalf' (1442), Short English Chronicle (1465), *Fakonbrige* 'Falcon-'; Cely Papers, *fawkyner*, *Tawbot* 'Talbot'; Gabr. Harvey Letters, *Mamsey* 'Malmsey'; Q. Eliz. *stauke* 'stalk'; Machyn writes *hopene*, 'halfpenny', and also the abnormal *swone* 'swollen', a type which is proved genuine by Surrey's rhyme *bemoan—swolne* (Tottel, p. 28; Surrey died 1547). Cooper (1685) notes the absence of *l* in *Holborn*, still pronounced [hóubən], although the influence of the spelling is tending to introduce an *l*-sound in the speech of some. Jones (1701) gives a long list of *l*-less words, which on the whole agrees with our present usage, except that it gives *hope*, *hopen* as the pronunciation of *holp*, *holpen*, the obsolete strong Pret. and P. P. of *help*, and *soldier*. The old-fashioned pronunciation [sóudžə] written *soger*, etc., by some of the Verney letter-writers, and in the next century by Lady Wentworth, and *sawgears* by Machyn, goes back to a different M.E. type (without *-l*) from our *soldier*.

Shud(d) 'should' appears in Elyot (1531); Gabr. Harvey's Letters (1573–80); Verney Mem. (1642).

Would appears as *wode*, *wood*, Verney Mem. (1656). These are all the weak, unstressed type. The poets rhyme *would— hold*, Wyatt; *should—behold*, *gold*, etc., Wyatt and Spenser; *cool'd—should*, Shakesp., etc.; Waller has *would—mud*.

Could, when stressed, was actually pronounced with *-l-*, cp. Spenser and Drayton, *could—behold*; Dryden, however, rhymes *could—good*. The genuineness of the *l*-pronunciation seems to be confirmed by the statements of Price, Wharton, and Cooper, who put together *could—cool'd*, as being pronounced alike.

(4) *Loss of r, finally, and before Consonants.*

(*a*) In Received Standard the sound of *-r-* has disappeared before consonants in *hard*, *harsh*, *church*, etc., and finally in *car*, *hear*, *fur*, etc. The preceding vowel has been lengthened.

So far as the evidence of the occasional spellings goes, it tends to show that the disappearance took place earliest before *-s*, *-sh*, *-ch* [s, ʃ, tʃ].

Bokenam (1439) rhymes *adust—wurst*; *wosted qwisshens* appears in a Lincs. Will (1450); Cely Papers have *passell* 'parcel', and also the inverted spellings *marster*, *farther* 'father', which seems to show that *r* + cons. was already eliminated in pronunciation; Gregory has *mossell* 'morsel'; in Rede me, etc. (1529), *church* rhymes *such*; *skarsly* 'scarcely' occurs in Robinson's translation of More's Utopia (1556), and in a letter of Sir T. Seymour (1544); Machyn (1550–2) writes *Wosseter*, *Dasset*, etc.; Surrey (Tottel) rhymes *furst* ' first ' with *dust* and *must*; Alleyne Papers (1593) has *posshene* ' portion '; Sir Edm.Verney (1635–6) writes *Fottescue*; a fair number of *r*-less spellings are found in Verney Mem.; *quater* ' quarter ', *doset* ' Dorset ', *passons* ' parsons ', *fust* ' first ', all in 1642; *drawers* ' draws ' (1674), and many others, and the inverted spelling *father* ' farther ' (1656). Cooper (1685) writes *wusted* for *worsted*; Jones (1701) states that *r* is not pronounced in *Worcester*, *harsh*, *marsh*; Lady Wentworth and her correspondents (1705–11) write *Gath* ' Garth ', *Albemal Street*, *extrodinary*, etc., etc.; Baker (1724) indicates the pronunciation of *nurse*, *purse*, *thirsty*, *Ursula*, *sarsanet* as *nus*, *pus*, *thusty*, *Usly*, *sasnet*.

These last spellings point to a very old loss of *r* before *s*, etc., which must have taken place before the preceding vowel was lengthened; they are of the same type as that seen in the rhymes given above from Bokenam, Rede me, and Surrey, and also in *cust* ' curst ', Roister Doister, and *burst*—*dust* in Dryden. The present-day vulgar or facetious *bust* ' ruined ', etc., and *cuss* ' curse ' are survivals. The fact that in Received Standard the vowel is invariably long in all these words shows that we now use a different type, in which the *r* was lost at a much later period. Our pronunciation may, however, be due to the spelling. *Dace* (name of a fish) was originally *darse*, and must have lost its *r* in M.E., and the vowel must in this case have been lengthened, since the present form can only come from a M.E. **dās*.

(*b*) *Loss of final -r.* On this point neither the occasional spellings nor the Grammarians throw much light. Lady Wentworth's spellings *Bavarior*, *Operar* show that she can have attached no phonetic value to the symbol. In words like *better*, *under*, etc., it seems probable that the murmur vowel is the result of weakening of syllabic *r*. The present spelling *-re* is a survival of this. We find such spellings as *remembr*, *undr*, Sir John Fortescue (1471–6), and *modre* ' mother ', Bp. Knight (1512), which probably represent [rimémbr, andr, mŭdr].

(*c*) *Development of murmur glide between a long vowel and -r.* The [ə] now heard as the second element of diphthongs, or the third of triphthongs, e. g. in *ere*, *air*, *tear*, *here*, *fire*, etc., etc., = [έə, tέə, hίə, fáiə] developed early after long vowels before *-r*. Already in the thirteenth century we find *eyer* ' ere ', St. Editha =

[ḗər]. There are several later examples of such spellings :— *desyer, requyer*, Anne Boleyn (1528) ; *hiare* 'to hire' Sir T. Elyot (1531) ; *devower, fyer, youers* 'yours', Gabr. Harvey (1572–80) ; *desiar, hiar* 'hear', Q. Eliz. The spellings occur also in Verney Mem., *desiar* (1642), *shewer* 'sure' (1657), etc. Dr. Watts rhymes *door—to her* [dūͧə(r)—tuə(r)]. Baker (1724) says that in *fire, hire*, etc., *-re* is pronounced like *-ur*. It seems that in *here*, etc. the development was [hīr < hḯər < hḯə < hḯə] and not [hīr < hḯə] as has been supposed.

(5) *Loss or Assimilation of d and t before other Consonants.*

(a) *Loss of -d-.* The examples are very numerous from the fifteenth century onwards ; many of the pronunciations suggested by the early spellings may be heard to-day from good speakers in rapid speech—e. g. [bl*d*inn*i*s] 'blindness', etc. [wénzd*i*] is universal except in affected speech. Examples :— *freenly* 'friendly', Hoccleve ; St. Editha, *bleynasse* 'blindness', *paunse* 'pounds' ; Shillingford (1447–50), *Wensday* ; Gregory, *Wanysday* ; Bp. Latimer, Sermons, *Wensdaye, frensheppe* ; Machyn, *granefather, Wostreet* 'Wood Street' ; Shakesp. rhymes *hounds—downs* (R. of Lucr.) ; Alleyne Papers, *stanes* 'stands' = [stænz], *hanes* 'hands' ; Verney Papers, *Wensday* (1639) ; Verney Mem., *Wensday*, passim ; *hinmost* (1674) ; Lord Rochester (d. 1680) rhymes *wounds—lampoons* ; Jones (1701) says 'men being apt to pass over *d* in silence between *-n-* and another consonant', it is not sounded in *Wensday, intends, commands* ; Lady Wentworth, *Wensday* (twice), *hansomly, Clousley* 'Cloudsley' ; Baker (1724), *hansome.* Jones gives a list of words where *d* is not pronounced before *-l-*, e. g. *land-lord, friendly, candle, fondle*, etc. ; and even in *children* he says *d* is omitted.

The pronunciation [lanən] 'London', which was still a fashionable pronunciation among the older generation into the seventies of last century, is found as *Lonan* at least three times in Mrs. Basire's Letters (1654), and once as *Lonant* ; Gray writes *Lunnon* jocularly in a letter to Walpole (1757), implying that this was the latter's form ; Elphinston (1787) says 'we generally hear *Lunnon*'.

(b) *Loss of -t-.* St. Ed., *fonstone* ; Marg. Paston (1448), *morgage* ; Machyn, *Brenfford* ; Q. Eliz., *attemps, offen* 'often', etc. ; Alleyne Papers, *wascote* 'waistcoat' (1593) ; Verney Papers, *wascott* (1639) ; *Chrismus* (1639) ; Verney Mem., *crismus* (1656) ; Sir P. Warwick, Memoires of Charles I (1707), *busling* ; Lady Wentworth (1708, etc.), *Crismass, Wesminster, crisned* 'christened' ; Jones (1701) notices loss of

-t- in a long list of words such as *Christmas, costly, Eastcheap, lastly, beastly, gristle, whistle, mostly, roast beef, wristband, christen,* etc., etc. ; also *colt's foot, maltster, saltcellar, Wiltshire,* etc.

(c) *Loss of -b- before consonant* :—*assemlyd,* Cely Papers ; *tremlyng,* Cavendish (1557); *nimlest,* Q. Eliz. Letters ; *before vowel* :—*Cammerell,* Machyn; *Camerwell* 'Camberwell', Alleyne Mem. (1607); *Lameth* ' Lambeth ', Archbp. Cranmer (1534).

(6) *Loss of final Consonants.*

(a) *Loss of -d.* The omission of final consonants, especially of *d* and *t,* but also of others after a preceding consonant, sometimes also after vowels, was a common tendency in the earlier centuries of the Modern Period. Examples :—*blyn* 'blind ', Norf. Guilds (1389); *God sene you* ' send ', Const. of Dynevor Castle, temp. Hen. IV ; *husbon,* Marg. Paston (1440), *hunder* ' hundred ', ibid. (1465) ; *my Lor,* Cely Papers ; *Edwar the IV,* Gregory ; *blyne,* Machyn ; Verney Mem., *friten* P. P. (1642) ; Cooper (1685) writes *thouzn* for the pronunciation of *thousand* ; Lady Wentworth has *dyomons, poun* ' pound ', *thousan, own* ' owned ', *Richmon, scaffels* ; Jones (1701) gives a long list of words in which *-d* is omitted, including *almond, beyond, despond, diamond, Edmond, riband, scaffold,* etc., etc.

(b) *Loss of -t.* *Synt Johan þe baptis,* Norf. Guilds (1389); *nex* ' next', Marg. Paston, and Cely Papers; *excep,* Cely Papers ; *uprigh,* Recept. C. of Aragon (1503) ; *Egype,* Machyn ; *prompe* ' prompt', Ascham Tox.; *stricklier,* Alleyne Papers (1608) ; Verney Papers, *respecks* (1629) ; Verney Mem., *respeck* (1650 and 1657) ; *Papeses* (1655) ; *honis* ' honest ' (1664) ; *Mundynex* (1647) ; Mrs. Basire, *the res of our neighbours* (1651). Jones (1701) says that *-t* is omitted in *rapt, script, corrupt, strict, direct, respect, sect,* etc., etc., also in *pageant,* sounded '*pagin* '; Lady Wentworth, *prospeck, riches* ' richest', *tex* ' text ', Peter Wentworth, *strick* ' strict '. Baker (1724) writes *Egip, poscrip, ballas* ' ballast ' ; Pope rhymes *sex—neglects* = [nigleks].

(c) *Loss of final -f.* *Kerchys* ' kerchiefs', Bokenam (1443); *Kerche, nekkerchys,* Marg. Paston (1469), *Sant Towleys* for *St. Olave's,* the origin of *Tooley* (street), Machyn ; *masties* 'mastiffs' (1513-30); *handkerchers,* Marston (1608); *masty,* Middleton (1608); Verney Mem., *baly* ' bailiff' (1642); Jones (1701) *mastee, bailee, hussee, hussy* ' housewife '; Baker (1724) *handkercher, mastee.*

(d) *Loss of final -b.* We have long ceased to pronounce *-b* in *lamb, comb, climb,* even in inflected forms when a vowel follows :

climber, combing, etc. We have, however, reinstated *-b* from the spelling in the Pl-Name *Lambeth*, from O.E. *lamb + hȳþ (hēþ)* 'landing-place', etc. But Archbp. Chichele writes *Lamhyth* (1418), and in a letter (1534) from Archbp. Cranmer (though not in his own hand) the form *Lameth* occurs ; *lameskynnes* is found in R. Sustr. Men. (1450) ; and to *clyme* 'climb' in Euphues (1580) ; Gabr. Harvey has *lamskin* (1573–80) ; and *come it* 'comb' occurs in Verney Mem. (1642). Cooper (1685) notes loss of *-b* in *climb, dumb, lamb*, etc., etc. The *-b* in *thumb* and *limb* is unhistorical.

(7) *Loss of open Consonants between vowels ; loss after vowel and before a Consonant.*

(a) *Loss of v between vowels.* St. Editha, *senty* 'seventy', *swene*, O.E. *swefen* 'dream', *pament* 'pavement'; Caxton, *pament* (1477) ; Machyn, *Denshyre*, etc. ; Marston, *I marle* 'marvel' (1605) ; Verney Mem., *senet* 'seven night' (1656) ; Aubrey, Lives (1669–96), *Shrineham* 'Shrivenham', Berks., now [ʃrivənəm] ; Jones (1701) gives *Dantry* for *Daventry*, now [déintri].

(b) *Loss of h before t, preceded by front vowel.* The original sound of *h* in *night*, etc. was [h̆]. In spite of the statements of some seventeenth-century Grammarians, this sound must have disappeared at least by the fifteenth century. Marg. Paston constantly has the inverted spelling *wright* for *write*, and so has E. of Surrey (1520) and Sir Thos. More (Letter in Ellis 1. 1. 199) ; Rede me spells *quight* 'quite'; Sir T. Elyot, *lyte* for 'light'; Cavendish, *whight* 'white'; Habington rhymes *weight* —*fate*, and *height*—*state* (1634) ; Spenser constantly writes *quight, bight* 'bite', and rhymes *fight* with *white* (often spelt *whight*).

(c) *Loss of h before t when preceded by a back vowel.* (For *ht < -ft* see § 282 (b) above.) The evidence for this loss is earlier than for that after a front vowel ; *broute* 'brought', Layamon (1200) ; *naut* 'naught', Hali Meidenhad (1225) ; *dowter* 'daughter', Songs and Carols (c. 1400) ; W. of Shoreham (1307) has the inverted spelling *foghte* 'foot'. From the fifteenth century onwards the evidence, from direct omission of *h*, or by inverted spellings where it is put in words that never had the sound, is more copious ; the following examples will suffice : Marg. Paston, *kawt* 'caught' (1450), *ought* 'out' (1461) ; Cely Papers, *dowttyr* ; Henry VIII in Letter (1515), *abought* 'about'; Elyot, *dought* 'doubt' (1531) ; Gabr. Harvey, *droute* 'drought', *thoat* 'thought'; Alleyne Papers, *datter, dater* (1593) ; Verney Mem., *dater* (1650), *slater* (1656).

§ 285. Addition of Consonants.

(1) *Development of y- [j] initially before Front Vowels.*

This process is probably Regional in origin, but its results are found early in documents written both in the East and West, and forms with *y-* appear in the London Dialect (Machyn) and even penetrate into literary works. In the seventeenth century these forms are found among the Verneys and their friends, and survive late into the eighteenth, though they seem to have been regarded as a sign of rusticity. 'Year' [jiə] for *ear* may still be heard from good old-fashioned speakers who have otherwise no trace of Class or Regional dialect. It seems doubtful whether even *yearth* has anything to do with similar spellings found in Kentish texts in M.E. Examples:—St. Editha, *ȝende* 'end'; Cov. Lt. Bk., *ȝeuery* 'every' (1430); Bokenam, *yorth* 'earth'; Shillingford, *yerly* 'early', *yeuen* 'even', *yese* 'ease'; Cely Papers, *yells* 'ells'; Thos. Pery (1539), *yending* 'ending'; Latimer, Sermons, *yere* 'ere', *yearth* 'earth'; Edw. VI First P.B. (1549), *yer*, 'ere', *yearth*, passim; Machyn, *yere*, passim; Lever's Sermons (1580), *yearth, yearthly*; Butler (1634) disapproves of *yere* 'ere', and *yerst* 'erst'; Verney Mem., *year(e)* (1665 and 1679), *yearnestly*; Cooper (1685) includes *yerb* and *yearth* amongst his barbarisms; Lord Chesterfield, Letter 149 (1749), includes *yearth* among the pronunciations of the vulgar man. Goldsmith (1759) puts *yearl* 'earl' into the mouth of a Club gossip, and a young squire in Humphrey Clinker (1771) italicizes *yearl* in a letter, as though to indicate a current pronunciation which he himself did not use. Elphinston (1787) notes that *yearth* and *yerb* are current both in England and Scotland, but not in good usage.

(2) *Addition of 'parasitic' Consonant, finally, especially after -r, -n, -m, -l, -s, -f.*

Palladius (1420), *spaniald* for *spaniol*; St. Editha, *to past away*; Capgrave, *lynand*; Sir J. Paston, *ilde* 'aisle'; Gregory, *loste* 'loss'; Card. Wolsey, *synst* 'since'; Lord Berners, *kneled downed*; Thos. Pery Letter, *varment* 'vermin; Gabr. Harvey, *surjiant* 'surgeon'; Lily, Euphues, *mushroompe*; E. of Shrewsbury (1582), *orphant*; Q. Eliz., *nonest* 'nonce'; Marston, *orphant*; Spenser, *vylde* 'vile', rhymes *milde*, F.Q.; Shakesp. First Fol. *vylde, vyldely*, passim; Verney Mem., *schollards* (1641); *micklemust* (1642), *hold yeare* 'whole' (1655); *night-gownd*(1688); Swift rhymes *ferment—vermin* [vāmĕnt]; Wentworth Papers, *made the house laught* (1710), *not saft* 'safe' (1710), *sarment* 'sermon' (1711 and 1713), *gownds* (1712), *lost of time*

(1711), etc., etc. ; Elphinston notes *sermont, drownd* inf., *gownd, scollard, wonst* ' once' as vulgarisms ; Pegge (1814) considered *verment, serment, nyst, margent,* as London vulgarisms.   It is interesting to note how old these forms are, how widespread they once were among persons who frequented the best society of their day, and how hopelessly vulgar they are now become.   The exception is *margent,* which is recognized by poets.

(3) *Development of Front glide between g-, k-, and a following Vowel.*

The results of this process, which produced such pronunciations as [kjād, kjai̯nd, skjai̯], etc., are no longer heard in Received Standard, though the type was fashionable in the early nineteenth century, and survived among old speakers here and there, into the eighties of that century.   The earliest certain traces are in Wallis's statement (1653) that *can, get, begin* were pronounced *cyan, gyet, begyin,* though it is possible that the spelling *gearl* 'girl', Lady Hobart, Verney Mem. (1644), may imply a pronunciation [gjéəl].   Elphinston and Walker (late eighteenth and early nineteenth century) are quite definite in emphasizing that this type of pronunciation is essentially refined and polite, as giving ' a fluent, liquid sound '.   Walker expresses this by the spellings *ke-ind, ke-ard,* etc.

(4) *Aspiration of Initial Vowels, popularly called ' putting in an h'.*

This takes place only in stressed syllables, and especially in those that have extra strong sentence-stress.   The habit has probably always, as now, been considered a vulgarism.   It is doubtful how far an initial aspirate added by a M.E. scribe can be considered conclusive of his pronunciation.   The following examples are probably all genuine : Norf. Guilds (1387) *her the* ' earth ', *hoke leaves*; a large number of *h-* spellings occur in St. Editha (1420), *houȝt* ' out ', *hende* ' end ', *hevelle* ' evil ', *harme* ' arm ', etc., etc. ; Bokenam, *hangyr* ' anger ', etc.; Gregory, *hasche,* the tree ; Cely Papers, *howlde* ' old '; Marg. Paston, *hour* ' our ', etc., etc. ; Machyn has more examples than any of his contemporaries, including *harme* (of the body), *her the, here* ' ear ', *Hambrose, haskyd* ' asked ', ' a gret dener as I haue be *hat* ', which is exactly what a vulgar speaker of to-day might say, only putting it ' the biggest dinner I was ever hat ', where very strong stress falls upon the last word.   Lady Sydenham, Verney Mem. (1642), writes *hobblegaschons* ' obligations '.   There is no evidence, apart from the occasional spellings, that the habit of 'putting in an *h*' was widespread as a vulgarism before the later eighteenth century. It is not till then that the Grammarians mention it, and it is then also (1771) that Smollet makes the vulgar fiancée of Mr. Jackson (Roderick Random, ch. xvi) write *hopjack* ' object ', *heys* ' eyes ', *harms*, etc. The fact that this practice is not found in America, nor in Ireland, also points to it being of late development as a common vulgarism.

§ 286. E. Voicing of Voiceless Consonants.

(1) *Voicing of Initial wh-* [w̥].

In Received Standard the vast majority of speakers make no difference between *while* and *wile*, between *why* and *Wye*, between *what* and *Wat*, pronouncing all alike with [w]. Only those speakers who have been influenced by Scotch, Irish, and North Country speakers, or who deliberately adopt the pronunciation, use the sound [w̥] at all. Although in Southern texts already in M.E. *w-* is occasionally written for *hw-* or *wh-*, London documents appear to preserve the latter spelling. In the fifteenth century a few *w-* spellings are found—*wen, werof*, in Creation of a Knight of the Bath (1493); Machyn has *wyped* ' whipped ', *warff* ' wharf ', and Cavendish *wyght* ' white ', *wye* ' why '. There are very few of these spellings in Verney Mem., though *anyware* (1644) and *wig* ' whig ' (1683) may be noted. The last is also used by Lady Wentworth (1709). All the seventeenth-century Grammarians state that *h* is pronounced in *wh-*. Elphinston (1765–87) admits the complete disappearance of *h* in *whale*, etc.; Dr. Johnson in 1765 still believed that he heard the *h*; Walker regrets the London use of *w* for *wh*. It looks as if the present [w] for [w̥] had passed into Standard English from some Regional dialect, probably in the first instance through the lower strata of society. The pronunciation seems to have established itself rather late, and only gradually. The available evidence is, however, inadequate for a final verdict.

(2) *Voicing of Consonants medially, between Vowels; between a Consonant and a Vowel; finally.*

St. Editha, *crebulle* ' cripple '; *peyndynge* ' painting ', *parde* ' part ', etc., etc. ; Fortescue, *treded* ' treated '; Bk. of Quint., *Jubiter* (twice) ; Gregory, *radyfyde*, ' ratified ', etc. ; Cely Papers, *jeberdy* ; Caxton, Jason, *Jubyter* ; Bury Will (1504), *cobard*; Sir Thos. More, Letters, *Jubardy* ; Machyn, *huntyd* ' hunted ', *cubard* ; Alleyne Papers, *conford* ; Verney Papers, *debutye* (1636) ; Verney Mem., *prodistants* (1642), *medigate* ' mitigate ' (1657), *Debity* ' deputy ' (1662) ; Mrs. Basire, *comford* (1655). Jones (1701) gives a long list of words where *p* is written though *b* is pronounced, including *Baptism, Cupid, Deputy, Gospel, Jupiter* ; Lady Wentworth (1705) writes *prodistant,* and Lady Strafford (1712) *prodistation.* Elphinston includes *proddestant, padrole, pardner* among London vulgarisms. Some of the words mentioned in the above list may still be heard pronounced as there indicated.

CHAPTER IX

HISTORICAL SKETCH OF ENGLISH INFLEXIONS

Definite Article and Demonstrative Pronouns

§ 287. The **O.E. Demonstrative Pronoun** meaning 'that', but also used merely as a definite article, has the following forms:

	Sing. M.	F.	N.	Pl.—all Genders.
N.	sē	seo	þæt	þā
A.	þone	þā	þæt	þā
G.	þæs	þ̄ǣre	þæs	þāra, þ̄ǣra
D.	þ̄ǣm, þām	þ̄ǣre	þ̄ǣm, þām	þ̄ǣm, þām
I.	þȳ, þon			

§ 288. The **O.E. Demonstrative Pronoun** meaning 'this' is as follows:

	Sing. M.	F.	N.	Pl.—all Genders.
N.	þes	þēos	þis	þās
A.	þisne	þās	þis	þās
G.	þisses	þisse	þisses	þissa
D.	þissum	þissum	þissum	þissum, þeosum
I.	þȳs			

The Definite Article in M.E.

§ 289. The M.E. development, in all dialects, is in the direction of a gradual loss of all distinctions of Number, Gender, and Case, and the use of a single form which is indeclinable. The process of loss went on very rapidly in the North and Midlands, comparatively slowly in the South-West, and in Kentish. The first thing that happens is that for the Nom. Sing. *sē*, *sēo*, a form *þe* is substituted which owes its *þ* to the analogy of the initial in the forms of all the other cases, Sing. and Pl. This indeclinable form is found to some extent, even in the South, in the earliest texts, alongside of the inflected forms.

§ 290. The South and S. West Dialects.

Twelfth Century. *H. Rd. Tree* (1170), which is copied from an O.E. text, preserves the O.E. forms of the Def. Art. to a great extent, though the distinctions of Gender and Case are already weakening.

The uninflected *þe* occurs once as an Acc. Sing. M., and once as a F. Sing. The Nom. *se* only occurs once. *þeo* is once used as Acc. S. Fem. instead of *þā*. The regular Acc. S. Masc. is *þone*; *þene* occurs, but rarely. The Dat. S. Fem. is *þāre*. The Neuter *þæt* is used uninflected as in *of þæt wætere*. *þet* is used three times with a Fem. Noun. The Gen. Pl. is *þāre, þārӕ*.

[I owe these statistics to Prof. Napier's Introduction to the text.]

Lambeth Homilies (before 1200) has the indecl. *þe* for both Sing. and Pl. In addition, however, it has full forms of the M. Sing.: N. *þe*; Acc. *þen, þene, þenne*; Dat. *þon, þan*. In the Fem. Sing. only the Dat. *þer* survives, and in the Neut. *þet*, and *þat* (Nom.). The Pl. *þā* is used without inflexions for all cases, but the Dat. *þan* occurs.

Trinity Homilies (before 1200) seems to have only the uninflected *þe*.

Thirteenth Century. *Ancren Riwle* (1210) uses the indecl. *þe* very commonly, but also preserves the Acc. *þene*, Gen. *þes*, Dat. *þen*, in the Masc. Sing. *þet* is used as an Article as well as demonstratively, without distinction of Gender. The Fem. *þer* is found in Gen. and Dat. In the Pl. *þeo* is used, undeclined, and *þen* survives in the Dat.

Moral Ode, and *Owl and Nightingale* (circa 1250) have *þe* indecl. regularly established; the former has also *se*, and the latter uses the indecl. Pl. *þeo*.

Robt. of Glos. (1298) uses chiefly the indeclinable *þe*, but occasionally *þen* after a preposition—*þorow þen ēye*, and the Neut. *þet, þat*, as a genuine Article.

Fourteenth Century. *Trevisa* (1387) has *þe* exclusively.

Fifteenth Century. *St. Editha* (1420), apart from such survivals of *þet* as *þe tōne, þe tōþer*, has only *þe* for all Genders and Cases, and for both Numbers.

We see that by the end of the twelfth century already the feeling for Gender and Case is much weakened, though the forms survive; that during the next two centuries, the indeclinable *þe* gains ground, the other forms being used more and more rarely, until by the end of the fourteenth century or the beginning of the fifteenth, *þe* is the exclusive form apart from a few fossilized phrases.

The Definite Article in the Midland Texts.

§ 291. The East Midland.

Twelfth Century. In the second continuation of the *A.-S. Chron.* (MS. Laud) written between 1122 and 1137, we find the indeclinable *þe* already in frequent use, and by its side the more archaic *se*, and sometimes *þa*. On the other hand, the inflected forms Sing. Masc., Acc., and Dat. *þone*, Gen. *þes*; Fem. N. and D. *þā*; Neut. Gen. *þes*, N. and Acc. *þet*, also occur. The feeling for Grammatical Gender is dying out. The usual Pl. form is *þā*, undeclined.

In the third continuation, between 1132 and 1154, the indeclinable *þe* is fully established for all Genders and Cases and both Numbers, but *þā* is often used undeclined in the Pl. *Seo ærcebiscop* occurs, which shows how the feeling for Gender was fading.

Thirteenth Century. *Orm* (1200) distinguishes only between Sing. and Pl., *þe* in the former, *þā* in the latter, and the same is true of *Gen. and Ex.* (1250), except that this text writes *þō* for the Pl. form. *Bestiary* (1250) has *þe* only, for both numbers.

We occasionally find *þat* in these texts, used rather as a Demonstrative than as a pure Art. We get also survivals like *þe tone*, and *G. and E.* sometimes uses *þō* as a Dat. Sing.

§ 292. The Definite Article in Kentish Texts.

Twelfth Century. The earliest M.E. Kt. text, a collection of *Homilies* (MS. Vesp. A. 22) (1150), has already the indeclinable *þe*, but uses also *se* in the Nom. Masc. Otherwise, the O.E. forms, or their representatives, are pretty well preserved, which may be accounted for by the fact that this text is based upon an O.E. original.

We have in the Masc., a Gen. *þes*, and a Dat. *þan* and *þam*; in the Fem., a Nom. *si*, Acc. *þō, þā*, Dat. *þare* and *þer*. In the Pl. *þā*, and Dat. *þan*.

Thirteenth Century. *Kentish Sermons* (1250) has *se*, and *þe* and *þō* (indecl.) in Sing. Masc., Gen. *þes*, Dat. *þan*, Acc. *þane*, and a Fem. N. *si*, Neut. *þet*. The Pl. has *þe, þa, þō* (indecl.).

Fourteenth Century. *Wil. of Shoreham* (1307–27) and *Aȝenbite* (1340) show the fully developed use of the uninflected *þe* irrespective of Number, Gender, and Case. *þet* is used, but appears to be chiefly demonstrative. Both texts make an occasional Acc. Masc. *þane.*

The Definite Article in the London and Literary Dialect.

§ **293.** The London Dialect of Hen. III's Proclamation (1258) has an Indecl. Sing. *þe*, Indecl. Pl. *þō*, but also Acc. Sing. *þane*, Dat. *þan*, a Neut. Sing. *þæt*, and the form *þære* used as a Gen. Sing. before *-riche* 'kingdom', that is an old Gen. Fem. of the Art. before a Neuter word. Davie has only *þe*, indeclinable.

Chaucer, Gower, and Wycliffe use the indeclinable *þe, the* both for Sing. and Pl. and retain no distinctions of Case or Gender. The earlier *þō*, which survives as the Pl. form, occurs in Gower, only as the Pl. Demonstrative. It is, however, preserved by Mandeville (1356) as the Pl. Art., side by side with *the.*

The London official documents of the fourteenth and early fifteenth centuries have practically the same usage. The uninflected *þe, the* is the commonest form for all Genders and Cases, S. and Pl. *þet oon, þet oþer* occur, and the specifically Pl. *þō* is actually found as late as 1427, in the Parliamentary Records. We must suppose that by that time it was an archaism as the Pl. of the article. The later fifteenth-century London Charters also occasionally use *tho, thoo*, but with a more definitely demonstrative force (Lekebusch, p. 111), and a few examples of it are also recorded as occurring in Caxton (Römstedt, p. 41), and, as a rarity, in Coverdale (Swearingen, p. 17).

The Definite Article in Modern English.

§ **294.** By the end of the M.E. period all forms of the article except *þe, the* had practically vanished. *þat* had become a pure Demonstrative, and its subsequent history falls under that head. Even the old distinction between Sing. and Pl., which survived in the literary usage of the late fourteenth century, had disappeared from common use.

All that remains, in the Mod. period, of the once varied declension of the Definite Art. must be sought in a few set phrases, and words which preserve, here and there, the fossil of a case ending.

For the nonce contains the old Masc. or Neut. Dat. *þen*, O.E. *þæm*. The name *Atterbury* preserves an old Dat. Fem.—M.E. *atter*, or *at þer, buri*, O.E. *æt þære byrig*. Such names as *Nash, Nalder*, and *Noakes* are all that is left of M.E. *at þen asche, at þen aldre, at þen ōke(s)*. The -*s* of the last is possessive with patronymic force.

DEMONSTRATIVE PRONOUNS THIS AND THAT

§ 295. We have seen that *þat*, the old Neuter N. and Acc. of Demonstrative Pron. and Article, is used with less and less of the general sense of the latter, and more and more with the more specific demonstrative sense, after the twelfth century. The old Pl. *þā*, later *þō*, except in the North, serves at first both as Pl. Art., and as that of the demonstrative 'that'. This is gradually displaced by *þās, þōs*, the old Pl. meaning 'these'. *þōs* is of course the ancestor of the Mod. *those, þō* being retained almost exclusively as the Pl. of the Def. Art. *þe. Tho* in the sense of 'those' occurs, however, at least as late as Caxton, and Gregory, and even in a letter of 1513 (Ellis, II. i. 218).

'This' is expressed by *þis, þes, þeos*, with gradual loss of distinction of Gender, until *þis*, the old Neuter form, becomes the prevailing one in the Sing.

A new Pl. *þeōse, þēse* is formed on the type of the Nom. Fem. Sing., or Dat. Pl., and this is the ancestor of *these*. In the Nth. *þir*, and occasionally *þer*, is found in the sense of 'these'; more rarely *þir* means 'those'.

Moral Ode (MS. Jesus 1250) has a Nom. Pl. *þeō* 'those'.

In the South, the Acc. Sing. Masc. *þesne* occurs in the early thirteenth century (*God Ureisun*). An inflected form *þise* is often used in the oblique cases in the Sth., in Kt. and Midl.

In twelfth-century Kentish (Vesp. A. 22) we find the inflected forms *þesses, þeses*, Gen. Pl.

þō as the Pl. of *þis* is found in *Kt. Sermons* (1250), *Lambeth Homilies*, and in *Allit. P.*

Morsbach's London documents have *þis, thys*, Pl. *thise*, but also *þees, thees, these*, etc.; *þat, that*, Pl. *þo, þoo, tho, thoo*, etc. This is also Chaucer's usage. Caxton has *this*, Pl. *thise, this*, and *these*.

Thoos (Pl. of *that*) occurs, but only sporadically (Römstedt, p. 41). In the later fifteenth-century London Charters, *thes, these* are the usual forms for the Pl. of *this*, but *those*, etc., is found fairly often (Lekebusch, pp. 111, 112).

The Personal Pronouns

§ 296. The O.E. forms are the following:

	1st.		2nd.		3rd Sing.			Pl., all
	Sing.	Pl.	Sing.	Pl.	M.	F.	N.	Genders.
N.	*iċ*	*wē*	*þū*	*ġē*	*hē*	*hēō*	*hit*	*hie, hi,* etc.
A.	*mec, mē*	*ūs*	*þē*	*eōw*	*hine*	*hīe, hi*	*hit*	*hie, hi,* etc.
G.	*mīn*	*ūre*	*þīn*	*eōwer*	*his*	*hire*	*his*	*hira* *hiera* *heora*
D.	*mē*	*ūs*	*þē*	*eōw*	*him*	*hire*	*him*	*him, heom*

Dual.

1st Pers.	2nd Pers.
N. *wit* 'we two'	N. *ġit* 'ye two'
A. *uncit, unc*	A. *incit, inc*
G. *uncer*	G. *incer*
D. *unc*	D. *inc*

§ 297. Compared with the inflexions of Nouns and Adjectives, those of the Pers. Pron. have been wonderfully well preserved in English.

The chief points to notice in the history of their usage are: (1) the generalizing of the Acc. Dat. *eōw—you* for the whole Pl. with the loss of the Nom. *ye*; (2) the loss of the Acc. *hine*; (3) the loss of the strong, aspirated *hit*; (4) the development of the form *she* for the old *hēō* in the Fem.; (5) the substitution of *they, their, them*, the Scandinavian forms, for the English; (6) the loss by the old Genitives *mīn, þīn, his*, etc., of the real Genitive force, and the reduction of them to mere possessive Adjectives; (7) the loss of the old Dual forms.

The Pers. Pronouns in M.E.

§ 298. **The First Person.** There is little change and variety to record here. Practically all the early texts have: N. *ic, ich*, but *i* is found in *Laud Chron.* (1137); Acc. Dat. *mē*, and in the Pl. N. *wē*, Acc. Dat. *us, ous*. The Sthn. texts usually write *ich*, the earliest (down to thirteenth century) having also *ic*. The E. Midl. *Orm.* has *icc*. Northern texts have *ik*, and *i*. The form *I*, the only form now surviving, except in a small district in the S.-West, where *uch* [utʃ] (M.E. *üch, ich*) still lingers, comes into frequent use in all dialects, apparently, in the fourteenth century. Chaucer has *I*, but still uses *ich*. *I* no doubt arose originally in unstressed positions. *Ich* continues in common use in the S. and S.-West during the whole M.E. period. *St. Editha* (1420), however, usually has *I*, but also *ich*, and still joins *ich* on to auxiliary verbs—*ichaue*;

ichulle ' I will '; *icham.* The author of *Piers Plowman* has *I* and *ich*, whereas Mandeville, Gower (*Confessio Amantis*), and Wycliffe use *I* as the only form.

Davie's poems in the London dialect of the early fourteenth century have both *ich* and *I*, the former being roughly five times as frequent as the latter.

The weak *i* had of course a short vowel. After the loss of *ich*, etc., *i* was used in stressed as well as in unstressed positions. In the former it was lengthened to *ī*, thus becoming a new strong form, distinguished by quantity from the unstressed form. It is from M.E. *ī* that the Mod. *I* [*ai*] developed, and this is now used in unstressed as well as in stressed positions.

§ 299. Dual of First Pers.

Traces of this are found in *Layamon* (c. 1205), and in *Owl and Nightingale* (c. 1250). The Possessive or Gen. *unker* ' of us two ', and the Dat. *unk*.

The Pronoun of the Second Person.

§ 300. The usual M.E. forms are :

	Sing.	Pl.
N.	*þū, þou, thou,* etc.	*ȝē, yē,* etc.
A. D.	*þē, thee,* etc.	*ēōw, ow, ȝou, ȝuw, you,* etc.

The Pl. *yē, you* are already used, as in Mod. Engl., by Chaucer and other M.E. writers in polite and respectful address, applied to a single person. Davie (1307–27) uses both *þee*, Dat. S., and *ȝee*, Nom., in addressing our Lord ; also *ȝou*, Dat. Pl., in addressing Edward II. The Angel speaking to Davie says *þou, þee.* In a general way the distinction between Sing. and Pl. was maintained during the whole M.E. period. The Sing. *thou, thee,* were used late into Mod. English, in addressing inferiors, and in affectionate, intimate relations. In Present-day Standard English, the Singular forms are never used except in addressing the Deity. According to *E. D. Gr.*, the Pron. of 2nd Pers. is in use in nearly all the dialects of England ' to express familiarity or contempt '. It has disappeared from use in S. Scotl., and is very rarely heard in other parts of the country. Among the Society of Friends, *thee* still lingers as a Nom.

Confusion of ye and you.

The Mod. *you* is of course the old Dat. Caxton still uses *ye* for the Nom. and *you* only in oblique case. The sixteenth-century language of the Prayer Book, and the seventeenth-century language of the Authorized Version of the Bible, preserve the old distinction—e.g. 'Ye have not chosen me, but I have chosen you'. This seems to be the polite usage, as noted by Hoelper, p. 48, with regard to *Tottel's Miscellany.* Otherwise confusion exists among sixteenth and seventeenth century writers, *ye* and *you* being used indiscriminately as Nom. or Obj. Apart from liturgical use, *ye* only survives in Stand. Engl. in a few phrases : [háudɪdú], where [ĭ], with loss of [j], is due to its unstressed position, [þǽŋkī] and [lúkī], now old-fashioned, and obsolescent. In the form [ĭ] it survives in many rustic dialects, chiefly, I believe, in unstressed positions [kam jᴀ̄r wɪl i; dɪdnt ai tɛl i?].

The use of *thee* as a Nom. among the Friends is doubtless due to the analogy of the other Nom. forms with the sound [ī]—*he, she, we,* and further to the Pl. *ye.*

The use of *ye* as an Obj. case is probably due to the analogy of the normal Early Mod. *thee* in the Sing., and the other Acc. Dat. form *me.*

The use of *you* as a Nom. may have been influenced by the Sing. *thou,* though certainly the two forms had not the same vowel.

There is no doubt that the various forms of the Pers. Pronouns have influenced each other in this way. In different periods, and among different divisions of the Community, there have been different starting-points—either [ī] as expressing an Obj. Sing. on the pattern of *me, thee*; a Nom. Pl. on the model of *ye, we*; or Nom. Sing. on the lines of *he, she.*

Pronouns of the 3rd Person in M.E.

§ 301. **Masculine Singular.**

The usual forms are, like the O.E., Nom. *he,* Dat. *him.*

The old Acc. *hine* is not very common in M.E. ; the Dat. *him* is used indifferently, even in early texts, for both Acc. and Dat. Even those texts which preserve *hine, hyne,* or *hin* use *him* also for the Acc. The old Acc. is found in *Lambeth Homilies, Owl and Nightingale,* and *Moral Ode* (Trinity MS.) ; in *Robt. of Glos.* (once after *mid*), the *Kentish Sermons,* and Shoreham's *Poems.* These texts, however, and the other Sthn. texts use *him* also. The earliest London sources have only *him, hym.* All the earliest E. Midl. texts use *him* indiscriminately for Dat. and Acc., though *Gen. and Ex.* has *hin* twice, once after *of,* and *hine* once.

The unstressed Dat. form *im* without the aspirate occurs in this text joined to the preceding verb—*madim* ' made for him ', and in the same text the weak *e* occurs—' And spac uneðes, so *e* gret, ðat alle hise wlite wurð teres wet.'

Seeing how common the modern descendant of *hine* [ən] is in the rural dialects chiefly of the South and S.-West (cf. Wright, *Dial. Gr.*, § 405 b), it is surprising that it is not to be found oftener in M.E. literature, where it survives only till the early fourteenth century (Shoreham), and only in scattered examples. The form [ən] is always unstressed and used chiefly of inanimate objects, so far as my experience goes (in Oxford-shire and Berks.), and though sometimes applied to men, it is never used of women. In Oxfordshire at any rate, the *stressed* form of the Acc. Pron. Masc. is now generally [ī], not [*i*m] and never [in].

§ 302. Feminine Singular.

The origin of the mysterious Nom. form *she*, which has been the only form in literary English at any rate since the middle of the fourteenth century, is a puzzle that has never been satisfactorily solved. It may be a kind of blend between the old Fem. Art. and Demonstr. *sēō*, M.E. [sjō] and the old Fem. Pers. Pron. *hēō*, M.E. [hjō], but this is pure conjecture.

It will be well to give first an account of the earliest appearance, and the distribution of those forms of the Fem. Pron. which are either the ancestors or close relations of Mod. *she*, and then an account of the numerous other forms used in early M.E. with the same meaning.

The earliest appearance of any pronoun at all like *she* is in E. Midl. in the latter part of the *Laud Chron.* (middle of twelfth century), where *scæ* is fairly frequent. *Orm.*, fifty years later, does not know the form at all, nor does the *Bestiary* of 1250. *Gen. and Ex.*, however, of approximately the same date, has *she*, and *sge* = [sje], together with other forms to be considered below. *She* and *sho* appear in *Havelok* (1300), but not in *King Horn*, about the same date.

It appears from this, since these are all E. Midl. texts, that the new form was established, on the whole, pretty firmly in the East Midlands, at any rate from the middle of the thirteenth century. The W. Midl. texts show *sche*, etc., coming in by the middle of the fourteenth century. Thus *Will. of Pal.* (1350) has *sche*, *she*, but also *he* and *hue*; *Allit. P.* has not the *she*-form at all, only *ho* ; the author of *Piers Plowman* has *sche* but also *heo*. Audelay (1430) has generally *heo*, but *che* and *she* occur a few times each ; *sheo* occurs twice (Rasmussen, p. 78). Myrc, however (c. 1430), has no instance of such a form as *sche*.

The more polished fourteenth-century writers of the Midlands, Mandeville, Chaucer, Wycliffe, and Gower, all have *sche* or *she* only, which coincides with the prevailing usage in the London dialect of this period. The London documents (Morsbach), however, still have a few examples of *ȝhe*. The later London Charters have *she, sche* only (Lekebusch, p. 107). Northern Engl. and Scots texts have *s(c)hō*.

Any form such as *sche, scæ,* etc., appears to be unknown during the whole M.E. period in any pure Southern text, whether Kentish or Saxon in dialect, apart from the quite exceptional *shee* which occurs once or twice in Trevisa instead of his usual *heo, hue* ; cp. Morris's *Introd. to Aȝenbite*, p. i.

We may say, then, that *she,* whether it actually arose in the Nth., or the E. Midl., or in both independently, must have penetrated into Literary and Standard Engl. from the E. Midl. dialect.

NOTE. There is, perhaps, something to be said for Lindquist's view, *Anglia* 44, that *she* arose from the *-s* of 3rd Pers. Pres. combining with [*heo* = jǭ] in versions such as *cumes heo,* etc., in the Nthn. dialect.

Other forms of the Pron. of 3rd Person Fem.

§ 303. Perhaps the commonest form (Nom.) in the South is *heo,* probably originally = [hǭ]. This was later unrounded to *hē,* which we find, together with *hī,* in *St. Ed.* *Hi* also appears in Kentish (*Aȝenbite*). The form *hi* is used occasionally as an Acc., though the Dat. *hire, hir* already in *Laud. Chr.* has come into use for that purpose. The inconvenience of *hi,* which was also, as we shall see, a common form for the N. and Acc. Pl., and of *hēo,* or *hē,* which was identical with the Masc. Pron., is obvious.

What appears to be an unstressed form, *ha,* occurs by the side of *hēo* in *A. R.* Late Sthn. (Trevisa) has, besides *hēo,* a form *hue* which may = [hy], and be due either to the analogy of the Gen. *hur, hure* (O.E. *hyre*), or to a special treatment of [ø] from *ēo* (cp. § 168 above). In the latter case *hue* would simply be a late form of *hēo.* *St. Ed.* (1420) has *hee, hē,* as the only forms.

Turning to the Midlands, we find a fair variety of forms besides *sche,* etc., already discussed. *Orm.* has *ȝho* which probably = [hjō] from *hēo* ; *Bestiary* has *ge,* probably = [hjē], also from *hēo* with unrounding of [ø] or monophthonging of *ēo* ; *Gen. and Ex.* besides *she, sge,* has *ge* and *ghe,* which mean no doubt the same thing and correspond to the form in *Bestiary* ; *King Horn* still writes *heo.* The W. Midl. *Wil. of Pal.* has *hue,* and *Allit. P. hō,* which presumably is due to a late O.E. **h(e)ō* ; *Jos. of Ar. heo* ; Myrc has generally *heo,* but also occasionally *ho* and *he.* This form is probably the ancestor of the Mod. dial. [hū] used in Derbyshire and Cheshire.

§ 304. Had the M.E. distribution of the forms of this pronoun remained undisturbed, we should apparently have had *she* [ʃī], in Standard Eng., in the E. Midl. and in the North generally ; we should have had [hī] in the Southern Area, including Kent, together with a weak form [ə], while in the West, and perhaps the Central Midlands, we should have [hū].

§ 305. The M.E. Dat. Fem. of the pronoun of the 3rd Pers. is regularly *hire, hir,* or *here, her,* and these forms are found in all dialects, though careful authors, or scribes (e.g. Gower), sometimes distinguish between *hir, hire,* on the one hand, which they keep for the Fem. Sing., and *here,* etc., which is the Possessive Pl., on the other. The majority of texts, however, write *hire, here,* indifferently. This is the case in some Chaucer MSS., though others use *hire* in the Fem. Sing., and *here* in the Possessive Pl. ; others again reverse this. The London official documents of the fourteenth century use *here, her* for the Fem. Sing. D. Mandeville and Wycl. have *hir, hire.*

Parallel to the M.E. levelling of the Sing. Acc. Masc. pronoun under the Dat. form is the use of the Dat. Fem. for the Acc. also, which is universal in all dialects. The Acc. *hi,* referring to a grammatically Fem. Noun, used in *O. and N.* and in Shoreham, is exceptional. Modern usage has fixed on *her* as the Acc. Dat. Sing. Fem. The weakened form of this, without the aspirate, must have been in use in M.E., though it is not so commonly recorded as the weakened form of *hit* (cp. § 306). *St. Editha* has *hoselder and aneled herre,* ' communicated her and gave her extreme unction '.

[On the distribution of *hir* and *her* in M.E. see § 311, under Possessive Pronouns.]

The Neuter Pronoun of the 3rd Pers.

§ 306. The usual Nom. and Acc. form in M.E. is *hit* in all dialects, and the other cases are identical with those of the Masc. Pron.

Weakening to *it*.

This is noticeable in E. Midl. texts of an early date: *Laud Chron.*, *Orm.*, *Bestiary, Gen. and Ex.* all have the weakened form. The W. Midl. have both *hit* and *it*. The earliest Sthn. and Kentish texts have *hit, hyt*, but the late thirteenth-century *Robt. of Glos.* has *it* as well as *hit*. This appears to be exceptional in the South, where *hit, hyt* are the typical forms.

The earliest London sources have *hit* only. Davie (1327) has *hit* and *it*.

The form *a* used by Trevisa as an impersonal pronoun should be noted. The same writer uses this form also as a weak (unstressed) form of the Masc. (or Neut. ?) Pron. It refers to the agate stone in the phrase *a ys blak as gemmes buþ*, ... *a brenneþ yn water*.

Of the fourteenth-century London documents the Charters generally have either *hit* or *it*; only once, according to Morsbach (*Schriftspr.*, pp. 121–3), do both forms occur in the same document; the Wills and State Records have both forms.

Gower generally has *it*, seldom *hit*; Chaucer has both, *hit* being commoner.

Caxton (*Troye*) still retains *hit, hyt*, though *it* is commoner. (Cp. also Römstedt, p. 40.)

The late fifteenth-century Charters have both forms, *it* being the more common (Lekebusch, p. 107).

Q. Eliz. frequently writes *hit* both in letters and transl.

The Plural Forms of the 3rd Person (Nom., Acc., Dat.).

§ 307. The normal M.E. continuations of the O.E. *hie* Nom. and Acc., *heom* Dat., and *heora, hira* Gen., are *hi, hem, here, hire*, respectively, or variants of these. (The Gen. forms will be considered below, § 312, under Possessive Pronouns.) The point of interest in the history of the Pl. forms is the gradual introduction and substitution for the native forms of the forms *þei, þeim, þeir*, and their variants, which are of Scandinavian origin.

It would appear that few *pure* Southern or Kentish texts have any of these *þ*-forms before the fifteenth century. The solitary form *þei* ' they ' occurs, strangely enough, in the *Trin. Homs.* The following table shows the N., A., and D. forms in the principal Sth. and Kt. texts down to the middle of the fourteenth century:

S. and S.W.

	Lam. Homs.	Trin. Homs.	Moral Ode.	O. & N.	R. of Glos.	Tre-visa.
N.	*he, ha*	*hie, he* (*þei*)	*hi, hy*	*hi, heo*	*hii, hi*	*hy, hi, a*
A.	*hes*	*hes, is*		*hom*	*hom* (*is*)	*ham*
D.	*heom, ham*		*heom, him*	*heom, hom*	*hem, hom*	*ham*

Kentish.

	Vesp. A. 22.	Kt. Sermons.	Shoreham.	Aȝenbite.
N.	*hi*	*hi*	*hi, hy*	*hi*
A.	*his, es*	*hi, hii*	*ham, hys*	*hise, his* (very frequent)
D.	*ham*	*ham*	*hem*	*ham*

The fifteenth-century *St. Editha* seems to be the first Sthn. text which has *þey, þai* in the N. Pl., as the only form, but the native forms *hem* Acc. and Dat., and *hure*, etc. (cp. § 312 below) are retained.

The E. Midl. texts tell rather a different story, and we find the Scandinavian forms coming in quite early, but even in this area the Nom. is earlier than the other cases.

	Laud Chron.	1200. Orm.	1250. Bestiary.	1250. Gen. & Ex.
N.	*hi*	*þeȝȝ*	*he*	*he, þei* 573
A.	*heom*	*hemm*	*hem, is*	*hem, is, hes*
D.	*heom, him*	*hemm, þeȝȝm*	*hem*	*hem*

	1300. Havelok.	1300. King Horn.	1303. Robt. of Brunne.	1440. Bokenam.
N.	*þei, he*	*hi, he*	*þey*	*they, þei*
A.	*hem, ys, es*	*hem*	*hem*	*þem, hem*
			hem	*hem*

Centr. Midland.   *West Midland.*

	1350. E. E. Pr. Ps.	1220. Ancr. Riwle.	1350. Allit. P.	1350. Jos. of Ar.	1426. Audelay.	1450. Myrc.
N.	*hii, hij*	*heo, ha*	*þai*	*þei, heo*	*thai*	*þey*
A.	*hem*	*hom*	*hem, hom*	*hem*	*hem, ham, hom*	*hem*
D.	*hem*	*hom*	*hem, hom*	*hem, heom*	*hom*	*hem*

The London official dialect of the thirteenth century, as shown in Henry III's Proclamation (1258), has only *heo* for Nom. Pl., and *heom* in Acc. and Dat.; Davie (1327) has still only *hij* in N. Pl.

All the London official documents of the fourteenth century have *þei, þey, they,* etc., in the Nom. In the earliest *Lond. Ch.,* for the other cases, *hem* alone is found, and even in the later

documents where *þaym, thaim, þam*, etc., appear, *hem* preponderates largely (Morsbach, *Schriftspr.*, pp. 122, 123).

The language of Mandeville, Chaucer, Gower, and Wycliffe
agrees in this respect with the fourteenth-century London
documents ; these writers all have *thei, þei, they*, etc., in the
Nom., but the Scand. forms are unknown in the other cases :
Acc. Dat. *hem.* Hoccleve and Lydgate (1420) have *þei, they*
in Nom. but *hem* in the oblique cases; Malory (1469) has
they in Nom., *theym, them* in Acc., *hem* in Dat. ; Caxton
(*Troye*, 1471) *they*, but *hem* more usually in Dat. Acc., though
I note also *them* in Acc. *Nut-brown Maid* (1500) and Skelton
(1522) have the *th*-forms throughout. I have noted the form
hem as late as 1605, several times in Marston's *Eastward Hoe*.

All the Present-day dialects have *they* or some variant of
it ; the old *hi*, etc., has completely vanished. In the oblique
cases, however, [əm], the descendant of *hem*, survives to this
day in the dialects and even in Standard English. This is
the form written *'em*, as though it were reduced from *them*.
Down to and during the eighteenth century, this form was
a recognized form even in serious, if somewhat colloquial
writing.

In good colloquial Spoken English [əm] is frequent, though
perhaps becoming obsolescent among some classes of society.
The loss of the initial *h* parallel to that in *it*, and the reduction
of the vowel, are of course due to the unstressed position, in
which alone [əm] can be used.

We may summarize the results of the above account of the
Pers. Pronouns in M.E. in the following table :

	First Person.	Second Person.
N.	*ic, icc, ich, I, y*	*þū, thou, þou*
Acc. Dat.	*me*	*þe, thee, þee*

Third Person.

	Masc.	Fem.	Neuter.
N.	*hē, ha, a*	*heo, hi, hue, ho, ȝe, ȝhe, ȝho, sìæ, schee, sche, she, scho,* etc.	N.A. *hit, it, a*
A.	*hine, hyne, hin, him, hym*	*hi, here, her, hire, hir, er*	
D.	*him, hym*	*hire, here,* etc., *hurre*	*him*

Plural.

N.	*hie, hi, hij, heo, þei, þai, þeȝȝ, they, thai*, etc.
A.	*hi, heom, hem, ham, hise, his, þaim, þeim, þem, thaim, them, theym*, etc.
D.	*heom, hem, hemm, ham, hom, þaim, þeim*, etc.

POSSESSIVE PRONOUNS

§ 308. The O.E. Genitives, *mīn, þīn, his*, etc., were used both as real Genitives and as purely possessive adjectives. In the former case they were often used after verbs and adjectives which in O.E. govern the Gen., e.g. *ič eom his geþafa* ' I consent to *it* (his) '; or *God helpe mīn* 'God help me', etc.

In the second case, some of these words (*mīn, þīn, ēower, ūre*) were declined in full like ordinary adjectives, agreeing in Number, Gender, and Case with the nouns before which they stood—*mid mīnum ēagum* (Dat. Pl.) ' with my eyes '.

In M.E. the purely Genitive force is very early lost, though there are some examples of a survival of this in early texts : e. g. *þe huile he mei his* (*es, hes*) *wealden* ' so long as he has power over it ', where *his* is the Gen. of the Neuter *hit*, governed by *wealden* ' rule, have power over, etc.' (*Moral Ode*, Egerton, Jesus, and Trin. MSS., l. 55) ; further, *ðog ic* is *haue drogen in wo, Gen. and Ex.* 2403, ' though I have borne *it* (is) in misery '.

Aȝenbite has *God his aurekeþ*, p. 70, ' God will punish it ' ; *bote he his ne knawe*, ' unless he know it not ', ibid. (N.B. In all these cases, however, *his, hes, es* may be the typical S.E. and S.E. Midl. Acc. Pl. Cp. § 307, p. 234.)

The Genitives of the Pers. Prons., then, become mere Possessives, and are usually uninflected, though occasionally they take a suffix -*e*, probably on the analogy of *hire, here* ' her ', ' their ', which preserved the *e* from O.E. *e*, and *a*.

The typical M.E. forms of the possessives are as follows, though it seems unnecessary to give an exhaustive list of every possible variant :

	1st	2nd	3rd M.	3rd F.	N.
Sing.	*mīn*	*þīn*	*his*	*hire, here*	*his*
	mi	*þi*	*hise*	*his, her*	
Pl.	*ure*	*ȝure*	*here*		
	oure	*youre*	*heore*		
		oure, etc.	*hare*		
			hor, hure, etc.		

§ 309. The First Person.

M.E. texts often—one might say generally—distinguish between *mīn* used before words beginning with vowels, and *mī* before those beginning with consonants.

In the Sth., *God Ureisun, Soules Warde, Owl and Nightingale*, and in the *Kt. Homilies*, Vesp. A. 22, the form *mĭre* occurs, probably formed from *mi-* on the analogy of *hi-re* (Fem.) (*mire* is found already in 991, in a Suffolk Ch.)

§ 310.   **The Second Person.**

The same distinction between *þīn* and *þī* is made as between *mīn* and *mī*. *Owl and Nightingale* and *God Ur.* have a form *þīre* (also Dat. Fem.) which may be explained on the same analogy as *mīre*, § 309 above. Or the analogy may be the Pl. *ʒou-re, ou-re.*

NOTE. Parallel to *mīre, þīre, Owl and Nightingale* and *Moral Ode* have *ōre* Dat. Sing. Fem. of *ō* 'one'. The O.E. forms are *ān, ānre*. *Ōre* is probably a new formation from M.E. Nom. *ō* (before cons.), which was often used by Chaucer as a kind of emphatic Indef. Art., 'a single one', etc.

The Possessive Pronoun of 3rd Person Feminine.

§ 311.   The O.E. form *hire* survives in M.E. as *hire, hyre,* in nearly all texts, and is far the commonest form. We find *here* but rarely in early texts. *St. Editha,* however, favours *herre,* but also has *hurre* and *hur.* The forms with *e* probably owe this vowel to the analogy of such a Nom. Fem. as *he*. *Hurre* probably represents an older *heore,* where the diphthong may be due either to the Nom. *heo* or to the diphthongized forms of the Pl.: *heom, heora,* etc. Of course M.E. forms with *u* may also represent an O.E. *hyre.*

The use of *her(e)* is of interest, since it is the ancestor of the Standard English form. In the West Midl. *Wil. of Pal. here* occurs, though *hire* is the commonest form, and *hure* occurs once according to Skeat (Glossary of *W. of Pal.*). *Allit. P.* seems generally to have *her* as Possess., though *hyr* otherwise; Myrc has *hyre.*

Turning to the London and Literary Dialect, the London Records have *her(e)* far more frequently than *hir* (Morsbach, p. 126); Gower and Chaucer have only *hir(e)*; Capgrave (1394–1460), *hire, here* being rare (Dibelius, *Anglia,* xxiv. 220); Lydgate (1420), usually *her* as Possess., *hir* in the other cases; Pecock (1449), *her*; the rather illiterate Cely Papers which give a good picture of Middle Class speech (1475–88) have *here, hyr,* and occasionally *har* (Süssbier, p. 77); Caxton has both *here* and *hir*; Coverdale generally has *hir,* but *her* occasionally (Swearingen, p. 37), Skelton (1522) only *her*; *Edw. VI's 1st P. B.* (1547) *her* only; *Tottel's Misc.* (1557) still has *hir* as usual form, with occasional *her* (Hoelper, p. 48), and I have noted the former in *Euphues* (1581).

It appears, then, that the introduction of *her* was very gradual, and its exclusive use comparatively late. In the later period, it may have developed from *hir* by a lowering of *i* in unstressed positions. It is not easy to ascribe the form to any particular dialect area, since it appears in various districts sporadically; quite early in Kent (*Wil. of Shoreham*), in the S. West, in W. Midl., and in the non-dialectal Pecock, who is supposed by some to represent the Oxford type of literary English. It may be noted that *hir* was a useful distinctive form for the Fem. Sing., so long as *her* was in use as the Possess. Pl. With the introduction and general use of *their*, etc., however, *her* could be used in the Sing. without ambiguity.

NOTE. POSSESSIVE NEUTER. The Possess. *its* is a late development. I have noted no example, even in the colloquial sources, in the sixteenth century. Q. Elizabeth and Lyly, to mention no more, still use *his*; Shakespeare has the uninflected *it* as a Possess. On the other hand, Charles Butler (b. *c.* 1570) includes *its* in his *Engl. Gr.* (1634) without any comment, whence we may perhaps conclude that the form was current, at least colloquially, and was no longer regarded as a novelty.

The Possessive Plural of the Third Person.

§ 312. The displacement of the English forms *here*, etc., by the Scandinavian *þeir*, etc., was like that of the O.E. Dat. *hem*, etc., of the Pers. Pron., a slow process in the Midlands and South. The earliest M.E. Northern texts, on the other hand, know only the *þ-*, *th-*forms of the Possessive Pl. In E. Midl., however, *Ormulum* is the only early M.E. text which has the *þ-*forms, though it still preserves the English forms as well. None of the Sthn. or Kentish texts, very few of the W. Midl., and none of the great fourteenth-century writers, Chaucer, Wycliffe, Mandeville or Gower, have any trace of *þeir*, *þair*, etc. The London Proclamation of Hen. III (1258) has a Gen. *her*, and this is also Davie's form. The London documents of the fourteenth and early fifteenth centuries utilized by Morsbach are the first texts, other than the Northern, and *Ormulum*, which make any considerable use of the *th-*forms, and they preserve *here*, etc., as well. The fifteenth-century Hoccleve and Lydgate use *her*, but Malory and Caxton have *ther*, *their*; the latter also *her*, *hir* a few times (Römstedt, p. 41). The later fifteenth-century London Charters have *here* comparatively rarely; *their*, etc., is the predominating form, and becomes more and more so with every decade (Lekebusch, p. 110). Henceforth these forms seem practically the only ones, but *Nut-brown Maid* (c. 1500) has *her* as well. As late as 1557, *Tottel's Misc.* has *her* a few times. *Machyn's Diary* (1550–53) has *her*, p. 141.

The following are the chief forms of the 3rd Pers. Possess. Pl. in the principal dialectal texts:

SOUTHERN.

God Ur.	Lambeth Homs.	Moral Ode.	Ancr. Riw.	Owl & Night.	Robt. of Glos.	Tre- visa.	St. Ed.
hore	*hare, heore*	*heora, heore*	*hore, hare*	*heore*	*hor, here*	*here*	*hure, hurre, here*

KENTISH.

Vesp. A. 22.	Kt. Sermons.	Shoreham.	Aȝenbite.
hare	*here, hire*	*hare*	*hare, hire*

E. MIDL.

Laud Chron.	Orm.	Gen. & Ex.	Havelok.	Robt. of Brunne.	Bokenam.
heore, here, hire	*heore, þeȝȝre*	*here, her, hure, þeir* 573	*here*	*here þeyr* (rarer)	*hyr, here, ther*

W. MIDL.

Layamon.	Jos. of Ar.	Allit. P.	W. of Pal.	Myrc.	Audelay.
heore	*heore, here*	*her, hor, here*	*here*	*hor, hur*	*here*

NORTHERN.

Cursor.	N. Psalter.	Metr. Homs.	Minot.	Bruce.
þair þar	*þair*	*thair*	*þaire*	*thair*

It seems evident from these statistics that *their* comes into Literary English through East Midland, from the North.

DECLENSION OF NOUNS

§ 313. **Gender.** English makes no distinctions of grammatical gender in nouns, but only recognizes the natural distinctions of sex. The confusion of genders which is observable in Early Transition texts (see account, §§ 289–93 above, of forms of article) was partly due to the working of analogy which levelled out distinctions in declensional types, partly to the weakening of vowels in unstressed syllables to *-e* which took place during the last quarter of the eleventh and the first quarter of the twelfth century, thus wiping out formal distinctions to a very great extent.

§ 314. **Case.** In Modern English the only case, in Nouns, distinguishable from the Nom., is the Genitive or Possessive. Of this case, only one type, that with the suffix *-s*, survives and is used both in Sing. and Pl. This suffix is written *-'s*: *dog's tail, king's crown*, etc. It should be noticed that although the spelling is fixed, the actual form of the suffix, as pronounced, varies according to the character of the final sound of the Noun. After voiceless consonants the suffix is

[-s] as in [kæts, ʃips], etc. After voiced consonants, and vowels, the suffix is [-z] as in [dɔgz teil, leidiz feis], etc. After the open consonants [ž, ʃ, z, s] the suffix is [-iz] in Standard English, but often [-əz| in Provincial and Vulgar English, as in [hōsiz hed, fiʃiz fin, bridžiz end], etc.

The origin of this suffix is the O.E. *-es*, a typical Genitive Singular suffix for Masc. and Neuter Nouns: *þæs cyninges sunu, sweordes eċġ* 'the King's son, sword's edge'. This suffix in O.E. and Early M.E. was confined to Masc. and Neuter Nouns of the Strong Declensions. It was very early extended to all Genders, and to original Weak Nouns as well: *þære eorþan sċēat* ' the bosom of the earth', becoming first **þer erþen sċēt* and then *þe erþes bōsme*; Mod. Engl. *earth's*, etc.

In O.E. there were other types of strong declension, both Masc. and Fem. Thus a fairly large class are the so-called ō-stems like *ġiefu* 'gift' (fem.), which in the Sing. is declined as follows:

> N. *ġiefu*
> A. *ġiefe*
> G. D. *ġiefe*

Another is that of *u*-stems which include words of all genders. The following is an example:

> S.
> N. *sunu* 'son'
> A. *sunu, -a*
> G. *suna*, etc.

NOTE. We should expect the Possess. of *wife, calf* to be [waivz, kāvz] instead of the actual [waifs, kāfs], which are new formations on analogy of Nom. We still say [kāvzhed] however, and [waivz] survived in seventeenth century, cp. spelling *wives* in Marston's *Eastward Hoe*.

The Possessive Singular in M.E.

§ 315. These types, whose cases are not very clearly distinguished, even in O.E., suffer in M.E. the further levelling of their suffixes to *-e*, so that there is nothing to distinguish one type from another. They are, however, distinguishable from the commonest type, in that they have *-e* in the Gen. Sing. instead of *-es*.

Sporadic examples of words with *-e* in the Gen. Sing. occur throughout the M.E. period.

The Sth. and Kt. texts have such forms of Gen. Sing. as *sune, his uncle deth*, in the Masc., and in the Fem. *huerte loue* 'heart's love', *soule fōde* 'soul's food', *senne slepe* 'sleep of sin', *thovene mouth* 'the oven's mouth', *oure leuedi soster* 'our Lady's sister', etc.

In the E. Midl. *Gen. and Ex.* has *helle niġt* ' the night of hell', *steore name* ' star's name', but as a rule the *-es* suffix is used for Fem. nouns as well as Masc. Cp. also *þes cwenes canceler* in Laud. Chron. ann. 1123. *St. Katherine* (W. Midl.) uses *-es* (*-is*) in Gen. S. for nouns of all genders—*lefdis* ' lady's ', etc. *Allit. P.* generally has *-es* in Fem. as well as Masc., but writes *honde myȝt* once.

In fourteenth-century London documents, Morsbach finds a few cases in which the suffix *-es* is omitted, or replaced by *-e* in Fem. words : *soule hēle* 'soul's welfare', *seint Katerine day* ' St. Katherine's day', *oure lādy chapell* ' our Lady's Chapel', etc. The last is the origin of the Modern *Lady Chapel.* Chaucer generally has *-es* for all genders, but omits *s* occasionally in old Fem. words : *herte* (also *hertes*), *widwe, cherche, lādy,* and once in the old Masc. *u*-stem *sune.* Caxton has a few survivals like *oure lady matins* (cp. *our Lady mattens,* Cavendish, 1577), *atte brydge foote,* etc. He also often omits *-s* after words ending in *-s*—*Kinge Menelaus, wyf, sir Patryse dethe,* etc. This practice is followed also by Coverdale—*Moses wife, righteous sake,* and is found later in the Authorized Version.

For the adverbial use of the Gen., see below under Adverbs, § 331. (3).

NOTE. The practice of writing *-'s* with an apostrophe, for the Possess. suffix Sing. is unknown in the sixteenth century, and in the first three quarters of the seventeenth century. Mr. Nichol Smith kindly informs me that *-'s* came in about 1680, and *-s'* for the Possess. Pl. not till about 1780.

The Plural of Nouns.

§ 316. In Mod. Engl. the only question we need ask concerning the declension of a Noun is, ' How does it form its Plural?'

Apart from foreign words like *seraph—seraphim, stigma—stigmata, rhinoceros—rhinoceri* (also *rhinoceroses*), etc., which take Hebrew, Greek, and Latin Plurals respectively, whose use must be confined to the learned, the types of Plural formation in English are very few. They are the following :

A. -s-Plurals: *cat—cats,* etc.; B. **Weak Plurals**: *ox—oxen*; C. **Mutation Pls.**: *tooth—teeth,* etc.; D. **Invariables**: *sheep, deer*; E. **Irregular, Double Pls.** : *children,* etc.

§ 317. A. -s-Plurals.

These include nearly all Nouns in the language; indeed, the number of each of the other types is so small that, although they include some very important words, many grammarians who deal only with English as it is consider them as 'irregular'.

The -*s*-suffix varies in pronunciation according to the same conditions which determine the form of the Possessive (§ 308, above): [kæts, dogz, le*i*d*iz*, hō*siz*], etc., etc.

There is also a class of words ending in *f* in the Nom. Sing., which take the suffix [z] and voice the [f] to [v] ; e. g. *loaf—loaves* [louf—louvz, kā*f*—kāvz], etc. The explanation of this is that in O.E. *f*, though voiceless finally, was voiced between vowels, so that the forms were *hlāf—hlāfas*, *f* in the Pl. being pronounced [v]. In M.E. the Pl. was *lōves*, and later, when the vowel of the suffix was lost, the combination [vs] naturally became [vz]. Thus the *v*-spelling in Mod. English indicates a phonetic change which took place in O.E.

The OE. forms of the Masc. type are :

	Sing.	Pl.
N. A.	*hām* 'home'	*hāmas*
G.	*hāmes*	*hāma*
D.	*hāme*	*hāmum*

§ 318. **B. Weak Plurals.**

The only surviving word of this type in common use in Standard English is *ox*, Pl. *oxen*. (*Brethren* and *children* will be considered under E, below.)

A few others survive in the Dialects, and a few such as *shoon*, *een*, are occasionally found in rather artificial literary usage.

The Weak Class was originally a very large one. In O.E. it included Masculine, Fem., and Neuter words. Examples are : Masc.—*guma* 'man', *hana* 'cock', *nefa* 'nephew', *steorra* 'star', *hunta* 'hunter', *nama* 'name', *mōna* 'moon', etc., etc. ; Fem.—*eorðe. folde* 'earth', *heorte* 'heart', *sunne* 'sun', *swealwe* 'swallow', *bēo* 'bee', *tā* 'toe', *clife* 'cliff', *pise* 'pea', *cwēne* 'woman' ; Neuter—*ēage* 'eye', *ēare* 'ear'.

The O.E. Weak Declensions run as follows :

	Masc.		Fem.		Neuter.	
	S.	Pl.	S.	Pl.	S.	Pl.
N.	*mōna*	*mōnan*	*heorte*	*heortan*	*ēage*	*ēagan*
A.	*mōnan*	*mōnan*	*heortan*	*heortan*	*ēagan*	*ēagan*
G.	*mōnan*	*mōnena*	*heortan*	*heortena*	*ēagan*	*ēagena*
D.	*mōnan*	*mōnum*	*heortan*	*heortum*	*ēagan*	*ēagum*

In M.E. this form of declension is largely extended in the Sthn. and Kentish texts, so that many originally strong words are included, and we find Pls. like *applen*, *bischopen*, *sustren*, *bruggen* 'bridges', *dawen* 'days', *dēden* 'deeds', *heveden* 'heads', *honden* 'hands', *wingen* 'wings', etc. Original Wk. nouns preserve their ending: *churchen*, *hunten* 'hunters', *pēsen* 'peas(e)', *herten* 'hearts', *tōn* 'toes', *eyen* 'eyes', etc.

Many Latin and N. Fr. Loan-words also take *-en* in Pl.: *develen*, *diaknen* ' deacons', *mylen* ' miles', *chambren* 'chambers', *joyen* 'joys', etc.

The texts of the Sth. and Kent. are very fond of a Wk. Gen. Pl. in *-ene*, O.E. *-ena*, which is used even with words originally strong, and otherwise regarded as such by the Sthn. texts themselves. Thus *king*, Gen. S. *kinges*, D. *kinge*, N. Acc. Pl. *kinges*, Dat. *kingen* (O.E. *cyn(in)gum*), but Gen. *kingene*.

The apparent spread of the wk. type in the Sth. may have been due to the analogy of the Dat. Pl., O.E. *-um*, M.E. *-en*. The latter would be indistinguishable from the M.E. representative of the O.E. wk. suffix *-an*. The Gen. Pl. ending *-ena* was also common in O.E. in the so-called *ō*-stem words (Fem.), which are of course a strong class—e. g. *ġ(i)efu* ' gift ', Gen. Pl. *g(i)efena*. This suffix, M.E. *-ene*, occurring here as well as in the regular Wk. declension, could easily be further extended. In the same way the M.E. N. and Acc. Pl. *-en* occurred already in a large number of words, and the same suffix resulted from every Dat. Pl. in the language. Hence it was natural to use it to express the Pl. generally.

In the Midlands, the use of the *-en* Pls. was very restricted. Thus in *Gen. and Ex.* the usual Pl. is *-es*, but a few *-en* forms occur, and some are new formations: *gōren* 'spears', O.E. *gāras* ; *sunen* ' sons', *wēden* ' garments', and the old wk. nouns *wunen* ' laws', *fōn* 'foes', *fēren* ' companions', etc.

In W. Midl. *Allit. P.* has *yȝen* ' eyes', *trumpen* 'trumpets', and the Gen. Pl. *bēsten* 'beasts', *blonken* 'horses', as the only forms of this class. *St. Katherine*, now generally considered to be W. Midl., confines the use of *-en* to Fem. nouns. The pre-Chaucerian London writer Davie (1307–27) has the shattered remains of the wk. Pl. in *ēren*, *halewen*, *fōn*, *honden* (Dölle, p. 63).

The fourteenth-century London documents dealt with by Morsbach have an overwhelmingly large proportion of *-es* Pls., the *-en* forms being only *hosyn* ' hose', *alle Halwen* ' All Hallows' (*Schriftspr.*, p. 114). Chaucer, who has more purely Southern characteristics, has a greatly preponderating number of *-es* Pls. but also *oxen*, *foon* 'foes', *pesen*, *asshen* 'ashes', *hosen*, *been* (and *bees*) 'bees', *toon* 'toes', *yèn* 'eyes', *fleen* 'flies', *sustren*, *doughtren* (and *doughtres*). Caxton's only

-en Pls. are *shoon* ' shoes' (also *shois*), *eyen* ' eyes', *oxen, hosyn.*
His usual form of the Pl. ends in *-es,* or *-is* (Römstedt). In
the fifteenth century Wk. Pls. are not infrequent, e. g. *horson*
' horses' (Cely P.). *Ewen* ' ewes' (Northumb. Will 1450),
bothen ' booths', *Al Haylwyn, Al Sawlyn* (Shillingford). In
the sixteenth century we still find—*shone* (Wilson, Elyot,
Gabr. Harvey), *All Sowllen College* (letter of Layton 1535),
Housen (Bury Wills, Ascham), and so on.

Some of the Mod. Dials. use the Pls. *housen, primrosen.*
Chicken is sometimes felt as a Wk. Pl. and used collectively :
to keep chicken. Possibly the form *chick* is felt to be the Sing.
of this word.

§ 319. C. Mutation Plurals.

A certain number of nouns in O.E., principally Masc. and
Fem., have in their N. and Acc. Pl. a change of vowel. This
change is always in the nature of fronting, and is due to the
original presence of an *-i*-suffix (cp. §§ 104–9 above, on *i*-
Mutation). The change occurs also in the Dat. Sing. This
suffix is no longer preserved after long sylls. in O.E., though
the results remain. The following are the principal words of
this class:

Masculine. fōt—fēt ' foot', *tōþ—tēþ* ' tooth', *mann* or
monn—menn ' man'; *frēond—frīend* ' friend'.

Feminine. hnutu—hnyte ' nut', *bōc—bēċ* ' book', *gāt—gǣt*
' goat', *gōs—gēs* ' goose', *mūs—mȳs* ' mouse', *lūs—lȳs* ' louse',
cū—cȳ ' cow', *burg,* or *burh—byriġ* ' city'.

Neuter. scrūd—scrȳd ' clothing' (cp. Mod. *shroud*).
These are declined as follows :

	S.	Pl.	S.	Pl.
N. A.	*fōt*	*fēt*	*bōc*	*bēċ*
G.	*fōtes*	*fōta*	*bēċ and bōce*	*bōca*
D.	*fēt*	*fōtum*	*bēċ*	*bōcum*

Rather more than half of these mutated Pls. are preserved
in Mod. Standard English ; *friend, cow, nut, borough, book,
goat,* and *shroud* have, however, succumbed to the influence of
the vast class of *-s*-Pls.

NOTE. The Dative Singular does not directly concern us here, but we
may note that the mutated forms hardly survive beyond Early M.E., with
the exception of *byriġ* (see § 322 below). I have noted the old Dat. S. of
bōc twice in the Kt. Gospels, as *bǣch, bēch.*

The form *fryndes* in Morsbach's fourteenth-century London

documents is probably the O.E. *friend* with the additional *-es* suffix (*Schriftspr.*, p. 114).

The mutated Pl. *kye*, etc., is found in M.E. in Midl. and Nthn. texts, and in W. Midl. *Allit. P. kuy* (see § 315). It survives as *kye* [*kai*] in the Mod. Dial. of the North, Nth. and E. and Central Midlands, and in W. Somers. and Devon (*E. D. Gr.*, § 381).

The form *geet*, etc., is fairly common, in all dialects down to and during the fourteenth century, by the side of *gootes*, etc. It is found as late as Caxton with the spelling *gheet* (C. also uses *gootes*). Caxton has *kyen* 'cows', and the Kentish *kēne* (Römstedt, p. 38).

On the whole, M.E. and Early Mod. agree with present-day Engl. in the group of words which have mutated Pls.

§ 320.   D. Unchanged or Invariable Pls.

In O.E. there is a group of Neuter Nouns which take no suffix in the N. and Acc. Pl. These are words of one syllable which has either a long vowel, or two consonants at the end : *dēor* 'beast', *scēap, scēp* 'sheep', *swīn* 'swine', *fȳr* 'fire', *word* 'word', *bearn* 'child'. The short-syllabled words of the same class take *-u* in the N. and Acc. Pl. This *-u* is lost after a long syllable in Early O.E., hence the uninflected form of *dēor*, etc.

These invariables survive to some extent in M.E., and while many pass into the common *-es* Pl. type, there are some additions, some of which are collective nouns, and others expressive of *measure*, or *number*, etc.

Examples : *schēp* 'sheep', *deor* 'deer, beast', *folc, yeer, thing, hors* (Chaucer), etc.

Caxton uses *myle* 'mile' in Pl. when preceded by a numeral, also *couple*, and *pound*.

The forms *yeres, thinges* are found by the side of the un-inflected Pls.

In present-day English *sheep* and *deer* are always invariable, while such phrases as *five mile long, two foot high, three stone ten*, are common though perhaps rather archaic. The words *dozen, couple, score* when preceded by a numeral are never inflected. Note also such phrases as a *three-year-old, five-pound note*.

Swine is now only used collectively—*a herd of swine*, except colloquially, as a term of abuse. Chaucer still uses *swyn* as an ordinary Pl. No doubt the analogy of *kīn* 'cows' may have helped to retain this form.

§ 321. **E. Irregular Plurals.**

In present-day English, the forms *children*, *brethren*, and the Provincial or poetical form *kine*, require some explanation.

Children. In O.E. the word *čīld* (neuter) is generally declined like *word* (see § 320 above) and has an invariable N. and Acc. Pl. *cīld*, but the form *čildru* is also found. In M.E. there are two chief types of Pl.: one *childre*, derived from *čildru*, found in *Orm*, and *Gen. and Ex.* (*childere*), *Allit. P. childer*; and the other *children*, found in the Sth. and Kt., used by Chaucer and Caxton, and in present-day English. This form is of course a double Pl., since the *-r-* is itself a Pl. suffix, and to this is added the Wk. suffix *-en*. Coverdale has a Pl. Gen. *childers*, otherwise *children*. *Edward VI's First Prayer Bk.* has both forms of the Pl. in the phrase—*childers children* (Marriage Service).

Brethren. This shows mutation of the vowel as well as the addition of *-en*.

In O.E. the usual W.S. Pl. is *brōþor* and *brōþru*, but it is worth noting that the Dat. Sing. is *brēþer*. Rushworth[1] (Mercian) has N. and A. Pl. *brǣðre*, by the side of *brōðer* and *brōðre*, and Lindisfarne (Northumbr.) has also mutated forms. The declension of *brōþor* is remarkable, as it belongs to a small class of words all expressing family relationships: O.E. *fæder* 'father', *mōdor* 'mother', *dohtor* 'daughter', and *sweostor* 'sister'. *Mōdor* and *dohtor* have Dat. Sing. *mēder*, *dehter*, but no mutation in the Pl. in O.E.

In Early M.E., in the Sth. and Kt. this whole group of words take the Wk. *-en*-suffix in the Pl.: *brotheren* and *bretheren*, *sustren*, *modren*, *douȝtren*, etc.; *Gen. and Ex.* also has *brethere*; W. Midl. (*Allit. P.*), *brether*, *deȝter*; Chaucer, *bretheren*, *doughtren* (and *doughtres*), *sustren*. Caxton has *brethren*, *bredern*, *bretherne*, *brothern*. The association of *brōþer* on the one hand with the mutation Pls. was effected through the Dat. Sing., since most words which had a mutated Dat. Sing. had also mutation in N. and Acc. Pl.

The association with the *-en* Pls. could be effected if any one member of the group acquired this suffix. *Sustren* may well have been the starting-point, as it is the most consistently used form in the Sth. As has been pointed out before, the origin of *-en* in M.E. need not in all cases have been O.E. *-an*, but it might arise from a generalization of the M.E. weakening of the Dat. Pl. suffix *-um*. When once *-en* arose in the Dat., the tendency to extend it to the other cases of the Pl. would be very strong, owing to the large group of words which already had the suffix from another source.

Apart from the group of relationship words which were associated by meaning, there were several other words—old neuters, like *ċildru,* which had *-ru* in the Pl. in O.E., and in M.E. *-re,* and *-ren.* When once *bretheren* and the rest were established, it would be natural to regard *-ren* as a Pl. suffix and to extend it to the words which normally had *-re.* These were, among others: O.E. *æ̇ġ* 'egg', Pl. *æ̇gru,* M.E. *ei,* Pl. *eire(n)*; O.E. *lamb—lambru,* M.E. *lambre, lambren*; O.E. *calf* 'calf'—*calfru,* M.E. *calfre* and *calvren.* Here again the Dat. Pl. *children, eiren, calfren* helped in the process. In this way, a considerable group of Pls. in *-ren* was formed.

Kine. This form is of course another example of a double Pl., showing mutation: O.E. *cȳ,* etc., + the weak *-n* suffix. The three types *kuyn, kīn, kēn* are all found fairly frequently in M.E. Chaucer has *kīn,* Caxton *kyen* and *kēne.* The *kīn-*type may have been assured permanence by a natural association with the collective *swīn,* which was invariable (§ 314). In Standard and Literary English, *kine* is archaic, and poetical. In the Mod. Dials. it is used in the W. of Scotland, the Nth. of England, Kt., and Devon (*E. D. Gr.,* § 383).

Other dialectal double Pls. of the same kind are [gīzn, mīzn, fītn].

§ 322. Survivals of old Datives in English.

Meadow is an old Dat., O.E. *mǣdwe, mǣdewe,* etc., from Nom. Fem. *mǣd.* This word, and *Leasowe* (Chesh. Pl. N.), *leasow* (Mod. Dial.) 'meadow' from O.E. *lǣs,* Dat. *lǣswe,* belonged to the so-called *-wō-*stems, a group of Fem. words which originally took the suffix *-wō-* after the 'root'. In the O.E. Nom. all trace of this has disappeared in long-syllabled words, but the *w* survives in the oblique cases.

In M.E. the forms *medwe, medoue, leseo, lesoue,* etc., occur, generally used indifferently as Nom. or oblique case. The forms *mead* and *leaze* are descended from the Old Nominatives.

Bury in Pl. Ns. is from the O.E. Dat. Sing. *byriġ* from Nom. *burh.* The usual pronunciation at present, when the element is stressed, is [bɛri] representing O.E. (Kentish) *beriġ,* but the spelling represents a M.E. type pronounced [y]. The word *borough* is descended from the old Nom. *buruh,* with a parasitic *u* in the second syllable.

THE ADJECTIVES

Declension.

§ 323. Old English.

The Adjective in O.E. has two modes of declension—the *Strong* and the *Weak*, which correspond, on the whole, to the Strong and Weak Declensions of Nouns. Nearly all adjectives can be declined in both ways. The Strong Declension is used when adjectives occur predicatively, or attributively, without the Definite Article. The Weak Declension of Adjectives is used after the Definite Article.

O.E. adjectives distinguish Gender, and Number.

STRONG DECLENSION.
Singular.

	M.	F.	N.
N.	*gōd*	*gōd, blacu*	*gōd*
A.	*gōd-ne*	*gōde*	*gōd*
G.	*gōd-es*	*gōd-re*	*gōd-es*
D.	*gōd-um*	*gōdre*	*gōd-um*
Instr.	*gōde*	—	*gōde*

Pl.

N. A.	*gōde*	*gōd-e*	*gōd, blacu*
G.	—	*gōd-ra*	—
D.	—	*gōd-um*	—

WEAK DECLENSION.
Singular.

	M.	F.	N.
N.	*gōd-a*	*gōd-e*	*gōd-e*
A.	*gōd-an*	—	—
G.	—	—	*gōd-an*
D.	—	—	—

M.F.N. Pl.

N.	*gōdan*
G.	*gōd-ena, -ra*
D.	*gōd-um*

NOTE. The forms of *blæc* 'black' have been given in the two cases, N. Fem. S. and N. A. Fem. Pl., in which short-syllabled words retain the suffix -*u*, lost after long monosyllables.

The cases which differ in their suffix from those of nouns are: Sing. Acc. M., Dat. M.; G. and D. Fem.; Dat. Neuter; in the Pl.—N. and A. Masc., G. of all Genders. The suffixes -*ne*, -*ra*, -*re* are formed on the analogy of the Pronouns: *hi-ne, hi-ra, hi-re, hi-e.*

§ 324. M.E. Adjectives.

The declension of Adjectives undergoes considerable modifications in M.E. by the natural process of levelling all the vowels of the endings under -*e*.

Further, since -*an* and -*um* are both levelled under -*en*, it is impossible to tell which suffix it represents; e.g. *to þe guoden* 'to the good', Dat. Pl., *Aȝenb.*, p. 72.

The Early Transition texts of the South preserve some of the strong adjectival endings, and distinguish to some extent between Strong and Weak endings.

Thus *Holy Rd. Tree* has D. Sing. Fem. *ludre, ðinre,* but often drops the *r* of the suffix; an Acc. Masc. *mucelne*; whereas the Dat. Pl. still preserves -*um* occasionally, by the side of

-on, -an, -a, -e. The Weak forms often drop the *-n*, and a strong Gen. Pl. *haligræ* occurs where we should expect *-ena.* (See on this text Napier's admirable Introduction, p. liv.)

The Weak suffix *-en* is disappearing from the language, perhaps by weakening and losing the *-n*, so that it is indistinguishable from the Strong ending *-e.* At any rate the *-en* suffix appears not to survive the close of the twelfth century, except in Adj. used as Nouns.

The Strong endings remain, here and there, considerably later. *Godne* is found in *Laȝamon*, 1388 ; *alnewan* in *Aȝenbite* ; *A. R.* (Morton's text) has *godere*, Dat. Sing., p. 428, and *to godre heale*, p. 194. *Orm* has *allre nēst*, 1054. Chaucer still has a few Gen. Pls. in *-r* in his poetry—*youre aller cost, oure aller cok*, and the fossils *alderbest, alderwers* (ten Brink, *Chaucers Spr.*, § 255). A belated *allermast* occurs in *St. Editha.*

For the Central M.E. period the ordinary suffix for attributive Adj., used without distinction of Gender, Number, and Case, is *-e* ; cp. Chaucer's ' smale foules maken melodie'. This *-e* remains in poetry until, together with all other unstressed *-e*'s, it is lost towards the close of the fifteenth century. It is often omitted in prose much earlier, especially after long vowels. It was probably archaic and disused in the spoken language considerably earlier.

§ 325. French Adjectives in M.E.

French Pls. in *-s* occur in Chaucer oftener in his prose than in his verse (ten Brink, *Chaucers Spr.*, § 243). These forms occur chiefly when the Adjective is used attributively and stands after the Noun: *places delitables, weyes espirituels, goodes temporeles.* But *-s* is found also when the Adj. precedes the Noun: *in the sovereyns devynes substaunces* ; and occasionally when the Adj. is used predicatively : *romances that ben royales* (rhymes with *tales*), Sir Thopas, 137. These Pls. are fairly common in the fifteenth century and even occur in the sixteenth, e. g. *most demures and wise sustris* (c. 1450), *noblez lettres* (1458), *letters patents* (Lord Berners); *clirristz days* (Q. Eliz. Transl.).

§ 326. Comparison of Adjectives.

In O.E. the ordinary suffixes of Comparison are—Comp. *-ra* ; Superl. *-ost*, more rarely *-ast, -ust*, and still more rarely *-est.* There were in Gmc. two types of suffix : *-ōza, -ōst,* ; *-iza, -ist-.* The latter occur in O.E. only in a few words, which are known by having *i*-mutation in the Comp. and Superl.

It is not otherwise possible to distinguish the two types in O.E., as *-ost*, *-est*, etc., may occur in the same word without mutation.

Examples of unmutated type:

> *heard—heardra, heardost*
> *fæger—fægerra, fægrost*

This is the normal type, and in M.E. occurs as *hardre, hardest*.

§ 327. Examples of type with i-mutation.

There are comparatively few of these:

eald 'old'	W.S. *ieldra*	*ieldest*
	non-W.S. *eldra*	*eldest*
grēat	W.S. *grīetra*	
ġeong	⎰ *ġingra,*	*ġingest*
	⎱ Merc. *ġungra*	*ġungest*
long		*lenġest*
strong		*strenġest*
brād	*brǣdra* (generally *brād-*)	
hēah	W.S. *hīerra*	W.S. *hīehst*
	non-W.S. *hērra*	non-W.S. *hēhst*

Comparatives are inflected weak, Superlatives nearly always weak, except in forms ending in *-ost*, *-est* (N. A. V. Neut.).

NOTE. In O.E. the Comp. either takes *þonne* 'than' after it, with the thing compared in the same case as that of the thing with which it is compared: *Sē wæs betera þonne ic* (Beow. 469), or omits *þonne*, and takes the Dat. of thing compared; *ne onġeat he nō hiene selfne bettran ōðrum gōdum monnum, Cura Past.*, p. 114. 23, cit. Wülfing, *Syntax*, p. 75.

In M.E. more of the mutated forms survive than in the Mod. period. Chaucer has *strenger—strengest, lenger—lengest*. At the present day we retain only *elder—eldest*, and these with a specialized meaning, defining usually the place or order in a family : *the elder of the two brothers, the eldest son*. *Eldest* was still used with the old force in seventeenth century. *Elder* as an ordinary comp. of *old* occurs in *Euphues England*, Arber's Reprint, p. 258. *Strenger, lenger*, are used by Sir T. Elyot (1531).

NOTE. The Comp. of *great* is generally *grĕttre, grĕtter* in M.E. (Chaucer, Caxton), with vowel shortening. Shakespeare rhymes *gretter—better* (Viëtor, *Shakesp.* 167). On the possible influence of this Comp. on the form [greit], see § 232, Note.

§ 328. Irregular Comparison.

Certain words form their Comp. and Superl. from a base other than that of the Positive.

	O.E.			M.E. (Chaucer).		
'good'	*gōd*	*betera* *bettra*	*betst*	*good*	*bettre*	*best*
'bad'	*yfel*	*wyrsa*	*wyrsta*	*evil*	*werse* *badder*	*werst*
'big'	*myċel* *miċel*	*māra*	*mǣst*	*muchel* *moche*	*mōre*	*moost*
'little'	*lȳtel*	*lǣssa*	*lǣst*	*litel*	*lǎsse*	*leest*

No comment is required on these words, as we have retained the irregularities. We generally use *smaller, smallest*, as the Comp. and Superl. of *little*. *Less* and *least* are generally adverbs at the present time, and we usually employ a Comp. *lesser* adjectivally.

§ 329.
Certain Adjectives derived from Adverbs and Prepositions are used with Comp. and Superl. forms in O.E.

'far'	*feor*	*fierra* *ferra*	*fierrest* *ferrest*
'near'	*nēah*	*nēarra*	*niehsta* *nēhsta*
'earlier, former'	*ǣr*	*ǣrra*	*ǣrrest*
'forward'	*fore*	*furðra*	*fyrrest* 'first'

Far represents O.E. *feor*, M.E. *fer, far*. Chaucer's *ferre* is the Comp. of this and represents the above O.E. form. We now use *further* or *farther* for this, the former being really the Comp. formed from O.E. *forð*, used, as we see above, as Comp. of *fore*. *Farther* is on the analogy of *further*, but owes its vowel to *far*.

Near is an old Comp. of *nēah*, and is derived from O.E. *nēarra*; it is still used, in the form *neer*, as a Comp. in Chaucer. We now feel *near* as a Positive, and have formed new Comp. and Superl. with -*er*, *est*. The real historical Positive is *nigh*, corresponding to, though not identical with Chaucer's *ney*, from O.E. *nēh* (cp. § 171 (3 b) for Mod. [nai]). Our word *next*, the old Superl., is quite isolated from *nigh*, *near* in form and meaning.

Erst. This is the old Superl. of *ǣr*, represented by our *ere* (Adv.). *Erst* is obsolete except in deliberate literary usage.

First. Now and in O.E. used as an Ordinal. The base is **fur-*, of which it is a normal Superl. with **-ist*. From the same base is O.E. *fore,* earlier **fura-.* The O.E. comp. *furðra* is from base *forð-.*

§ 330. Superlatives in -most.

The words *foremost, utmost, inmost,* etc., require some explanation. There is an old superlative suffix *-ma* which survives in O.E. in *for-ma* 'first' (cp. Lat. *pri-mus*) and other words indicating for the most part position or direction. *Forma* means literally 'most forward'.

In O.E. already a form *fyrmest* existed, which is a double superlative, having both suffixes, *-m-+-ist.* A large number of other words with the double formation exist in O.E., e. g. *sīðemest* 'last', *lætemest* 'last, latest', *innemest* 'inmost', *norð-mest,* etc. The suffix *-mest* was identified with O.E. *mæst, māst* 'most', and forms with *-mæst,* rarely *-māst,* are found. In M.E. this latter normally became *-mōst,* the association with *mōst* preventing shortening. To all appearances, therefore, we get superlatives with *mōst* used as a suffix, though historically they are nothing of the kind.

The old superlative (used as an Ordinal in O.E.) *forma,* where no longer felt as such, received the normal Comp. suffix *-er* and appears as *former,* while *fyrmest* was altered to *fore-most,* the first syllable being associated with *former,* the second with *mōst,* as we have seen.

Utmost stands for E. M.E. *ūtmōst,* with shortening of *ūt-* to *ŭt-* before *-m-. Outmost* is a new formation on the same model, from *out.*

Other new formations of the kind are *topmost, hindmost.*

Uppermost, uttermost, outermost have the supposed superlative suffix added to a Comp. ending *-er.* The O.E. Comp. of *ūt* was *ȳterra,* and *ūterra.* The latter becomes *utter* (§ 176).

ADVERBS

§ 331. There are three main ways of forming Adverbs in O.E.

(1) By the suffix *-e* added to Adjectives: *wīde* 'widely', *sōðe* 'truly'.

(2) By the addition of an adverbial suffix—(*a*) *-līce* 'like' = Mod. *-ly*: *sōðlīce, frēondlīce* 'friendly wise'; or (*b*) *-unga, -inga*: *ierringa* 'angrily', *eallunga* 'altogether'; or (*c*) *-lunga, -linga*: *grundlunga, -linga* 'from the foundations'; (*d*) *-mælum*: *styccemælum* 'piecemeal'; (*e*) *-rādum*: *floccrādum* 'in troops', etc.

(3) By the addition of the Genitive or Dative case ending to an adj. or noun : *ealles* ' completely ', *dæges* ' by day ', and by association with this, *nihtes* ' by night ', *dearnum* ' secretly ', *micclum* ' much, very '.

§ 332. The Adverbs in *-e* are very common in O.E. and equally so in M.E.; cp. Chaucer's *Wel coude he sitte on hors and faire ryde*. With the disappearance of unstressed *-e* in the fifteenth century these adverbs become indistinguishable from adjectives, e. g. to run *fast*, to sleep *sound*, to work *hard*, etc., etc.

The *-linga* type survives in a few more or less obsolete words—*darkling*, and formerly *noseling* ' on the nose ', *flatling* ' with the flat of the sword ', and others were used ; *lunga* survives in *headlong*, *sidelong*. *Piecemeal* has already figured above. Old Dat. Pls. survive in *seldom*, and the archaic *whilom*.

Genitives occur in *needs* ' he must needs do it ', *now-a-days* (=*nū on dæge*) with an *-s* suffix as well as the old preposition, and similarly *o' nights* (=*on nihte*), *always, once*, etc., etc. *Twice* and *thrice* are M.E. formations—*twies, pries* on the analogy of *ōnes*. The O.E. forms are *twiwa, ðriwa*.

Once = O.E. *ānes* (see § 240, Note (2) for explanation of [wans]). Chaucer has the phrase *for the nōnes* ' for the nonce ' —*for ðen ōnes*, where the adverbial *ōnes* is used as a noun.

VERBS

§ 333. The inflexions of verbs in English express distinctions of Person, Tense, and Mood.

The inflexions of Person are chiefly confined to the Pres. Indic. and the 2nd P. Past Sing., there being no distinction made between the persons of the Pl.

The Tense endings distinguish between the Present, used also in a Future sense, the Preterite, or Past Tense. The Indic. and Subj. Moods are distinguished by different personal endings.

The most important formal distinction of verbs into classes is that made according to the mode of forming the Past Tense and Past Participle.

Those verbs which, like Mod. Engl. *follow—followed, laugh —laughed, weld—welded*, form their Past by the addition of the suffix *-ed* [d, t, *id*] are known as *Weak*, and those which, like *ride—rode, sing—sang*, express the difference between Past and Present by a change in the vowel, without the addition of a suffix, as *Strong* verbs. This vowel change is known as *Gradation*. Its origins lie in the remote past, before English, or even Primitive Germanic, in the Aryan period.

The history of the forms of English verbs is partly merely that of ordinary sound change, as in O.E. *wrītan*, Pret. *wrāt*, Present-day *write—wrote*, which is covered by the general statement that O.E. [*ī, ā*] become Modern [*ai, ou*]. On the other hand, the principle of Analogy has fashioned the forms of Modern English Strong verbs, in some cases, to a degree which is probably in excess of its influence in other parts of speech, though, as we have seen, Analogy has indeed been active among the Pronouns and Nouns.

§ 334. **Personal and other endings in O.E. Verbs** (cp. Sievers, *ae. Gr.*, § 352 and following sections).

PRESENT TENSE.

Indicative.		Subjunctive.		Imperative.
Sing.	Pl.	Sing.	Pl.	
1. -*e*		1.		2. Sing.—; -*e*
2. -(*e*)*st*	-*aþ*	2. }-*e*	-*en*, -*on*, -*an*	1. Pl. -*an*
3. -(*e*)*þ*		3.		2. Pl. -*aþ*

Infinitive.	Participle.
-*an*	-*ende*

PRETERITE.

	Indicative.			Subjunctive.	
Sing.		Pl.		Sing.	Pl.
Strong.	Weak.	Strong.	Weak.	Str. & Wk.	Str. & Wk.
1. —	-*e*				
2. -*e*	-*est*	}-*un*, -*on*, -*an*	-*on*	-*e*	-*en*, (*on, an*, wk.)
3. —	-*e*				

PAST PARTICIPLE.

Strong.	Weak.
-*en*	-*ed*, -*od*

NOTE 1. In W.S. texts syncope of the vowel usually takes place in the endings of the 2nd and 3rd pers. Sing. This produces the various combinations of consonants with -*st* and -*þ*, and certain changes in the consonants result : *winst, winþ* from *winnist, winniþ*; *bitst* for *bidst from *bidist; *bit* for *bitþ from *bidþ from *bidiþ; *grēt* for *grētþ* for *grētiþ; *cīest* for *cīes(i)st*, also for *cīes(i)þ*, etc., etc. In non-W.S. we get full forms *cēoseþ*, etc.

NOTE 2. Already in O.E. the 3rd Sing. Pres. Indic. appears as -*es* in Nthmb., by the side of -*eþ*, and the Pl. as -*as* by the side of older -*æþ*. The other dialects preserve the old endings. These early Nth. forms are important in the light of later developments.

NOTE 3. When the order of pronoun and verb is inverted, as often happens in O.E., instead of the endings -*aþ*, or -*on* in the Pl., the ending is -*e* : Pres. *we bindaþ*, but *binde we*; Pret. *we bundon*, but *bunde we*.

VERBAL INFLEXIONAL ENDINGS IN M.E.

§ 335. Present Indicative.

The main features are preserved, allowing for the loss of distinction between -*aþ*, -*eþ*, -*on*, -*an*, -*en* which arises from the levelling of these under -*eþ*, -*en*.

There arise, however, certain characteristic modes of distribution of the endings of the Pres. Indic. in the various dialects. On the whole, these are as follows :

	Sthn. & Kt.		E. Midl.	W. Midl.	E. Midl.	W. Midl.	Nth.	
	Sing.	Pl.	Sing.	Sing.	Pl.	Pl.	Sing.	Pl.
1.	-*e*		-*e*	-*e*			-*e*	
2.	-*est*	-*eþ*	-*est*	-*es*, -*est*	-*en*, *es*	-*es*, *en*	-*es*	-*es*, -*is*
3.	-*eþ*		-*eþ*, *es*	-*eþ*, -*es*		-*us*, -*un*	-*es*	

Taken together with other features, and allowing for variety of usage within a given dialect group, the forms of the 2nd and 3rd Pers. Sing., and those of the Pl., are useful tests of dialect.

The Present Indicative. A. The Singular.

The Southern dialects generally retain the old endings in the Sing. The E. Midl. on the whole agrees with this, but the N.E. Midl. (*Rob. of Brunne*, 1303) by the side of the usual -*eþ* in 3rd Sing. has also -*s*, especially in rhymes, e.g.:

> þe holy man *telleþ* vs and *seys*
> þat þe lofe made euen *peys*.

The W. Midl., owing no doubt to Nthn. influence, frequently has -*s* in 2nd and 3rd. In the Nth. -*s* is universal in 2nd and 3rd Sing.

NOTE. *Wil. of Pal.* has -*es*, -*us* and -*eþ*, -*uþ* in 3rd S. about equally (Schüddekopf, p. 74). The late *Audelay* has -*is*, -*ys*, -*s* most frequently, but also a fair number of examples of -*eth*, -*yth*, -*uth* (Rasmussen, p. 82).

In the London Dialect and Literary English, the -*s* type gained ground but slowly. The earliest London documents to first quarter of fourteenth century have only -*eþ* (Dölle, p. 72) ; the later fourteenth-century documents have only -*iþ*, -*ith*, -*eþ*, -*eth*, except for one Nth. -*s* form (Morsbach, *Schriftspr.*, pp. 134, 136, 137) ; Chaucer with one exception in rhyme, *telles*—*elles*, has only -*eth*, -*ith*, in Verse and in Prose (ten Brink, § 185 ; Frieshammer, p. 95) ; the fifteenth-century London Charters, etc., have an enormous preponderance of -*ith*-forms, but about three examples of -*es* (Lekebusch, pp. 121 and 123) ; other official London documents of late fifteenth century have also a sprinkling of -*s*- forms. Caxton has only -*eth*, or -*ith* (Römstedt, p. 45).

The Oxford writers, Wycliffe and Pecock, employ only -*th*, but Lydgate has frequent -*es* forms, while Capgrave has only one (Dibelius, *Anglia*, xxiv, p. 247). The -*es* forms certainly become more frequent both in prose and verse during the sixteenth century, though until the third quarter of the century the -*eth*, -*ith*, forms greatly predominate in both the formal and the familiar prose styles. The poets Wyatt, Surrey, Sackville use frequent -*s*- forms, but an examination of the instances appears to show that they occur instead of the -*th* type chiefly in the interests of rhyme or of metre. It has been suggested by Hoelper (on Tottel's Misc.) p. 54, that the -*s* forms were first made current by the usage of the poets, and that they passed from poetry into prose, and thence into the colloquial forms of standard English. This does not seem to be supported by the evidence. The poets practically only employ these forms when they are obliged, while, with a few exceptions, such as Latimer and Ascham, writers of elevated prose hardly use them at all before the end of the sixteenth century. The -*es* endings are found chiefly in more or less colloquial private letters ; Machyn, the last person to be influenced by literary usage of any kind, uses them in his Diary, in the rare instances where he uses the third Sing. Pres. at all. Such stately prose as that of the first and second Prayer Books knows only -*th*, and the same is true of the much later Authorized Version of the Bible. We must regard -*es* as definitely colloquial in origin. (See full discussion of this, and the other question of the dialectal origin of these forms, in my *Hist. Coll. Engl.*, pp. 332–37.) The ending -*es* in the third S. Pres. has usually been regarded as of Nthn. origin in literary and standard spoken Engl. Since direct Nthn. influence upon the dialect of London is out of the question, we must suppose that it was exerted, if at all, indirectly through the E. Midl. But the documents written in Lincs., Norf., and Suffolk, in the fifteenth century, that is just when the -*es*, -*ys* forms begin to make a sporadic appearance in London documents, hardly show a greater number of these forms than do the latter, Bokenam, for instance, having hardly any at all. The ending -*eth*, -*yth*, predominates in E. Midl. as in London itself. On the other hand, the Wilts. text, S. Editha (c. 1420), actually has a few -*s* forms, and it would surely be fantastic to suppose that Nthn. influence could have been exerted here ! Holmquist (see Bibliography E.) appears to wish to derive the forms from Leicestershire (see p. 145 of his book), but even supposing it to

be established that -*s* was the characteristic form of Leics., it
is difficult to see that the solution of the problem how -*s* got
into London Engl. is helped thereby.   How could a feature of
the Leics. dialect pass into the colloquial speech of London?
On the whole it seems probable that the -*es* form has nothing
whatever to do with the Nthn. dialect, but has been developed
quite independently in the South through the influence of, and
by analogy with, the common Auxiliary *is*.

The Present Indicative.   B.   The Plural.

The Sthn. dialects preserve the O.E. -*aþ*, in the weakened
form -*eþ*.   While the typical Midland ending is -*en*, from the
Subj., later weakened to -*e*, W. Midl. texts, by the side of this
ending, and the typical -*un*, very frequently use the Nthn.
-*s* (-*es*, -*us*).   Nthn. dialects have regularly -*s*, which as we saw
in § 334, Note 2, is found already in O. Northumb.

It is interesting to observe the encroachment of the Midl.
type in the London dialect, and the gradual elimination of
the Sthn. -*eþ* form.   The earliest Charters have -*aþ*, -*eþ*, but
Henry III's Procl. (1258), while still retaining -*eþ* in *habbeþ*,
beoþ, shows already a preponderance of the Midl. -*en* forms:
willen, hoaten, senden, beon (twice).   Davie (1327) has only one
example of -*eþ*.   In Morsbach's fourteenth-century documents,
Sthn. -*eth* still lingers occasionally, but Midl. -*en* or -*e* are
very much commoner (*Schriftspr.*, pp. 134, 136, 137) ; Chaucer's
Prose has -*en* oftener than -*e*.   In rhymes, -*e* is nearly universal,
-*en* rare.   Frieshammer (p. 96) mentions only four examples
of -*th* Pls.   Pecock and Caxton have -*en*.   The late London
Charters, etc., have most often -*en*, or, after a vowel, -*n* ; by
the side of this, but considerably less often, -*e* ; -*eth* is found
rather more than twenty times, and once -*ith* ; -*es* occurs
twice.   A certain number of forms without any ending are
used, but these are not very frequent (Lekebusch, p. 124).

Shakespeare has 'and wax*en* in their mirth' (cit. Morris's
Hist. Outlines, ed. Kellner-Bradley, p. 257), where the suffix
is obviously used for the sake of the metre.   Ben Jonson,
writing 1640, says that the suffix -*en* was used in the Pl.
'till about the reign of Henry VIII', but adds that 'now it
hath quite grown out of use' (cit. Kellner-Bradley, p. 257,
footnote).   Pres. Pls. in -*en*, -*in* occur occasionally in the
sixteenth century : *bin*, St. Papers of Henry VIII (1515) ; *ben,*
Surrey, Æneid Bk. ii. 735 ; *you that blamen*, Wyatt, Tottel 37 ;
they loaden, Euphues, p. 144 ; and as late as 1695 *we sayn*
in Congreve's *Love for Love*, Act III, Sc. VI.

§ 336.   **The Preterite.**

In O.E., whereas the 2nd Person Sing. of Weak Verbs had
the suffix -*est*, like the Present, Strong Vbs., on the other
hand, had only -*e* in this Pers. The vowel of the base is
different from that of the 1st and 3rd Pers. in O.E. and M.E.
So long as this distinction was preserved by the Strong Vbs.
the ending remains unchanged, but later, when the vowel of
the 2nd Pers. is levelled under that of the other Sing. forms,
this Pers. takes -*est* on the analogy of the Present.

Chaucer preserves the old distinction of vowel in the 2nd
Sing. Pret. only in verbs of the *sing*, *find*-type, and not always
here. He often has such forms as *thou founde*. He also has
forms without -*est* in vbs. whose vowel in 2nd Pret. has been
levelled under that of 1st and 2nd Pers.—*thou drank*. On the
other hand, forms like *begonnest* are also found (ten Brink,
§ 193).

Caxton habitually inflects the 2nd Pret. Sing. with -*est*, -*ist*,
both in Wk. and Strong Vbs., but exceptionally has *thou
took, had, fond, gate, sawe, knewe* (Römstedt, p. 37 ; Price,
p. 188). In Wycliffe, Bokenam, Pecock, and Capgrave, the
-*est* forms greatly predominate, though the old forms are also
found (Dibelius, *Anglia*, xxiv, p. 256). Price, p. 188, gives
examples of the uninflected forms from Shakespeare and
Heywood.

§ 337.   **The Present Participle in M.E. and afterwards.**

In a general way, the form of the Pres. Part. is a useful
indication of dialect in M.E., but it must not be relied upon
absolutely, without considering the other dialectal features of
a text. The Sthn. and Kentish texts have -*inde*, the Midland
generally -*ende*, and the Nthn. always -*and*. The more
Northerly portions of E. Midl. dialect, however, e. g. as seen in
R. of Brunne (Lincolnshire), have -*and* after the Nthn. use,
and the Sthn. Midl. has -*inde* according to the Sthn. dialect.
The West Midl. texts have very commonly -*and*, except *Jos.
of Ar.*, which has habitually -*inde*.

By the side of these forms, a new type of Pres. Part. comes
into use, first in the Sth. during the M.E. period, one in -*inge*.
The origin of this is uncertain. It is first used in the Sth.,
and is the ancestor of the Present-day form.

Kellner-Bradley, p. 263, mentions *ridinge* in *Laȝamon*, used
in the same sentence with the older and more usual *goinde*.
Handlyng Synne has already a fair number of forms in -*yng*,
but otherwise the Nthn. type -*and*, especially in rhymes.
The Sthn. Trevisa, according to Morris, Introd. to *Aȝenbite*,

p. lxiv, has always *-inge, -ing,* never *-inde.* The Kentish
Aȝenbite has only *-inde, -ynde.* In W. Midl., *Earliest Engl.
Pr. Ps.* has generally *-and,* but also *in keping hem*; *Jos. of
Ar.* several forms in *-inge,* by the side of *-inde*; *Allit.
P. -ande*; *Wil. of Pal. -and* thirteen times, Midl. *-end*
twelve, and *-ing* ten times (Schüddekopf, p. 75); *Audelay* has
almost exclusively *-ing,* twice *-and* in rhyme, and once *-and*
in the middle of a line (Rasmussen, p. 82).

The earliest London documents have *-inde* in Procl., but
Davie only *-ing* (Dölle, p. 73); Chaucer's Prose *-ing(e),* rarely
-enge (Frieshammer, p. 97); Morsbach's Charters, etc., only
-yng(e) (*Schriftspr.,* pp. 175, etc.); the later Charters have
only *-yng, -ing,* or *-eng* (Lekebusch, pp. 122, 123, 125).

It is worth noting that Chaucer's contemporary Gower very
rarely uses the *-ing(e)* form, but almost invariably *-ende,* with
the accent upon this suffix (Macaulay's Introd. to the small
ed. *Conf. Amant.,* p. xliv). *Mylkand Kyne* occurs in Paston
Letters in 1450, i, p. 98.

THE WEAK VERBS

§ 338. It should be noted that the distinguishing feature
of a weak verb is that it has the ending *-ed, -t* in the Past
Tense. Some weak verbs show a change of vowel, as *teach—
taught,* O.E. *tǣcan—tāhte,* where one form has *i*-mutation,
and the other has not (§ 106); others show a change of vowel
due to gradation, *bring—brought.*

Classes of Weak Verbs.

There are originally three classes of Weak Verbs:

(1) Those in *-*jan* which have *i*-mutation whenever the
original vowel is a back.

(*a*) When the original vowel of the base is short, the
following consonant, other than *r,* is doubled in the Inf., in
all forms of the Present except the 2nd and 3rd Pers. Sing.
and the 2nd Imperat.

Examples:

Inf.	Pret.	P.P.	
nerian 'save'	*nerede*	(*ġe*)-*nered*	from **nazjan,* etc.
temman 'tame'	*temede*	(*ġe*)-*temed*	from **tammjan*
cnyssan 'strike'	*cnyssede*	(*ġe*)-*cnyssed*	from **knussjan*
settan 'set'	*sette*	(*ġe*)-*seted*	from **sattjan*

(*b*) When the vowel or syllable of the base is long, no
doubling of the consonant takes place. The Pret. ending is

usually *-de*, earlier *-ida*, the *-i-* having been syncopated, except after *-r*, and often *l*.

Examples:

Inf.	Pret.	P.P.	
dēman 'judge'	*dēmde*	(*ġe*)-*dēmed*	from **dōmjan*
frēfran 'comfort'	*frēfrede*	(*ġe*)-*frēfred*	from **frōfrjan*
dǣlan 'divide'	*dǣlde*	(*ġe*)-*dǣled*	from **dāljan*
(W.S.) *hīeran* 'hear'	*hīerde*	(*ġe*)-*hīered*	from **hēarjan*

(2) *-ōjan* Verbs. This suffix appears in O.E. as *-ian*, having passed through *-ējan*, *-ījan*, and then being shortened to *-ian*. The bases of these verbs have no mutation. The Pres. Indic. Sing. normally runs *lōciġe*, *lōɼast*, *lōcaþ*. The Pret. ends in *-ode*, and the P.P. in *od*.

Examples:

Inf.	Pret.	P.P.	
lōcian	*lōcode*	(*ġe*)-*lōcod*	from **lōkōjan*
hālgian	*hālgode*	(*ġe*)-*hālgod*	from **hāl(a)gōjan*
þancian 'thank'	*þancode*	(*ġe*)-*þancod*	from **þankōjan*
wilnian 'desire'	*wilnode*	(*ġe*)-*wilnod*	from **wilnōjan*

(3) *So-called -e- Verbs.*

These verbs, whose formation offers some difficulties, are those in which the suffix *-ja-* interchanges with Gmc. *-ai-*, or *-ǣ-* in the various forms. The Inf. and Pres. Indic. 1st Pers. Sing. and the Pres. Indic. Pl. have doubling of the consonant, and *j*-mutation of preceding vowel in these forms; the suffix of the Pret. is added to the base directly, without any intervening vowel.

Examples:

	Inf.	Pret.	P.P.
	hæbban 'have'	*hæfde*	(*ġe*)-*hæfd*
1st	*hæbbe*		
2nd	*{hafast / hæfst*		
3rd	*{hafaþ / hæfþ*		
Pl.	*habbaþ*		
	libban (*lifian*)	*lifde* (also *leofode* like *-ōjan* vb.)	*ġelifd*
1st	*libbe* (*lifiġe*)		
2nd	*leofast* (*liofast*)		
3rd	*leofaþ* (*liofaþ*)		
Pl.	*libban* (*leofaþ, liofaþ*)		
1st	*seċġan* 'tell, say'	*sæġde*	(*ġe*)-*sæġd*
2nd	*sagast* (*sæġst* W.S.)		
3rd	*sagaþ* (*sæġþ* W.S.)		
Pl.	*seċġ(e)aþ*		

NOTE 1. The difference between *temman* from **tammjan* and *temede* from **tamida* is due to the interchange of *-ja-* and *-i-* in the suffix. Before *-j-* a consonant is doubled, but not before *-i-*.

NOTE 2. In *dǣlan* from **dāljan* the double consonant has been simplified after a long vowel.

NOTE 3. The *bb* in *hæbban* is from **-ɓj-*. The *æ* in this form and in *hæbbe* is the *j*-mutation of *a*. **Haɓjan*<**hæbbjan*, which would become **hebban*. *Hæbban* is a new formation **habbjan*, on the analogy of **haɓ-as*, **haɓaþ* 2nd and 3rd Pers. Sing. Cp. also § 107 Note.

Irregular Weak Verbs.

§ 339. There is a certain number of verbs which have *-ja-* in the Inf. and Pres. (all except *bringan*), but which have often lost the *-i-* of the stem, before the suffix *-de* in the Pret. and P.P. Many of these survive to the present time. The combination of the Pret. suffix with the final consonant of the base often brings about considerable changes in the latter.

Inf.	Pret.	P.P.
sellan 'give, sell'	*sealde* (Angl. *sālde*)	*ġeseald* (Angl. *sāld*)
tellan 'tell, count'	*tealde* (Angl. *tālde*)	*ġeteald* (Angl. *tāld*)
settan 'set, place'	*sette*	*ġeset(t)*
leċġ(e)an 'lay'	*leġde*	*ġeleġd*
byċġan 'buy'	*bohte*	*ġeboht*
reċċ(e)an 'narrate'	*reahte*	*ġereaht*
streċċ(e)an 'stretch'	*streahte*	*ġestreaht*
þeċċ(e)an 'cover'	*þeahte*	*ġeþeaht*
lǣċ(e)an 'seize'	*lǣhte*	*ġelǣht*
rǣċ(e)an 'reach'	{ *rǣhte* / *rāhte*	*ġerǣht*
tǣċ(e)an 'teach'	{ *tǣhte* / *tāhte*	*ġetǣht, ġetāht*
reċċ(e)an 'reck'	*rōhte*	—
sēċ(e)an 'seek'	*sōhte*	*ġesōht*
þenċ(e)an 'think'	*þōhte*	*ġeþōht*
þynċ(e)an 'seem'	*þūhte*	*ġeþūht*
wyrċ(e)an 'work'	*worhte*	*ġeworht*
bringan	*brōhte*	*ġebrōht*

NOTES 1. *sellan, tellan* have mutation of *æ* (§ 107), but Fracture of *æ* in Pret. (§ 102). The Sthn. and Kt. representative of *sealde* in M.E. is *sēlde*. *sōlde* and Mod. *sold* are from Anglian *sālde* (§§ 126, 164, 165).

2. *sette* is from **satda*, **satta*, and owes its *e* to the Pres. and Inf.; *leġde* is also an analogous form.

3. *byċġan* is from **bug-jan* (§ 109); *bohte* from **buχ-ta*, with change of *u* to *o* before *a* in next syllable.

4. *reċċan—reahte* and all the verbs which have *ċċ* or *ċ* in Inf. and Pres. and *-ht-* in Pret. illustrate the Gmc. and O.E. change of *kt* to *ht*: **rǎkjan* <*reċċan*; **rakda*<**rakta*<*rahta*<**ræhtæ*<*reahte*. This form, as well as *streahte, þeahte*, has Fracture (§ 102).

5. The normal Prets. of *tǣċan, rǣċan,* are *tāhte, rāhte,* from **taikta,* etc. There is nothing to cause mutation here, and the by-forms *tǣhte, rǣhte* owe their vowel to the analogy of the Pres. and Inf.

6. On the changes in *sēċan, þenċan, þynċan, wyrċan* and their Prets., cp. §§ 105, 109 and Note, 108, 113.

7. *bringan—brōhte* shows a gradational change **briŋȝ- — *braŋχ-,* comparable to *sing—sang,* but **braŋχ-* instead of **braŋȝ-* is rather a puzzle. We must assume a primitive **braŋχ-,* otherwise the suffix *-te* in O.E., and in O.H.G. *brāhta,* cannot be accounted for. Perhaps the analogy of **þaŋχ-ta* (O.E. *þōhte*) may have produced *braŋχ-ta,* or again the existence of the pairs **faŋȝ- —faŋχ-, *haŋȝ- —*haŋχ-* (cp. § 98) may have helped to form **braŋχ-* by the side of **bra ȝ-.* The latter survives in O.E. *brenȝan* from **braŋȝ-jan.*

Weak Verbs in M.E.

§ 340. The points to be considered are the treatment of the Inf., the Pret., and the Past Part.

In the Nth. and Midlands the *-jan* vbs. with long first sylls., and the *-an* class, are practically both levelled under one class, in *-e(n).* Thus O.E. *dēman—dēmde* becomes *dēme(n)—dēmde,* just like *have(n)—havde* or *hadde.*

The *-ōjan* class, on the other hand, while losing, except in the Sth. and Kent, the *-i-* in Inf., and Pres. Indic. 1st S., retains the vowel *e* before the ending of the Pret. Thus O.E. *lōcian—lōcode* becomes *lōke(n)—lōked(e).* The *-jan* vbs. with short first sylls., whether of the O.E. *werian* or *temman* type, appear in M.E. as *wěre(n), temme(n)* respectively, but retain the *-e-* before the *-de* in Pret.—*wěred(e), temed(e),* being thus levelled under the *lōcian* type, since *-ode, -ede* both appear as *-ed(e)* in M.E.

Thus from the point of view of the Pret. there are two classes, one which has the suffix *-de* or *-te* added to the base direct, and the other which has *-e-* between the base and the *-de* suffix. The Inf. and Pres. Indic., however, show only one type: *hǎue, lōke, mǎke, wěre, hēre, dēme,* etc.

§ 341. A further confusion involving the Pret. also arises in later M.E. Forms like *axede, werede, wunede, luvede* lose the final *-e* and appear as *wered, luved, axed,* etc., though often written full, the loss being proved by the metre in poetry. This gives two types of Pret.—*dēmde, hērde,* but *luved, axed,* etc. Now a cross analogy works between the two types, so that we get *dēmed* on the analogy of *luved,* but also *luvde* on the analogy of *dēmde.* The result is that poets often use both forms of Pret. for the same word, *luved(e)* or *luv(e)de, cry(e)de* or *cryed(e), clēped* or *clepte,* etc., etc. In a general way, however, one or other of these forms must be used—either *clēped* with loss of final *-e*, or *clepte* with loss of medial *-e-*. Such a form as *clepede* (three sylls.), if it occur, must be regarded as a new formation from a blending of both types. In the Pl. the forms which do not syncopate the medial vowel lose the suffix *-en*, such forms as *yelleden*, *strēmeden* being rare, and being of course, like similar forms in the Sing., the result of blending (cp. ten Brink, *Ch. Spr.*, § 194).

The O.E. -ian Vbs. in Sthn. and Kentish in M.E.

§ 342. This type is very common indeed in the Sth. and Kt., and originally obtained in the London dialect, though it disappears through the encroachment of the Midl. tendencies in the fourteenth century. Before this, such Infinitives as *ġepauien, werien, makien, tholie* are found (Dölle, pp. 72 and 73). In fourteenth-century Kentish (*Aʒenbite*) the typical ending is *-ie, -ye,* or *-y* : *louie, louye, louy* ; *māki, māky* ' make ' ; *hātye, hātie* ' hate ' ; *polie, polye* ' suffer ' ; *lōki, lōky* ' look ' ; *ponki, ponky* ' thank ', etc. Many foreign verbs also have this ending : *troubli, excusi, stonchi* ' to staunch ', etc., etc.

STRONG VERBS

Old English Period.

§ 343. These are divided into six classes, according to the vowel series represented in the forms. The forms which show the various gradation vowels are (1) Inf., (2) Pret. S., (3) Pret. Pl., (4) P. P. The type of the Inf. occurs also in Pres. Indic., Imperat., and Subj. The vowel of the Pret. Sing. occurs in 1st and 3rd Pers. of that; that of Pret. Pl. occurs also in 2nd Pers. of Pret. Sing., and in Pret. Subj. S. and Pl. The vowel of P.P. sometimes agrees with that of Pret. Pl., but in other classes is an independent vowel, not found in any other form of the verb.

§ 344. **Class I.**

Inf.	Pret. S.	Pret. Pl.	P.P.
bītan 'bite'	*bāt*	*biton*	*(ġe)-biten*
drīfan 'drive'	*drāf*	*drifon*	*drifen*
ġewītan 'depart'	*ġewāt*	*ġewiton*	*ġewiten*
rīdan 'ride'	*rād*	*ridon*	*riden*

So also *slīdan* ' slide ', *snīpan* ' cut ', *bīdan* ' wait, bide ', and several others.

§ 345. **Class II.**

Inf.	Pret. S.	Pret. Pl.	P.P.
bēodan 'announce'	*bēad*	*budon*	*boden*
sēoþan 'boil'	*sēaþ*	*sudon*	*soden*
ġēotan 'pour'	*ġēat*	*guton*	*goten*
flēogan 'flee'	*flēah*	*flugon*	*flogen*

So also *ċēosan* 'choose', *hrēowan* 'have pity, rue', *clēofan* 'cleave, split', *sċēotan* 'shoot', etc.

NOTE. *dūfan* 'dive', *sċūfan* 'thrust', *brūcan* 'enjoy, use', *lūcan* 'lock', belong to this class. The *ū* may go back to Idg. *ēu̯*.

§ 346. **Class III.** The original series in this class was Gmc. *e, a, u, u*. In West Gmc. and O.E. various combinative changes affect these vowels, according to the consonants which follow.

Group (*a*). Verbs whose base ends in nasal + another consonant :

bindan 'bind'	{ *band* } { *bond* }	*bundon*	*bunden*
findan	*fand*	*fundon*	*funden*, etc.

So also *cringan* 'double up, fall', *grindan* 'grind', *windan* 'wind', *ġelimpan* 'happen', *climban* 'climb'.

Group (*b*). Verbs whose base ends in l + consonant :

| *helpan* | *healp* | *hulpon* | *holpen* |
| *meltan* | *mealt* | *multon* | *molten* |

So also *sweltan* 'die', *delfan* 'delve, dig', *swelgan* 'swallow', etc.

Group (*c*). Verbs whose base ends in r, or h + consonant :

| *weorpan* 'hurl' | *wearp* | *wurpon* | *worpen* |
| *ċeorfan* 'carve' | *ċearf* | *curfon* | *corfen* |

Also *weorþan* 'become', *hweorfan* 'turn, go', *steorfan* 'starve', in sense of 'die', *beorgan* 'protect', *beorcan* 'bark'.

| *feohtan* 'fight' | *feaht* | *fuhton* | *fohten* |

Group (*d*). The following verbs either show the vowel series unchanged, or slightly modified by Fracture, or early change of *u* to *o* :

Inf.	Pret. S.	Pret. Pl.	P.P.
breġdan 'draw, brandish' a sword	*bræġd*	*brugdon*	*brogden*
berstan 'burst'	*bærst*	*burston*	*borsten*
friġnan 'ask, find out'	*fræġn*	*frugnon*	*frugnen*
spurnan	*spearn*	*spurnon*	*spornen*

NOTE. *Spurnan* owes its vowel perhaps to the Pret. Pl. *Frignan* may owe its *i* to the analogy of *friġ(e)an* 'ask', from same base = **fregjan*, Idg.**prek-.*

§ 347. Class IV.

Inf.	Pret. S.	Pret. Pl.	P.P.
beran 'bear'	*bær*	*bæron*	*boren*
brecan 'break'	*bræc*	*bræcon*	*brocen*
stelan 'steal'	*stæl*	*stælon*	*stolen*

Also *cwelan* 'kill', *helan* 'conceal'.

NOTE 1. *Niman* 'take', *nōm, nōmon, numen,* and *cuman, c(w)ōm, c(w)ōmon, cumen* are only irregular in appearance. *Nim-* instead of **nem-* is due to the influence of *m.* *Cum-, num-* in P.P. are also due to change of *o* to *u* before *m.* The type *cum-* of 1st Pers. Pres. Indic. and Inf. is from earlier **cwuman* from **cweoman* from *cwiman.* Cp. Goth. *qiman,* and § 110 and Note. *Nōm, c(w)ōm,* instead of *năm,* etc., are due to the analogy of the Pl. where *ō* is regular before a nasal (§ 99). We also get Pl. *nāmon* and Sing. *năm* (W.S. and Kt.).

NOTE 2. In non-W.S. these vbs. have of course *ē* in Pret. Pl. (§ 123).

§ 348. Class V.

Inf.	Pret. S.	Pret. Pl.	P.P.
cweþan 'speak, say'	*cwæþ*	*cwǣdon*	*cweden*
sprecan	*spræc*	*sprǣcon*	*sprecen* (Late O.E. *spec-*, etc.)
tredan	*træd*	*trǣdon*	*treden*

W.S. *ġiefan* 'give', *on-, be-, ġietan* 'perceive, obtain', etc., have the forms :

ġiefan	*ġeaf*	*ġēafon*	*ġiefen*
ġietan	*ġeat*	*ġēaton*	*ġieten*

The non-W.S. dialects have no diphthongization, and therefore *ġefan, ġæf, ġēfon, ġefen,* etc. (§§ 115, 120, 123). The following belong to this class :

Inf.	Pret. S.	Pret. Pl.	P.P.
sēon 'see'	*seah*	*sāwon*	*sewen* and *sāwen*
ġefēon 'rejoice'	*ġefeah*	*ġefǣgon*	—

sēon from **sehwan* (§§ 102, 112), *seah* from **sæh, sāwon* from **sǣwum* (cp. § 99 (*b*)) ; *sāwen* formed on the analogy of Pret. Pl.

biddan 'pray', *sittan* 'sit', *liċgean* 'lie down', are peculiar as forming the Inf. and 1st Pers. Pres. Indic. with a *-ja-* stem. This is responsible for *i* instead of *e* (W. Gmc. change) and also for the double consonants and *ċġ: biddan* from **beddjan, sittan* from **settjan, liċgan* from **legjan.* Gothic has *bidjan* where *i* for *e* is a characteristic isolative change. In other respects these verbs are quite regular : *sittan, sæt, sǣton, seten.*

§ 349.   Class VI.

Inf.	Pret. S.	Pret. Pl.	P.P.
faran 'go'	*fōr*	*fōron*	*faren*
bacan 'bake'	*bōc*	*bōcon*	*bacen*

So also *wascan* 'wash', *galan* 'sing', *hladan* 'lade', *wadan* 'go, pierce', etc., etc.

sceacan 'shake'	*sc(e)ōc*	*sc(e)ōcon*	*sceacen*

owes its diphthong to a late tendency which affected back vowels.

Inf.	Pret. S.	Pret. Pl.	P.P.
standan	*stōd*	*stōdon*	*standen*
slēan 'strike'	*slōg*	*slōgon*	*slagen*, *sleġen* (cp. § 107 on
swēan 'wash'	*þwōg*	*þwōgon*	p.p. of *slēan*)

These verbs have Fracture, loss of *h* and contraction in Inf. (§ 112).

A certain number of verbs of this class form Inf. and Pres. with *-j-*: *sceppan* 'injure' from **skappjan*, *swerian* 'swear', *steppan* 'proceed', *hliehhan* 'laugh', etc.

These have mutated vowels and double consonants in the forms mentioned, but are otherwise normal:

steppan	*stōp*	*stōpon*	*stapen*, etc.

REDUPLICATING VERBS

§ 350.   A few verbs in O.E. retain signs of reduplication in Pret. The reduplicated forms are chiefly used in poetry, though *heht* occurs by the side of *hēt* in prose.

hātan 'order'	*hēht*	cp. Goth *haíháit*
rǣdan 'advise'	*reord*	„ *raírōþ*
lācan 'play'	*leolc*	„ *laíláik*
lǣtan 'let'	*leort*	„ *laílōt*

§ 351.   The following verbs have assimilated the reduplicated syllables :

Inf.	Pret. S.	Pret. Pl.	P.P.
fōn 'catch, take'	*fēng*	*fēngon*	*fangen*
hōn 'hang'	*hēng*	*hēngon*	*hangen*
feallan 'fall'	*fēoll*	*fēollon*	*feallen*
hlēapan 'leap'	*hlēop*	*hlēopon*	*hlēapen*

NOTE.   For explanation of *hōn, fōn,* and *fēhþ*, etc., cp. §§ 98, 112, 105, 352.

Mutation of 2nd and 3rd Pers. Sing. in Strong Verbs.

§ 352.   As the usual suffixes of these Pers. are *-is(t)*, *-iþ*, the preceding vowel if back, or a diphthong, is fronted : *cēose—*

cīesþ, cume—cymþ, fō—fēhþ; if *e* it is raised to *i*: *cweþe—cwiþ, helpe—hilp(e)þ, ġiefe—ġifþ*, etc.

NOTES ON POINTS CONNECTED WITH THE VERB IN O.E.

(1) The prefix *ġe-* (unstressed), generally used in the P.P. in O.E., without modification of meaning, is found in Gothic in the form *ga-* and in O.H.G. as *gi-*. It becomes *ȝe-* and simply *i-* in Transition and Early Middle English. It disappears altogether in the Nth. in M.E., and to a great extent in Midland, but survives longer in the South.

The survival of *i-* in the fourteenth-century dialect of London (Davie and Chaucer) must be regarded as one of the Southern features of that dialect. The prefix *ġe-* is also used in O.E. with all parts of Verbs with the function of making intransitive verbs transitive, e.g. *sittan* 'sit', but *ġesittan* 'occupy, take possession of', etc.; *gān* 'go, walk', but *ġegān*, 'overrun, take' (a country, etc.).

Verner's Law.

(2) An interchange between *h* and *g*, *þ* and *d*, often appears in O.E. Strong Verbs. This has primarily nothing to do with verbs as such, but is merely an illustration of a general principle of Sound Change which was active in Primitive Germanic, and it may appear in any class of words where the necessary conditions are present. It should be remembered that *g* and *d* stand for sounds which were originally voiced open consonants [ȝ, ð] and not stops. The change, therefore, of *h* to *g*, *þ* to *d* is simply one of voicing to start with, the original sounds being [χ, þ]. These represent Aryan *k*, *t* (later *kh*, *th*), which by the so-called *Second Sound Shift* are merely opened in Gmc. In positions other than initially (where χ, þ always remain), these sounds are voiced in Gmc. *when the accent in Aryan and Early Gmc. fell on any other syllable than that immediately preceding the* χ *or* þ. Thus O.E. *weorþan* from **werþan* from Aryan **wért-*, but O.E. *wurdon*, Gmc. **wurđúm*, Aryan **wr̥túm*. Similarly O.E. *fæder*, Gmc. **fađér*, Aryan **pətér*, which used to be regarded as an 'exception to Grimm's Law', is satisfactorily explained from the position of the primitive accent which still survives in Gk. πατήρ. This far-reaching law is called after the name of its discoverer, Karl Verner, who formulated it in 1877 in Kuhn's *Zeitschrift*, vol. xxiii, pp. 97–130. Under the same conditions primitive *s* was voiced to *z*, which usually appears in W.Gmc. as *r*—O.E. *wæs* but *wæron*, *cēos-an* but *cur-on*, etc.

THE STRONG VERBS IN M.E. AND LATER PERIODS

§ **353.** The changes in the forms of Strong Verbs since the O.E. period have been determined partly by normal sound change, partly by the action of analogy working in various ways. The results of the latter factor have been (*a*) the levelling out of what proved to be an unnecessary variety of forms, and the reduction under fewer gradation-types ; (*b*) the transference of verbs from one class to another. These points may be briefly illustrated.

Normal Sound Change since O.E. Period.

§ **354.** The series of vowels found in Cl. I in O.E. $\bar{i}$, $\bar{a}$, $\bar{i}$, $\breve{i}$: *rīdan—rād—ridon—riden*, etc., became in M.E. $\bar{i}$, $\bar{o}$, $\breve{i}$, $\breve{i}$ by the change of $\bar{a}$ to $\bar{o}$ which took place in the Sth. and Midlands. In the Mod. Period a further set of changes made the series into [*ai*, *ou*, *i*], giving the Present-day [*raid—roud—ridn*]. Again, Cl. IV, which in O.E. had short vowels in all forms except the Pret. Pl. : *brĕcan—brăc—brǣcon—brŏcen*, developed in M.E. —apart from other changes—long vowels in all forms except the Pret. Sing., through the M.E. process of lengthening which affected the short vowels of open syllables, thus giving *brēken—brăk* (also *brāk*)—*brēken* (also *brāken*)—*brōken*.

Levelling of Pret. Pl. under type of Singular (Northern Preterite).

§ **355.** This mode of levelling is an early characteristic of the Northern dialects, and in the Nthn. Homilies, and *Cursor Mundi*, etc., we find Pret. Pls. such as *faand, dranc, bigan, rāde* (O.E. *rād*), *sagh* (O.E. *sæh* 'saw'), etc. This type of Pret. spread later to the London literary dialect, and to it we owe our forms *sang, drank, forbade* = [bæd], etc.

In M.E. this mode of reduction is an important sign of Northern origin, or at least Nthn. influence, when found in a doubtful text. It is referred to by German writers as *nördlicher Ausgleich*, and we may call such Prets. *Northern Preterites*.

Levelling of Preterite under type of Past Participle (Western Preterite).

§ **356.** While the dialects of the Sth. and Midlands preserve, on the whole, the distinction between the Singular and Plural of the Pret., where this existed in O.E., with fair

completeness during the whole M.E. and into the Modern
Period, a tendency exists, especially among writers of the
South-West and the Southerly West Midlands, to use the P.P.
type in the Pret. as well. *Gun, bygun, flow, fought, bounde,*
which occur severally in La3amon, *S. Marharete, Rob. of
Glos.,* Trevisa, and Wycliffe, as Pret. Sing., cannot be derived
from O.E. *-gan, flēow, feaht, bānd,* which normally produce
M.E. *-gan, flēw, fauht, bōnd.* The vowels in the form mentioned,
or their ancestors, do however occur both in the Pret. Pl. and
the P.P. (except in the case of *fought*)—O.E. *gunnon, gun-
nen ; flōwon, flōwen ; fuhton ; bundon, bunden.* The new
M.E. forms might therefore at first sight be derived from the
Pret. Pl. type, and some writers explain them in this way,
but as Bülbring points out (*Abl. d. starken Zeitw.,* pp. 116–17),
the Pret. Pl. type is the least permanent of the various forms
of the Strong Verbs, and never survives in Mod. Engl. unless
it be the type also of the Past Participle. While therefore
the Pl. may have helped to fix its type in the Pret. Sing., it
seems probable that the main influence was exerted by the
P.P. The form *fought* in M.E. is ambiguous. While it
cannot represent the old Pret. Sing., it may represent either
fūht with *ou* for *ū,* in which case it might be derived from the
Pret. Pl., or the *ou* may stand for a diphthong, in which case
it would represent the type of the old P.P. *fohten.*

The Mod. form [fɔt] cannot be descended from *fūht,* which
would give [faut], but can perfectly well represent the old
P.P. type, just as O.E. *dohter,* M.E. *douhter* (*ou =* diphthong)
has become [dɔtə]. The spelling of the Present-day form
points to the P.P. and not to the Pret. Sing. type *fauht,* which
though it would also become [fɔt] would be spelt *faught.*

This mode of levelling is known as the *Western type*
(German, *westlicher Ausgleich*).

Transference of Verbs from one Class to another.

§ 357. The verb *spēken,* O.E. *sprecan,* belonged originally
to Class V, and ran *sprecan, spræc, spræcon, sprecen,* but in
M.E. a P.P. *spōken,* from which, of course, our form is derived,
is found. It is clear that this form with *o* is on the analogy
of the P.P. of Cl. IV, e.g. *brōken.* This class differs from V
only in having *o* in the P.P. Other verbs in M.E. undergo
the same transference, such as 3euen ' give ', for which a P.P.
3ouen is often found, though this form can also be explained
by assuming Scandinavian influence (see Price, p. 100, and
references there given), and the Preterites *slew, drew* (O.E.

slōg, drōg) which show the influence of the reduplicating verbs *grōwan, grēōw*, M.E. Pret. S. *grēw*. The contact must have arisen from the existence of a form (Inf.) *slō*, which would be parallel to *grōw-, blōw-*, etc. *Slo* actually occurs in Shakespeare, and may be from Scand. *slā*, or *slew, drew* may both be explained as loan-forms from the Nth., where **slā(wen)*, **drā(wen)* would be parallel to *blāwen—blēw, prāwen— prēw*, etc.

NOTE. Owing to the very large number of questions, many of them of great interest, which arise in the history of the English Strong Vbs., it is utterly impossible, within the limits of a small book, to attempt to deal with the subject in any but the most superficial manner. A full treatment would mean to a great extent the discussion of each individual verb, the enumeration of all its forms at every period, and an account of how each form arose, in so far as it was not the normal representative of the O.E. form. Most of the vagaries fall, as a matter of fact, under one or other of the principles mentioned above. It is the details of the application of Analogy between one class and another which cause most difficulty. We can only deal here with a few outstanding verbs under each class. For a thorough treatment of the problems, and an enumeration of the chief facts, the student must refer to the works of Bülbring, Dibelius, and above all to the illuminating book of Price, with its copious collection of the forms of each verb found among writers from Caxton to Elizabeth. The following account is chiefly based on Price's work. I have had to resist the temptation to enter into many an alluring discussion, and have necessarily restricted the treatment mainly to the elucidation of the forms of Present-day Literary and Standard English. Further material from texts ranging from fifteenth to early eighteenth century will be found in my *Hist. Coll. Engl.*, pp. 342–55.

The Classes of Strong Verbs in M.E. and Mod. English.

§ 358. **Class I** (O.E. *ī—ā—ĭ—ĭ*). Type: *write, wrote, written.*

This class preserved its integrity to a great extent in M.E., and added the French *estriver*, M.E. *strīve, stroof, strĭven*. The *e*-forms in P.P., *wrēten, smēten*, etc., found in M.E. and down to the seventeenth century, may be explained according to Luick's principle (§ 174) or from the non-W.S. *wreoten*, etc.

Bite preserves the old Pret. *bote* as late as 1557. The form is found in Caxton and Coverdale.

Chide, originally a Weak Verb (O.E. Pret. *cīdde*), passed into this class in fifteenth and sixteenth centuries. Coverdale and Authorized Version of the Bible have *chode*, and P.P. *chid* and *chidden* appear in Shakespeare.

Slide retains *slode* in Caxton, and Ben Jonson allows it. Present-day *slid* may be explained from the P.P., but also may be due to *hide, hid*.

NOTE. *Hide*, an old weak verb, like *chide*, has been drawn partly into this class, the Pret. M.E. *hǐdde* suggesting the Pret. Pl. and P.P. type of Cl. I. The suffix *-en* in the P.P. shows that it is felt as a Strong Verb. When once *hidden* had arisen, comparable to *slidden*, it was natural for the latter verb to develop a Pret. Sing. *slid*.

Strike in M.E. had the normal Pret. *strōk*, O.E. *strāc*. This became Early Mod. *stroke*. In early seventeenth century *strook*, *struck* began to take its place. By the side of M.E. *strōk* there existed also a form *strake*, and a P.P. *strōken*, on analogy of *brāke*, *brōken*, helped by *sāte*, *sitten*, parallel to *strāke*, *stricken*. *Struck* may be due to analogy of *stuck*. *Stick*, earlier *stēken*, had forms *stāke*, *stōken* parallel to *strāke*, *strōken*, and it seems possible the latter may also have had an Inf. *strick*, when the analogy would be complete. *Stuck* itself may owe its vowel to the *sting*, *stung* Class.

The regular Verbs of this class in Present-day Engl. are *write*, *ride*, *stride* (P.P. doubtful), *smite*, *rise*, *drive*.

Bide, *abide*, *shine* retain the old Pret. but have lost the P.P., the latter being either Weak, or having the vowel of the Pret. *Shone* is now pronounced both as [ʃɔn] and [ʃoun].

§ 359. **Class II** (O.E. *ēo—ēa—u—o*). Types: *freeze*, *froze, frozen*; *choose, chose, chosen*.

In this class the interchange of *s—r*, *ð—d*, etc., has been eliminated.

Freeze. In O.E. *-frēosan*, *-frēas*, *-fruron*, *-froren*. The Present-day Inf. is normally derived from the O.E. form. The Old Pret. Sing. and Pl. have disappeared, and their place has been taken by the P.P. type, with *z* from the Inf. Caxton still has a Pret. *frore* with no alteration of the medial consonant. *Frore* is found in 1494, and *froze* first in Shakespeare. Milton's ' parching air burns *frore* ' is the old P.P.

Flee, fly. The O.E. verbs *flēon* and *flēogan* differed only in the Inf. The former meant *flee*, the latter *fly*. *Flee* is descended from *flēon*, M.E. *flee(n)* ; *fly* from the type seen in 2nd and 3rd Pers. Sing. Pres. O.E. *flīehst*, *flīehþ*, which produce a new M.E. Inf. *flīen*, *flȳe(n)*, the latter being found in Chaucer, etc. Chaucer uses the Pret. Sing. *fleih*, *fley* (O.E. *flēh* from *flēah*) indifferently in the senses ' flew ' and ' fled ', and indeed the Infinitives are also confused during the whole M.E. and well into the Mod. Period. The new Pret. *fleu* is found in *Rob. of Glos.*, and is the ancestor of our *flew*. It is due to the analogy of the Reduplicating Verbs *blōwan*, *blēōw*, M.E. *blēu*, etc., and was encouraged by the form of the P.P. *flōwen* (O.E. *flogen*) parallel to *blōwen*, etc. Our P.P.

flown is of course descended from the O.E. and M.E. forms.
It is possible that a further association with O.E. *flēōw* from
flōwan 'flow' may have existed. Chaucer has also a Pret.
Sing. *flough* 'didst fly', and a Pret. Pl. *flowen* in the sense of
'fled'. The former is from the old P.P. type *flŏg*-, M.E.
flouh-; the latter is probably also from this type. In Early
Mod. the new weak Pret. for *flee* comes in, and Tyndale has
fleed which may simply be a new formation from *flee + d*, or,
if *ee* represents a short vowel, it may be derived, as has been
suggested, from O.E. *flēdan* 'flow' (cp. *flōd*), Pret. *flēdde*, M.E.
fledde. This would be the ancestor of our *fled*.

Choose. The O.E. *cēōsan—cēās—curon—coren* is normally
represented in Chaucer, so far as the Inf. and Pret. Sing.
types are concerned, by *cheesen* [ē], and *chees* [ē]. The Pret.
Pl. and P.P. are both *chosen*, which show the O.E. P.P. type
as regards the vowel, the *s* [z] introduced from Inf. as in
frozen, and *ch* generalized from the Inf. Pres. and Pret. Sing.
The *chese* (Pret.) type is last found in the second quarter of
the sixteenth century. *Chose* occurs in Pecock and in Caxton,
but the latter also has Chaucer's form, and a form *chāse*, the
explanation of which is doubtful.

The former is of course the 'Western' penetration of the
P.P. type into the Pret.

It remains to explain the form *choose* [tʃūz]. This may be
derived from O.E. *cēōsan* by a shifting of stress, giving M.E.
chōsen instead of *chēsen* from O.E. *cēōsan*. This type of Infin.
is found before 1530. As early as 1300 *chuse* occurs in
S. Marharete (W. Midl.), and in 1510 the spelling *chewse* is
found, and this rhymes with *refuse*. This type, spelt *chuse*,
continues side by side with *choose*, etc., during the sixteenth,
seventeenth, and eighteenth centuries. It is not infrequent in
first quarter of the nineteenth century. The *chuse*-type, as
seems to emerge from the rhyme, had the sound of [ȳ], and
this would point to an origin from O.E. *ēō*, which was written
u in M.E. in the Sth.-West, and W. Midl. We may derive
this type, then, from a Western form of O.E. *cēōsan*. *Chuse*
[tʃȳz] and *choose* [tʃūz] would later be levelled under the
latter pronunciation. See § 265 on Early Mod. [ȳ].

Lose. O.E. *lēosan—lēās—luron—loren*. This has now
been merged in the Wk. Verb. It owes its spelt form to O.E.
losian, and its vowel sound possibly to association with *loose*,
or as suggested in the case of *choose*, by a stress-shifting in
O.E., that is, a form *lēosan*, M.E. *lōsen*. The normal descendant
of the O.E. Inf. is M.E. *lēsen*, which occurs as late as

Shakespeare, and the Authorized Version. In Sth. M.E.,
Pret. Sing. *-lēs*, Pl. *-luren* are found. Early Mod. has the
Wk. *lost.* The old P.P. *lorn* and *forlorn* are often used in
sixteenth century, and a case is recorded as late as the
eighteenth. The Adj. *forlorn* with an independent meaning
is now quite dissociated from its original connexions. It is
used as an Adj. as early as the middle of the twelfth century.

§ 360. **Class III** (O.E. *in—an—un—un*). Types: *sing,
sang, sung*; *find, found, found*; (*el—(e)al—ul—ol*): *swell,
swollen.*

Most of the old verbs with nasals have preserved the
original forms. In *find*, etc., the lengthening of the vowels
before *-nd* has produced the interchange [*ai—au*].

*Cling, sing, spin, begin, spring, ring, swim, drink, stink,
sink* preserve the three types of the old Inf. and Pres., the
Pret. Sing., and the P.P. *Swing, win, slink, sting, sling, fling,*
on the other hand, have levelled the Pret. under the P.P. type.
Wan, span are still found in sixteenth century, *clang* in
fifteenth, *wrang* in Shakespeare, *wroong, wrong* in Spenser,
flang in Ascham, *flong* in Kyd.

Of the verbs with *e—help, delve, melt, swell,* and *yield*—the
form *swollen* is still used, but more as an adj. than a P.P.,
the ordinary form of which would be *swelled*, while the Pret.
is always weak; *molten* is purely adjectival, *delve* is practically
obsolete except in mannered speech or writing, and is always
weak; *holpen* survives in the public mind simply on account
of its occurrence in the *Magnificat. Yield* is now a Wk. Verb.
The old Pret. *yold(e)* from O.E. *gēald*, or perhaps from the
O.E. P.P. type *golden*, is found in Caxton, and in Spenser.
P.P. *yolden* is found as late as Gascoigne (died 1577).

Turning to the *find*-group—Late O.E. *findan, fānd, fundon,
funden*—we find this preserved in Chaucer as *finden, fond,
founden, founen,* and the *fond*-type in Pret. survives in Caxton
and his contemporaries, and into the sixteenth century. But
Caxton and other fifteenth-century writers also use the P.P.
type *founde*, and this is the exclusive form in the principal
sixteenth-century writers.

The verbs *bind, grind, wind* have very much the same
history as *find.*

Run demands a few words to itself. The O.E. forms were:
irnan, iernan, yrnan, eornan (Merc.), *arn, urnon*; *rinnan,
rann, runnon, runnen.* The M.E. Inf. and Pres. type is usually
renn- which is probably Scandinavian. The earliest example
of *run* as Pres. type is about 1325 (*Metr. Hom.*), and this form

in a Northern dialect is difficult to explain. It is hardly the
ancestor of our form, unless indeed it be a borrowing from the
Sth. or Midlands. The old Sthn. *yrnan* would become M.E.
ürnen, which with metathesis would give *rünnen* and Mod.
run. On the other hand, this might be derived from Merc.
eornan, which would also become *ürnen* in W. Midl. (*y* from *œ*).

§ 361. **Class IV** (O.E. *e—æ—ǣ—o*). Types: *bear, bare*
(*bore*), *born* ; *break, brake* (*broke*), *broken*.

Bear. In non-W.S. the Pret. Pl. was *bēron*, etc., in O.E.,
and in Kentish, and part of the Merc. area, the Pret. Sing.
was *bĕr*. In M.E. we find *bēr—bēren* in the Sth. The
lengthening may be a natural process in syllables ending in
a single consonant (though this is doubtful), but it may also
be explained from the analogy of the other forms of the verb,
which all had long vowel—*bēren, bēre, bōren*, with lengthening
in open sylls., in Pres., Inf., and P.P., and *bēren* with an
original long vowel in Pret. Pl. Those dialects which retained
O.E. *æ* retracted this to *ă* in M.E., and here we get a Pret.
Sing. *băr* and *bār(e)*, where the lengthening may be explained
like that in *bēr*. This M.E. *bār* was the ancestor of *bare*, so
common in fifteenth, sixteenth, and seventeenth centuries.

In *Gen. and Ex.* we already find a Pret. Sing. *bore* which
need not be due entirely to the P.P. type of the same verb, but
partly also to the analogy of *swōr*. The two verbs would then
run *swēren—swōr—swōren* ; *bēren—bōr—bōren*. In this case
the *ō* in the Pret. would be tense, that in the P.P. *bōren* slack,
unless the two verbs were completely levelled under one type,
probably that of *swēren*, with tense *ō*, in Pret. and P.P. The
only form changed then would be *bōren*.

Modern *bore* in Literary and Standard Engl. is clearly the
P.P. type. This Pret. begins to come into use in the sixteenth
century.

Break, shear, tear, wear, steal. The M.E. forms of these
verbs are parallel to those of *beran*. Both *brăk* and *brāk(e)*
existed in Pret. Sing., as is seen from the rhymes. The latter
gave the Biblical and general sixteenth- and seventeenth-
century *brake*. *Broke* of course comes from the P.P., and the
same is true of *shore, tore, wore, stole*. The Pret. *stale*, as well
as *brake, tare, ware*, all occur in the Authorized Version, the
first and last being much less common than the others.

Come. O.E. *cuman, cwōm, cōm, cwōmon, cōmon, cumen*.
This verb is quite irregular already in O.E., the normal vowel
sequence being seen in the verb *niman, năm, nōmon, numen*

(cp. Gothic *qiman—qam—qēmum—qumans*). The Present-day Inf. may be the normal descendant of M.E. *cŭmen* (written *comen*), or, as Luick believes, it may be from M.E. *cōmen*, with lengthening and lowering of *u* to *ō* in *cū-me*. Our Pret. *came* presupposes a M.E. *cām*, which certainly existed by the side of *căm*. This latter may be either a survival of a normal O.E. *cam* or *cwam* unrecorded, or it may be a M.E. formation on the analogy of *năm*, a comparatively common word in M.E. It is clear that no other verbs of this Class could have influenced the forms of *come*, as they are quite differentiated from it by various combinative changes. The *ā* in *cām* can be accounted for by the influence of the quantity of the Pret. Pl. *cōmen*. Caxton and the Latest London Charters (Lekebusch) have *cāme*, but other fifteenth-century writers still use the old *come*, written sometimes *coome*, and (in Cely Papers) *cwm* [=kūm]. Chaucer has *căm—cāmen*, and *coomen* in the Pret.

§ 362.   Class V (O.E. *e—æ—ǣ—e*).

None of the verbs in this class are in all respects the absolute representatives of the O.E. forms. *Speak* has passed completely into Class IV; *bid* from O.E. *biddan* has become blended with O.E. *bēodan*; *sit* has abandoned its P.P. type altogether; *fret* has become quite isolated from *eat*, and is weak; *eat* itself alone among these verbs preserves the old P.P. type, but has lost its old Pret. *Give* and *get* have undergone changes of various kinds not only in the vowels of all the types, but also in the initial consonants. It will be seen that most verbs of this class developed, at one time or another, P.P.'s in *ō*, which vowel penetrated to the Pret. as well. Mod. Engl. has in some cases got rid of the *ō*-forms.

Speak needs no particular comment. Its history is very similar to that of *break*. *Spōken* is found in Pret. Pl. in E. M.E., and it must have got there presumably from the P.P., which had been formed from *brōken* by the complete association of the two verbs in their other forms. The usual M.E. form in the Pret., however, is *spăk*, and Chaucer has a Pret. Pl. *spēken* [ē]. *Spoke* does not become the usual Pret. form till after 1600.

Tread. Parallel to *spake*, etc., Caxton has Pret. *trad, trade*. Sixteenth-century writers have also Pret. *troad*, P.P. *troaden*. Other writers in this and the following century have both *trŏd*, *trōde*, *trodden*, *trōden*.

Bid, forbid. O.E. *biddan, băd, bǣdon, bĕden*, ' pray'. From this we can explain our Pres. and Inf. type, and the Pret.

forms [bæd] and [be*i*d] from M.E. type *bāde*. The P.P. *bidden*, found already in M.E. and common in the Elizabethan period, is less easy to explain. It is difficult to establish an association between this verb and the *ridden* group of P.P.'s except through the Pret. *bōde* which may have existed in the sixteenth century. The spelling is often found, but Price finds it difficult to settle the length of the vowel. If long it could be explained from a P.P. *bōden*, and this in the same way as *trōden*, *spōken*. Having formed a Pret. *bōde* like *rōde*, it would be easy and natural to form a new P.P. *bidden* like *ridden*. On the other hand, it seems certain that short forms *bod*, *bŏden* also existed, and these can be explained as due to M.E. *bŏd(e)n*, a by-form of *bō-den*. The short *bod* in the Pret. may be due to this type of P.P.

By the side of *bid* in the Pres. and Inf., M.E. and Early Mod. (Chaucer and Caxton) have *bede*, and also *bēden* in the P.P. The latter is the normal descendant of the O.E. form. The former may be explained from confusion with O.E. *bēodan*, M.E. *bēden* 'to command'. The P.P. of this verb would be *bōden* or *bŏden* (from *bod(e)n*), and the short type would account for a Pret. *bŏd*.

Eat has now usually the Pret. [ɛt], though in Ireland people often say [īt] from the P.P. type. The short type of Pret. is found already in the fourteenth century, and is probably due to the analogy of the weak Prets. *led*, M.E. *ledde* from *lead* E. Mod. and M.E. *bet* from *beat*, etc. The archaic Pret. *ate*, preserved to some extent in the spelling but rarely in speech, presupposes a M.E. *āte*, and *frate* from O.E. *fretan* is found. The explanation of these forms is the same as that of *bade*, *spake*, etc. The P.P. *eaten* is quite normal, and the Scotch [ɛtn] is due to M.E. *ĕtn*.

Get, beget, forget. O.E. *-ġietan* (non-W.S. *ġetan*, *-ġeotan*), *-ġeat* (non-W.S. *-ġæt*, *-ġet*), *-ġēaton* (non-W.S. *ġēton*), *-ġeten*, is always compounded with *on-*, *bi-*, *for-*. The use of uncompounded *get*, the short vowel, and its initial consonant are alike due to Scandinavian influence (O.N. *geta*). The M.E. native forms of the Inf. and Pres. are *ʒēten*, *yēten*, *yuten*, etc. The M.E. Pret. Sing. was *ʒat*, *yat* from *ġæt*, and *ʒet* from *ġet*. The Pret. Pl. was either *yāten*, etc., by the side of Sing. *yāt*, *yăt*, or the normal *yēten* from the non-W.S. *ġēton*. By the side of these, forms with initial *g-* are also found, and Chaucer has *gēte*, *gat*, *gĕten*. The existence of *gāte* (Pret. Sing.) is also established by rhymes for M.E. and Early Mod.

Caxton has Pret. *gat*, *gatte*, and *gate*, and usually *-yeten*,

-yete in P.P.   He has, however, the *o*-forms *for-* and *be-goten*,
and these are common in the Latest London Ch. (Lekebusch).
The *o*-forms, according to Price, are not established till near
the end of the sixteenth century. While *forgotten* has remained
in Standard English, the uncompounded *gotten* was rarer than
got after 1600, except in the Authorized Version and two other
writers cited by Price.

As might have been expected, long forms such as *gōte*
(rhyming with *wrōte*) occur in sixteenth-century English.
Price sums up this question by saying, ' It looks as if at the
beginning of the period (E. Mod.) there were in the Inf.
alternative forms with long and short *e*, in the P.P. with long
and short *o*, in the Pret. two sets, with long and short *a* and
with long and short *o* ; that the long forms in Inf. and Pret.
with *ō* were already obsolescent, while the long *a* lasted through
the whole period '.

Give.   O.E. (W.S.) *ġiefan, ġeaf, ġēafon, giefen* ; non-W.S.
ġefan, ġeofan—ġæf, ġef—ġefon, ġefen, ġeofen.   It may be said
at once that the two chief problems are the initial consonant
and the vowel, in Mod. *give*.   It is quite certain that O.E.
ġ- could not become [g] and we may put this down to
Scandinavian influence.   As regards the vowel in *give*, this
has been variously explained as due to the analogy of the 2nd
and 3rd Pers. Pres. *ġifst, ġifþ* (from **ġeƀis, *ġeƀiþ*), or from
a W.S. form *ġifan*, P.P. *ġifen* (from *ġief-*).   Another possibility
is the analogy of *begin* through *gan* parallel to *gaf, yaf*.   The
normal M.E. forms from non-W.S. are *yēuen, yaf, yāue (yef)*,
yāuen, yēuen.   By the side of these, *giue, gaf, gēven, given*,
etc., are also found in M.E., which are a blend between the
O.N. and the English types.   Again, a Pret. *yōue, gōue* also
occurs.   The latter may be either pure Scand. (O.N. *gǫ́fom*
Pret. Pl.) or derived from the W.S. Pl. *ġēafon* with a shifting
of stress to the second element of the diphthong.   The form
ȝāfen from *Laud. Chron.* may conceivably be the ancestor of
yōue, etc., but this is very doubtful.   Since P.P. forms *youen*,
govyn are found in the fifteenth century, these may be due to
the same analogy as the other *ō* P.P.'s in this class, and the
type then extended to the Pret.

The *yēve*-forms in Inf., etc., are very usual in the London
dialect of fifteenth century, though Caxton besides this form
has also *geue*, but more often *gyue*.   In the London Charters
(Lekebusch) *yeue* is most frequent, but *geue* is also common,
and *giue, gyue*, etc., are much rarer.   During the sixteenth
century *yeve* practically dies out, but *geue* still predominates

over *gyue*, *gyve*, *give*, etc. There is reason for thinking that the spelling *give*, etc., often stands for the pronunciation [gīv], so that the *geve*-type is really commoner than appears at first sight. It may be noted that the final consonant appears both as *v* (or *u*) and *f*. The latter is due to generalizing the final sound of the Pret. Sing., the former to the other inflected forms.

The *give*-forms are fixed by seventeenth century.

In the Pret. the *y*- dies out during the sixteenth century. Sir T. Smith refers to *yaf* and *yave* as antiquated. Henceforth the struggle is between the short *găf* and the long *gāve*, and the latter becomes the only form in most of the principal writers before the end of the century. In the P.P. the *y*-forms die out by the end of the fifteenth century, but the two forms *geven*, *given* (in various spellings) remain during the whole sixteenth century, *geven* becoming gradually less and less frequent, until, after the first quarter of the seventeenth century, it apparently disappears from Literature altogether.

At least two examples of *geven* [gīvən] occur, however, in the Wentworth Papers in 1706.

See. O.E. *sēon—seah*, *sæh—sāwon* (also, poetical), *sǣgon—sewen*, *sawen*. The adj., W.S. *ġesīene* 'visible', non-W.S. *ġesēne*, is also used as a P.P. already in O.E. in Anglian. This form spreads, and becomes the usual one in M.E., e.g. Chaucer, etc., *yseene*, Present-day *seen*.

The M.E. forms of the Pret. are : *sauh*, whence *saugh* and *saw*, from Angl. *sæh* through *săh*; *seih* which may represent a Sth. *seh*, with diphthonging before a fronted *h*; *sȳ* = *sī*, also *sīh* from the O.E. Pl. type *sǣgon*, *sǣh*, *sēh*, *sīh* (cp. *ī* 'eye' from *ēh*).

The *saw*-type appears to be Anglian in origin ; it does not occur early in the South. The -*w* is presumably due to the influence of the Pl. It is possible that *sei*, etc., may sometimes be due to the Pl. *sǣʒen*, M.E. *sēʒen*, *sēyen*.

In Early Mod. the London dialect seems generally to have used the ancestors of our present forms, though such P.P. forms as *sayn*, *seyne*, etc., still survive, from earlier -*sēʒen*.

Sit. O.E. *sittan—sæt—sǣton* (non-W.S. *sēton*)—*seten*. The only noteworthy point about this verb in Present-day English is the disappearance of the old P.P., which has been replaced by the Pret. type. In Early Mod. *set* was often used, generally with the auxiliary *be*—'I am, was *set*,' etc., which may be either a survival of the old P.P. or that of the wk.

settan. In Early Mod. a P.P. *sitten* is sometimes used, and also *sat* and *sate.*

Bequeath, quoth. The former of these two is now always weak and seems to have been so during the whole Mod. period. The uncompounded verb appears only in Pret. during Mod. period, sometimes as *quod,* sometimes as *quoth.* The *o*-forms are found both in the Pret. and P.P. during E. M.E. —*quod, quoðen,* etc., as well as the normal *quaþ, quāden, queden.* Various explanations have been suggested to account for *quoth,* but since it is found in the P.P. as well as in the Pret., it is difficult to see why it should not be due, like the *o*-forms of so many verbs in this class, to the analogy of the P.P. of Class IV. We know that *spōke—spōken* existed, and the association in meaning between *spōke* and *quōth* or *quōd* is surely close enough. In the now antiquated and half jocular expression *quotha,* we have *quoth + a,* the Sthn. form of the Pers. Pron. which we saw already in Trevisa (§ 306). Against the above explanation of *quoth,* it must be recorded that this form occurs in early texts where *spāk,* etc., are the usual Pret. forms. It may, as Bülbring suggests, be due to the influence of *w,* and that perhaps chiefly in unstressed positions. In this case it is from *quăþ* and is short.

Lie. O.E. *licgan—læg—lǣgon—legen.* The direct descendant of the old Inf. and Pres. is M.E. *liggen* (lidžen). As with so many verbs of this type, a new Inf. and 1st Pers. Pres. are formed from the analogy of the 2nd and 3rd Pers., O.E. *lig(e)st, lig(e)þ,* which give in M.E. *liȝest, liȝeþ,* whence the new forms, ich *liȝe,* or *lye,* Inf. *lyen,* etc. *N.E.D.* records *ligge* (probably= [lig] a Nthn. type) as late as 1590. The Mod. forms *lay, lain* are normal descendants of the O.E. forms. After 1400 a type of P.P. *lyen,* on the analogy of Inf. *lye,* is common. This form still remains in the Prayer Bk. version of the Psalms—*though ye have lien among the pots.*

Weave is like *speak* in having *o*-forms in Pret. *wove,* and P.P. *woven.*

§ 363. Class VI (O.E. *a—ō—ō—a* ; also with *i*-mutation in Inf. type, *e—o—o—a*).
This class has had a varied fate. Some verbs have preserved the old forms, or their Mod. equivalents, like *shake* ; others have passed into the group of Reduplicating Verbs like *slay,* but more have become wholly weak, or preserve a strong form, constantly, or occasionally.

Shake, take (of Scand. origin), **forsake,** all have now the gradation [*ei, u, ei*—(ən)], though *wake* and *awake* have *woke, awoke,* and also weak forms.

Stand (understand) has lost its old P.P. *standen* and uses the Pret. type, just as *sit* does. This form of P.P. was introduced in the fifteenth century and gradually won, though *stande, stonde* are also in use during the fifteenth and sixteenth centuries. By the side of these a weak -*standed* is common in the fifteenth and sixteenth centuries, in the P.P., but not, apparently, in the Pret.

Swear has [ɔ] in the Pret. before *r,* instead of [ū] (§ 238). The P.P. *swōre* occurs already in the fourteenth century. It may easily be accounted for on the analogy of *bōre(n).* The Biblical Pret. *sware* also shows the influence of Cl. IV.

Draw, slay, with their Prets. from the Reduplicating group, have already been discussed above, § 357. **Gnaw** also shows some instances of a Pret. *gnew* in sixteenth century. The P.P. *gnawen* is less rare, in fact it may be heard to-day. Already in the fourteenth century the weak Pret. was in use, and this is found in Auth. Vers. and other sixteenth and seventeenth century texts. The verb is often spelt *knaw* from fifteenth to eighteenth century.

Bake has long been a weak verb. O.E. *bōc* was replaced by a weak Pret. in the fifteenth century, but the P.P. *baken* is found in the sixteenth century.

Wash already in E.M.E. formed a Pret. *weeshe, weoshe* after the model of the Reduplicating Verbs. This is still in use in Caxton's works, but the wk. Pret. is found in Coverdale. The strong P.P. still survives in the adj. *unwashen.*

Wax. Tottel and Spenser still have the old Pret. *wox,* but a commoner form, in Caxton and later, is *wex,* the ancestor of which is found already in O.E. *weōx.* Here we have the influence of the Reduplicating Verbs. The P.P. *waxen* is still found in Shakespeare, and the Auth. Vers.

Shape. The Pret. *shope* is still found in Surrey, Coverdale, and Spenser. The strong P.P. is found in Caxton and in Coverdale. The compounds with *mis-, un-, ill-,* which are of course Adjectives, from the old P.P., still survive.

Shave has now only *shaved, shaven,* is now an Adjective, but was used as a P.P. during the whole Elizabethan period. The old strong Pret. *shōve* occurs in Caxton and Coverdale.

Heave is now usually weak throughout, but the strong Pret. *hove* is still in colloquial use.

Laugh. The Pret. *lough*, normally descended from O.E. *hlōh*, was frequent down to the end of the fifteenth century, but is not found often after 1500. See § 260 and Note on relation of our [lāf] to the form recorded by the spelling.

§ 364.   Reduplicating Verbs

A. Beat. This is the only survivor of the class. But for the P.P. in -*en* we should probably feel this verb as weak. The O.E. forms were *bēatan—bēot—bēoton—bēaten*. Though now levelled, the Inf. and Pret. must in Late M.E. or early Mod. have been [bēt—bīt] respectively. The Early Mod. forms collected by Price do not show any distinction made in the spelling.

The new *bet*, Pret. or P. P., on the analogy of such weak forms as *met*, now only jocular, was used by Scott.

B. Blow-Class. *Blow, blew, blown* represent O.E. *blāwan, blēōw, blēōwon, blawen*. To this class belong also *crow* (also weak), *know, throw, mow* (now only weak).

Sow still retains strong P.P. but has weak Pret. and often a weak P.P.

Flow is now only weak, though its old strong P.P. may have helped to fix *flown* as P.P. of *fly*.

Hew, now generally weak, has also a strong P.P., especially in passive—*hewn down*, Adj. *rough-hewn, unhewn*, etc.

Snow has long lost its old Pret. *snew* and P.P. *snow(e)n*, but these survived in literary English in the sixteenth century, and the Grammarian Charles Butler (1632) still recognizes them.

C. Fall-Class. O.E. *feallan—fēoll—fēollon—feallen*. Our *fell* and *fallen* are normal representatives of the old forms. The common M.E. *fill* (Chaucer) has not been satisfactorily explained.

Hold is from the Angl. *hāldan*. The Sthn. and Kt. *hēlden* still survives, though rarely, in Chaucer (§ 165). A few cases of *held* as an Inf. are found in M.E. Nthn. texts. Here they must be either loan-forms from Sth. or new formations from 3rd Pers. Sing. (see § 166 Note). A few scattered forms are found in the sixteenth-century Acts of Parliament, and Price explains these from the Pret. This is certainly right, for seeing how rare the non-Anglian forms are in M.E. these can hardly be survivals of the old Sthn. form.

The old P.P. *holden* survives still in official language—'*at a meeting holden* on such and such a day'. The compound *beholden*, now rather archaic, is still used. Price's *holden*-forms seem to occur mostly in official sources. The Pret. *held* is shortened from M.E. *hēld*.

IRREGULAR VERBS

§ 365. To be.

O.E. Pres. Indic. Pres. Subj.

'am'-type.

	W.S.		Merc.	Nthmb.	W.S. & Merc.	Nthmb.
Sing.	eom		eam	am	sīe, sī	S. and Pl.
	eart		eart	arð		sīe, sē
	is		is	is		
Pl.	we	sindon	earun	aron	sīen	
	ge	sint	sind	sint		
	hie		sindon	sinden		

'be'-type. Pres. Indic. Pres. Subj.

	W.S.	Merc.	Nthmb.	W.S. & Merc.	Nthmb.	
Sing.	bēo	bīom	biom			Inf. *beon, beon.*
	bist	bis(t)	bist	bīo	bīa	Part. Pres. *bēonde*
	bið	bið	bið	bēo	bīe	
Pl.	bēoð	bioð	bioðun	bēon		Imperat. *bēo,* Pl. *bēoþ*
	bioð		biað	bīon		

Preterite Indic.

Sing.   Pl.

ic, þe wæs   Inf. *wesan*
þu wǣre   } *wǣron* (non-W.S. *wēron*)   Part. Pres. *wesende*
he wæs

Pret. Subj. S. *wǣre*; Pl. *wǣren*   Imperat. *wes*; Pl. *wesað*

M.E. *1st Pers. S.* All dialects agree in having *am* (*æm, ham*), as the usual form ; *bēo* is also found in E. Midl.

2nd Pers. S. Nth. has *es* ; E. and W. Midl. *art* ; Southern and Kt. *bēþ, art.*

3rd Pers. S. Nth. *es* ; Midl. *is, ys,* W. Midl. also *bēoþ* and *buþ* ; Sthn. *bēoþ, bēþ, is* ; Kt. *bīoþ, bīeþ, byēþ.*

Pl. (all Pers.) Nth. ar. *are, er, ere, bēs* (*bēn*) ; W. Midl. *bēn, arn, bēoþ, bēþ* (P. *Plowm.*) ; E. Midl. *aren, bēn* (*Orm.* has also *sinndenn*) ; Sthn. *bēoþ, bēþ* ; Kt. *bīoþ, bīeþ.*

The London sources before Chaucer have *is*; Pl. *bēoþ, bēon, bēn*; *beo, be* Subj. Pres.; Pret. *wæs, wes, was*; Pl. *weren, were*; Inf. *beon, be* (Dölle, p. 76).

Chaucer has *am, art, is*, Pl. *been, bee*, rarely *arn* (ten Brink, § 197). The fourteenth-century London documents agree on the whole with this, but occasionally have the Sth. Pl. *beþ* (Morsbach, *Schriftspr.*, p. 149). Caxton's usage agrees with that of to-day in Sing. In Pl. he has *ar*, but also *bēn, bē* (Römstedt, p. 50).

The later London Documents show some variety in the Pl.: London Charters *been, ben*; State Records *are*; Parliamentary Records usually *been, bēn*, occasionally *byn, buth* twice; *ar, arne, arn* not infrequently (Lekebusch, pp. 126, 127, 128).

The other parts of this verb in M.E. are: Inf. *been, be*, Kt. *bi*; Imperat. Nth. *bē*; Midl. *bē*, Pl. *bēþ*; Sth. *bē, bēþ*; Subj. Pres. *bēo*, Pl. *bēon*, etc., *bēoþ*.

Pret. *was, wes* (*wast* 2nd Sing. L. M.E. *-t* on analogy of *ar-t*), *wēren, wēre*; Subj. Pret. *wēre*.

Pres. Part. (Chaucer) *bēing*; Past Part. (*i*)-*bēn*, (*i*)-*bē*.

Be in the Pres. Indic. survives in many Regional Dialects, used both as S. and Pl. In Standard and Literary it is extinct, except as a poetical archaism in the Pl. and in the Subj. *Are*, originally Nth. and Nth. Midland, penetrated early into the London Dialect, probably from E. Midl., but was not exclusively used, even in the literary language, till the seventeenth century.

Preterite Present and other Anomalous Verbs

§ 366. Pret.-Pres. Verbs have, with the function of a Present Tense, one which is a strong Pret. in form. They form new Pret. forms with the weak suffix *-de, -te*.

Can.

O.E.   Inf. *cunnan* 'to be able, to know'.

Past Part. *cūþ* 'known', cp. *un-cūþ* 'unknown', formally identical with *uncouth*.

Pres. Indic. S. *can, canst, can* (also *con*, etc.); Pl. *cunnon*.

Pret. S. *cūþe* 'knew, could', *cūþest, cūþe*; Pl. *cūþon*. (O.E. *cūþe*, Goth. *kunþa* have never been satisfactorily explained.)

Pres. Subj. S. *cunne*; Pl. *cunnon*.

Pret. Subj. S. *cūþe*; Pl. *cūþon*.

M.E. (Chaucer's forms), cp. ten Brink, § 198. Inf. *connen*; P.P. *kouth*.

Pres. Ind. S. *can, canst, can*; Pl. *conne(n)* [kŭnen].
Pret. *kouthe, koude.*

The London Documents preserve distinction between S. *can*,
Pl. *conne* in 1425, and in Pret. have *coude, koude* (Morsbach,
pp. 148, 150, 151); Pecock (1449) has Pres. Pl. *kunnen*, and
coupist in Pret.

Caxton still appears to distinguish the Pl. *conne* from Sing.
can occasionally (Römstedt, p. 48).

Coverdale (1535) has Pret. *coude*, and also the new spelling
coulde, on analogy of *would, should* (Swearingen, p. 42).

§ 367.   Dare.

O.E.   Pres. Ind. S. *dear(r), dearst, dear(r)*; Pl. *durron.*
Pret. *dorste*; Pl. *dorston.*
Subj. *dyrre, durre.*

M.E. (Chaucer).   Pres. S. *dar, darst, dar*; Pl. *dor.*
Pret. *dorste.*

In Mod. Engl. there is a tendency to inflect *dare* like an
ordinary Pres.—*he dares not do it*, by the side of the more
historical *daren't*. Similarly a new Pret. *dared* has been
formed, used both intransitively and transitively—*I dared him
to do it. Durst* is now felt to be old-fashioned, and is becoming
obsolete.

§ 368.   May.

O.E.   Inf. *magan*; Part. Pres. *magende.*
Pres. Ind. S. *mæġ, meaht* (and *miht*), *mæġ*; Pl. *māgon* (and
mægon).
Pret. *meahte, mehte* (Late W.S. *mihte*).
Subj. *mǣġe* (L. W.S. *māge*); Pl. *mǣġen* (L. W.S. *māgon*)
Latest O.E. *muge.*

M.E. (Early). Sth. S. *mei*, Kt. *mai*; Midl. *maʒʒ* (*Orm*),
may, mayst; Pl. Sth. *mahen, moʒe, muwen*; Kt. *muʒe, mowe*;
E. Midl. *muʒhenn* (*Orm*).
Inf. (W. Midl.) *mow.*
Pret. Kt., E. Midl. *mihte, michte, miʒte, mighte*: Sth. *mahte.*
Pl. E. Midl. *mihten, muhten.*

Chaucer has S. *may, might* (*mayest*), *may*; Pl. *mowen, mowe,
mow, may*; Pret. *mighte.*

The London Documents and Caxton agree with Chaucer,
except that Caxton has, as in Present-day English, *may* in the
Pl. instead of the older *mowe* (Römstedt, p. 49).

§ 369.   **Shall.**

O.E. Inf. *sculan, sceolan.*
Pres. Indic. S. *sceal* (non-W.S. *scæl, scal*); Late W.S. *scel,*
scealt, scælt, sceal, scæl, etc.; Pl. *sculon, sceolon,* Late W.S.
scylon.
Pret. Indic. S. *sceold, scolde*; Pl. *sceoldon.*
Subj. (W.S.) *sciele, scyle, scile.*

M.E. Pres. Indic. S., Sthn. *scal, schal*; Pl. *schulen, ssullen*;
Kt. *scel, ssel, sselt, ssalt*; Pl. *scule, ssollen*; E. Midl. *shall,*
schal, sal, salt, schalt, shalt; Pl. *schullen, shulenn, sulen, schulle,*
shul; W. Midl. *schal, shall, schalt*; Pl. *schul, schulle*; *Allit. P.*
has also the curious forms *schin, schyn* 'shall', once each in
Cleanness; Nth. *sal* S. and Pl. *(salle).*
Pret., Sth. *sceolde*; Pl. *sceolden, scholde, schulde*; Kt. *sceolde,*
sceolden, ssolde, (Aȝenb. has 2nd S. *ssoldest)*; E. Midl. *schollde,*
shollde, sholden, sulde, sulden, scholde, shuld; W. Midl. *schulde*;
Nth. *suld.*

London Dialect. Earliest London sources *shal*; Pr. *schullen,*
shullen; Pret. *sholde, shuld* (Dölle, p. 76). Chaucer: *shal,*
shalt, shal; Pl. *shullen, shul (shold)*; Pret. *sholde.* Later
Official Lond. Documents: *shall*; Pl. *shullen, shul, shalle,*
shal; Pret. *sholde, shold, shulde, shuld.* Pecock distinguishes
between the S. and Pl. types, *schol, schullen.* Caxton still
sometimes distinguishes Pl. *shul, shulle* from Sing. *shal(l)*, but
more usually levels both under the type of the Sing. (Römstedt, 48).

§ 370.   **Ought.**

This word is the descendant of the old Pret. *āhte* of O.E.
āgan 'possess, own', a Pret. Pres. verb. In its present force
expressing moral obligation, it occurs in Pres. as well as Pret.
as early as the middle of the twelfth and beginning of the
thirteenth century. Thus, *bename him al ðet he ahte to hauen*
'deprived him of all that he ought to have', *Laud Chr.* Ann.
1140; *We aȝen þene sunnedei swiþeliche wel to wierþen* 'we
ought to honour Sunday exceedingly', *Lambeth Homs.*, Morris
and Skeat, I, p. 20.

§ 371.   **Owe**

is the normal descendant of *āgan* 'possess', M.E. *ōwen*
'possess obligations, to be bound, obliged'; in M.E. therefore

not isolated in meaning from the Pret. *āȝte*, *ōughte*. *Rob. of Glos.* has *þe treuþe ich ou to þe*, and Wycliffe *ȝeld þat þou owist* (Kellner-Bradley, p. 272). The word gradually loses the sense of *possess* and means 'owe an obligation', and finally 'owe money', etc.

§ 372. Own

is from O.E. *āgnian* 'own, possess', and has entirely taken the place of the O.E. *āgan* in meaning.

§ 373. Will.

O.E. Inf. *willan*; Pres. Part. *willende*.
Pres. Indic. S. *wile, wilt, wile*; Pl. *willaþ*.
Pret. *wolde*; Pl. *wolden.*
Ne wille, etc., becomes *nylle*, the *w* first rounding *i* and then being lost.

M.E. The forms are *wile, wille, wulle, wule, wol(e)*. Of these the *wule*-type is from *wille*, with rounding of the vowel after *w*. *Wol*, on the other hand, is a new formation, derived by Analogy from the Pret. *wol-de.*

The following shows the distribution of the types:

Wille ⎫ Kt. Vesp. A. 22, Shoreh., *Aȝenb., Trin. Homs.*
Wile ⎬ *O. and N., P.M., Orm., Gen. and Ex., Havelok, Horn, Bokenam.*

Wulle ⎫ *Lambeth Homs., Laȝ., A.R., Horn.*
Wule ⎬

Wol(e) P.M., Laȝ., Robt. of Glos., Hendyng, Havelok, Horn, Wil. of Pal. (only form).

Wol appears to become more common after the beginning of the fourteenth century; it is found both in the E. and W. Midl., chiefly in the latter, and to some extent in Sthn. It appears to be absent from Kt. texts, and does not occur in Morris's Glossary to *Aȝenbite*. It does not occur in the earliest London sources (Dölle, p. 76). In Gower it is very common, and is in fact the only form in Macaulay's *Glossary* to *Selections*. Chaucer has *wil*, but more often *wol*, especially in his prose. In the London Documents *wil, wille* (S. and Pl.) appears to occur in Morsbach's references about fifteen times, as against *wol* about thirty-five times (*Schriftspr.*, pp. 149, 151, 152). Caxton, according to Römstedt (p. 49), has only *wil(le)* in 1st and 3rd Sing., but *wolt* as well as *wilt*, and *woll* as well as *wil(le)* in Pl. The later London Documents have both *will* and *wol*; in the Lond. Ch. *will* predominates; in State Records and Parliamentary Records both forms seem equally frequent (Lekebusch, pp. 126, 127, 128).

Coverdale has only *wil*, *wyl* (Swearingen, p. 42), and the same is true of Edward VI's First P. B. (1549).

The *wol*-type survives in *won't*, from *wol not*.

INDEX

U

-*oi*-, in unstressed sylls., 280.

Old English, limitation of period, 19; relation of to other old Gmc. Dialects, 18; literary sources of, 75-9; mode of writing, 80; pronunciation of, 81-93; Isolative changes in, 97; combinative changes, 98-114; Dialectal characteristics, summary of, 145; Vowel Lengthening, 113, 114.

one, present pronunciation, antiquity of, survival of older type, 240, Note 2.

open syllables, M.E. lengthening of short vowels in, 173 (2); an early process, ibid., Note 4; lengthening of *ĭ* and *ŭ*, 174.

Orm, individualism of his system of spelling, 149 (1); throws important light on vowel quantity in M.E., 155 (6).

ou diphthong, (M.E.) levelled with *au* under [ɔ(u)] in sixteenth century, 264.

'*Palatal*' *Mutation*, 111.

Participle Present, 337.

Personal Pronouns, main points in history of, since O.E., 296; details of, 296-312.

Peterborough Chronicle, latter part of (middle of twelfth century) shows drastic changes in spelling, inflexions, style, compared with O.E., 148.

Pitch of Vowels, 51.

Place-Names in M.E., forms of, throw light upon phonology of Dialects, 150; methods of using in dialectal investigation, p. 90.

Pl. of nouns, 316; Pl. in -*s*, 317; Weak Pls., 318; Mutation Pls., 319; Unchanged Pls., 320; Irregular Pls., 321.

Pope's rhyme, state—great, quoted by Dr. Johnson, 232 (3).

Possessive suffix-es, extension of to Fem. nouns in M.E., 315; uninflected possessives, ibid.

Quantity, in vowels, 52.

r, lost before -*s*, -*sh*, 284 (4 a); loss of final -*r*, 284 (4 b).

Received Standard, character and origin of, p. 149; changes in since sixteenth century, 212.

Reduplicating Verbs, 350-2.

Regional and Class Dialect, 211.

Rhymes, information concerning pronunciation to be derived from, 214.

Rome, formerly pronounced 'room' [rūm], 337, Note 3.

Rounding of vowels, 48; degrees of, 49; rounding in O.E., 100.

Rowe (1673-1718), rhymes *seat—great*, 232 (3).

Runes, 80.

-'*s*, -*s*', introduction of apostrophe, 315, Note.

Scandinavian words, vowels of, 179.

She, appearance and origin of, 302.

Shortening of vowels in M.E., before consonantal combinations, 175; in first syll. of words of three syllables, 176; in unstressed sylls., 177.

Shortening of M.E. long vowels in Mod. Period; of [ē] 235; of [ū] from *ō*, 236; of M.E. *ō²* as in *hot*, 243.

-*si*-, -*ti*-, pronounced '-*sh*-' [ʃ], 283 (1).

Smoothing, an Anglian process 127.

Sound Laws, apparent exceptions to, 65.

South Eastern Dialects in M.E., p. 93; list of texts representing, pp. 102-3.

Southern Dialects, 151 (4), p. 92; list of texts representing, pp. 102-4.

South Western Dialects in M.E., 151 (4), p. 92; list of representative texts, p. 104; chief features of, 204.

Spelling in M.E., 152; changes from O.E. system which are purely graphic, 153.

Standard of Speech, recognized in sixteenth century, 210.

Strong Verbs in O.E., 343-9; in M.E. and later, 353-63.

su-, pronounced '*shu*-' [ʃū], 283 (2).